Applied Ethnobotany

People, Wild Plant Use and Conservation

Anthony B Cunningham

Earthscan Publications Ltd, London and Sterling, VA

First published in the UK and USA in 2001 by
Earthscan Publications Ltd

A catalogue record for this book is available from the British Library

ISBN: 1 85383 697 4

Typesetting by PCS Mapping & DTP, Newcastle upon Tyne
Printed and bound in the UK by Redwood Books Ltd, Trowbridge, Wilshire
Cover design by Yvonne Booth
Cover photo by A B Cunningham
Panda symbol © 1986 WWF
® WWF registered trademark owner

For a full list of publications please contact:
Earthscan Publications Ltd
120 Pentonville Road
London, N1 9JN, UK
Tel: +44 (0)20 7278 0433
Fax: +44 (0)20 7278 1142
Email: earthinfo@earthscan.co.uk
http://www.earthscan.co.uk

22883 Quicksilver Drive, Sterling, VA 20166–2012, USA

Earthscan is an editorially independent subsidiary of Kogan Page Ltd and publishes in association
with WWF-UK and the International Institute for Environment and Development

This book is printed on elemental chlorine-free paper

Contents

List of Figures, Tables and Boxes

Figures

Tables

Boxes

The People and Plants Initiative

Conservation is directly linked to people's values and behaviour. It is therefore ironic that the people–conservation interface has been neglected in the past. Part of this neglect has been due to a lack of appreciation of the roles that the knowledge, institutions and cultural perspectives of local people can play in resource management and conservation. To see conservation areas or natural resources through the eyes of resource users is an instructive and important process for any conservation biologist or national park manager. Research in ethnobiology (of which ethnoecology and ethnobotany are parts) is a useful element in this process. Ethnobotany stands at the interface of several disciplines, including anthropology, botany, ecology, geography, economics and others. To work in ethnobotany applied to conservation or rural development may therefore seem a daunting intellectual challenge. Progress is greatly dependent on the ability to recognize priorities – an ability which the *Applied Ethnobotany* manual is designed to promote.

People and Plants is an initiative of WWF, the United Nations Educational, Scientific and Cultural Organization (UNESCO) and the Royal Botanic Gardens, Kew. It aims to increase the capacity for community-based plant conservation worldwide. Training is undertaken at field sites in selected countries, with case studies and other information made available to a wide audience through various publications, training videos and an Internet service. Publications include working papers, issues of a handbook and discussion papers, in addition to the People and Plants conservation manuals series, to which the present work contributes.

The People and Plants website can be visited at http://rbgkew.org.uk/peopleplants. It contains full versions of several of the smaller People and Plants publications, and contact information for organizations involved in applied ethnobotany.

Alan Hamilton
Head, International Plants Conservation Unit
WWF-UK

Preface

Ironically, although conservation is directly linked to people's values and behaviour, in landscapes changed by people, the people–conservation interface is often neglected. Part of this neglect results from a lack of appreciation of the role that local people's knowledge, institutions and cultural perspectives can play in resource management and conservation. To see conservation areas or natural resources through the eyes of resource users is an instructive and important process for any conservation biologist or national park manager. Research at the interface between several disciplines, using methods derived from anthropology, geography, economics and ecology – in what is becoming the 'new' discipline of *ethnobiology*, of which *ethnoecology* and *ethnobotany* are part – is a useful part of this process.

Confusion or clarity in conservation practice?

Tropical ecosystems are the most diverse on earth, yet they have been poorly studied by scientists. Although these habitats have received increasing attention in the past decade, many species in the tropics remain undescribed. Even less is known about the biomass production of most tropical species, or about the ways in which species interact, so that the ecological impact of the loss of species through over-harvesting is difficult or even impossible to predict. Under these circumstances, it is no wonder that field researchers and national park managers ask themselves: how can a policy of sustainable use be implemented when hundreds of species may be involved?

Many researchers or national park managers, whether expatriates or nationals, have grown up in an urban environment, and end up in positions where they have to make decisions on resource-sharing arrangements on the basis of limited theoretical background or field experience. Many, like myself, were trained in university or college systems where undergraduate courses start at a micro-level, full of detail (cell biology, taxonomy, physiology), rather than at the macro-level of pattern and process across landscapes. Many university courses have limited linkage between subjects such as zoology, botany or geology that are closely interconnected in the field, and even fewer graduates have training in both the biological and the social sciences.

It is no wonder, therefore, that graduates who end up in conservation areas are often confused by the detail of the hundreds of species and life forms, or by the patchiness within and between vegetation types. It is even more perplexing for those working at the interface between parks and people, trying to straddle social and biological issues in an effort to resolve land-use conflicts or to set up sustainable harvesting systems. Where do we start (or stop) in the information-collecting process? Do we collect everything or focus only on key issues, and if so, what are those issues?

The answers to these questions depend on the objectives of the research, on time constraints, and on the available money and manpower. In many developing countries, the problems facing conservation areas are urgent, and time, funding and trained researchers are scarce. Long-term monitoring therefore has to be limited to key issues, with initial guidelines set through short-term research of less than two to three years. The first step is to 'make haste slowly'. This should be done by systematically working through the social, economic and ecological components that all influence resource management and conservation at different spatial and time scales. The chapters that follow deal with different steps in this process.

At one stage, during the long process of writing this manual, it crossed my mind that it would be better to produce a manual on methods which was composed of just one Zen-like sentence: 'The only method is that there is no method.' There would have been method in this. In a field as complex as conservation, one cannot hope to produce a 'recipe book' of methods, applicable to every situation. What is suitable in one case may be completely unsuitable in another. Some problems are unique to a particular region, posing new challenges for innovative methods that need to be designed in the field. For this reason, I cover some general principles, conceptual models and methods as tools to keep in mind when faced with particular problems, to take out where appropriate, field test, modify and test again. This is far better than blindly transplanting field methods from one place to another. However, any choice of methods needs to be informed by theory, research design and an understanding of basic concepts. For this reason, the 'how to do it' part of methods is given in the context of the practical and theoretical background to those methods.

The advantage of applied ethnobotanical research is that a great deal can be achieved with simple, inexpensive equipment: pencils, paper, a tape measure, a compass and a ball of string. In common with any science, a healthy dose of scepticism is also an excellent ingredient! In the complex world of conservation, it is unlikely that we will get to know all the answers. It is to be hoped that this manual is a guide to asking the right questions – and also to answering some of them.

This book is dedicated to the students and young professionals from local communities who work so much in isolation, but who are at the forefront of conservation effort and ethnobotanical research.

Introduction

This manual is a product of the People and Plants Initiative, a joint programme of WWF, UNESCO and the Royal Botanic Gardens, Kew. It is a companion volume to two other methods manuals in the People and Plants series: *Ethnobotany: a methods manual* by Gary J Martin (1995; second edition forthcoming) and *People, Plants and Protected Areas: a guide to* in-situ *management* by John Tuxill and Gary P Nabhan (1998; reissue 2001). Gary Martin's manual, the first in this series, provides practical guidelines for work in regional floras of ethnobotanical importance and describes the botanical, anthropological, phytochemical, linguistic and ecological approaches used to collect information on useful plants. John Tuxill and Gary Nabhan's manual focuses on in-situ conservation of crop plant varieties and useful wild plants. *Applied Ethnobotany: people, wild plant use and conservation* focuses on practical steps to develop a better understanding of the values, vulnerability and resource management options for wild, non-cultivated plant resources. All three manuals stress the essential collaborative nature of ethnobotany, linking scientific and folk knowledge. They also contribute to efforts to build local capacity for plants conservation by promoting applied research on biodiversity conservation which strengthens connections between biological and social sciences.

Over the past 30 years, conservation efforts have broadened from the earlier emphasis on increasingly insular, strictly protected areas to a broader approach involving land users in 'bioregional' management at an ecosystem level. This broader approach is evident in the different World Conservation Union (IUCN) categories of protected areas which were developed in the mid 1980s and recently modified at the IV World Congress on National Parks and Protected Areas (Chapter 1, Box 1.1). It also represents a change from one where intervention by the state (by government) through proclamation of national parks was seen as the solution, to one where the role of private landowners and residents of communal lands are recognized. Despite increased awareness of environmental concerns and international backing for conservation, many national parks have inadequate staff or funding to control often large protected areas.

The focus of this manual

This manual focuses on an issue crucial to rural development and conservation: the impact of harvesting of wild plants by people. It thus covers the borderland between cultural and biological diversity. It is intended as a practical guide to approaches and field methods for participatory work between resource users and field researchers. In particular, it is aimed at African students or professionals working in conservation, rural development or as national park managers who have to make resource management decisions.

The emphasis of the manual is on how to identify the most urgent problems, needs and opportunities relating to wild plant use and resource management. It also aims to provide practical guidelines for research which interface applied ecological approaches with the knowledge and expertise of local resource users.

The excellent ecological primer written by Charles Peters (1994) provided guidelines for the sustainable harvest of non-timber forest products, focusing primarily on examples from South-East Asia and Latin America. This manual looks beyond tropical forests to other vegetation types as well, with many of its examples drawn from Africa.

There are three reasons for this. The first is that despite the great importance wild plant use plays in African people's lives, far more attention seems to have been given to plant use in Asia or Latin America than in Africa. Secondly, it is the continent where I was born and have spent most of my life. Thirdly, plant use by people is an increasingly important issue to take into account at the interface between conservation areas and local communities, and African conservation areas are a prime example of this. Understaffed, with limited money and manpower, and sometimes overrun by warfare, many conservation areas exist virtually only on paper. Examples over the past decade alone are national parks in Angola, Chad, Ethiopia, Liberia, Mozambique, Rwanda, Sierra Leone, Somalia, Sudan, Uganda and the Democratic Republic of Congo (formerly Zaire) (Figure I.1). Projections for the future of prime conservation areas such as forests are considered to be bleak (Barnes, 1990). It will become even bleaker if planning of protected areas does not take local land and plant use into account. To some extent, similar problems are faced in parts of Latin America and Asia, affecting not only the future of land set aside for biodiversity conservation, but also the lives of people surrounding national parks and nature reserves. Whether effective answers to these questions can be found that can benefit both people and conservation remains to be seen, and careful monitoring of resource sharing and participatory management projects is essential (Kremen et al, 1994).

Figure I.1 *Can protected areas survive under these circumstances? A patrol ranger in Mgahinga Gorilla National Park, a Ugandan conservation area in the Virunga Mountains on the border of Rwanda and the Democratic Republic of Congo*

Why use the term 'wild' plants?

Some people are uncomfortable with the term 'wild' in the title of this manual, feeling that it sidesteps issues of indigenous peoples' intellectual property. What is important is the context in which 'wild' is used. As you read through this manual, you will see that I have stressed that there are few landscapes in the world that are not affected by human disturbance. Some of these were deliberately burned, manipulating plant production with fire as a tool to 'domesticate' some landscapes. There is no controversy about this. Few virgin habitats exist on earth, and landscape 'domestication' using fire predates plant species domestication by people by about 200,000 years. At a species level, I use the term wild to distinguish between wild and domesticated plant species, where domesticated plant species are those whose breeding systems have been so changed through genetic or phenotypic selection that they have become dependent upon sustained human assistance for their survival. Wild and domesticated species are at opposite ends of a continuum (Figure I.2). 'Wild' is also a lot shorter than alternative terms, such as 'traditional non-domesticated plant resources'.

PLANT-EXPLOITATIVE ACTIVITY	ECOLOGICAL EFFECTS (SELECTED EXAMPLES)	FOOD-YIELDING SYSTEM	SOCIOECONOMIC TRENDS			TIME
Burning vegetation Gathering/collecting Protective tending	Reduction of competition; accelerated recycling of mineral nutrients; stimulation of asexual reproduction; selection for annual or ephemeral habit; synchronization of fruiting Casual dispersal of propagules Reduction of competition; local soil disturbance	Wild plant–food procurement (foraging)				
Replacement planting/ sowing Transplanting/sowing Weeding Harvesting Storage Drainage/irrigation	Maintenance of plant population in the wild Dispersal of propagules to new habitats Reduction of competition; soil modification Selection for dispersal mechanisms: positive and negative Selection and redistribution of propagules Enhancement of productivity; soil modification	Wild plant–food procurement (with minimal tillage)				
Land clearance Systematic soil tillage Propagation of genotypic and phenotypic variants: DOMESTICATION Cultivation of domesticated crops (cultivars)	Transformation of vegetation composition and structure Modification of soil texture, structure and fertility Establishment of agroecosystems	Cultivation (with systematic tillage) Agriculture (farming)				
		Evolutionary differentiation of agricultural systems				

Column labels (vertical) under SOCIOECONOMIC TRENDS: Increasing sedentism (settlement size, density and duration of occupation); Increasing population density (local, regional and continental); Increasing social complexity (ranking → stratification → state formation).

Running vertical label: PLANT-FOOD PRODUCTION.

Source: Harris, 1989

Figure I.2 *A schematic continuum from wild to domesticated plant species, from foraging of wild species to farming domesticated species*

Problems in conservation

Seen from the outside, the problems facing conservation and resource management seem insurmountable. Indeed, many efforts to solve these problems through interventions planned from the 'outside' by urban-based planners or policy makers have failed. For this reason, there has been a move away from centralized planning and identification of problems to a decentralized, local approach. Ethnobotanical methods are part of this decentralized approach, where people contribute to solutions in resourceful ways, rather than being part of the problem.

Innovative, decentralized approaches also have a way of catching on and spreading. Two examples are CAMPFIRE (Communal Areas Management Programme for Indigenous Resources) in Zimbabwe (Child, 1996) and Joint Forest Management Programme projects spread across India and Nepal (Poffenberger et al, 1992a, b; Fischer, 1995). Although small, and begun in isolation, these programmes have built up experience and common ground that have been more widely applied. Norman Reynolds's experience with community forestry in India, for example, led to recommendations for Community Land Companies (CLC), aimed at combining local people's control of natural resource harvesting with effective resource management. CLCs were later proposed for rural development in southern Africa (Reynolds, 1981) and for strengthening traditional fisheries management (Scudder and Conelly, 1985).

Some creative projects give signs of hope, however, even under the bleakest of circumstances. Two Central African examples highlight the need for training hand-picked local people in protected area management. One of the strongest tests of conservation strategies is how resilient they are to the chaos of civil conflicts. Recent tests of this stem from conservation areas in Rwanda and the Democratic Republic of Congo, engulfed by conflict (Hart and Hart, 1997; Fimbel and Fimbel, 1997). These Central African examples highlight the crucial need for appropriate training for hand-picked local people at various levels (rangers, technical staff, research professionals and managers) to take responsibility for conservation programmes. International non-governmental organizations have key roles in this process, and one of these is to support this training process. In both cases, international funding was disrupted and expatriate staff left or were evacuated due to conflicts in or around the Nyungwe Forest Conservation Project in Rwanda and four World Heritage Sites in the Democratic Republic of Congo. What maintained these conservation areas during the conflicts was the presence of local people connected to these projects.

The important lesson from both cases is summed up from the Rwandan case, where Nyungwe Forest, an Integrated Conservation and Development Project (ICDP) and a priority area for conservation, was held together in the face of lawlessness and land-grabs. Four local people with exceptional leadership qualities continued to collect and safeguard project records and liaise with people neighbouring the park and local government representatives. Of 45 local staff, all from villages bordering the conservation area, 40 remained, continuing to undertake forest patrols without salaries or communications from former supervisors or senior staff, who had fled. The main lesson is:

> '... *that vehicles, buildings, and short-term consultants supported by large multinationals do not make a conservation project. Instead, conservation is achieved by people with commitment. Project personnel recruited from the local population who demonstrate qualities of leadership and commitment, who receive regular hands-on training that empowers them to take responsibility for the management of their natural resources, are the formula proven to sustain long-term conservation efforts under difficult conditions. The combination of a few dedicated individuals, together with the support of a non-governmental organization (independent of political constraints) with a long-term commitment to conservation, is the best recipe for achieving lasting success in countries where political stability is in question, or perhaps anywhere.*' (Fimbel and Fimbel, 1997)

People and Plants Partners

WWF

WWF (formerly the World Wide Fund For Nature), founded in 1961, is the world's largest private nature conservation organization. It consists of 29 national organizations and associates, and works in more than 100 countries. The coordinating headquarters are in Gland, Switzerland. The WWF mission is to conserve biodiversity, to ensure that the use of renewable natural resources is sustainable and to promote actions to reduce pollution and wasteful consumption.

UNESCO

The United Nations Educational, Scientific and Cultural Organization (UNESCO) is the only UN agency with a mandate spanning the fields of science (including social sciences), education, culture and communication. UNESCO has over 40 years of experience in testing interdisciplinary approaches to solving environmental and development problems in programmes such as that on Man and the Biosphere (MAB). An international network of biosphere reserves provides sites for conservation of biological diversity, long-term ecological research and testing and demonstrating approaches to the sustainable use of natural resources.

ROYAL BOTANIC GARDENS, KEW

The Royal Botanic Gardens, Kew, has 150 professional staff and associated researchers and works with partners in over 42 countries. Research focuses on taxonomy, preparation of floras, economic botany, plant biochemistry and many other specialized fields. The Royal Botanic Gardens has one of the largest herbaria in the world and an excellent botanic library.

The African component of the People and Plants Initiative is supported financially by the Darwin Initiative, the National Lottery Charities Board and the Department for International Development (DFID) in the UK, and by the Norwegian Funds in Trust.

DISCLAIMER

While the organizations concerned with the production of this manual firmly believe that its subject is of great importance for conservation, they are not responsible for the detailed opinons expressed.

Acknowledgements

This manual is dedicated to the students and young professionals from rural communities in developing countries who often work in isolation, sacrifice a great deal, and who are at the forefront of conservation efforts and ethnobotanical research. It is also dedicated to my family, who have spent so much time without me when I have been in the field – or immersed in this manual.

A manual of this type is not just based on years of field work, but is a product of discussions with many colleagues over a long time: too many to acknowledge individually here. Nevertheless, I must thank a few people: William Bond, Charles Breen, Bruce Campbell, Bekazitha Gwala, Margie Jacobsen, Jeremy Midgley, Eugene Moll, Jackson Mutebi, Bev Sithole, Ken Tinley, Fiona Walsh, Rob Wild and Siyabonga Zondi for inspiring discussions; my colleagues in the People and Plants Initiative for their support and for reading through parts of this manual at different stages: Alan Hamilton, Gary Martin, Robert Hoeft and Yildiz Aumerruddy. Richard Cowling, Martin Luckert, Jeremy Midgley, Jack Putz and Trish Shanley also commented on sections of the manual, as did the series editor, Martin Walters.

I must thank both Martin Walters and Alan Hamilton for their interest, patience and understanding during the long process of writing this manual between field trips and supporting students. Wendy Hitchcock is thanked for drawing several of the figures. Reprinted figures are acknowledged in the text, but I must thank Charles Peters for the use of several figures from his ecological primer, Terry Sunderland, De Wet Bösenberg, Robin Guy, Glen Mills, Fiona Walsh and Yildiz Aumeeruddy for contributing photographs, and the McGregor Museum, Kimberley, South Africa, for permission to use an unpublished photograph (Figure 4.6) from the Duggan-Cronin collection. Where not acknowledged, the slides are my own.

Finally, I should like to thank the organizations that have funded the African component of the People and Plants Initiative, as this has also supported production of this manual: funds to WWF from the Darwin Initiative, the National Lottery Charities Board (NLCB) and the Department for International Development (DFID) in the UK, and to UNESCO through the Norwegian Funds in Trust.

Chapter 1

Conservation and Context: Different Times, Different Views

Introduction

Throughout the world, wild, naturalized or non-cultivated plants provide a 'green social security' to hundreds of millions of people, for example in the form of low-cost building materials, fuel, food supplements, herbal medicines, basketry containers for storage, processing or preparation of food crops, or as a source of income. Edible wild foods often help prevent starvation during drought, while economically important species provide a buffer against unemployment during cyclical economic depressions. This is particularly important for people living in areas with drought-susceptible soils of marginal agricultural potential, such as the vast areas of sub-equatorial Africa covered by leached, nutrient-poor sands (Figure 1.1). Despite the immense importance of these plant resources, their value is rarely taken into account in land-use planning; and when it is, it is often assumed that these species are sustainably harvested and that this 'green social security' will always be available to provide a safety net for resource users. This is not always true. Although many ecosystems and harvested species populations are resilient and have a long history of human use, they can be pushed beyond

recovery through habitat destruction or overexploitation.

Cultural systems are even more dynamic than biological ones, and the shift from a subsistence economy to a cash economy is a dominant factor amongst all but the remotest of peoples. In many parts of the world, 'traditional' conservation practices have been weakened by cultural change, increased human needs and numbers, and by a shift to cash economies. There is a growing number of cases where resources which were traditionally conserved, or which appeared to be conserved, are today being overexploited. The people whose ancestors hunted, harvested and venerated the forests that are the focus of enthusiastic conservation efforts are sometimes the people who are felling the last forest patches for maize fields or coffee plantations, often on slopes so steep that sustainable agriculture is impossible. In other areas, local human populations have decreased due to epidemic disease or even urbanization, with swidden agriculture only occurring on old secondary forest. While some resources are being overharvested due to cultural and economic change, the majority are still used sustainably, and the

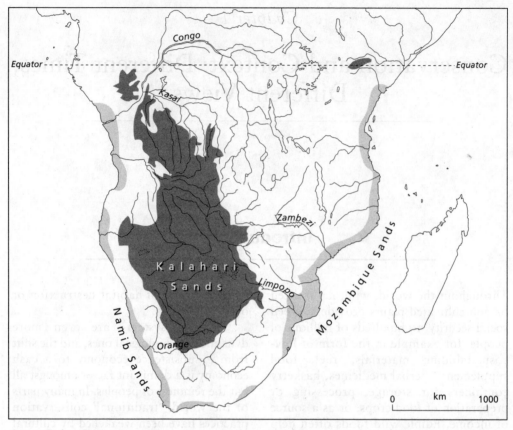

Source: Cooke, 1964

Figure 1.1 *Soils are a major determinant of reliance on plant use. In Africa, for example, the distribution of leached, nutrient-poor and drought-susceptible sands of the coast (light grey shading) and Kalahari basin (dark grey shading) affects most land users. Whether they are hunter-gatherers, pastoralists or farmers, people remain dependent to some extent upon wild plants (and the associated edible insects) for food supplements, housing, fuel, furniture and fibre for household containers*

impact on others has lessened because of social change. In the most extreme cases, 'islands' of remaining vegetation, usually created by habitat loss through agricultural clearance, then become focal points for harvesting pressure, and are sites of conflict over remaining land or resources.

For all interest groups, whether resource users, rural development workers or national park managers, it is far better to have proactive management and to stop or phase out destructive harvesting in favour of suitable alternatives before

overexploitation occurs, than to have the 'benefit' of hindsight in the midst of a devastated resource. Marilyn Hoskins (1990) puts this well in her paper on forestry and food security:

All research and management by outsiders must remember that their activities come and go, but food security – land and resources surety – is a long-term, life and death issue for rural peoples.

2

Historical context

Since the 1960s, the approach to conservation in developing countries has broadened from its past emphasis on strictly policed protected areas, or land set aside for large mammals or spectacular landscapes. Nowadays the emphasis has shifted to sustainable resource use and the maintenance of ecological processes and genetic diversity and a broader approach involving land users in 'bioregional' management at an ecosystem level.

This broader approach is evident in the different IUCN categories of protected areas which were developed in the mid 1980s and recently modified at the IV World Congress on National Parks and Protected Areas (Box 1.1). It also represents a change from one where intervention by the state (by government) through proclamation of national parks was seen as the solution, to one where the conservation roles of private landowners and residents of communal lands are recognized. It also became widely accepted that the future of most conservation areas largely depends upon the acceptance and support of the surrounding human populations. In Africa, for example, the consequences of political turmoil, changes of government and a 'brain drain' of park biologists and policy makers, reinforce Jonathan Kingdon's (1990) point that:

'... the realities of power are exactly the opposite to those perceived by most of the participants of this struggle to conserve key areas of high endemism and biodiversity because the long-term future of Africa's Centres of Endemism lies with local peasantries rather more than with transient governments or enthusi-astic conservationists; yet locals seldom receive the respect that is generally accorded to those that wield power. Meanwhile, both populations and resentments grow.

... The conservationists' answers should not lie in propaganda campaigns, which are generally seen for what they are, but in a shared growth of knowledge and debate. The minimal demands of local communities will include sustained, not ephemeral, programmes of action in which their own people can find meaningful, decisive and dignified roles.'

At a meeting in Tanzania in the 1960s, Sir Julian Huxley suggested that the means to justify conservation as a form of land use to local people or national governments centred upon 'pride, profit, protein and prestige'. Little attention was paid to wild plants and their importance to rural people. This is no longer the case. There is now a strong emphasis on sustainable use of resources, including wild plants, and the involvement of national governments and local people in conservation. Buffer zones, formed around strictly protected core conservation areas, have been one of the tools in this process and are a characteristic planning tool of biosphere reserves established by the UNESCO Man and Biosphere programme. This approach is embodied in many recent policy documents, such as the World Conservation Union's (1991) strategy document *Caring for the Earth*, and more recently, the World Resources Institute's

Box 1.1 IUCN Protected Area Categories: the modified system of protected areas categories agreed at the IV World Congress on National Parks and Protected Areas, 1992

1 Strict Nature Reserve/Wilderness Area

Areas of land and/or sea possessing some outstanding or representative ecosystems, geological or physiological features and/or species, available primarily for scientific research and/or environmental monitoring; or large areas of unmodified or slightly modified land, and/or sea, retaining their natural character and influence, without permanent or significant habitation, which are protected and managed so as to preserve their natural condition.

2 National Park

Protected areas managed mainly for ecosystem conservation and recreation. Natural areas of land and/or sea, designated to:

- Protect the ecological integrity of one or more ecosystems for this and future generations.
- Exclude exploitation or occupation inimical to the purposes of designation of the area.
- Provide a foundation for spiritual, scientific, educational, recreational and visitor opportunities, all of which must be environmentally and culturally compatible.

3 Natural Monument

Protected areas managed mainly for conservation of specific features. Areas containing one or more specific natural or natural/cultural features of outstanding or unique value because of their inherent rarity, representative or aesthetic qualities or cultural significance.

4 Habitat/Species Management Area

Protected areas managed mainly for conservation through management intervention. Areas of land and/or sea subject to active intervention for management purposes in order to ensure the maintenance of habitats and/or to meet the requirements of specific species.

5 Protected Landscape/Seascape

Protected areas managed mainly for landscape/seascape conservation and recreation. Areas of land, with coast and sea as appropriate, where the interaction of people and nature over time has produced areas of distinct character with significant aesthetic, cultural and/or ecological value, and often with high biological diversity. Safeguarding the integrity of this traditional interaction is vital to the protection, maintenance and evolution of such areas.

6 Managed Resource Protected Area

Protected areas managed mainly for the sustainable use of natural ecosystems. Areas containing predominantly unmodified natural systems, managed to ensure long-term protection and maintenance of biological diversity, while providing at the same time a sustainable flow of natural products and services to meet community needs.

Source: IUCN

(1992) *Global Biodiversity Strategy* (WRI, 1992) and the World Convention on Biological Diversity (see Glowka et al, 1994).

Policies on sustainable development or calls for sustainable use of resources by local people within protected areas (for example, Ghimire and Pimbert, 1997) are fine on paper. The challenges arise with their implementation. In their review of conservation projects, trying to make a link between parks and people through planning of buffer zones and links to development (which they termed Integrated Conservation and Development Projects), Michael Wells and Katrina Brandon (1992) found very few buffer zone models which they were convinced worked well. As usual, 'the devil is in the details': and if policies are impractical, they are worthless. If implementation results in resource degradation rather than the sustainable use intended, then the self-sufficiency of resource users is further reduced, increasing the likelihood of land-use conflict between national parks and people. This manual is about one of those details: the sustainable harvesting of wild plant resources.

Management myths and effective partnerships

Policy changes towards sustainable use of resources in conservation areas have placed many field researchers and national parks managers in a dilemma. How do we go beyond the rhetoric of policy on human needs and sustainable resource use without jeopardizing the natural resource base or primary goal of the conservation area: the maintenance of habitat and species diversity? This is no easy task. The higher the number of harvesters, the more uses a plant species has. The scarcer the resource, the greater the chance that resource managers and local people will get embroiled in a complex juggling of uses and demands, in an attempt at a compromise that could end up satisfying nobody.

In theory, sustainable harvesting of plants from wild populations is possible, but is often more complex than the urban biopoliticians and policy makers think. Sustainable management of wild plant use by people depends as much upon an understanding of the biological component as it does on the social and economic aspects of wild plant use. Without an understanding of ecological, political and socio-economic factors (Figure 1.2), plans for sustainable use are likely to fail.

Sustainable use of resources by local people and the concept of 'extractive reserves' appear to have been promoted in developing countries on the basis of two commonly held assumptions that:

1 Local (or indigenous) peoples have been harvesting these resources for thousands of years, with no detrimental effects on harvested populations. Traditionally, many useful biological resources have been valued and conserved. Therefore if 'resource sharing' between national parks and neighbouring peoples takes place in buffer zone areas, then the people living around that national park will have an interest in conserving resources for the future, and will harvest these resources in a sustainable way.

2 Wider recognition for wild plant products, whether from forests, savanna or wetlands, will result in more appropriate values being placed on vegetation currently being damaged

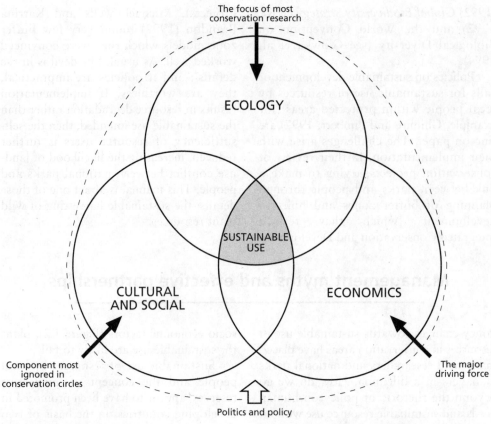

The focus of most
conservation research

ECOLOGY

SUSTAINABLE
USE

CULTURAL
AND SOCIAL

ECONOMICS

Component most
ignored in
conservation circles

The major
driving force

Politics and policy

Source: Martin, 1994

Figure 1.2 *Achieving sustainable use of resources requires cross-disciplinary work at the confluence of the social sciences, economics and ecological studies, all within a political (and policy) framework*

for a few products (hardwood timber-logging, charcoal) or cleared for agriculture or pasture, ignoring other protective (eg watersheds) and productive (nuts, oils, fibres, etc) functions.

While there is some truth in these assumptions, they have reached almost mythical proportions, with the result that local resource users are often considered natural conservationists who have always used natural resources sustainably. There is no doubt that 'traditional' conservation practices existed in many societies, and that these have buffered the effects of

people on favoured species and in selected habitats. Customary restrictions can also be an important guide to culturally acceptable limits on the harvesting of vulnerable species (see Chapter 6). Equally, there are many examples of resource overexploitation prior to the introduction of firearms and more efficient hunting technologies or large-scale, species-specific commercial trade.

Also often glossed over is the fact that protected areas, particularly those with a high species diversity and vulnerability to overexploitation, require a level of detailed management that is not possible with the

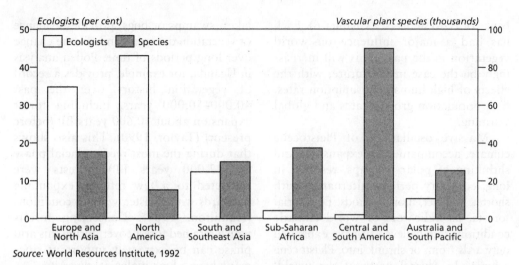

Source: World Resources Institute, 1992

Figure 1.3 *The distribution of professional ecologists in relation to the distribution of plant species richness*

economic constraints that are a feature of many conservation departments. Despite increased awareness of environmental concerns and international backing for conservation, many national parks have inadequate staff or funding to control often large protected areas. The level of responsibility faced by two young Ugandans supported through the People and Plants Initiative provides a typical example: one Ugandan is the only ecological monitoring officer for Rwenzori Mountains National Park, 1300km² in extent. The other is warden of Semliki National Park, 219km² in size. While similar sized parks in the US would have a team of ecologists or park managers, these young professionals carry immense responsibility for huge areas on their own. This is not an unusual situation in developing countries, and worldwide there is an inverse relationship between plant species richness and numbers of ecologists (Figure 1.3).

Vegetation change: spatial and time scales

Lack of communication between disciplines has led to a number of misconceptions, myths and inaccuracies in conceptual models. Limits on a 'cross-pollination' of concepts have occurred at two levels: firstly, between different academic disciplines, principally between the biological and social sciences; and secondly, between formally trained researchers and local peoples and resource users. The resultant misconceptions have had important implications for biodiversity conservation, and have prevented a clear understanding of how ecological systems function and how dynamic biological and cultural systems change over time. Climate change over long time scales can be superimposed by human-induced changes on vegetation, for example, while cultural change can be rapid.

To facilitate informed decision making, plant use and conservation policy have to be seen against the background influences of climate and human disturbance of ecosystems (see Chapter 6). Each has had a major influence on world vegetation in the past. This will increasingly be the case in the future, with the effects of high human consumption rates, high population growth rates and global warming.

Massive oscillations of Pleistocene climate, accompanied by expansions and shrinking of polar ice caps, resulted in long, cool, dry periods, alternating with shorter, warmer, moist periods. Equatorial forests, as indicators of world climatic conditions, are believed to have expanded outwards from, or shrunk into, Pleistocene refugia. In several parts of the world, pollen analysis from cores, usually taken in lakes, swamps or bogs, provides evidence of vegetation dynamics and climate change over long periods of time. Pollen analysis in Uganda, for example, provides a record of vegetation history over the past 40,000–50,000 years, including forest expansion about 10,600 years BP (before present) (Taylor, 1990). This also shows that during the most recent glacial phase (pre-12,000 years BP), forests were restricted to a few refugia, expanding outwards with moister, warmer conditions (Hamilton, 1981). Conserving forests which retained forest cover during this arid phase can be extremely important since many have a high biological diversity.

Human influence: landscapes and species

Human disturbance and deliberate modification of vegetation have been superimposed on natural disturbance, sometimes in the relatively recent past. Local people in many parts of the world have also favoured certain useful species through traditional conservation practices, dispersal and planting. Anthropogenic changes caused by agricultural clearing, burning patterns or species-selective overexploitation are sometimes overlooked at a policy level. Archaeological studies similarly show the extinction of mammal and bird species on islands such as Hawaii and New Zealand, or the complete disappearance of forest habitat and palm woodlands on Easter Island after the arrival of Polynesians (Diamond, 1992; Flannery, 1995). Human-induced or anthropogenic changes due to the use of fire, for example, have long been recognized by ecologists as contributing to the maintenance of African savanna or of prairie grasslands in North America. Archaeologists have also provided detailed evidence of how long-lasting such changes can be in creating small-scale patches within savanna woodlands, as in the 1000-year-old *Cenchrus ciliaris* grass patches on early Iron Age dung accumulations in Botswana.

In tropical forests, this has been less commonly recognized until recently. To many city people who support rainforest conservation, whether they are from urban areas of the tropics such as São Paulo or Bangkok, or temperate cities such as London and New York, even disturbed secondary rainforest might appear to be pristine. This is understandable, given their unfamiliarity with these environments – but until biologists started talking to people, they had also often been misled. Darrell Posey, for example, working with Kayapo people of the Brazilian Amazon, has shown that certain 'wild' plants along paths through 'pristine' forest are in fact planted by the Kayapo as a source of food, medicine and other resources (Posey, 1984). Expanding this approach to the entire Amazon terra firma forest, William Balee (1989), of the New York Botanical Garden, estimates that at least 11.8 per cent of this forest is anthropogenic. Even biologists well aware of the dynamic nature of vegetation change can be surprised by what they find in seemingly 'undisturbed' forests in remote areas. Thus biologist Alan Hamilton, digging soil pits in 'remnant' forests of the Usambara Mountains of Tanzania, East Africa (which had been selected as soil sample sites for their 'undisturbed' status), regularly found charcoal and pottery; the sites had been occupied by people with iron-smelting and agricultural technology from about 1800 years ago (Hamilton and Bensted-Smith, 1989).

If human influence and cultural landscapes are so widespread, why then use the term 'wild' plants in the title of this manual? I raise this point because a colleague involved in policy and intellectual property rights issues was uncomfortable with the term 'wild'. The main reason for this concern is that the term is linked to the word 'wilderness', usually taken to mean an uninhabited or uncultivated tract of land. Use of the word 'wild' was then considered to undermine the issues of indigenous peoples' intellectual property rights. The sense in which the word 'wild' is used here is explained in the introduction. At a species level, I use the term 'wild' to distinguish between wild and domesticated plant species, not to suggest that the landscapes where they occur are virgin land, unaffected by human influence or tenure.

Out of a global flora of 270, 000 plant species, relatively few are domesticated (species whose breeding systems have been so changed through genetic or phenotypic selection that they have become dependent upon sustained human assistance for their survival). The vast majority of species are wild. Others along the continuum are replanted from wild-collected seed or seedlings, self-sown species which are managed or tolerated in fields, or semi-domesticates in the process of domestication, where phenotypic (and genotypic) modifications have arisen through people deliberately selecting favoured characteristics. The quantitative ethnobotanical studies by Alejandro Casas and Javier Caballero (1996) on selective management of *Leucaena* by Mixtec Indians is a good example of this process. Innovative quantitative studies like theirs that carefully document this process are extremely useful.

Also important is the development of quantitative methods and predictive models, rather than lists of species or anecdotal data. Such models can lead to a more effective conservation of the remaining habitats. These sites may hold the wild relatives of domesticated species, or wild species which are too slow growing and take such a long time to reach reproductive maturity that in situ conservation is their only option.

Chapter 2

Local Inventories, Values and Quantities of Harvested Resources

Introduction

The methods outlined in this chapter are the steps used to get a better understanding of people's preferences and the demand for particular plant species. Although some plant uses such as harvesting of wood for fuel, building or commercial woodcarving are more obvious, occurring throughout the year and in large volume, wild plant gathering is often part of a 'hidden economy' unnoticed by outsiders. Consequently, careful field observation, sensitive consultation with local harvesters and strategic planning are required before any monitoring takes place. Even the identity of some commonly harvested species, often well known to local people, is often poorly known to protected area managers or outside researchers. Each

method provides useful information on its own, but ideally should be cross-checked against data collected using different methods.

If alternatives are to be provided to prevent overexploitation of resources or to defuse land-use conflicts before demand exceeds supply, it is also important to know what quantities of plant material are being harvested. If this is not known, it is very easy to underestimate quantities of the resource required, or to provide only piecemeal alternatives in such small quantity that they are of little practical value. The 'resource demand' component discussed here and in Chapter 3 leads on to the 'resource supply' components covered in Chapters 4, 5 and 6.

Local priorities: vegetation types, resource categories and species

A reversal of roles has always been implicit in ethnobotanical work. Formally trained outsiders, whatever their experience, have a lot to learn from the insights of local people who are acknowledged within their own communities as experts on local

vegetation. As a result, local people play a crucial role at several parts in the research process, including research design, specimen and data collection, interpretation of data and, less commonly, the presentation of research results back to the community.

Amongst development practitioners, this type of approach, where local people help in conducting research, has given rise to the term 'participatory research'. It is important to realize that this does not refer to a single research method, as Brian Pratt and Peter Loizos (1992) point out:

'Although some writers make it sound as though there is a separate "participatory" research method, this is misleading. The idea of participation is more an overall guiding philosophy of how to proceed, than a selection of specific methods. So when people talk about participatory research, participatory monitoring and participatory evaluation, on the whole they are not discussing a self-contained set of methodologies, but a situation whereby the methods being used have included an element of strong involvement and consultation on the part of the subjects of the research. Not all methods are equally amenable to participation.'

Considerable common ground for joint work in resource management often exists. Resource users, development workers and protected area managers often have a common interest in cases of conflicts over valued but vulnerable plant resources. This can be due to restrictions on harvesting of rare species or vegetation within protected areas, to overexploitation arising from demand exceeding supply for useful wild plant species, or to conflicts between local harvesters and people from outside the community. Involvement of resource users as research partners is an essential part of a successful conservation strategy for useful plant species that are vulnerable to overexploitation. There are three main reasons for this.

Firstly, the knowledge and perceptions of resource users such as traditional healers, craft workers and commercial medicinal plant harvesters provide valuable insights into the scarcity of useful plant species. It is these resource users who walk further or pay more for scarce resources, and are thus aware of scarcity long before any conservation biologists. Their knowledge therefore provides a 'short-cut', saving time and money, and enabling biologists to monitor key species. Local knowledge represents a practical and cost-effective method for identifying possible key species. In some cases, as with small, cryptic and low-population density plants such as *Schlechterina mitostemmatoides* (Passifloraceae), it provides the main evidence of occurrence as commercial trade items, and can direct specialist monitoring and conservation programmes. The validity of local knowledge can also be tested against data in herbaria and in literature on the geographical distribution, rarity and extent of exploitation of species. Thus, local traders' conceptions of scarcity may be a result of limited geographical distribution rather than overexploitation – for example, in the case of the medicinal plant *Synaptolepis kirkii* (Thymelaeaceae) in South Africa.

Secondly, dialogue with resource users is a crucial part of developing conservation and resource management proposals with, rather than for, resource users. This includes interaction with resource users about their perceptions as to why scarcity has arisen, setting quotas and human carrying capacities if practical, and identifying appropriate alternatives and how these can be implemented.

Thirdly, it enables specialist user groups to be identified. Rural communities are not homogeneous, but are complex networks, divided on the basis of power, gender and specialist interest groups. People who specialize in harvesting specific resources such as medicinal plants, basketry fibres or woodcarving timber can have a direct interest in maintaining rural self-sufficiency and in ensuring that further resource degradation (or alterna- tively, restoration of diversity and self-sufficiency) takes place. Identifying different user groups plays an important role in the social side of resource manage- ment (see Chapter 7).

Choosing the right methods

Choices of methods should be made case-by-case on the basis of preliminary planning, bearing in mind timetable and budget constraints. More detail is given on these methods in this chapter and in Chapters 3 (ethnobotanical surveys of markets), 4 to 6 (harvesting impacts and vegetation dynamics) and Chapter 7 (tenure).

Once permission for research work has been granted at a national and local level, then researchers need to decide on the survey methods that are appropriate. Commonly used methods are:

- discussions with individual resource users;
- group interviews and discussions;
- rapid rural appraisal (RRA), partici- patory rural appraisal (PRA) and participatory assessment, monitoring and evaluation (PAME);
- social surveys using various sampling techniques and structured or semi-structured interviews;
- participant observation;
- ethnobotanical inventory methods;
- sample surveys based on field records with local resource users;
- surveys of plants sold in local markets (see Chapter 3).

In the past five years, several excellent manuals and reviews have been published that give detailed descriptions of different methods. Many of these are readily avail- able through organizations supporting field work in developing countries. Rather than repeat the detail contained in these manuals, I will first give an overview of social survey methods that are commonly used, such as interview surveys and various participatory methods. I also recommend that, if at all possible, researchers or the organizations they are working for should obtain these useful methods manuals that are suggested for further reading at the end of this chapter. I then describe ethnobotanical survey methods and approaches in more detail. Ethnobotanical methods mentioned by Gary Martin (1995) or by John Tuxill and Gary Nabhan (1998) are then described in more detail in this chapter. Other recent and useful reviews of methods covered in this chapter are Oliver Phillips's (1996) review of quantitative methods, and Darna Dufour's and Nicolette Teufel's (1995) description of methods for assess- ing food use and dietary intake.

There are four recent methods manuals that I would recommend for field researchers planning to use social survey methods: *Social Survey Methods: a Field-Guide for Development Workers* (Nichols, 1991); *Choosing Research Methods: Data Collection for Development Workers* (Pratt and Loizos, 1992); *The Community Toolbox: the Ideas, Methods and Tools for Participatory Assessment, Monitoring and Evaluation in Community Forestry* (FAO, 1990) in the FAO Community Forestry field manual series available from FAO/SIDA Forests, Trees and People

1 **Resource users identify problem:** which species, where, why?
2 **Are background data available?** Formal or informal sales data? How do trends in sales (up) compare to natural resource supply (down)?
3 **For key species, translate 'user units'** (bundles, bags, baskets) **into 'natural resource units** (leaves, stems etc → plants per hectare → total area → production rates → yields)
4 **With resource users: map, measure, mark, evaluate** (resources, harvest methods, impacts, 'harvest per unit effort')
5 **Identify practical alternatives** (and local opinion on how these could best be implemented, evaluation, adjustment of methods)

Basketry materials

Number of respondents

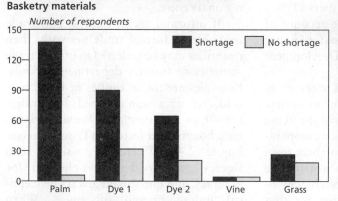

Legend: Shortage / No shortage

(Bar chart, y-axis 0–150; categories: Palm, Dye 1, Dye 2, Vine, Grass)

Botswanacraft total sales

Total sales value (Pula) (thousands)

Legend: Total sales / Local basket sales / Export basket sales / • No data

(Bar chart, y-axis 0–500; years 1972 through 1987)

Best method: palm cultivation

Producer plants own 57%
Do not know 1%
Large plantations 8%
Individuals and group 2%
No preference 3%
Communal groups 29%

Etsha interviews (n=123)

Figure 2.1 *Five basic steps in dealing with plant-resource management issues*

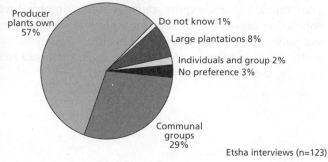

13

Programme; *Participatory Learning and Action: a Trainer's Guide* (Pretty et al, 1995), produced by the International Institute for Environment and Development (IIED), London, in their Participatory Methodology series.

These all give detailed and well-illustrated descriptions of social survey methods that are very useful in ethnobotanical work. Robert Chambers (1992) also provides a very readable account of PRA approaches in a discussion paper produced by the Institute for Development Studies.

Once the geographic focus of the study has been decided, it is useful to review relevant studies that have been done in the same region, or on the same or comparable resource species. For researchers from outside the region, it is also worthwhile finding out whether cross-references of vernacular to botanical names for that region are available. Background biological, social and economic information can come from a wide variety of published or unpublished reports, as well as from discussions with people who have lived and worked in the region for a long time. These may include, for example, previous ecological or social science studies published in journals, or unpublished reports of non-governmental organizations (NGOs) or government departments. A considerable amount of time can be saved by consulting and obtaining data from annual reports, export statistics and population census information in reports and publications of departments of health, trade and industry, agriculture and forestry, survey and lands, or geological survey. These may be available in a university, herbarium or government library. In each case, it is useful to have an introduction to someone in these organizations who is aware of the aims of the research. If not, despite the delays that may be caused by bureaucracy and poor filing systems, time can be saved through visiting these departments in the capital city or regional centre.

If informal sector harvest and trade feeds into a formal trade network, then quantities may be reflected in official trade statistics or forestry department records. Examples are the quantities of Brazil nuts sold, in data summarized by Prance (1990), or the quantity of *Prunus africana* bark bought by a factory in Cameroon (see Figure 2.4). Wherever possible, such figures need to be cross-checked for accuracy, and one should always be sceptical unless proved otherwise. When cross-checking, you may need to work 'backwards' from marketing surveys or export data to field studies. Although certain assumptions can be made from trade statistics on the basis of what part of the plant is harvested, and from the population biology, abundance and distribution of the species, trade data have limited value unless they are combined with field studies providing a link between volumes traded and what is happening to these species in the wild. In many cases, however, plant species are traded by the informal sector and no trade records exist: so if you need to document the quantities involved, you need to collect the data yourself (see Chapter 3).

Before starting: attitudes, time spans and cross-checking

Identifying local values or quantities of resources used is extremely difficult without community support: something that requires courtesy, consideration and time. Local support, in turn, is influenced by the social survey methods used, and the approach and attitude of the researcher, whether local or not. Ideally, it is best to carry out surveys with the help of a team, which should also include local researchers. In reality, however, this may not always be possible, and it is then even more important to ensure that all efforts are made to obtain as much relevant background information as possible before undertaking a survey. Before starting any field work, it is also worth thinking about the social context of the research: 'who watches whom' and 'whose priorities' are questions worth bearing in mind before field work begins.

In contrast to research studies whose hypotheses and objectives are set in urban laboratories, the objectives and methods for resource management research are best decided on in the field through preliminary work with local resource users and resource managers. In this process, it is important to consider the following:

- Who are the resource users: are they men, women or children and are they specialist plant users such as herbalists, weavers or midwives?
- What is their socio-economic and formal educational status?
- Is harvesting for commercial or subsistence purposes, or a combination of both?
- Which species or resource categories (eg fuelwood, thatch) are most in demand or most valued (culturally, economically, nutritionally)?

- When, where and how does collection take place – for instance, season, vegetation types (and patches within a vegetation type): what skills and technology are required?
- What are the effects of harvesting on plant populations and which species are most vulnerable to overexploitation?
- Are overexploitation and increased resource scarcity of concern within local communities (rich vs poor), nationally or internationally?
- In the case of multiple-use species, what are the effects of harvesting one species on the availability of other desired natural products?

Field observation: who watches whom?

With few exceptions, the resource users you are working with are not only perceptive observers of the environment, they are equally good observers and judges of human nature. Furthermore, they are often aware that outsiders, whether researchers, government officials or people from NGOs, may have worked in this or nearby communities in the past and made promises which were never kept, arrived with hidden agendas or took far more than they gave. Be well aware that this is a learning period on both sides, and a crucial one that can set a positive or negative tone for later work.

Field surveys with local people are more than just asking about uses and local names of plants; they also enable local people to ask questions of the researchers, such as: what attitudes do researchers show to local people and to one another? How serious and interested are they in addressing the problems raised at the community meetings preceding the research? How much do they know about the local vegetation? How do they measure up in working, camping or merely walking through the forests or woodland? Do they act like a bunch of city slickers or like people used to the bush? If they are completely ignorant, what hope is there of their resolving the problems that have been raised? Demonstrating some of your knowledge does not mean that you should shift away from your role as a person quietly questioning and stimulating discussion so that local people, as experts in their own right, contribute to the discussions. Your field knowledge will be apparent to local resource users from the questions you ask, the local terminology you use or the approaches you follow in identifying plants.

The 'walk in the woods' approach in the first stages of field work is an important opportunity to work in the field with the local people who know it best, as a stimulus for discussions and an opportunity for field observation. The emphasis is on relaxed and open-minded fieldwork, avoiding repetitive questioning and encouraging free-ranging discussion on plant uses and plant ecology. It may also be a time to observe and discuss signs of harvesting or patterns of plant distribution in relation to soils and disturbance. It also gives the local people the opportunity to observe and get to know the researchers, which is particularly important if they are outsiders; this is an important step which is often lost in 'rapid' surveys.

Short-term 'snapshots' or 'long-term surveys'

Do the aims of the research match up with the time and funding available? How accurate do you want to be? Fluctuations in volume of wild plant resources used,

with season, site differences of vegetation or markets as well as cultural factors, make estimates from short-term 'snapshots' difficult, and the results will be doubtful, whatever the short-term technique used.

In the early 1980s, for example, I started a study of the palm-wine trade, developing appropriate forms and training local enumerators at four palm-wine sale points. All palm-wine sales were monitored (the sale days being Monday, Wednesday, Friday); as the first few months of data accumulated, I excitedly did rough calculations, extrapolating from monthly sales volumes to the whole year. These preliminary estimates of total annual sales based on a few months' data were interesting, but with the benefit of hindsight, completely wrong. Once I had 12–18 months of sales data, I realized the extent of seasonal variations, with palm-wine sales rising in early summer (October–December), then plummeting between January–March when a much tastier local beer from *Sclerocarya birrea* fruits was available (see Figure 2.2b).

In addition, there were variations between markets and changes in yields of palm sap to take into account (see Figure 2.2c). If such survey work had been limited only to 'snapshots', the results would have been very different. If I had estimated total annual volume of palm wine sold on the basis of three months of sales records for October–December or, alternatively, records from January–March, they would have given totally different results, both incorrect. The same danger of extrapolating from short-term surveys also applies to other resources, including edible plants (see Figure 2.3), fuelwood or building materials. Long-term monitoring of quantities sold is expensive and time consuming, however, so you also need to ask yourself 'what level of precision is required?'

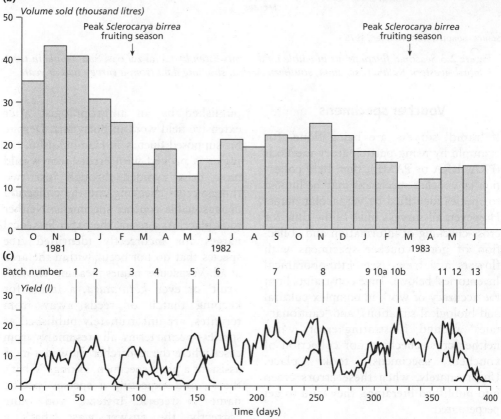

Figure 2.2 *The palm-wine trade and variation in volumes sold. (a) Daily measurements of sap yields to an individual tapper, keeping different 'batches' of sap separate. (b) Regional volumes sold at a single sales point. (c) Variation in yields from different groups of palms tapped by a single tapper*

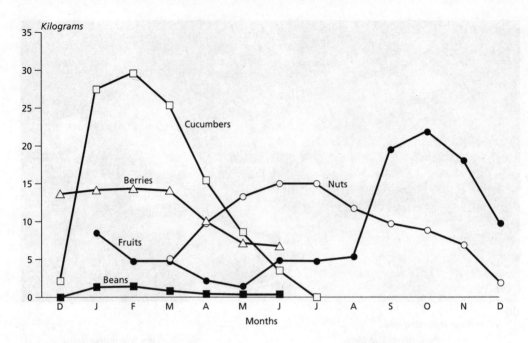

Source: adapted from Wilmsen, 1978

Figure 2.3 *Seasonal fluctuations in edible wild plants eaten by /ai /ai zu/ oasi San people in the north-western Kalahari savanna, southern Africa, showing data from a survey over a year*

Voucher specimens

If 'rapid' surveys are being done, for example by using participatory methods (PRA, RRA or PAME), then field collection of voucher specimens may be limited to species identified by vernacular name. However, all surveys must allow time for cross-checking of information and collection of good voucher specimens with flowers and fruits (see 'Ethnobotanical Inventories' below). Time constraints limit the accuracy of work in complex cultural and biological situations, and 'cautionary tales' abound, illustrating errors when neither cross-checking nor collection of voucher specimens took place. Unfortunately, when these errors creep into published literature, they tend to get perpetuated.

One such example is a paper on the ethnobotany of Hambukushu people,

published by an anthropologist after extensive field work in Botswana. Despite his supposed fluency in Hambukushu, the paper is packed with errors that would have been avoided through just two things: cross-checking and the collection of reasonable voucher specimens. Neither took place. As a result, the paper lists local names for incorrectly identified tree species that do not occur within the area at all. Vernacular names meaning 'flower', 'fruit' or even *kataratara*, a frame for keeping thatch or reeds away from termites, are unfortunately published as species-specific terms, all presumably from cases where the researcher showed a local assistant a plant specimen, asking: 'What's that?', and expecting a species-specific name in return. Instead, and quite correctly, the answer was: 'that's a flower...a fruit...a drying frame for reeds' (instead of the local name for the reed species). Similarly, throughout the world local terms for 'I don't know' have been published as species-specific names. Be careful!

Cross-checking

In addition to cross-checking the scientific and folk names of plants through collecting voucher specimens, it is important to cross-check information with different people and compare the results from different methods.

Whatever method or set of methods you use, it is important to consider the accuracy of the responses you receive. How appropriate (or inappropriate) are the methods and questions? No single method has all the answers – all have advantages and disadvantages. Nor can you always expect the answers you are given by local people to reflect your measures of time or quantity. 'Informant' accuracy, the responses you get from the people you interview or discuss things with, can vary greatly according to how they view your intentions. They may also see the issue in a different way (see Bernard et al, 1984). If someone says she walked for six kilometres to fetch fuelwood, then did she? If she really walked 3.7km to collect fuelwood, is this accurate enough or not? Is our use of 'kilometres' as a measure of effort appropriate or not, and if not, what is a more valid measure? It is crucial to cross-check information from a mix of different methods, even if you only compare the results from just two methods. If every researcher did this, there would be far fewer misunderstandings than is commonly the case.

Five cautionary examples are given here, where cross-checking showed discrepancies between methods. The first example deals with information from official records; the second compares records from conservation permit data with field studies of pole-wood cutting; and the third is a comparison of interview data with two sets of field data. The fourth example compares results from PRA and interview methods, and the final case shows how and why the role of wild plant foods in diet were underestimated.

Official data versus other sources

In some cases, long-term data are available from official statistics, such as where there are commercial sales for export, or where harvesting is allowed on the basis of permits. Scott Mori and Ghillean Prance (1990), for example, were able to obtain data from government reports for Brazil nuts over more than 50 years (1933–1985). If at all possible, this type of data needs cross-checking, since official statistics may be rather unreliable. Comparisons of quantities of medicinal *Prunus africana* bark exported from Cameroon from forestry department annual reports showed large discrepancies compared to primary data cross-checked from weigh-bridge returns from the single factory processing the bark (see Figure 2.4). The same applies to data from forestry permits or social surveys, whether interviews or PRA approaches.

Conservation department permit records versus cut bundles of poles

Working in Hlatikulu forest, South Africa, Dirk Muir (1990) assessed permit data accumulated by the conservation department where local woodcutters specified which tree species they would harvest for building poles. He compared these data against a large sample of poles already cut and bundled by the same woodcutters (593 poles, 2647 laths). This showed great discrepancies between the two sets of data (see Figure 2.5). Permit data on pole harvesting implied, for example, that 18

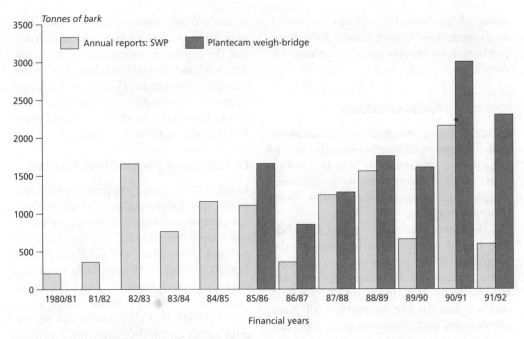

Figure 2.4 *Maintain a healthy skepticism and cross-check where possible: discrepancies between forestry annual report data and weigh-bridge returns for* Prunus africana *bark harvests in South-West Province, Cameroon*

species were harvested, with the top 10 species carrying 90 per cent of the utilization. By contrast, the cut-wood sample data showed that 37 species were harvested, with the top 10 species carrying 74 per cent of the utilization. Twenty-three of these 37 species are canopy tree species; this implied that there would be a long-term impact on the forest canopy from overexploitation of poles.

Interviews versus cut bundles versus cut stumps

Charlie Shackleton's (1993) study of fuelwood use also provides a cautionary example for field workers relying on information from a single method. Shackleton used three different methods (interviews, assessment of fuelwood bundles and identification of cut stems) to assess which fuelwood species were avoided or preferred (see Table 2.1).

PRA versus interview methods

Comparisons are made when different sets of people in the same area give very different responses to the same method. This often generates more questions than answers. PRA enthusiasts, for example, like to promote the use of PRA in recording quantitative as well qualitative data to express the numbers of people, cattle or relative amounts of resource collected. This may even be used to estimate annual or seasonal consumption rates. Working in Zimbabwe, Allison Goebel (1996) compared the results of PRA surveys with groups of people with information from individual interviews about the sale of different plant resources (fuelwood, poles, thatch-grass, herbal medicines, fruits, and wild collected and garden vegetables). She found that with the exception of garden vegetables, the PRA exercise greatly overestimated the extent to which local

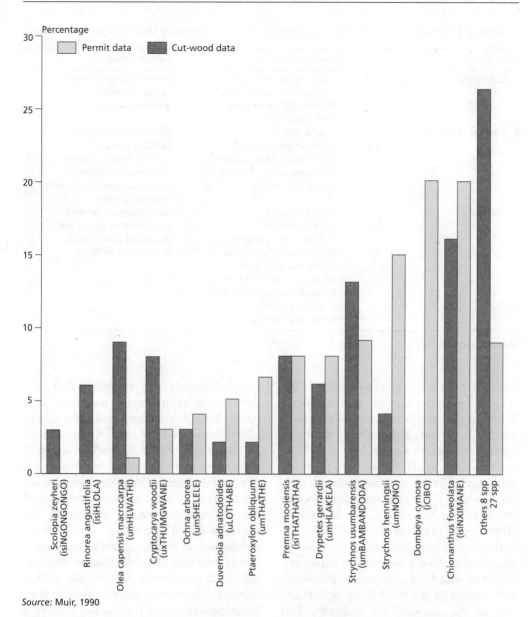

Source: Muir, 1990

Figure 2.5 *Comparison of the proportional species of pole harvests at Hlatikulu Forest Reserve from permit data and counts from a large sample of poles (n = 593) showing the inaccuracy of responses given in permit forms*

plant resources were sold. As a result, she suggested that it is extremely risky to accept PRA data as quantitatively reliable.

Methods for surveying gathered plant foods

Food lists and food records are commonly used for studying patterns of food selection and consumption. A useful reference on

Table 2.1 *A comparison of fuel wood preference or avoidance using three different methods*

Data source	Preferred species	Avoided species
1 Cut stems	Combretum collinum	Dichrostachys cinera
	Diospyros mespiliformis	Lantana camara
	Maytenus senegalensis	'pooled species'
	Terminalia sericea	
2 Fuelwood bundles	Acacia swazica	Dichrostachys cinera
	Combretum collinum	Lantana camara
	Combretum hereroense	Lonchocarpus capassa
	Peltophorum africanum	Maytenus senegalensis
	Terminalia sericea	Strychnos madagascariensis
		'pooled species'
3 Interviews	Acacia swazica	Lonchocarpus capassa
	Albizia harveyi	Maytenus senegalensis
	Combretum collinum	Pilotstigma thoningii
	Dalbergia melanoxylon	Sclerocarya birrea
	Dichrostachys cinera	
	Diospyros mespiliformis	
	Peltophorum africanum	
	Strychnos spinosa	
	Terminalia sericea	

Source: Shackleton, 1993

methods for studying people's diet is the chapter by Darna Dufour and Nicolette Teufel in the excellent book on common standards for data collection in studying human societies by Emilio Moran (1995). In a systematic study of the extent to which wild greens and fruits are used in diet, Anne Fleuret (1979) gathered data among the Shambaa people of the Usambara Mountains, Tanzania. Several different methods were used, including interviews at 40 different periodic markets, to gather the names of wild foods consumed, combined with counts of the wild foods and fruits sold at the markets. In addition, 200 women were asked, in open-ended interviews, to list the wild greens their families preferred, and to estimate the frequency of their consumption.

The key finding of this study was that wild plants are important in the local diet and that they contribute significantly to nutrition, even though earlier studies, using the '24-hour recall method', had implied otherwise, and had indeed concluded that the Shambaa diet was deficient in many major nutrients. It is particularly noteworthy that wild foliage plants accounted for some 81 per cent of instances of *michicha* (wild spinach) consumption, being found in 45 per cent of all meals eaten. Village surveys involved house visits by local assistants who asked the householders what was eaten the previous day. These village surveys were conducted at three different seasons – April, June and October. Despite employing local assistants to do the village surveys, however, they missed fruit consumption, since fruit is not usually a part of meals; rather, it is an occasional snack taken during the day at any time. Observations of children, ranging from 6 months to 14 years, revealed that a range of fruits was eaten in this way, typically gathered by the older children as they went about other tasks.

Participatory methods with groups of people

Participatory methods have become very popular for use in conservation and rural development projects. Many people using this manual are probably already familiar with the terms rapid rural appraisal (RRA), participatory rural appraisal (PRA), participatory assessment, monitoring and evaluation (PAME) or participatory action research (PAR). These approaches developed from a need to involve local communities in analysing their own circumstances. Respect for local knowledge and the desire to move away from 'top-down' approaches to conservation or development make these attractive methods to use. Pratt and Loizos (1992) point out the need, however, to maintain a healthy scepticism and critical view of processes described as 'participatory': the word has been used to describe anything from obligatory, through to genuinely democratic and enthusiastic involvement in a research project. It is crucial that local participation is genuine. It is pointless to bring local people into a data-gathering exercise which is of no interest to them in an effort to legitimize research through 'participation'.

Very useful and detailed descriptions of a wide range of participatory methods are given in *The Community Toolbox: the Ideas, Methods and Tools for Participatory Assessment, Monitoring and Evaluation in Community Forestry* (FAO, 1990) and in *Participatory Learning and Action: a Trainer's Guide* (Pretty et al, 1995). Good examples are also given in the *Joint Forest Management* manuals (Poffenberger et al, 1992) and in the recent manual by John Tuxill and Gary Nabhan (1998). The most useful PRA methods for work at the interface between ethnobotany and resource management are listed below. All of these can stimulate local insights that may have arisen during informal discussions or during interview surveys, but some (the last two methods, in particular) may be too sensitive to use in short-term surveys unless you have a great deal of local credibility.

Mapping

This includes mapping of land or resource tenure, resource distribution, and social maps showing where different resource-user groups stay in a village, or mapping the flow of resources after harvesting. This method and some of its disadvantages are covered in more detail in Chapter 6.

Transect walks

Transect walks combine well with initial ethnobotanical surveys and discussions. These are usually done with key informants through the area of interest by asking, observing, identifying different vegetation types and land-use impacts, and by indicating problems or possible solutions.

Time lines

Time lines can lead on from or be developed during transect walks, and identify important historical events which people remember. It can be useful to correlate these with known dates, which are then related to historical trends. Examples of this are the 'stick graphs' showing trends in resources and population numbers around Bwindi Forest from 1940–1990 (see Figure 2.6).

Seasonal calendars

Preferences and demand for different products will also change according to season. Seasonal calendars are a useful PRA technique, where local seasons form one axis of a matrix and products the other, enabling local people to rank

(a) Herbal medicines outside forest reserve

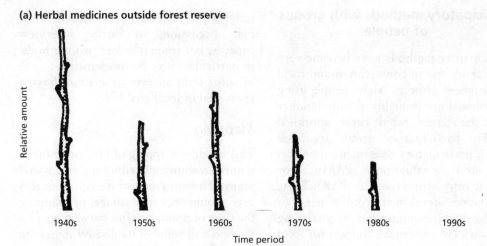

- 1940s — no need to go to forest reserve for medicines, as enough on own land;
- 1950s — about half amount of 1940s due to land clearance for farming;
- 1960s — as people left, herbs on farms increased;
- 1970s–1980s — people migrated from Rwanda and they know herbs well;
- 1990s — no forest medicinal species left outside forest reserve – they were finished.

(b) Human population

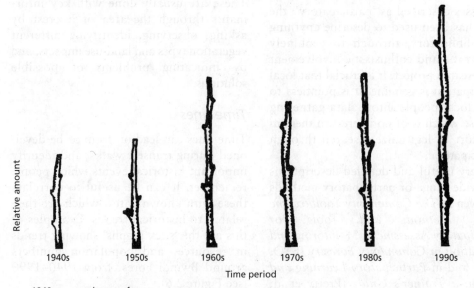

- 1940s — people were few;
- 1950s — people came from Rubuguli, encouraged by the County chief;
- 1960s — immigration from Rubanda;
- 1970s — people left the area;
- 1980s — immigration from Rwanda and Zaire;
- 1990s — more immigrants and families increasing.

Source: Wild, 1996

Figure 2.6 *Resource and population trends from 'stick graphs' made by a group of people from the Nteko area adjacent to Bwindi-Impenetrable National Park, Uganda. Sticks are gathered and, after explanation by a facilitator, broken into lengths representing relative abundance (long sticks) or scarcity (short sticks) of a resource*

harvesting or availability of products by season.

Matrix ranking and scoring exercises

These can be done on the ground or on paper, using symbols, picture cards or names for different resource categories or species. The first step is to list the categories or range of species that are available or which you have decided to rank. On the basis of their experience in India with this method, Poffenberger et al (1992) suggest a listing of 5 to 15 products for ranking. Different sized markers, such as small stones or seeds, are then placed under each category, building up a matrix of preferences based on different positive and negative qualities of each species, or multiple uses of each species or even of different vegetation types. Examples of qualities could be flavour of edible plants, durability and regeneration capacity of building timber, flexibility of different craft-work fibres, and so on. Ranking exercises can also list and rank problems with harvesting or resource availability, and the reasons for these problems.

Venn (or 'chapatti') diagrams

Understanding the relationships between different institutions and how community members relate to them is an important issue in resource management (see Chapter 7). Venn diagrams can give very interesting (and counter-intuitive) insights. The power of a local chief may be far less influential than one is led to believe, for example. Circles are used to represent people, groups and institutions. These are arranged by local participants to show their perceptions of overlap. Lines can be drawn between the different circles, with thick lines showing strong relationships, or thinner lines weaker ones.

Wealth ranking

Where households are listed, their names are written on separate cards; then local research participants can be identified. After discussion with each person about local perceptions of wealth, the cards representing each household are sorted into piles or wealth classes. Discussions then revolve around the main aspects of each household's livelihood strategy and the differences between the different wealth classes. This can give useful insight into which groups rely most on (or control) plant resource use.

Village mapping

Participants are invited to draw a sketch map of their neighbourhood, either on the ground using stones, tins, etc as symbols, or on paper. It can be useful to divide participants into groups, depending upon their gender or background. Maps vary according to perceptions and knowledge, and are a useful discussion point on how long people have been in an area, where they came from and what they do for a living.

Matrix ranking data can also be cross-checked or compared with information from field observations, discussions, market surveys or social survey methods that may have been carried out in similar vegetation or social situations. It is often wise to work with a homogeneous group selected on the basis of their interest in, and knowledge of, that particular resource category, such as groups of woodcutters or carvers (generally men) who have knowledge of building or carving timber, the production of fuelwood or edible wild greens, and the women who gather these resources. Herbalists or midwives can be consulted on traditional medicines. In other cases, it can be very useful to compare the insights of different user groups within or between communities or vegetation types. Men, women and children, for example, may have very different insights on the values of edible fruits, with children eating a much wider range of species as 'snacks' than adults, or women who gather 'top of the range' species most favoured for size, flavour and abundance for home consumption.

Individual interview surveys

Depending on time, funding and the aims of the research study, individual interviews may be case studies, where the researcher gains insights from discussions with individuals who 'typify' a particular situation. These do not yield quantitative data, but can give detailed insights into people–plant relationships.

Alternatively, discussions could be with **key research participants**, who have detailed knowledge of the topic of the research. Nichols (1991) distinguishes case studies and key participant interviews from a third category, **individual indepth interviews**, as the former have a wider scope and are more open-ended in nature and do not follow a strictly set pattern. All three of these approaches are important exercises to undertake before designing the format for a larger-scale structured interview survey, just as the inventory phase is important in recording local vernacular names and uses of harvested plants. Individual indepth interviews prior to larger-scale structured social surveys may be **unstructured** or **semi-structured**:

'In an unstructured interview, the person interviewed is free to voice their own concerns, and to share in directing the flow of conversation. The interviewer relies on open questions to introduce topics of interest. The aim is, literally, an "inter-view": a mutual exploration of the issues, without the researcher imposing his or her ideas. In a semi-structured interview, the researcher has a prepared list of topics – though still not a series of questions. Interviewers deal with the topics in any order, and phrase questions as they think best in the circumstances' (Nichols, 1991).

In individual semi-structured interviews at each homestead, for example, a woman could be asked which edible wild greens she gathered in different seasons, leaving her to list the species she collects (by local name). In a study on edible wild foods in Swaziland (Ogle and Grivetti, 1985), for example, interviews were done by seven siSwati-speaking students studying home economics, using a questionnaire which took 40 to 60 minutes to complete. Adults and children from four different ecological zones were interviewed separately in semi-structured interviews, which asked respondents first to identify species available near their homesteads, then how frequently each of these was consumed (see Figure 2.7).

Food lists, such as the 24-hour recall method, are commonly used in dietary surveys (Dufour and Teufel, 1995). Food lists take less time than food records, which require descriptions of the food eaten at the time of consumption, with records made either by an outside observer or by a trained household member. Food lists may be unreliable, however, largely because they depend upon memory. They involve asking people to recall the types and amounts of food consumed over a particular time period, often 24 hours. Interviews are best conducted in the area where the food is prepared or consumed, and all items, including drinks, noted. A common problem arises from the fact that participants may be reluctant to admit to poor feeding habits or low-standard

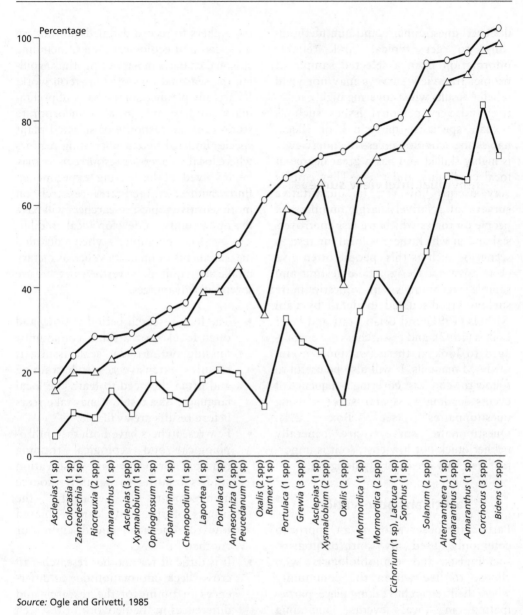

Source: Ogle and Grivetti, 1985

Figure 2.7 *Reported frequency of consumption by 211 adults of 47 edible wild greens*

meals. The presence of visitors (including researchers!) may prompt the preparation of special, untypical food, or food may be taken from a shared vessel, making the assessment of amounts consumed difficult. Like other methods, this is worth cross-checking against other methods, as Anne Fleuret (1979) did in her study of the

Shambaa people's diet in Tanzania.

Structured interview surveys can be appropriate survey methods in some situations but not in others, where information can be more efficiently gathered through field and participant observation, discussions, RRA/PRA methods or by market surveys. Interview surveys use a carefully designed questionnaire and aim methodically to get typical and reliable information from a selected sample of people. Interview surveys may not yield reliable results when covering highly sensitive and very personal issues such as sexual, specialist medicinal or illegal harvesting activities, unless the interviewer is highly skilled and has a great degree of local credibility and trust. They can be very useful, however, in quantitative surveys of relatively large numbers of people on topics which are less controversial and in which there is local interest; in scenarios such as this, people often give clear answers. Design, field testing and sample techniques in questionnaire surveys are discussed in detail by Paul Nichols (1991) and Brian Pratt and Peter Loizos (1992), and researchers are encouraged to look at these two most useful OXFAM manuals. It will also be useful to follow the checklist covering a sequence of events leading to social surveys using questionnaires (see Box 2.1). Questionnaire surveys are generally neither quick nor low-cost, so it is important that they are carefully designed.

Participant observation

Participant observation is an approach commonly used by anthropologists, sociologists and ethnobiologists who choose to live within the community where their research is taking place, participating in local events, including harvesting of natural resources. Participant observation usually takes place over a relatively long period of time, enabling detailed observations to be made and informal discussions held on the topic of the research. In common with any method, it has advantages and disadvantages that need to be weighed up on a case-by-case basis.

A long research period enables researchers to record detailed information on social and ecological issues, including seasonal changes in harvesting, thus avoiding the seasonal bias of short-term work. If carefully planned on the basis of preliminary studies, it can also incorporate studies on the response of selected plant species under different harvesting regimes where local villagers or resource users may be involved in harvesting experiments. Furthermore, it facilitates research on more sensitive topics; researchers will have the opportunity to develop local credibility – for example, when detailed measurements of quantities such as dietary intake are required. Nevertheless, there are several disadvantages.

- The long research period is slow, and often focused on a single community, missing out broader scale issues; it requires extensive research training and often the need to learn the local language. As a result, it may take years before results are available.
- Few researchers have both the anthropological and ecological training required for participant observation studies relating to natural resource management. Consequently, the results of the study can be biased towards one academic discipline or another.
- It is difficult for another researcher to cross-check information due to differences in timing of the research and differences in the network of research contacts (Pratt and Loizos, 1992).

For these reasons, participant observation studies on resource management in the people/protected areas situation would either be part of, or develop from, postgraduate academic study. In cases where answers are needed for urgent resource management problems, the time and expense required for participant observa-

Box 2.1 Steps in Questionnaire Design and Implementation

Questionnaire Construction: Content and Form

The content of the questionnaire is determined by what information is sought and from whom. What is the best way to elicit answers? Aspects for consideration include the following.

- Question construction: does the question pinpoint the issue? Will its meaning be clear to all respondents (see Nichols, 1991; Pratt and Loizos, 1992)?
- Length of the questionnaire: although this depends upon the type of questionnaire and the skill of the interviewer, many people feel that an hour is the maximum amount of time that interviewees are prepared to spend answering questions.
- Language of the questionnaire: it is usually desirable to have interviewers speak the same language as the interviewee, rather than work through an interpreter; however, this may be unavoidable in some cases. The questionnaire should preferably be in the language of the interview to ensure as much consistency as possible among interviewers. It is also preferable to have the answers recorded in the language in which they will be analysed. Decisions on these issues need to be made in terms of what local information is sought, the number of interviews and the linguistic abilities of the interviewers.
- Amount of interview coding required of interviewers during interviews: unless very basic, all coding requiring any discrimination or decision making should be left until processing of the questionnaire data occurs. The issue of open-ended questions needs to be carefully taken into account in cases where the researcher is unable to anticipate likely responses or is trying to raise new issues.
- Clarity and simplicity of layout: the layout of questions and responses should enable smooth, efficient progress through the questionnaire.
- Pilot testing: this should be completed, and all major alterations made before interviewer training. The training period then provides the opportunity for double-checking on the effectiveness of questions when asked by interviewers and to check translations.

Questionnaire Implementation: Interviewers and Interviewing

Aspects to consider are the following.

- Type of interview: will the interviews be structured, providing a precise list of questions to the interviewer, or semi-structured, listing the general agenda of issues to be covered? Structured interviews are necessary if the project requires a repeatable, uniform approach, and if it uses several interviewers over a relatively large sample population.
- Who and when to interview: choice of 'unit of analysis'. Does the information required relate to the individual, family, household or the community? Who is the best person to respond to questions in the survey? When would it be most convenient to be interviewed?
- Establishing an appropriate sample frame: this is very project-specific and you may need to get statistical advice. Nichols (1991) gives a good introduction to sample selection, which may be random, systematic, stratified or clustered, depending upon the type of project and resources you are dealing with.

- Selection, training and supervision of interviewers:
  1. Selection: this will depend upon: (a) the local acceptability and previous experience of potential interviewers; (b) the attitudes, empathy and sensitivity of the interviewers; (c) linguistic ability; (d) literacy and numeracy. It may be better to work with a smaller number of skilled interviewers than with a larger number of less skilled ones – but if so, beware of the problems of bias. Ideally, final selection of interviewers should be made after an initial training period has enabled potential interviewers to learn exactly what the project requires and the project manager/researcher has had the opportunity to observe potential interviewers during training.
  2. Training: all questionnaires differ, and thorough training is usually required. Resist the urge to move into the field too quickly. Training should include detailed discussions of each question and/or probe question. This can also serve as an opportunity to double-check wording and meanings of questions. Make sure that interviewers have a clear understanding of administrative details: expected work schedules, amount and frequency of pay, transport arrangements, anticipated length of interviews.
  3. Supervision: this is essential. It is also time consuming. Cross-checking of completed questionnaires should not be delayed, so that incomplete or inconsistent information can be corrected when necessary.

Computer Processing of Questionnaire Responses

The availability of good statistical computer packages and portable computers can facilitate faster processing of data. If researchers are not familiar with a particular computer program, they need to get advice from the first stage of questionnaire construction. They also need to consider: keeping a code book which shows a number or letter for each possible answer; and checking that the computer can read the codes used. Poor classification of responses can have a disastrous influence on survey results.

Sources: Prinsloo, 1982, with reference to Nichols, 1991; Pratt and Loizos, 1992

tion can be a major problem. For this reason, it may be possible to compromise by working with the same community, by making a series of short-term visits, and by participating in local events and harvesting expeditions in appropriately timed visits over a number of years.

Ethnobotanical inventories

Inventory of plant and animal species is a common basic step in field surveys, whether this includes all species or is limited to identifying useful or unique species. Collecting plant specimens is an important step in this process so that voucher specimens can be identified by scientific as well as local names. If at all possible, it is important to collect good quality herbarium specimens which not only have leaves and stems, but also flowers and/or fruits and, where necessary, samples of bark, wood or the roots or bulbs that characterize the species. These have to be well preserved, and accompanied by detailed field notes on the collection locality, characteristics of the plant, its local uses and vernacular names and their meanings.

Duplicate specimens need to be collected and, as voucher specimens, should be located in a recognized herbar-

BOX 2.2 COLLECTING PLANT SPECIMENS: FIVE IMPORTANT REMINDERS

1 Specimen Size and Quantity

Make sure you collect plant samples that are the right size – enough to fit across a standard newspaper page (30cm wide x 45cm long) – and that there is enough material for duplicates, so that a specimen is retained in the national herbarium. If the material is unusual, or from an undercollected region, it can be sent for identification to a regional herbarium and to an international herbarium. Four specimens may be required from an unusual plant species collected, for example, in western Uganda: one for the field-station herbarium, one for the national herbarium, one for the East African Herbarium in Nairobi and one for a large herbarium which specializes in African plants, such as those at either Missouri or the Royal Botanical Gardens, Kew.

2 Quality

Ideally, your specimens should be 'fertile' (with flowers and fruits), rather than being 'sterile' – material consisting of leaves and twigs or underground plant parts. In some cases, however, ethnobotanists (and ecologists), no matter how hard they look for fertile specimens, are faced with the necessity of collecting sterile specimens or none at all. Although this drives many taxonomists to distraction, if you have no choice, it is better to collect good sterile material than not to collect any specimens at all. It is essential that the specimens are pressed properly, each carefully flattened on individual 'flimsies'– the sheets of paper that support the specimen when you regularly change the drying papers. Particular care should be taken with certain specimens. Flowers of plant species with very delicate flowers (such as in the Aristolochiaceae, Asclepiadaceae, Balsaminaceae, Bignoniaceae, Commelinaceae, Curcurbitaceae, Passifloraceae and Scrophulariaceae) should also be preserved in spirit preservative such as 50 to 79 per cent ethanol, FAA (formalin-acetic acid alcohol) or 'Kew cocktail' (Bridson and Forman, 1992). Specimens of plants such as fig species (Moraceae) and succulents (Cactaceae, Euphorbiaceae and *Aloe* species), which grow well from cuttings and are tough survivors, should be killed off quickly by immersing them in boiling water or preservative (ethanol or even petrol).

3 Thorough Documentation

Specimens without thorough documentation have little value. Field notes on characteristics of the plant such as smell, sap colour and bark slash can be very important in identifying sterile material. In addition to information required for standard botanical specimens – collection locality (ideally with latitude and longitude coordinates); colour of fresh flowers/fruit/sap/leaves; ecological notes on habitat; collector's name; collection number and date of collection – ethnobotanical collections should include information on the vernacular name(s) of the species, their meaning, part(s) used, method of preparation and whether commercially traded or not, and the name of the person who supplied the information. In addition to writing this information on labels, you also need to maintain a field notebook where these records are written alongside your collection number for each specimen.

4 Proper Curation

When good quality specimens have been identified, they are poisoned, mounted and are usually placed in a recognized herbarium where they are accessible to other researchers. The location of your voucher specimen, indicated by an internationally used list of herbarium codes, the *Index Herbariorum* (Holmgren, 1990), should be recorded in scientific publications in addition to the specimen collection number.

5 Sensitivity to Conservation and Cultural Concerns

Although collecting duplicate specimens and accurately recording localities, plant uses, methods of preparation and the name of the local person providing the information is the ideal, you need to be sensitive to conservation and cultural issues. If a plant is very rare and the population small, you have to be aware of the dangers posed by overcollecting and drawing the attention of commercial collectors to the site by giving locality information that is too precise. You should be equally sensitive to concerns the local people may have regarding religious aspects of plant uses or fears about commercialization of the information they provide. These concerns need to be taken into account, and the ethical guidelines proposed by professional organizations such as the Society for Economic Botany and the International Society for Ethnobiology should be followed by researchers (Cunningham, 1993,1996).

ium. Three recent manuals give detailed information on how to collect, preserve and label herbarium specimens and I recommend that you read at least one of these: Diane Bridson and Leonard Forman's *The Herbarium Handbook* (1992), Miguel Alexiades's *Selected Guidelines for Ethnobotanists* (1996) or Gary Martin's *Ethnobotany: a Methods Manual* (1995). For those who do not have access to any of these manuals, I have summarized five important points to remember when collecting plant specimens (Box 2.2). I then give more detail on two important, linked, aspects of ethnobotanical inventory work. Firstly, there is the need to document and use a wider range of field characters than are normally used by formally trained botanists; and secondly, it is important to be aware of both the potential and the pitfalls of folk taxonomy and terminology in field work with local resource users.

Taxonomy with all your senses: the use of field characters

Although plant taxonomists rely strongly on flower or fruit characters, it is very useful to be able to describe and use the characteristics of sterile material as an aid to identification. As this manual is for field researchers, I have concentrated on describing macroscopic characters that you will find useful, not microscopic ones. Many field workers in the tropics and subtropics will already be familiar with some of the excellent field guides based on the vegetative characteristics of woody plants, such as those by Al Gentry (1993) for north-west South America, Eugene Moll's (1981) guide to 700 tree species in KwaZulu/Natal, South Africa, or Alan Hamilton's (1983) guide to trees of Uganda. Although plant growth form and leaf characteristics such as simple or compound leaves, arranged alternately or opposite, are a basis of field identification, so too are other vegetative characteristics. Learning about the vegetative characteristics of plants also makes field work more interesting and enables field workers to recognize many plant families from the combination of three or four characteristics. This can be of practical value when identifying the family or genus of a species from sterile material – something which led the late Al Gentry (1993), a superb botanist and field worker in the most diverse tropical forest area of the world, to observe that:

'Most neotropical plants are surprisingly easy to identify to family, even in sterile condition. Indeed, in many ways it is probably easier to identify woody tropical plants in sterile condition to family than it is identify the fertile material to which many systematic botanists tend to restrict themselves. This is true both because of the strong convergence by many different families that share a common disperser or pollinator, and because the technical characters on which plant families are defined are so obscure and esoteric (typically involving a determination of ovule number, placement and orientation) that they are of limited practical use...vegetative characters, on the other hand, are always available, mostly macroscopically obvious, and at least in the rainforest, apparently have been subjected to much less of the kind of convergence-inducing selection on taxonomically useful characters than have flowers and fruits.'

The same applies in other tropical forest areas. For these reasons, it is very important to use all your senses to record field characters based on vegetative criteria such as smell, texture, sap colour, skin irritant qualities or taste. It is also useful to describe characteristics of fresh and dried plant material to assist identification. In some cases, it can be useful to construct your own key for the most commonly used species, based on bark, bulb, root or wood characters. Part of a key to medicinal bulbs commonly sold in southern Africa is given as an example in Box 2.4.

Local people's knowledge is an important guide to these characteristics. In contrast with most taxonomists, who usually concentrate on dried specimens of leaves, flowers and fruits in herbaria, local people harvest and work with live, whole plants through different seasons. They consequently have the opportunity to perceive important characteristics of the plants, other than those commonly used by taxonomists. These are very useful to record during field work in addition to collecting voucher specimens, and there are a number of other reasons for this. Firstly, as discussed earlier, it may be difficult to obtain fertile plant specimens that bear flowers or fruits, or sometimes even leaves of a particular plant. They may be inaccessible, such as on the top branches of rainforest trees. Alternatively, you may be working during a time of the year when no leaves, flowers or fruits are available, such as during the dry season in arid zones, deserts and savanna, or in the cold season of alpine or arctic sites or temperate woodland. Similarly, in village and urban markets, medicinal plants and chewing sticks are often sold without any leaves, flowers or fruits attached.

Wood anatomists are an exception to the taxonomist's normal focus on herbarium specimens which consist of leaves, flowers and fruits. Their work provides an outstanding example of how macroscopic characteristics of wood (which can be seen with the naked eye or with a 'x 10' hand lens), well known to local resource users, can best be combined with microscopic characters to form definitive keys to wood identification (Gregory, 1980; IAWA, 1981, 1989; Miller, 1981). At an early stage, however, it is possible that systems of bark, root and bulb identification could similarly combine the best of indigenous and formal scientific approaches, using macro and microscopic characters to develop identification keys similar to those developed for wood identification.

Local people have an excellent knowledge of bark, root or bulb characters and make slashes in bark or roots with a machete to determine the identity of forest trees, rather than use leaf or flower characteristics (see Figure 2.8). Some of these are so characteristic that they are referred to in the local names for that species. In Zulu, for example, two Afromontane trees in the Rutaceae, *Clausena anisata* and *Zanthoxylum capense*, are called respectively *umnukambiba* ('smells like a striped field mouse') since its crushed leaves smell like mouse urine, and *umnungamabele*, since the knobs on its trunk are shaped like breasts. Identification of species by a fragment of bark, roots or stem on the basis of a combination of scent, sap, colour or texture has its parallels in urban industrial society. People employed as 'noses' by perfume companies, for example, can identify a single perfume variety from hundreds of others. Similarly, 'wine tasters' are able to identify the origin and year of production of a particular variety of wine. Descriptions of the smell of bark, roots, wood or leaves of different tree species are reminiscent of the way in which wine varieties are described.

Be careful to record whether these are characters of fresh or dried bark, roots,

wood or leaves, as some features characterize dry rather than fresh material. The shiny calcium oxalate crystals are best seen in the broken cross-section of dried rather than fresh Bersama (Melianthaceae) bark, for example, and the leaves of pressed specimens in the Scrophulariaceae, Loranthaceae and Olacaceae often turn black (sometimes olive) only when they dry out. Examples of field characters you need to look out for in bark, bulb, root and wood identification are listed below.

Colour of roots, bark and wood

This can be a useful first step in identifying unknown samples of harvested plants. Wood colour characteristics are well documented, with characteristics of roots and bark better known by 'undergound botanists' – herbalists and hunter-gatherers. The roots of many Celastraceae (*Maytenus*, *Pleurostylia*, *Salacia*), for example, are covered in orange, flaky 'root-bark', as are the roots of *Cardiogyne africana* (Moraceae). The roots of many Ebenaceae, such as *Euclea* and *Diospyros* species used for dyes and 'chewing sticks' (traditional toothbrushes), are characterized by an almost black outer root-bark and a yellow or orange cross-section in the inner root. The unusual colours of the cross-section of roots of parasitic plants such as *Hydnora* (Hydnoraceae, pink) and *Cycnium* (Scrophulariaceae, purple) are useful guides when all you see on herbal traders' shelves are root material. You also need to take note of colour changes, as exudates or inner roots oxidize on exposure to air. As an aid to identification, for example, Tembe-Thonga herbalists sniff the roots of *Albertisia delagoense* (Menispermaceae), which are used to treat toothache, and watch as the inner root colour darkens to a yellow-brown when twisted open.

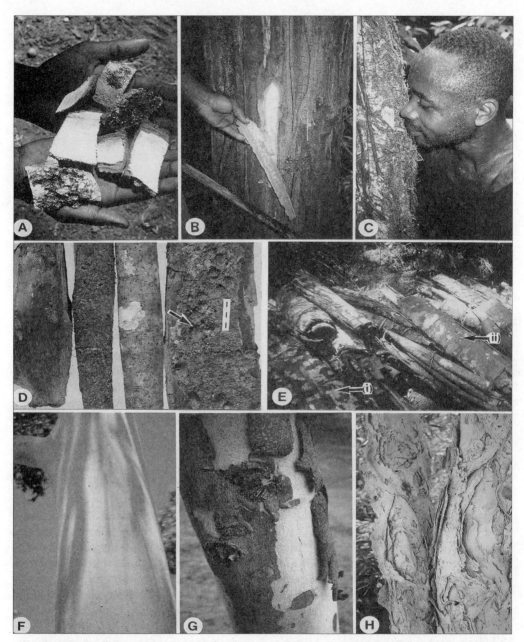

Figure 2.8 *Examples of bark characteristics. (a) Smooth pale inner bark of* Cassine transvaalensis *(Celastraceae). (b) Bright-yellow bark slash (*Enantia chlorantha *(Annonaceae)). (c) Ndumbe Paul checks the onion-like smell of a bark slash on* Afrostyrax lepidophyllus *(Huaceae). (d) 'Warts' on the bark of older* Ocotea bullata *(Lauraceae) trees (arrow), but not the smooth younger bark (centre), with both characterized by the pig-dung aroma when the bark is broken and the smooth chocolate-brown inner bark (left). (e) Two species harvested for commercial export as one:* Pausinystalia macroseras *bark, characterized by extensive lichen growth (arrow (i)) distinguished from* Paunsinystalia johimbe *bark (arrow (ii)), with limited lichen growth (both Rubiaceae). Three Myrtaceae, different bark texture: (f) Smooth bark (*Eucalyptus citriodora*); (g) Loose bark flakes (*Eucalyptus leucoxylon*); (h) Irregular papery bark flakes (*Melaleuca quinquinerva*)*

35

Scent

In your field notes, think of the best way of describing the scent of the bark, leaves, roots or wood you are examining. If you have the opportunity, crush or cut them to get a better scent. Some will already be familiar. Crushed leaves of many Fabaceae smell like green beans and the leaves of many African Myrtaceae like guava fruits. The bark of several *Croton* species (Euphorbiaceae), for example, smells like pepper; *Prunus africana* (Rosaceae) bark and leaves like almonds (or cyanide); the roots of some Polygalaceae, such as *Securidaca longipedunculata* in Africa or *Polygala paniculata* in Fiji, smell like methyl salicylate (or 'wintergreen' ointment); *Ocotea bullata* (Lauraceae) bark smells like pig-dung; *Clausena anisata* leaves smell like striped field-mouse urine; *Maesopsis eminii* (Rhamnaceae) bark smells like cold, cooked chicken; while *Olinia usambarensis* (Oliniaceae) bark has a burned smell.

Some woods also have a characteristic fragrance, particularly trees in the Lauraceae (*Aniba*, *Cinnamomum*, *Ocotea*), Santalaceae (*Santalum*) and the genera *Spirostachys* (Euphorbiaceae), *Cedrela* (Meliaceae) and *Viburnum* (Caprifoliaceae). The most familiar of these are the smell of camphor (from *Cinnamomum camphora*), cinnamon (from *C. zeylanicum*, *C. aromaticum* and others) and the incense smell of *Santalum* species. These characteristics are often encountered in the roots and leaves as well. In some cases they are absent from the fresh leaves, for example in *Mondia whitei* (Periplocaceae), a commonly used appetizer and aphrodisiac root which has a 'fresh' smell of cinnamon in the roots but not in the leaves. As in any field work, however, you need to be cautious. You wouldn't want to crush *Mucuna* (Fabaceae) leaves or *Euphorbia* stems to smell them (and get covered in irritant hairs or toxic sap). Based on his work in South American forests, Al Gentry emphasized the need to take care when you smell anise (liquorice), as this can be the smell of a liverwort which lives on tree leaves, rather than the tree itself; so cross-check.

Texture

The texture of bark, roots, corms, bulbs or wood, when combined with other characters, can be a useful guide to identification, whether you are working in local markets which sell medicinal plants or in tropical forest where the trees are so tall you cannot collect any leaves. For many tropical botanists and foresters, wood characteristics and bark texture, combined with the colour, odour and exudate from small blazes (slashes) in the bark are very important means of identifying tall forest trees (see Figure 2.8, the following section on describing bark characters and Box 2.7). For this reason, bark characteristics form an important component of field guides such as Polak's (1992) guide to timber trees of Guyana, Whitmore's (1962) studies of the Dipterocarpaceae, or Tailfer's (1989) guide to trees in tropical Africa. Nobody would fail to be impressed by a master field worker, whether forester or herbalist, who is dwarfed by a towering forest tree and makes an accurate identification on the basis of a quick slash, a sniff and a pause to look at colour and exudate. It is important to keep bark slashes to a minimum and avoid them where possible, however, as some rare forest trees in the Proteaceae and Podocarpaceae, such as the South African endemic *Faurea macnaughtonii*, are very susceptible to fungal attack following a deep bark slash.

Sound

Even your hearing can be an aid to identification. There is an audible 'squeaking' when *Parinari excelsa* (Chrysobalanaceae) bark is slashed, as air is drawn into the xylem tubes, apparently a characteristic of some other tropical tree species as well. In Burma, the resin-impregnated bark of *Canarium resiniferum* (Burseraceae) is so hard that it makes a ringing sound when hit with the back of a machete.

Taste

Many people would be familiar with the taste of spices such as cinnamon bark or the bitter flavour of quinine (*Cinchona* bark). Bark can also have a hot, peppery flavour (*Warburgia* species, Canellaceae) or taste sweet and aromatic (root bark of the climber *Mondia whitei*). Some plants are toxic and/or taste absolutely awful – so be careful.

Exudates

Certain families are characterized by the exudates that seep from the inner bark or leaves when they are damaged. Milky latex is well known as a character of the bark, leaves and roots of many members of the Apocynaceae, Asclepiadaceae, Caricaceae, Euphorbiaceae, Moraceae and Sapotaceae family. Also watch for any colour change when the exudate is exposed to air. The white exudate of *Trilepsium madagascariense* (Moraceae), for example, oxidizes from white to a russet brown after a few minutes. Bright orange or yellow latex is common in the Guttiferae family, red sap a characteristic of *Pterocarpus* species (Fabacaeae) and many Myristicaceae. Exudates are a feature of fresh rather than the dry plant material that you would encounter when working with a herbalist or during a market survey. They may be still visible, however, in resin canals or congealed lumps. While these will have changed colour, they can still be a useful clue in the combination of characters that help identify a specimen to family or genus.

The elastic threads that form when latex-containing roots, leaves or bark are broken and gently pulled apart are used by botanists and local herbalists as useful field characters. Elastic threads characterize some roots (such as *Asclepias cucculata*, which is used as a love charm in Zulu traditional medicine), bulbs (such as *Crinum* species) or in bark and leaves (such as *Maytenus acuminata*). Plant exudates are typically classified as sap, gum, latex and resins, but this can be confusing, as it is sometimes difficult to tell what is sap, resin or latex. For this reason, it is useful to describe exudates by their physical characteristics and source (see Box 2.3).

Ash and charcoal

If you think of the hundreds of species and tonnes of trees burned by local people each year in household fires, or when clearing forest or woodland for swidden agriculture, it is not surprising that insightful local people are familiar with the ash or charcoal characteristics of particular woody plants. Wood anatomists also use ash and charcoal characteristics. They first check whether a wood splinter burns to ash, or whether it burns to charcoal instead (a characteristic of *Shorea negrosensis* (Dipterocarpaceae) wood). Then they look at the colour of the ash or charcoal: is it grey or white; black; brown; or none of these options (Miller, 1981)? Just as local names for plants often say something about their colour or smell, so names can reflect their ash characteristics. A southern African example is the tree *Antidesma venosum* (Euphorbiaceae), known in Zulu as *isibangamlotha*, which literally means 'ash-causer' due to the quantity of white-coloured ash it produces. This local knowledge needs to be better documented and used by ethnobotanists.

Box 2.3 Plant Exudates: Standardizing Botanical Descriptions

Plant exudates are typically classified by botanists either as sap, gum, latex or resins, which can be confusing. For practical purposes, it is better to use Leo Junikka's (1994) system of describing exudates by their physical characters. It is best to break off fresh leaf material and check the petiole for the presence or absence of exudates. This avoids having to make a bark slash and wait for the exudate to be produced. If you make a bark slash, however, look to see whether the blaze (slash) is dry (no exudate and feels dry when touched) or wet (slight exudation and feels moist). Is the exudation abundant (profuse for a while) or scanty (some families or individual plants supposedly characterized by exudate only produce minute amounts)? Also be aware that it can take several minutes for the exudate to appear.

The rate of exudation also depends on the season. Exudates may be clear (transparent) or opaque, coloured (white, yellow, golden, red, brown, blackish), may discolour within a few minutes on contact with air, be frothy (forming a foam when you rub it with your fingers), liquid (flowing readily, often transparent) or viscous (flowing slowly, but not necessarily sticky), sticky (sticking to your fingers) or non-sticky. Does the exudate have a smell or not? Although deciding whether something smells pleasant or not can be subjective (do you like the smell of garlic or not?), you can group exudates according to whether they are odorous (smelling pleasant, like incense) or whether they are smelly (smelling like excrement, urine or rotten eggs).

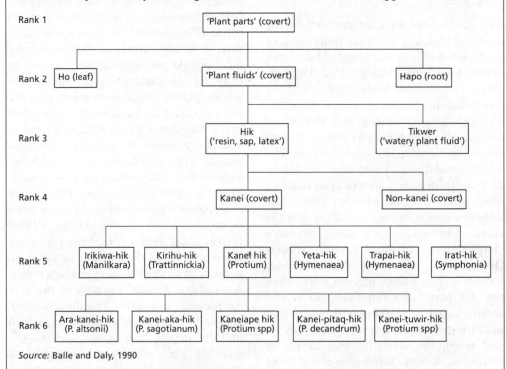

Source: Balle and Daly, 1990

*The hierarchical system of exudate classification used by the Ka'apor Indians of the Brazilian Amazon. Plant families represented are the Burseraceae (*Protium* and *Trattinnickia*), Sapotaceae (*Manilkara*), Guttiferae (*Symphonia*) and Fabaceae (*Hymenaea*)*

Folk classification of exudates can also be very detailed (see the figure above). In their study amongst the Ka'apor Indians of the Brazilian Amazon, for example, Bill Balle and Doug Daly (1990) found that although the Ka'apor had a detailed hierarchical classification based on their uses (particularly inflammability for lighting purposes) this differed from their classification of the plants themselves. This leads to distinct differences between Ka'apor and Linnaean classification. For example, morphologically different species (*Protium giganteum, P. pallidum* and *P. spruceanum*) are given the same folk-specific name due to the similar properties of their exudates. *Protium giganteum* and *Protium decandrum*, which look very similar, had different folk names due to the different properties of their exudates.

Crystals

Wood anatomists commonly use the presence and type of calcium crystals, silica bodies and cystoliths (calcium carbonate deposits) as important microscopic characteristics of wood (IAWA, 1981). Prismatic crystals are common in the wood of *Terminalia* (Combretaceae) and *Diospyros* (Ebenaceae), for example, but are usually absent from *Dipterocarpus, Betula* and *Tilia* wood. Cystoliths have only been found in wood of Opiliaceae, *Sparattanthelium* (Hernandiaceae) and *Trichanthera* (Acanthaceae) (Miller, 1981). While these microscopic characters do not help a field botanist with just a hand lens, shiny calcium oxalate crystals can be seen with the naked eye in some cases. The presence of calcium oxalate crystals, for example, is used by herbalists to identify the bark of medicinal species being sold in urban African markets. Calcium oxalate crystals are a useful character that are best seen glinting in the broken cross-section of dry bark in full sunshine. This helps to distinguish the crystal-packed bark of trees such as *Cassine papillosa* (Celastraceae) and *Bersama* species (Melianthaceae) from bark with a similar thickness and colour.

Describing bark characters

Whether you are working with people in the field and observing fresh bark or are observing dried bark collected by herbalists or bought in village markets, it is useful to record bark characters that will aid identification at a later stage. While wood anatomists clarified the terminology used in wood identification (IAWA, 1957, 1989), the terms used to describe macroscopic features of bark were not standardized and were confusing. This has been corrected in a recent publication by Leo Junikka (1994), a Finnish botanist, on the basis of his field experience in South-East Asia and an extensive literature review.

Very few herbarium specimens record details of bark characteristics. Ethnobotanists have a great opportunity to change this, since they work with local people who are not only knowledgeable about bark, root or bulb characters, but who often have insightful folk classification systems for bark texture or characters such as exudates. Because of the value to field workers of a standard system for describing macroscopic bark morphology, the terms Junikka (1994) suggests are summarized in Box 2.7. I would also recommend his publication for additional reading.

His first step was to standardize the terms used to describe the main components of bark, and to clarify terms such as **cork** (the trade product from cork oak – *Quercus suber*), **bast** (any fibres from the outer part of the plant, but mainly from secondary phloem), and **phloem fibre**, the taxonomically important and often conspicuous fibre which can occur in the secondary phloem, often making tough bark. He then suggested terms which could be used to describe **bark texture** (**consistency**), **bark patterns** (see Box 2.7) and **exudates** (see Box 2.3). Bark varies considerably from species to species in its thickness and texture. For a particular species, bark thickness also varies with tree age, rate of growth, genotype and location of the tree (see Figure 2.8). In southern Africa, for example, *Rauvolfia caffra* trees growing along the coast have a very different outer bark texture from those growing in upland sites. Examples of other bark features are the smell, presence or absence of latex or oxalate crystals, or elastic threads seen when the bark is broken, or the appearance of inner or outer bark and its cross-section.

Some local people, notably woodcutters and herbalists, have an excellent knowledge of bark characters and take small bark slashes with a machete to determine the identity of forest trees, rather than using leaf or flowers. Be careful to record whether these are characters of fresh bark, dried bark or both, as some bark features are more evident in either a dry or a fresh state. An obvious example would be the presence or absence of latex, which is clearly evident in freshly slashed bark, but less so in the dry bark that you might encounter when working with a herbalist or during a market survey. At this stage, latex will not be exuded when the bark is cut, but may be seen in resin canals or as congealed lumps and will often have changed colour.

Underground botany: identification of bulbs, corms and roots

If, in your field work with herbalists, food

gatherers or ethnobotanical surveys of local markets you are unable to identify roots, corms, bulbs or tubers, do not feel alone! With the emphasis that Linnaean taxonomy has placed on flowers, fruits and leaves, and because above-ground plant parts are easier to observe, formally trained botanists and plant ecologists generally have limited knowledge of underground plant parts. Ironically, in large areas of Africa, and possibly elsewhere in frequently burned tropical savannas, underground plant biomass is greater (and often more selectively used) than the above-ground biomass. Frank White (1976), for example wrote of the 'underground forests' in the vast Kalahari sands region, stretching south of the Democratic Republic of Congo into southern Africa and dominated by woody dwarf shrub genera (suffrutices). In the red syringa (*Burkea africana*) sandy savanna, for example, which is on Kalahari sands, underground plant biomass is 2.2 tonnes per hectare compared to total above-ground biomass of leaves, stems, flowers and fruits of 1.7 tonnes per hectare (Huntley, 1977).

In contrast with many formally trained taxonomists, craft workers, fishermen, herbalists and food gatherers frequently have an excellent knowledge of the characteristics of the roots and tubers used for dyes, fish toxins, floats and netting fibre, medicines or food. Underground plant parts can be very distinctive (see Box 2.4). In common with above-ground plant parts such as shoots and branches, root structure and patterns of root architecture are to some extent genetically determined, and it is often useful to record these important morphological characters in ethnobotanical work. As you will frequently find – since underground plant parts are sold in markets with no leaves, flowers or fruits attached – the characteristics used by local resource users are important to record and use in field work. They may also have added value in formal taxonomic work (Pate and Dixon, 1982).

Obermeyer (1978), for example, uses bulb characteristics to distinguish certain *Ornithogalum* species, also noting how bulb morphology varies with climate and habitat. *Ornithogalum* bulbs from winter rainfall areas are generally small in relation to plant size, while bulbs in summer rainfall areas are large, firm and globose. The two *Ornithogalum* species, which grow in permanently wet habitats, also differ markedly from other species as they do not form swollen bulbs at all, presumably due to a lesser need for storage of food and moisture. The morphology of underground plant parts has also been used to distinguish between reseeder and resprouter categories of dicotyledons and Restionaceae in western Australia (Pate et al, 1990; Pate et al, 1991). Insights from such studies provide valuable information relevant to resource management and how plant species will respond to disturbance and harvest (see Chapters 4 and 5).

Some of the characteristics of underground plant parts are shared by the bark and leaves of the same species. More detailed examples are given in the section 'Taxonomy with All Your Senses' and in Box 2.7. Such details include sap occurrence/absence, colour and odour; **root-bark** texture and colour; **elastic threads**; and so on. As expected, this applies to the presence and colour of latex of the Apocynaceae, Asclepiadaceae and Clusiaceae family or to the strong, fibrous root-bark of Thymelaeaceae. Root-bark of *Warburgia*, for example, has the same peppery flavour as its bark and leaves.

Although many bark and root characteristics are shared, other characteristics are not and these need to be carefully noted. Examples are the characteristic 'cracks' along roots when they dry out (as seen in *Acridocarpus* (Malphigiaceae)

roots sold in village markets), the way they twist, or their shape, size, elastic threads or cross-sectional appearance. Similarly, bulbs and corms are characterized by a combination of colour, shape, thickness and structure of scale leaves, latex, occurrence of irritant chemicals, and markings on the compressed stem that forms the 'base plate' of the bulb or corm.

Discussions with local resource users can facilitate development of detailed field notes or even keys (see Box 2.4) to different categories of fibrous roots or bulbs and corms. Although keys of this type can be very useful in improving communication and understanding between researchers and resource users, such as herbalists, it is very important that verification and cross-checking are done. In some cases, you can grow bulbs bought at markets. In others, as with pieces of root, you need to confirm root characters and make fresh voucher specimens while collecting with resource users in the field.

Describing macroscopic characteristics of wood

Wood anatomists have developed sophisticated ways of classifying wood and charcoal based on macroscopic and microscopic characters, primarily due to the great economic importance of timber. Wood collections made for this purpose, found in many parts of the world, are listed in the *Index Xylariorum* (Stern, 1978). Early identification guides to woods using **dichotomous** keys (based on a choice of one of two characters) have given way to systems of hardwood identification using **multi-state characters** (sets of alternative options for a feature such as heartwood colour, crystal types or geographic origin) which are used in computerized keys in addition to dichotomous characters.

These well-developed keys for wood

Box 2.4 Bulbs and Corms

Corms, for example from *Crocus* and *Gladiolus*, are short, swollen food-storing stems surrounded by protective scale leaves. One or more buds in the scale-leaf axils produce new foliage leaves. A bulb, of which the onion is a well-known example, consists of a modified shoot with a short flattened stem. A bulb is covered on the outside by papery scale leaves which surround swollen leaf bases. A terminal bud sits at the centre of the upper surface and produces the foliage leaves and flowers. This is an example of part of a key to bulbs and corms commonly sold for traditional medicinal purposes, illustrating characters that may be worth recording in similar studies. In this case, bulbs and corms were divided into two main groups (group 1: exterior with fleshy or thin scale leaves; group 2: exterior without scale leaves apparent). Only part of the key to group 1 is shown here.

1 Outer surface of bulb covered in dense fibrous 'hairs'
 obscuring scale leaves   *inGcino* (*Scilla nervosa*)
 Outer surface without dense fibrous 'hairs'   see 2

2 Scale leaves fleshy   see 3
 Scale leaves thin, not fleshy   see 4

3 Exterior generally smooth; usually pale green in colour,
 small bulbs almost translucent; scale leaves only
 conspicuously visible towards the top of the bulb *iGibisila* (*Bowiea volubilis*)
 Exterior not smooth; scale leaves conspicuously visible see 4

4 Scale leaves on exterior conspicuously pointed *uMhlogolosi* (*Urginia spp*)
 Scale leaves on exterior not pointed   see 5

5 Scale leaves with persistent leaf-base
 fibres   *uMaphipha-intelezi* (*Albuca fastigiata*)
 Scale leaves without leaf-base fibres *iCubudwana* (*Ledebouria* spp)

6 Inner cut surface reddish or light purple in
 colour; sap stings skin *inDongana-zibomvana* (*Drimia* spp)
    or *isiKlenama*
 Inner cut surface green, white, yellow or cream in colour see 7

7 Bulbs with wide, compressed stem base bearing conspicuous striations see 8
 Bulbs without compressed stem base bearing conspicuous striations. see 9

8 Elongated bulb with length about twice the size of base
 diameter; exterior with glossy brown scale leaves *inGuduza* (*Scilla natalensis*)
 Bulb with length approximately equal to base diameter; *uMathunga* (*Eucomis*
 exterior with dark-brown scale leaves; cut interior surface *autumnalis*)
 reveals yellowish leaf bases and white compressed stem or *iMbola*

9 Inner cut surface without sap; large elongate brown bulb *iNcotho* (*Boophane*
    distica)
 Inner cut surface with sap   see 10

10 Sap very mucilaginous and stings skin *uMababaza* (*Ornithogalum* spp)
 Sap milky-white, not sticky and does not sting skin *umDuze* (*Crinum* spp)

Source: Tait and Cunningham, 1988

classification provide a challenge for ethnobotanists and innovative taxonomists. Wood identification systems have been developed using excellent collections of voucher specimens of woods from many tree species. As a result, wood identification guides provide a standard for which ethnobotanists working on non-timber products should strive to develop for bark, roots, bulbs and corms. The advantages that ethnobotanists have in achieving a similar standard of identification for bark, roots, bulbs and corms are, firstly, that many of the characteristics of wood, such as odour, frothiness, fluorescence, and types of crystals, also apply to bark and to some bulbs, corms and roots. Secondly, local uses already provide information on what characteristics would be expected. Saponin-containing fish poisons are well documented (Acevedo-Rodriguez, 1990), so that frothiness (a wood identification character) can also be used as a field character to identify bark, roots, or fruits of many Sapindaceae, Pittosporaceae and Theophrastaceae, for example. The same applies to local knowledge of plant dyes (wood, exudate, bark or root colour), odour or ash colour.

To avoid confusion, and enable international cooperation, the International Association of Wood Anatomists (IAWA) has developed a standard list, terminology and computer codes for characters used in wood identification (IAWA, 1981, 1989; Miller, 1981). These and Sherwin Carlquist's (1991) review of the wood anatomy of vines and lianas are recommended reading for ethnobotanists studying wood use. The IAWA wood identification system needs both macro and microscopic characters to be used to their full extent, and the IAWA (1981) standard list of characters, together with Miller's (1981) explanations, should be referred to for full details.

The most basic questions you need to ask yourself (and local people) in trying to identify a cut wood sample are: where does the wood come from, and what are its vernacular name(s), use(s) and growth form (is it a tree, shrub or vine?). These can all help narrow down the options about the identity of the wood. Bear in mind that boot polish or stains produce look-alike substitutes for scarce, more valued woods (such as ebony – *Dalbergia melanoxylon*). In these cases, the heaviness of an ebony carving compared to the light-weight black boot polish alternative is one indicator. For greater precision, wood anatomists use basic **specific gravity** (based on green volume and oven-dry weight) as one of the tools in wood identification.

The next questions you need to ask yourself are: is the heartwood colour similar to the sapwood (or not), and what colour is the heartwood? In most Flacourtiaceae and Sapotaceae, or well-known trees such as *Polyscias* (Araliaceae) or *Tilia* (Tiliaceae), there is no differentiation between heartwood and sapwood, whereas it is very distinct in many Fabaceae, such as *Dalbergia*, *Acacia* and *Robinia*. Although brown and pale white woods are found in many genera, heartwood colour can be a good macroscopic character. Yellow heartwood, for example, is a complete giveaway, found only in *Berberis* species (Berberidaceae), a source of medicine and dye. Red heartwood is also uncommon, characterizing *Berchemia zeyheri* (Rhamnaceae) and several species of *Pterocarpus* (Fabaceae), *Brosimum* (Moraceae) and *Simira* (Rubiaceae). Other examples of macroscopic characters which can be used in wood identification include the following.

- Are growth rings distinct or absent?
- Is the wood ring-porous, diffuse-porous or semi ring-porous? Take care, however: the same species can

sometimes be ring-porous and at other times, diffuse-porous. Woods that are ring-porous also have distinct growth rings. Most Proteaceae have pores in a characteristic festoon arrangement.

- Does the wood include phloem (interxylary phloem which is embedded in the secondary xylem of the stem or root) or intruded phloem? Included phloem commonly characterizes genera within the Fabaceae, Loganiaceae, Nyctaginaceae, Menispermaceae, Solanaceae and Urticaceae family. Included phloem is usually destroyed by drying, so small wood samples have to be preserved in 70 per cent alcohol or formalin-acetic acid alcohol (FAA).
- Is there any odour (or not)?
- Is the parenchyma banded, aliform (wing-shaped) or confluent (joined together)?

Other creative methods used by wood anatomists are the wood characteristics under fluorescent (long-wave ultraviolet) light, the colour of wood ash, water and ethanol extracts or **frothiness** (due to saponins). Simple tests for frothiness (which indicates natural saponins in the wood) and the **presence or absence of fluorescence** (heartwood, water and ethanol extracts) are also useful in identifying some Fabaceae, Sapotaceae and Rutaceae. The test for frothiness has added ethnobotanical interest, as plants with saponins have many uses, including use as fish poisons, molluscicides and in herbal medicine. Use enough heartwood shavings (rather than splinters or chips whose saponin extraction takes too long) to cover the bottom of a clean vial (2cm x 7cm). The shavings are then covered with distilled water, the vial blocked with a cork and then shaken vigorously. If a large quantity of saponins is present, then a froth will form on the surface of the water. If you have access to long-wave ultraviolet light, the same sample should immediately be placed under the light to check for fluorescence. Extracts of *Zanthoxylum flavum* (Rutaceae) and *Pterocarpus indicus* (Fabaceae), for example, will fluoresce a brilliant blue (Miller, 1981). The same vial with the sample can then be placed on a hotplate and brought to the boil, with the liquid then checked for colour. While brown or colourless extracts are not particularly useful in identifying an unknown sample, reddish (*Brasilettia*) or yellowish (some *Albizia* species) can be diagnostic characters.

You could also check on the fluorescence colour of the freshly sanded or shaved heartwood, water extract and ethanol extract under long-wave ultraviolet light. Some will not fluoresce at all, whereas others have a characteristic fluorescence colour. Wood of several genera in the Fabaceae (*Enterolobium*, *Robinia*) glow yellow-green, for example, while *Symphonia* (Clusiaceae) and *Vatairea* (Fabaceae) fluoresce orange.

Potentials and pitfalls: combining skills in inventories

Taxonomy is the branch of biology dealing with the naming and classification of living things. Internationally, biologists use what is known as the Linnaean classification system. Each species is given a name consisting of two words. This, the binomial, consists of the **genus** or **generic** name, followed by the **specific epithet**. Both words together denote the species, and the binomial is conventionally written in italic font. The Linnaean classification system is an international link in naming plants with considerable precision. All cultures have their own classification systems to facilitate communication from person to person in naming a particular species. Alternatively, specialists such as local healers may use special names for plants to obscure the identity of species with religious, medicinal or ritual significance from people who have not undergone initiation processes or specialist training. Detailed studies have been carried out in the field of **ethnotaxonomy** or **folk classification systems** by Brent Berlin (1992) and are covered in detail in Gary Martin's manual (1995), so will not be covered in detail here.

Biological inventories of even the best-known national parks in the tropics and subtropics are often incomplete or inadequate. In most planning exercises, inventories are done on the basis of Linnaean taxonomy. This is a perfectly valid approach. It can also be useful to carry out surveys which link with the skills of knowledgeable local people on the basis of folk taxonomies, particularly when skilled biologists and taxonomists are a scarce resource. Folk taxonomic knowledge can be invaluable in inventory work for conservation purposes, whether for botanical or zoological surveys. Baker and Mutitjulu Community (1992), for example, point out from their work in Uluru National Park, central Australia, that:

'In a number of instances Anangu provided names of animals which did not match any that were caught at the survey sites. One such animal was tjakura. Anangu provided a detailed description of this reptile and brought the animal to the scientists, who identified it as the great desert skink (Egernia kintorei). This species was not caught on any of the survey sites,

and was found to be restricted to a particular locality within the Park. The woma python (Aspidites ramsayi) and Stimsons python (Bothrochilus stimsoni) were also recorded for the survey only by Anangu.'

It is important to be aware of some of the pitfalls in this process. Firstly, you need to avoid confusion of local plant names with local names for plant parts, such as 'flower', 'fruit' or 'leaf', or with general categories for 'tree', 'shrub' or 'vine'. You will be surprised how many botanists unfamiliar with the local language have published names which are supposed to be the specific local name for a plant species, but which actually refer to a plant part or a life form. Embarrassingly, some have even recorded the response: 'I don't know' as a 'local name' from a perfectly honest local helper! Sometimes folk biological classification systems may also have totemic links, so that on Groote Eylandt, Australia, an Anindilyakwa man seeing a red-winged parrot (*wurruweba* – *Aprosmictus erythropterus*) flying overhead may say, 'There goes my brother-in-law' (Waddy, 1982), which could well confuse a biologist unaware of the totemic connection of the species!

You also need to be aware that while some species may be what linguistic anthropologists term **underdifferentiated**, others are **overdifferentiated** (Martin, 1995). The nine Zulu names for the medicinal plant species *Curtisia dentata*, in South Africa, are an example of overdifferentiation, a fairly common occurrence with species of great cultural importance (see Box 2.5). With underdifferentiation, a single local name can be a generic term for several different plant species. In Afromontane forest in Uganda, for example, the single Rukiga name *bitindi* applies to two *Memecylon* species – M.

BOX 2.5 MULTIPLE NAMES, SINGLE SPECIES

The tree *Curtisia dentata* (Cornaceae), endemic to Afromontane 'islands' of forest, is one example. It is a multiple-use species with hard, durable timber but is best known amongst traditional healers for its red bark, used by sorcerers to cast spells (*ukuthakatha*), causing hysteria. Even within a small part of its range in Natal province, South Africa, I recorded eight Zulu names for this tree. Three names (*inkunzi-twalitshe*, *ijundu-mlahleni* and *umphephelelangeni*) are *hlonipha* (respect) names used only by herbalists. One name (*igejalibomvu*) is only known by people (specialists and non-specialists alike) within a few districts near the Nkandla and Qudeni forests; one (*umgxina*) is known only in the southern KwaZulu/Natal, where the name is more commonly used amongst Xhosa-speaking people. Only three names are more common regionally (*umlahleni* and *umlahleni-sefile*, and *umagunda*). Lastly, a ninth name, *umhlibe*, was recorded by ethnobotanist-linguist and missionary extraordinaire Jacob Gerstner in the 1930s, but not at all in my regional medicinal plants survey 50 years later. All have meanings alluding to collection or use, additional factors that can be confusing to people from outside the immediate area of use or outside the professional ranks of traditional healers. In discussions, *umlahleni* and *umlahleni-sefile* mean 'throw him away' or 'throw him away, he's dead'; *ijundu-mlahleni* also refers to a person being 'thrown away', and *ijundu* to medicine that kills a person outright. *Umphephelelangeni* means 'something that escapes to the sun' and *igejalibomvu* refers to a 'red hoe', and so on.

---

jasminoides and an undescribed *Memecylon* species only found in Bwindi forest; *omushabarara* applies to at least three *Drypetes* species, including the rare *Drypetes bipindensis*; *omurara* applies to at least four *Macaranga* species with different regional distributions; and *nyakibazi* applies to three locally endemic *Rytigynia* species in one area, as well as to the widespread tree *Bersama abyssinica*. For this reason alone, it is very important to collect voucher specimens and record both local and scientific names for species.

Using several methods in inventory work can be useful. Firstly, there is what Brian Boom (1989) terms the 'artefact/interview' technique, which is a common approach used by anthropologists, where people are asked the names of materials used to make a particular item. Secondly, there is the reverse approach, termed the 'inventory/interview' technique, which involves the active collection of plant specimens and subsequent interviewing of informants about their names and uses (Boom, 1989). This has been applied in several studies where specimens are linked to one-hectare forest plot surveys (Prance et al, 1987; Boom, 1989). Thirdly, there is the 'walk in the woods' approach, where records are made with key helpers directly from whole plants while in the field, rather than in subsequent interviews from fresh specimens. This avoids misidentification which is a danger in the 'inventory/interview' technique in forest areas, where formally trained botanists collect botanical specimens (leaves, flowers, fruits) to show to local resource users who often use criteria of bark, roots or stem morphology as the main classification criteria.

These approaches are outlined in more detail in Gary Martin's (1995) *Ethnobotany Manual*, published in this series. On their own, neither vernacular nor botanical names are sufficient for thorough work, although the value of using agreed scientific

---

BOX 2.6 MISMATCH: LINNAEAN NAMES TO FOLK TAXONOMY AND VICE VERSA

Discrepancies between Linnaean and folk taxonomy are widespread, and these differences must be taken into account. Firstly, they may refer to chemical, genetic or morphological differences not considered by Linnaean taxonomists, and which indicate useful qualities for plant breeding or phytochemistry. They also indicate the need to get scientists to take note of folk taxonomy. Secondly, they are important when resource management priorities are being discussed – for example, species recorded under a single name which actually represent more than one species of different conservation status, as when an endemic species with restricted distribution has the same name as a widespread, non-endemic species. This can apply to both Linnaean and folk taxonomic systems. In the early 1980s, I collected several voucher specimens of a commonly eaten wild spinach in the Ingwavuma district, South Africa. These were all identified scientifically as *Asystasia gangetica*, yet locally identified as two separate species with different habitat preferences and local Tembe-Thonga names. The first, known as *isihobo*, was widespread, growing in fallow fields and along forest margins, with thin leaves that were not particularly tasty. The second local name, *umaditingwane*, referred to a robust, fleshy-leaved species growing on coastal dunes with leaves 'as good as meat' to eat. These were even selected for cultivation at home because they were so tasty. A few years later, on the basis of this local knowledge, *umaditingwane* was more carefully examined and described as a 'new' separate species, *Asystasia pinguifolia* – a regional endemic along the Mozambique coastal plain – in belated accordance with the local folk taxonomy.

---

names is paramount, particularly for international communication and for publications. What we also need to know in the supply-demand balance of sustainable use is which species are most favoured, or which individuals within a species population are selected for harvest. This is an important issue in setting conservation or resource-use policies for plant species.

Although individuals with the richest traditional knowledge often live in remote areas and are frequently marginalized by urban-industrial society, their skills are often recognized within their own communities. As Gary Nabhan and his colleagues (1991) point out:

> '*More often than not, conservation biologists are unaware that indigenous people have detailed knowledge of a particular rare plant or animal that is under study. Even when not biased against traditional peoples, these biologists often lack the skill of ethnographic interviewing and the incentives to learn from indigenous people who live in close proximity to rare species. To date, only one US endangered species recovery plan, which recommended local Navajo participation in the habitat protection and plant population recovery efforts for Carex specuicola, has included ethnobotanical data derived from indigenous people.*'

Similarly, social scientists with training in cross-cultural communication lack the taxonomic skills or ecological insight of conservation biologists. For this reason, a team approach involving local traditional experts, biologists and social scientists can be very useful.

Matching folk taxonomy with Linnaean taxonomy

A cross-reference of vernacular to botanical names provides an invaluable guide when using the methods that follow, as well as in general discussions or interview surveys. There is no substitute for work in the field with a range of local resource users – men, women or children – who are locally acknowledged to be experts on different categories of plant uses. Inventory work can often be done by local people themselves, after guidance on the requirements for good herbarium specimens. Researchers need to be aware of gender issues that may be involved in field work. Work with midwives, for example, is often best done by female researchers, or work with hunters done by men. There is also a need to be aware of differences and complexities in different naming systems.

'Rapid' approaches advocated by rapid rural appraisal (RRA) and participatory rural appraisal (PRA) practitioners that fail to match local names with international taxonomic nomenclature are the poorer for it. Information from the inventory and field-based discussion phase with a few key resource users can be invaluable for cross-checking information from ranking and scoring exercises (see 'Participatory Methods with Groups of People'). If species are identified by vernacular name only, communication amongst local people within a district or region may be limited, and this limits local people's access to information on uses of the same species in most published forms as well.

Some vernacular names may only be used by specialists, others only in a very limited area, while use of some vernacular names may be widespread. In certain cases, this obscurity is for a good reason, as in traditional medicines used with powerful and magical symbolism (see Box 2.5). In others, there is a need to improve communication and link local names to internationally used botanical names (see Box 2.6). In any language, words can be used both to communicate or to obscure meaning, and you have to be aware of this in discussions and interviews. Although they may initially sound awkward, there is no getting away from using Latin names to refer to plant species; even though they may seem strange at first, they are part of an internationally used naming system. This enables you to work from vernacular names and opens the door to published information on distribution, qualities, uses, population biology, conservation and cultivation which may be highly relevant to local agroforestry, health care or conservation programmes.

Quantitative methods: species use values

Although individual or group survey methods are required to determine preferences for some plant uses, such as for edible or medicinal plants, in several cases quantitative assessments of wild plant use can be made from work with local resource users. In other cases, quantitative assessments can be done as part of ethnobotanical surveys of marketplaces (see Chapter 3).

Three **quantitative ethnobotanical methods** are commonly used: **informant consensus, subjective allocation** and **uses totalled**. A fourth, less commonly used, **interview/resource assessment** method is useful for resource management purposes, since it records resource users' assessments of individual plants in terms of their utility. These quantitative approaches add a new and important component to ethnobotanical work. The informant consensus method, in particular, allows for hypothesis testing. These methods also enable comparisons of use between vegetation types or ecological zones, between different cultural groups or between people of different ages, gender or occupation within or between communities. Several of these approaches have recently been reviewed by Phillips and Gentry (1993a,b) and Phillips (1996).

Informant consensus

In this method, the relative importance of each use is calculated directly from the degree of consensus in the responses of the people interviewed. The advantages are that this yields data which can be tested statistically, and it is relatively objective. However, it is time consuming, as individuals or households must be interviewed separately. Oliver Phillips used the following formula to analyse the results of a study in Peru:

$$UV_{is} = \frac{\Sigma U_{is}}{n_{is}}$$

UV_{is} stands for the use value (UV) attributed to a particular species (s) by one informant (i). This value is calculated by first summing (indicated by the symbol Σ) all of the uses mentioned in each interview event by the informant (U_{is}), and dividing by the total number of events in which that informant gave information on the species (n_{is}).

Phillips and Gentry (1993a) worked in plots of six types of forest in the Zona Reservada Tambopata in southern Peru. They recorded the uses of trees and vines of 10cm diameter at breast height (dbh) or more in a total area of 6.1ha. Use data were recorded from 29 *mestizo* (mixed Spanish-Indian descent) people who were interviewed in the forest plots or in their communities. In terms of data analysis, each act of interviewing a local person on one day about the local names and uses of

one species was classified as an 'event'. If a species was encountered more than once in a single day, the person's responses were combined. During 12 months of field work spread over 5 years, the researchers and local people participated in 1885 independent events.

Results from different events can be added to use-values derived from other local people ($\Sigma_i UV_{is}$). This is then divided by the total number of people interviewed about that particular species n_s to yield the overall use-value (UV_s), as indicated in the following formula:

$$UV_s = \frac{\Sigma_i UV_{is}}{n_s}$$

Although this statistic was used initially on results from interviews that took place in forest plots, it could be applied to any data-gathering technique in which numerous people give information on a range of plant resources. For example, if you work with local collectors who make a large number of ethnobotanical collections, each voucher specimen with its accompanying data sheet could be considered an 'event'. It is likely that each species will be encountered numerous times by each collector, so the number of uses on each data sheet can be added together to obtain UV_{is}, the individual use-value. These can be summed for all collectors to calculate the overall use-value for a particular species (UV_s).

Subjective allocation

This is a semi-quantitative method, where the relative importance of each use is subjectively assigned by the researcher on the basis of the assessment of its cultural significance (Lee, 1979; Turner, 1988). Its advantage is that it is quicker than the informant consensus method; however, the results are not so amenable to statistical analysis since they are more subjective. It also does not allow for more than one use for each species within each category (Phillips, 1996).

Turner (1988) developed an index of cultural significance for each plant species. The index is made up of a range of plant use attributes as recognized by the researcher. The index of cultural significance (ICS) for each species is then calculated as:

$$ICS = \Sigma(qie)ui$$

where, for use *u*, *q* is quality value, *i* is intensity value and *e* is exclusivity value. Therefore, the use value of each species is the total of all (*q* x *i* x *e*) calculations for each use. This index allows an indepth analysis of species usefulness.

Uses totalled

In this method, no attempt is made to quantify the relative importance of each use, the numbers of uses simply being totalled, by species, category of plant use, or vegetation type. This method is fairly quick and simple. Oliver Phillips (1996) points out two problems with this method. Firstly, it does not distinguish between the relative importance of different uses or species. Secondly, the results are not weighted by the intensity of sampling effort. As a result, the quantity of useful plants reported can be a result of research effort rather than reality. He considers that these problems may be less important for country or ecosystem-wide comparisons (such as Toledo et al, 1992), but that they may become a problem with small-scale studies.

Interview/resource assessment method

A simple method that gives useful information for resource management purposes

is where local resource users grade the usefulness of plants within plots. This exercise can be repeated independently with several resource users (or with small groups of people), giving insights into which species are most favoured within broader use categories (such as trees for fuel, building poles or carving) and why favoured individuals are selected within those species based on size class, shape, health of the plants or possibly even genetic factors. As each stem (or leaf or whatever is the focus of the study) is measured by the researcher, the local resource user rates it either very good, good, acceptable, poor or not useable, giving the reason(s) why (see Figure 2.9). Cut stems (or leaves) that have already been harvested or have been damaged in other ways (such as eaten by animals) are also recorded.

Essentially combining standard ecological plot methods with the added benefit of work with local harvesters, this method not only gives insight into what has been harvested, but also into selection criteria, what level of harvesting might be expected and whether this will be sustainable or not. As this can be time consuming, either due to high density of stems of a single species or high species diversity within plots, it is important to have time available and to select an appropriate plot size. Alternatively, assessments based on transects or quantitative plots can be done in sites where harvesting has already taken place, such as from the proportion of cut stumps or root or bark damage assessments within plots (see Chapters 4 and 5).

In some cases, it may be necessary to work with small groups of harvesters. Although this means that independent ratings by individual harvesters are not possible, it has the advantage, in common with participatory-group interview methods, of being able to listen to

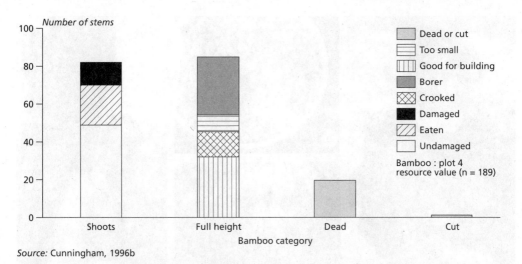

Source: Cunningham, 1996b

Figure 2.9 *Local harvester assessments of bamboo utility in Bwindi-Impenetrable National Park, Uganda, showing the high proportion of stems that are unsuitable for building purposes and the reasons why, the low level of harvesting and number of stems eaten by non-human primates*

harvesters debate the merits of different qualities of the resource. In Botswana, for example, I worked with groups of four to five basket makers who assessed the suitability of leaves of *Hyphaene petersiana* palms which were experimentally cultivated as an alternative basketry fibre supply source. The unopened leaves usually harvested for basketry were checked by women basket makers in two study plots on different soils: 70 palm stems in one plot and 74 palms in another.

Women in each group inspected each potentially suitable leaf (one per palm stem), had a brief discussion, then concluded why the leaf was acceptable for basketry or not. The majority were not considered suitable because they had poor qualities: 'too hard as they hadn't been softened by frequent harvesting' (33 per cent and 51 per cent respectively); 'too thick' (8.5 per cent and none); 'too short' (23 per cent and 13 per cent); 'leaves a yellowish colour' (1.7 per cent and 3 per cent); and 'leaf apex skew' (none and 1.4 per cent). The remainder had good qualities: 'soft and pliable' (43 per cent); 'not rough (good texture, fewer spines)' (6.7 per cent and 5.7 per cent) and 'sharp straight tip' (none and 1.4 per cent). These insights would probably be missed in the informant consensus approach which records whether the species (rather than individuals within the species) is useful.

Local to international units

Measuring the quantity of plant products sold can be valuable in linking with other quantitative studies on plant biomass production, such as fruit or sap yields per plant or per hectare (see Chapter 4). To be of most value, however, the measurements need to accurately reflect the quantities that really are being harvested, consumed or sold. Inaccurate measurements of volumes used are of limited value. Quantitative market surveys are expensive and time consuming, just as interviews are

Figure 2.10 *Local units, whether bundles, baskets, bicycle or vehicle loads, can be useful units of measure convertible to international units of mass (tonnes, kilograms) or volume (litres, cubic metres) for comparison to other studies on biomass production or yields*

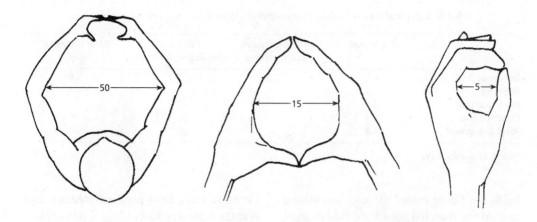

Figure 2.11 *Commonly used local estimates of circumference for different-sized bundles of plant products*

a more time-consuming and expensive social survey method than RRA or PRA methods, yielding a different type of data that will take longer to process. It is therefore important to focus on key resources to ensure that the research funds and available time are well used.

The size, shape, and weight of the 'units' in which plant resources are transported are very variable, coming in bundles, bags or bottles of varying types (see Figure 2.10). Units will also be determined by which storage or transport containers are most commonly available, and this will often vary with time. Despite this variation, some local 'units' may be fairly constant over a wide area since some bundle sizes are dictated by the easiest way of transporting that particular product. Thus, similar-sized reed bundles are sold throughout southern Africa, measured by 'arm-circumference' diameters. Other bundles, such as thatch grass or weaving material, may be measured in subunits which can be useful in discussions and PRA work, such as hand-circumference bundles or bundles the same circumference as thumb and forefingers (see Figure 2.11). Measuring large samples of local 'units'

(at least 30 of each local unit) gives the mean mass or volume and standard error for each unit, enabling conversion to international units and estimates of quantities used.

Recovery rates and quantity used

It is important to avoid under or overestimating the quantities of plant material being used. One way of avoiding this is to assess the quantity harvested at source, so that you measure unprocessed amounts, which can then be related to wild-harvested material. If this is not possible, such as when you are working from long-term sales data, you need to take recovery rates into account, whether due to air-dry versus wet weight of material harvested or to loss of volume during harvesting.

In some cases, processed products can represent a high proportion of harvested material. In other situations there may be a deceptive increase in volume – for example, when palm wine is diluted before resale (Cunningham, 1990). You also need to watch for cases where recycling of harvested resources takes place. Some studies of wood consumption by house-

Table 2.2 *Total annual wood consumption (tonnes per household per year)*

	Live wood	Recycled from construction	Dead wood (including leftovers)	Total domestic fuel
Domestic fuel	1.8	1.3	2.7	5.8
Brewing	1.3			
Brick burning	0.4			
Construction	1.3			
Total live wood	**4.8**			

Source: McGregor, 1991

holds have been biased through not taking note of the recycled use of old timber used for housing construction as fuel. In her study of this in Zimbabwe, Joann McGregor (1991) showed that 1.3 tonnes of wood per household per year were recycled as fuel (see Table 2.2).

In woodcarving or in the case of some edible foods, very little of the unprocessed plant material becomes the final product (see Figure 2.12). Ebony (*Dalbergia melanoxylon*), for example, is a prime woodcarving timber used in the tourist trade. It is also the main wood used for several musical instruments, including clarinets, flutes and recorders. Since it is overexploited in many parts of Eastern and South-Central Africa and is a very valuable timber, it is useful to determine the volume of cut timber exported for musical instruments. The only data available during a survey of ebony use in

Tanzania were **final product volumes** and **average recovery rate**. Only 7 per cent of total log input was recovered as a 'final product' of wooden blocks or billets exported for the musical instrument industry (Moore and Hall, 1987). Data from the Sawmill Industry of 125 m³/yr during 1987 were then converted, to give an estimate of the volume of **total log input** used annually:

$$\frac{Final\ Product\ Volume}{Average\ Recovery\ Rate} = \frac{125\ m^3}{0.07} = 1785\ m^3\ of\ logs/yr$$

In other cases, recovery rates can be high. This facilitates a far more accurate assessment to infer quantities of raw materials harvested. Weaving material is one such example. In a study of commercial trade in crafts in South-eastern Africa, for

Table 2.3 *Basket makers' assessments of* Hyphaene petersiana *palm leaves rejected or considered acceptable for basketry*

Reasons given	ETSHA-5 % (No)	ETSHA-8 % (No)	Reasons given	ETSHA-5 % (No)	ETSHA-8 % (No)
a) Good qualities			b) Poor qualities		
'Soft' (pliable)	43.4% (26)	30.1% (21)	'Too hard'	33.3% (20)	51.4% (36)
			'Too thick'	8.3% (5)	0
'Not rough' (good texture, fewer spines)	6.7% (4)	5.7% (4)	'Too short'	23.3% (14)	12.8% (9)
Sharp tip	0	1.4% (1)	Yellow colour	1.7% (1)	2.9% (2)
			Leaf apex skew	0	1.4% (1)

Source: Cunningham, 1992

Figure 2.12 *Low recovery rates from an edible fruit: steps in the processing of (a)* Strychnos madagascariensis *fruits – (b) cracked open after harvesting, (c) seeds and pulp removed and sun-dried, (d) then smoked and (e) the pulp finally removed for storage or consumption*

Box 2.7 Standardized Terms for Describing Bark Components, Bark Texture, Patterns and Exudates

Bark Texture (Consistency)

This is the composition of the bark, mainly resulting from the characteristics of the cells making up the tissue and the extent of decay of the outer bark (rhytidome). Bark texture may be **corky** (like cork), **fibrous** (the outer and/or inner bark dominated by fibres), **brittle** (outer or inner bark hard, breakable), **loose** (outer and/or inner bark breaks up on cutting into coarse or fine grains or flakes), **granular** (inner bark mainly composed of sclereids), **mealy** (outer bark falls off like powder), **homogeneous** (either fibres or sclereids occur) versus **heterogeneous**, **soft** (outer and/or inner bark is soft and easy to cut versus **hard**), **laminate** (layers in the phloem formed by sclerenchyma).

Bark Patterns

Four aspects of bark texture provide useful macroscopic characteristics: firstly, those seen in cross-section or in a bark slash (blaze); secondly, bark fissuring; thirdly, bark scaling; and finally, the external appearance of the bark.

Patterns in cross- and tangential section

This includes the following: **corrugations** (inner bark surface corrugated, matching similar pattern on sapwood), **dilatation (growth)** (patterns from the process of tangential widening of the bark during growth seen in bark slash), **flame marks** (a pattern like flames seen in bark cross-section, formed by phloem rays), **phloem, mottled** (coloured spots seen in bark slash), **phloem, scalariform** (in cross-section, the phloem rays form a ladder-like structure, with radial 'rungs'), **ripple marks** (fine parallel horizontal lines seen in the bark slash), **streaks** (striations on the surface of the bark slash usually formed by phloem rays and sclerenchymatic tissue), these may be **longitudinal**, as in *Wormia triquetra* (Dilleniaceae) bark, which has dark streaks like coconut wood, or **reticulate** (regular or wavy lines), like the bark of the West African timber tree *Terminalia superba*.

Bark fissuring

Fissured bark is cracked lengthwise into fissures (generally longitudinal grooves) between ridges in the outer bark (or rhytidome). Bark fissures may be **parallel** (usually long and regular), **reticulate** (with grooves joining each other and dividing again) or **oblique** (short or long grooves, joining and splitting again – anastomosing, but not as regularly or distinctly as with reticulate fissures). Fissures can also be classified according to depth and length: **deep** (at least half as deep as total bark thickness), **shallow** (less than half as deep as total bark thickness), **boat-shaped** (oval or elliptical fissures which are not continuous), **short** (<15cm long), **long or elongated** (>15cm long), **V-shaped** (sharp V-shaped cross-section), **round** (concave in cross-section), **square-shaped** (fissures flat-bottomed in cross-section), **irregular** (different-sized gaps and furrows), **compound** (anastomosing shallow fissures in the bottom of main fissures), **wavy** (coarse longitudinal grooves with irregular, wavy faces). Also take a good look at the bark **ridges**, the raised part of the outer bark between the fissures. These can be **flattened**, **hollow** (concave in cross-section), **rounded** (convex in cross-section), **V-shaped** or **reticulate**, joining each other, irregularly dividing and enclosing non-continuous fissures.

Bark scaling

Many tree species have flaky, 'shaggy' or 'scaly' older outer bark which becomes detached, such as *mvule* (*Milicia excelsa*) in Africa or many Australian *Melaleuca* and *Eucalyptus* species. Following Wyatt-Smith's (1954) work in Malaysia, **bark flakes** are those patches of outer bark more than 7.5cm long which become detached, whereas **bark scales** are less than 7.5cm long. Flakes and scales can vary in shape or thickness and may be **rectangular, irregular, circular, papery, scrolled** (thin flakes rolled up at their edges) or **shaggy** (loosened, usually curved rectangular or irregular flakes which may hang for a while on the stem). In addition, **bark scales** can be **flat-sided** (one or several layers thick), **chunky** (with irregular rough faces and an irregular shape), **scallop-shaped** (thickest in the middle, tapering to the edges, leaving a scalloped-shaped depression on the tree stem when they drop off).

Bark may be **heterogeneous** (with more than one type of bark on the same stem), as in the miombo tree, *Brachystegia bussei*, **patchy** (usually with two colours dominating, often with lighter blotches due to irregular dehiscence), **powdery** (with a fine powder-like crust which rubs off easily), usually found on smooth barks like the fever-tree, *Acacia xanthophloea*, **stringy** (thick, loose-fibred bark, never deciduous), **surface rotten** (bark has short fissures, varying in depth and cross-section, scaly, rugose or smooth, with variable bark scales – small, adherent, chunky or flat-sided; in cross-section, the inner edge of the outer bark follows the surface shapes and is not parallel to the cambium), **tessellated** (with fairly regular, square or oblong plates or blocks on the bark surface, which remain on the stem for a long time) or **ring-bark** (a type of outer bark where periderms are formed parallel to the first one, resulting in concentric cylinders of outer bark which detach, often annually, in large sheets).

External markings

The outer bark surface may be **dippled** (covered with shallow, usually circular depressions >1cm in diameter which are the scars of the scaled-off old bark), **pock-marked** (covered in depressions <1cm in diameter), **scribbly** (with characteristic 'scribble' patterns caused by insect larvae), **rugose** (which looks smooth from a distance, but is covered by wrinkles, depressions, shallow fissures or irregular scales), **rough** (with an uneven surface, such as scaly, flaky or fissured barks), **smooth** (thin and unbroken, although it may have lenticels), **lenticellate** (covered with raised, sometimes corky spots or lenticels).

These vary in their shape, size, frequency, grouping and consistency. Lenticels may be **linear** (like button-holes), **round, stellate** (star-shaped) or **diamond-shaped**, and can also be described according to their diameter as **large** (>5mm), **medium** (3 to 5mm) or **small** (<3mm). They may be **numerous** (or **scarce**), **solitary** or **compound**, occurring in **vertical, horizontal** or **oblique lines**, and may be **soft, powdery** or **compact**. Bark may also be characteristically marked by **eye-marks** (eye-shaped marks which often correspond to old leaf or lateral branch scars) common on *Bridelia micrantha*, **hoops** (raised transverse rings which partially or completely circle the trunk), **ring-grooves** (transverse grooves which partially or completely circle the trunk) as in *Alberta magna*, **scroll marks** (similar to dippled bark, but where sinuous marks are formed between depressions when scales are detached), **prickles** (which can be detached without tearing the wood), **spines** (which tear the wood if detached), and may be **simple** (versus **branched**), **straight** (versus **curved**), **hard** (versus **supple**), tapering or conical. Finally, the tree trunk or branches may be characterized by **burls** (hard woody outgrowths), **cankers** (localized lesions on the bark or cambium) and **warts** (bumpy outgrowths which are not spines, prickles or burls).

Figure 2.13 *Be careful not to make incorrect assumptions of recovery rates from quick surveys, and take part in harvesting expeditions if at all possible to determine selection procedures. (a) Smilax anceps – but vertical stems are not selected. (b) Processed horizontal runners. (c) Completing the final product*

example, I was able to use sales records from the sole craft work organization in the area to determine annual sales, which fortunately had been kept according to the materials from which the crafts were made. All craft items were weighed to convert records of numbers of baskets sold to mass of material. Recovery rates were then determined by working with local basket makers. With the exception of palm leaves, other plant fibres were not reduced in volume after they had been selected by leaf size class and dried. Ilala palm (*Hyphaene coriacea*) leaves were also amongst the most favoured material (see Table 2.3). Recovery rates were high as only the leaf mid-rib and petiole were discarded. Air-dry weight of whole leaves of favoured length was 310g (SE ± 97g). This provided 249g (SE ± 95g) of weaving material. Taking this recovery rate into account, the estimated number of leaves used per year varied: 5554 leaves (1978), 6622 (1979), 5884 leaves (1980), 10,584 leaves (1981), 7963 (1982) and 9902

leaves (1983). This could then be related to leaf-production rates in the palm savanna mapped from aerial photographs.

Other cases are not as simple, emphasizing the importance of field observation and participation in harvesting expeditions before conclusions are made on quantities of material used. *Smilax anceps* (Smilacaceae), known locally as *ensuli*, is the most favoured basketry material in western Uganda and is easy to identify and frequently pointed out by local people (see Figure 2.13). What is less obvious, unless one participates in harvesting, is that it is not the vertical stems, as one might expect, that are used. Basket makers carefully select horizontal 'runners', and any inference on impact of harvesting has to take this into account.

It is in these cases that participant observation and careful discussion by ecologically aware researchers can avoid some of the inaccuracies that may result from rapid surveys.

Chapter 3

Settlement, Commercialization and Change

Introduction

Understanding trade networks is a key to designing practical conservation, resource management or rural development programmes for species in trade. Knowing which species are sold, how much they sell for, or the quantities sold, is not enough. It is equally important to know who is involved in sales along often complex marketing chains, how this is organized and how it is changing, where source areas used to be or are today, and how demand and supply are likely to change in the future. In this chapter, I give a general introduction to ethnobotanical surveys of markets, then discuss the theoretical background to studying the location and classification of markets, market schedules and the different sellers within them, and suggest a checklist of guidelines to assist researchers in conducting market surveys.

Rural people, moving from a subsistence lifestyle to a cash economy, have relatively few options for generating income. They can sell agricultural or pastoral produce, work for a cash wage in agriculture or industry, or retail goods in local or regional marketplaces. For the rural poor without land or livestock, harvesting of wild plant resources is a common option, particularly for people in ecosystems with low arable potential. A growing demand from urban areas catalyses this trade, drawing in resources from rural areas to towns and cities, often for favoured fuelwood, building materials, medicinal or edible wild fruit species.

Many people who harvest and sell wild plants are from what is termed the **informal sector**: self-employed people, generally unrecognized in official statistics, who have little access to capital and who earn money from labour-intensive enterprises. From first harvest to final sale, the trade in wild or naturalized plants for local, national or regional trade forms part of an informal 'hidden economy' sector. International trade in these plant products is more obvious, as middlemen link the informal sector to an export sector for which export or import records are sometimes kept.

This trade provides an important opportunity for systematic ethnobotanical surveys and a rich source of information for conservation, rural development and resource management programmes. There are several reasons for this.

Firstly, the species that are sold are a 'short-list' of a much wider range of species that are available which can be

Table 3.1 *A summary of methods used at different levels of detail in the study of exchange and distribution*

Level	Type of data	Information obtained	Problems
Minimum	Government records and published information	Government price records and other market information; market calendars	Reliability
	Key informant interviews	Trader types; commodity types; overview of organization of exchange – who, where, when, what, how; transportation information; units of measures and standard of value; bargaining methods	Reliability and knowledge of key informant(s)
Second	Household surveys	What is bought/sold/exchanged	Resource limitations in carrying out surveys
	Trader surveys	Demographic information; information on organization of exchange; social relationships, credit bargaining; movements of traders	Design of appropriate questions
	Market surveys (where marketplaces are main sites for exchange)	Number of vendors and types of vendors; number of commodities and types of commodities; functional groupings	Determination of set markets to study
Third	Market surveys	Movement of people (vendors, consumers), movement of vehicles and commodities	Resource limitations
		Number of commodities (functions) and vendors as basis for determining central-place hierarchy of market system	Modify central-place methods for specific system, especially separate wholesale and retail functions
Most comprehensive	Observation and in-depth interviews	Details on social organization of exchange – bargaining, customer relations, social networks, etc; additional information on basic questions (who, when, what, how)	Time and intensive work by research

Source: Trager, 1995

cross-checked with information from social surveys (see Table 3.1, and Chapter 2). If demand for a species or resource category such as fuel, basketry fibre or herbal medicine is high and supplies are still available, then these species or resource categories will be sold in many marketplaces. Conversely, a species or category of plant use in low demand would be less common in marketplaces.

Systematic ethnobotanical surveys of local markets not only classify the species on sale, but also arrange them into hierarchical levels – which may reflect their relative demand. There is an important exception: some of the most useful and popular species no longer feature in markets due to overexploitation.

Secondly, the shift from subsistence use to commercial sale can have important

Figure 3.1 *As roads reach further and further into remote resource-rich regions, initiating settlement and clearing habitat, commercial harvest and trade usually increase. This photograph shows road construction through tropical forest in Côte d'Ivoire, West Africa*

implications for resource management since it results in larger volumes being harvested, a higher frequency and intensity of harvesting, and can affect resource tenure. In some cases, commercial harvesting strengthens resource tenure and the incentive to conserve individual plants. Commercial sale of wild fruits, for example, maintains the incentive to conserve wild fruit-bearing trees in parts of Africa where development of a social stigma against gathering wild fruits as a food resource is undermining the 'traditional' practice of conserving wild fruit trees. In other cases, the shift from subsistence use to commercial harvesting weakens resource tenure and undermines customary controls of resource use. Harvesters are often people with low incomes and few resources in reserve. In some cases, the species producing the tastiest fruits, strongest fibres, the most effective medicinal plants, or finest timbers – those with the greatest value to local people, and with potential for national or international horticultural or industrial development as new crops – are those most likely to be overexploited.

As roads reach further and further into remote resource-rich regions, initiating settlement and clearing habitat, commercial harvest and trade usually increase (see Figure 3.1). Improved transport networks strengthen the link between rural resources and urban demand. They also result in an influx of outsiders, frequently disrupting traditional resource tenure systems and increasing the scramble for economically valuable resources. Species identified in market surveys are an important component in a matrix of biological and socio-economic criteria that can be used to prioritize species for conservation purposes (see Box 3.2).

Thirdly, systematic surveys of local markets are a good way of identifying information on indigenous species which have already been domesticated or which have a high potential for domestication.

Local markets: order within 'chaos'

An outsider, walking into a busy rural or city marketplace for the first time, is faced with unusual scents, exotic sounds, bright colours and densely packed crowds. At first sight, marketplaces may appear totally chaotic. To local people, however, there is a clear pattern in the crowded market indicated by types of sellers, what they are selling, where they come from and by the location of particular categories of goods or sellers within the marketplace. In addition to these patterns within market-places, there is generally also a pattern in where markets are located within rural or urban areas, and when these markets are held.

Before deciding on how or where to perform detailed ethnobotanical surveys in markets, it is useful to view markets in a stepwise, systematic way – firstly, from the perspective of an economic geographer or anthropologist, and then as a botanist. The question is: where do we start (or stop) collecting information? Just as harvesting impacts have to be viewed at different scales, from a regional landscape level to species-populations and individual plants (see Chapters 4 to 6), with mapping and an understanding of vegetation dynamics as tools in this process, so trade and markets need to be viewed from a systems perspective. One of the tools frequently used by geographers to under-stand how markets are organized is derived from central place theory, which uses a hierarchical approach to systemati-cally classify market systems. One of the best-known examples of this approach is Skinner's (1964, 1965) seminal study of markets in China. Despite the shortcom-ings of **central place theory** pointed out by some archaeologists (Crumley and Marquardt, 1987) and geographers

(Vance, 1970), it continues to be the basis for many studies of exchange and distrib-ution (Trager, 1995). To understand market networks as systems, we need to step back from the exotic and seemingly chaotic and crowded market and work downwards from a regional landscape (or even global scale in the case of the inter-national export trade) to finer levels of detail at smaller spatial or time scales.

Survey methods will also depend upon whether you are doing a short- or long-term survey, on the gender of the sellers with whom you will be working, and on the types of products and markets on which your survey will focus. Detailed surveys can cross-reference with informa-tion collected from other methods, such as participatory mapping, seasonal calendars and ranking of products described in Chapter 2. If you are working in a large study area, you will need to decide on which markets to survey, when to survey them and what to survey (see Box 3.1). You will notice factors that influence your survey, such as the following.

- Markets are often located at predictable places in the landscape, such as at stopping-off points on transport routes along major rivers or roads, in villages and at predictable sites within urban areas (taxi ranks, bus stops).
- Within markets, sellers are often distributed according to the type of goods they are selling. Their location within markets and the types of goods they sell are also indicators of their socio-economic status.
- The timing of markets will vary according to a variety of factors, including the size of the village,

seasonal availability of the resource, or daily activity. For this reason, you need to be well aware of the bias that can occur due to poorly timed surveys.

- Observe, discuss and think carefully about what units you will use to monitor which products in more detailed surveys. Survey forms may also need to be designed according to the literacy levels of people involved in monitoring, such as the palm-wine survey form in Figure 3.2.
- Where do plant resources sold in the market come from? Some items, and the people selling them, may travel long distances from other vegetation types, with very specific products.
- Is species substitution occurring and if so, why? In some cases, less scrupulous harvesters mix in similar looking species to bulk up bundles of harvested plant material when they sell to unsuspecting traders. In other cases, species substitution is a warning 'flag' for increasing scarcity. In South Africa, for example, Zulu women harvesting medicinal plants find it increasingly difficult to obtain aromatic bark of the forest tree *Ocotea bullata* (Lauraceae). As a result, bark of two forest trees in the same family (*Cryptocarya latifolia* and *C. myrtifolia*), each with a similar bark aroma to *Ocotea bullata*, are substituted and sold by urban herb traders as the real thing.

As the volume of products sold varies from one market to another, as well as by season or on a daily and weekly basis, quick surveys may indicate the main products sold, but may miss out important details such as competition between different products. In a detailed medium-term (12 to 18 months) daily-sales survey of palm-wine sales in South-Eastern Africa, 'primary sale points' were located, as expected, within the *Hyphaene* palm ecological zone. These were distinguished from palm-wine sales outside the zone, where palm wine from primary sales points was diluted with water for resale (see Figure 3.2). Monitoring resale points would have given a complete overestimate of sales volumes. Only later in the study, however, was it clear how palm-wine sales varied not only weekly, but also with a distinctive decrease in sales when a fermented beer from the popular wild fruit *Sclerocarya birrea* was available – and this did not appear in markets at all, as it is traditionally never sold due to its cultural and religious importance (Cunningham, 1990a,b; see Figure 2.2).

Location and mapping of marketplaces

Marketplaces of different sizes and function in rural areas, or in cities, towns or villages of different sizes, can be identified from maps or aerial photographs, depending upon the size of the study area. Initially, you might work from 1:250,000 or 1:50,000 scale. In cities or towns, work on a smaller 1:10,000 scale.

Local knowledge is very important in identifying rural periodic markets that are not located in places that are obvious to an outsider – for example, at periodic cattle sales or on days when pensions are paid out in rural areas. During this mapping process, you will also have the opportunity to categorize marketplaces in different ways. One example is the map of markets along the Zaire River in Central Africa made by anthropologist Yuji Ankei (1985) (see Figure 3.3). For this reason, it

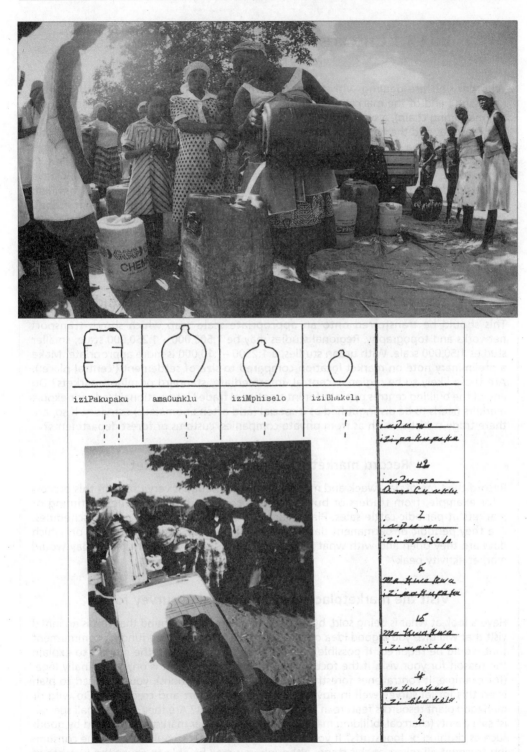

Figure 3.2 *Case study example: survey form and involvement of selected local people in monitoring palm-wine sales*

Box 3.1 Checklist: Ethnobotanical Surveys of Marketplaces

Whether you are dealing with the rural harvest ('supply') end or the urban retail ('demand') end of the marketing chain (or possibly supply and demand at points along the marketing chain), a systematic approach is useful in developing an understanding of marketplaces and the networks of resource supply and demand that support them. This checklist assumes a stepwise process, from a regional 'coarse grain' approach downwards to more detailed surveys. The cut-off point will be determined by time and funding. In some cases, you may be starting from scratch. In others, you may already have background information on which species are commercially harvested, either from field observation in local markets, discussions, participatory rural appraisal (PRA) methods, standard interview surveys or informant indexing methods of species/vegetation utility or cultural importance (see Chapter 2). This can put information from field observations as well as rapid, broad-scale (PRA, RRA) or detailed (interview, informal indexing) methods into geographical perspective. The following steps are recommended.

Map the location and names of marketplaces in your study area

This should be transferred onto an appropriate scale map which shows transport networks and topography. Regional studies may be 1:500,000 – 1:250,000 scale; smaller studies 1:50,000 scale. With urban studies, a 1:2500 –1:10,000 is more appropriate. Make a preliminary note on market location compared to size of settlement ('central place'). Are these likely to be regional, central, intermediate, standard or minor markets? Do any of the bulking centres operate for international trade? International trade for export markets needs to be distinguished as a special (and often anomalous) category. If so, are there trade statistics, such as from private companies, customs or forest departments?

Record market schedules for each market

Record the time of day, week and month. Local knowledge is very useful in this process – for example, from traders or buyers, or according to boat schedules or timing of markets at periodic cattle sales. Plan your visits according to these market schedules. Are they periodic or permanent daily markets? If they are periodic markets, on which days are they open and with what frequency? On open days, what time of day would market activity peak?

Visit the marketplaces before designing survey forms

Have a look at what is being sold, by whom and where. Bear in mind that this is an initial visit that will give you a good idea of the scale of sale and the time/funding commitment that would be required. If possible, meet the person controlling the market to explain the reason for your visit. If the focus of your study is trade that is only marginally legal (for example, it contravenes forestry or conservation regulations), you will need to plan even this initial survey well in advance with local support and credibility. Do wild or managed plant resources feature at all, and if not, why not? Are they sold at small specialist sale points (charcoal, building materials, fuel) or in larger markets dominated by goods such as clothing or foodstuffs? If you are in large markets, it would be too time consuming to count all sellers at this stage, although you may be able to count the number of people selling the products that are the focus of your study (herbal medicines, wild fruits, crafts). Where are sellers positioned in the market: in permanent stalls, under temporary shelters, on the ground in the market or outside of the market (where they may not have to pay fees)? Are the sellers men or women? Are they harvester-sellers, long-distance traders, itinerant traders, travelling merchants or permanent sellers? Do the quantities look as if this is a bulk-sale centre (wholesale) or bulk-breaking centre (retail)? Would it be possible to categorize a range of 'standard' bundles/bags/bottle sizes? Keep in mind criteria that characterize different types of markets and sellers.

Logistics, project planning

Plan your work on the basis of available time and funding. At this stage, you may already start to wonder whether you are being too ambitious or not. Using information from the guidelines above, make an initial grouping of markets according to location, size and market schedule. You will then have a more realistic basis on which to plan more detailed work. Are you being too ambitious regarding the number of marketplaces? If so, you may need to: focus on wholesale (bulk buying) markets and subsample retail markets; or scale down the size of the study area.

Have you allowed for seasonal differences that affect wild plants on sale and their prices? You may be recording alone in a broad-scale survey or, if you have the funds, you may decide to recruit reliable local assistance with the market surveys. Work out practical forms for the survey. Depending upon the sensitivity and credibility of your study, you may/may not want to record uses and prices at this stage – they create suspicion. Prices are also likely to be inflated for outsider researchers and are best recorded by local researchers/assistants. Follow up initial visual surveys with longer-term detailed work. Count and categorize sellers. Categorize the type of market. Survey species being sold by each seller and collect voucher specimens, parts of plants used and local names; record whether the material is sold fresh or dried. Compare with data from other survey methods. Select key species. You need to decide what your focus will be: value, volume or vulnerability, or a combination of these. Key issues in group/individual interviews are the interrelated issues of price, scarcity and popularity, source areas and long-distance trade. Is there a 'moving front' of depletion where harvesters overexploit a resource-rich frontier then move on, or not?

Choose 'indicator' species for field assessment and/or monitoring

Focus on populations of species that are indicators of demand which exceed their capacity to regenerate after harvesting. In some cases, you will be able to overlay the map of marketplaces onto a map showing distribution of these 'indicator' species (see Box 3.2 and Chapters 4 to 6). Field check harvester-seller or trader perceptions of scarcity in the following different sites:

- · the major harvest areas where resources are considered to be 'finished';
- 'frontier' sites which have recently become a focus of harvest; and
- 'indicator' species populations beyond the 'frontier', where commercial harvest has yet to take place.

For a discussion of changes in resource tenure with commercialization and competition from outsiders, see 'Social Surveys', Chapter 7; for methods used for damage assessment, biomass comparison, size-class selection, increased intensity/frequency of harvest, see Chapters 4 and 5.

is important to select local people as key helpers to find out about the location and schedules of markets, who sells which products, and where they, and the products they sell, come from.

In some cases, marketplaces and market schedules are easily identified. In others, location of marketplaces can be extremely difficult, particularly where major river systems rather than roads are the main transport route. Anthropologist Christine Padoch, for example, found that there were almost no stable marketplaces wholesaling wild-collected plants in Iquitos in the Peruvian Amazon: most wholesale buying was done on moving river boats before they entered any port. Informal markets also shifted with the seasonal rise and fall of the river (Padoch, 1988). A similar situation probably applies on the Zaire River.

Local knowledge, including advice from buyers and sellers themselves, can be useful in resolving these challenges to field research. Despite the complexity of marketing in Iquitos, Christine Padoch was able to focus on key species such as the *aguaje* (*Mauritia flexuosa*) palm, and identify the wholesale (land-based) market for these fruits where they were sold in open 50kg sacks. This enabled her to quantify the more than 700 metric tonnes of *aguaje* palm fruit sold each day in Iquitos and estimate that about 500 people, primarily women, relied upon this sale as a source of funds.

Records of product prices recorded within the same season over longer time spans can also tell a story, sometimes 'flagging' overharvesting as prices rise with increasing scarcity. Working in the same market in Iquitos, for example, botanist Rodolfo Vasquez has also been able to carry out regular surveys of wild-collected plants, and the harvesting methods and the retail prices paid for them over a period of more than ten years,

highlighting species such as *aguaje* (*Mauritia flexuosa*) palms in this process (Vasquez and Gentry, 1989).

Conceptual framework: location theory, central places and resource use

Two simple but useful theoretical models are still widely used by economic geographers to explain the location of central places in a landscape and the activities around them. These two models have primarily been used by geographers interested in urban or agricultural planning. Despite the simplicity of these models and the much greater complexity of harvesting wild plant resources compared to agricultural or urban expansion, they are a useful basis for considering patterns of resource harvesting in response to demand from growing towns and cities.

The first, the **von Thünen model**, was developed in the early 1800s by a young German farmer called Johann von Thünen to determine the best way of using land on his farming estate. This led to the publication of a book called *The Isolated State*, which developed a theory of the most economical land use around a city that formed the only market in an isolated, flat plain. Assuming that farmers wanted to maximize their income and that transport costs increased with distance, he visualized a series of concentric land-use zones around the city, with the most intensive activity closest to the market. He also considered a situation where transport along a river or good road would influence land use, in bands of decreasing intensity in parallel zones away from the river or road.

The second, the **Christaller-Lösch model**, was independently developed in Germany by two economic geographers, Walter Christaller and August Lösch in the 1930s (Christaller, 1966; Lösch, 1954). While von Thünen was interested in

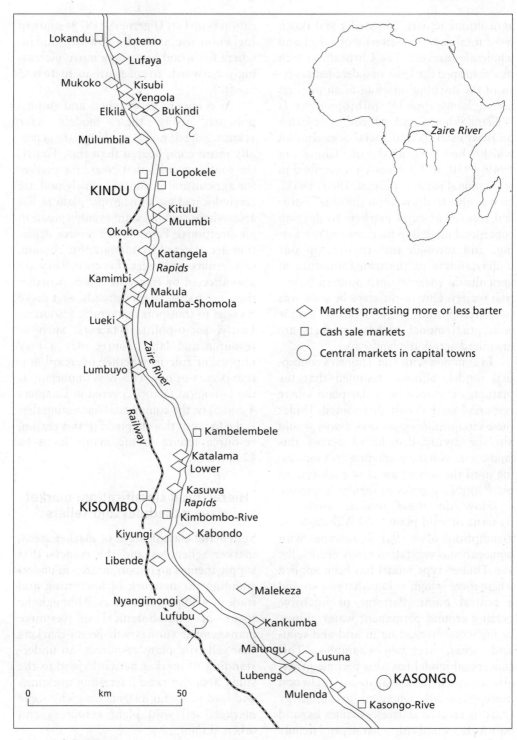

Figure 3.3 *Map of markets along the Zaire River in Central Africa*

agricultural activity, Christaller and Lösch were interested in patterns of retail and wholesale markets. The Christaller-Lösch model formed the basis of a detailed analysis of the distribution of agrarian markets across landscapes by anthropologist G William Skinner, underpinned by research on rural markets and social organization which he conducted in China in 1949–1950. In his research, described in two seminal papers (Skinner, 1964, 1965), he was able to draw upon the long historical records of rural markets to develop conceptual models of markets and marketing, and through this to develop our understanding of the transformation of agricultural societies into modern industrial society. One of the steps he took was to develop and work from a simple conceptual model of how markets are organized across the landscape.

In common with von Thünen's conceptual model, Skinner assumed that the markets developed on a flat plain where resources were evenly distributed. Under these circumstances, market towns would also be evenly distributed across this landscape, with the marketing area increasing until the service areas of each central place formed a series of regular hexagons.

How do these models apply to patterns of wild plant use? Although the assumption of a flat landscape with homogeneous vegetation rarely occurs, the von Thünen type model has been applied where there is high-volume harvest around a central point. Patterns of intensive grazing around permanent water points, or fuelwood harvesting in arid and semiarid areas, are two examples. This conceptual model has also become generally accepted as a feature of fuelwood overexploitation, where an 'urban energy crisis' is created as treeless zones expand outwards around cities that depend mainly on fuelwood, with fuel getting more and more expensive. One example of its application is in Turi Digernes's (1979) study of fuelwood use around a town in Sudan, where fuelwood harvesters move increasingly outwards to meet urban fuelwood needs.

As economic geographers and anthropologists using these models have acknowledged, however, things are generally more complicated than this. Firstly, the towns or cities that create the market for agricultural products or fuelwood are rarely located on an isotropic plain (a flat area where resources are evenly spread in all directions). Patterns of resource depletion are affected by topography, climate, soil fertility and vegetation type. They are also affected by transport routes, whether these are paths, rivers or roads, that make it easier to transport marketable resources. Lastly, socio-political factors, such as resource and land tenure, play a very important role in whether overexploitation occurs or not. This is as important as the biological factors covered in Chapters 4 and 5, or the commercial harvesting that is the focus of this chapter. For this reason, resource tenure is the major focus of Chapter 7.

Hierarchical classification: market sizes, schedules and sellers

Systematic classification of market areas, market schedules and the traders that supply them is an important step in understanding the network of harvesting and trade in wild plant resources. Although the focus of ethnobotanical or resource management studies will be on markets that sell wild plant resources, an understanding of market networks within the study area can raise interesting questions and lead to useful insights into why some markets sell wild plant resources and others do not.

The process of mapping and classifying markets can help to guide research

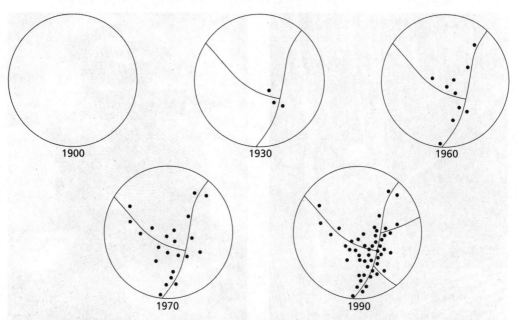

Figure 3.4 *Sequence of a 'node' becoming what geographers call a 'nucleated' settlement, and developing into a town and then a city*

design, providing a basis for deciding whether to sample all markets in a small study area or which markets to subsample if there are too many involved for detailed ethnobotanical surveys. It can also impart some predictive value on what to expect from cultural, socio-economic or environmental change. Although many more detailed studies of markets have been conducted in agricultural societies than of wild plants in trade, they provide useful background to developing a systematic approach to ethnobotanical surveys in marketplaces.

Marketplaces often evolve from barter and trade at small 'nodal points' at river crossings or road junctions. Some of these 'nodes' become what geographers call nucleated settlements, developing into towns and cities (see Figure 3.4).

The towns, cities and other settlements which support markets are called central places by economic geographers. As central places grow, the markets within them exert a stronger pull on rural resources. Over the past century, there has been an unprecedented flood of people moving from rural to urban areas. In 1800, for example, there were only 50 cities of more than 100,000 people. By 1950, there were 900, and by the end of the century more than a quarter of the global population will live in cities exceeding one million people.

Today, the highest rate of urbanization, 6 per cent per year, is in sub-Saharan Africa. In South Asia, the rate is 4 per cent per year. Godoy and Bawa (1993) suggest that economic development 'encourages rural to urban migration, lowers population growth, and supports more productive agriculture, all of which should decrease pressure on the forest as a source of livelihood'.

The urban-rural divide is rarely clear cut, however, and cultural and family ties to rural communities and rural resources are often strong. Urbanization may result in a reduction in the diversity and quantity of some wild plant resources in trade as

Figure 3.5 *(a) A seller of hardwood poles from mangrove and coastal forest tree species at a daily market in Malindi, Kenya. (b) A woman harvester-seller of edible wild spinach,* Cucumella cinerea, *at a market in Maputo, Mozambique*

people enter the cash economy and alternative foods, utensils or roofing materials become available. In other cases, however, the continued cultural and economic importance of wild plants to urban people is evident in continued trade in plant resources from rural to urban areas. Common examples in many cities in Africa, Asia and Latin America are the informal sector trade in fuelwood, charcoal, medicinal plants, basketry and construction materials such as bamboo or hardwood poles (see Figure 3.5).

In these cases, urbanization has tended to increase rather than reduce the demand for wild plant resources, resulting in a commercial trade that stimulates overexploitation. Cities and towns are characterized by the people that live in them, and part of this identity is reflected in the types of plant resource that are used and sold. A good example is the interview survey of chewing stick use in Ghana (Adu-Tutu et al, 1979), which showed the high proportion of chewing sticks commercially harvested from the wild to supply people from different-sized settlements and from different educational backgrounds (see Figure 3.6).

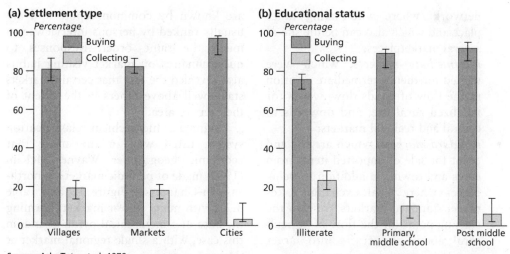

Source: Adu-Tutu et al, 1979

Figure 3.6 *An interview survey of chewing stick use in Ghana showed the high proportion of chewing sticks commercially harvested from the wild to supply people from (a) different-sized settlements and (b) different educational backgrounds*

Characteristics of markets

Depending upon the size of your study area, several methods could be used in combination to identify where these markets are located, what they are called, when they are held, and which market-places sell wild plant resources.

Size of market areas

In general, the types of goods and functions of a market increase in proportion to the number of people in the market area. As settlements get bigger, more and more people are attracted from greater and greater distances into the central market point. In a study of rural marketing systems in rural China, using information from interviews and historical records, Skinner (1964, 1965) developed a five-level classification of markets, based on their service areas; this has been widely used by economic geographers.

The basis for this regional analysis was the central place theory developed by Christaller (1966) and Lösch (1954), described earlier in this chapter. Although central place theory is a theory of retail distribution centres, rather than of whole-sale distribution (which is often a feature of the initial sale of wild plant products after harvest), it still provides useful background to understanding patterns of supply and demand for wild plant resources. Skinner concentrated on analysing rural markets and the flow of agricultural produce from rural areas to city markets, or the flow of goods from cities to rural markets. He recognized different levels of market in an approach which has since been used by many other economic geographers seeking to understand marketplaces within an exchange system:

- *regional markets,* which cover the largest area and which generally support several marketplaces;
- *central markets,* usually found at a strategic point in the transportation

network, where wholesaling takes place and which also can be the site of several marketplaces;

- *intermediate markets,* which were named for their intermediate position in the flow of goods downwards for localized rural use, and upwards to central and regional markets;
- *standard markets,* which are the end point for sale of imported items from cities and towns, in addition to being places where local exchange takes place; standard markets are also the starting point for the flow of agricultural goods and crafts into larger central or regional markets;
- *minor markets,* characterized by local exchange of goods between local people, which Skinner termed 'horizontal exchange'; minor markets deal with few goods that are imported into the area – Skinner also called these 'incipient standard' markets as they represented an early stage in the development of markets.

It is well worth checking your interpretation of the regional hierarchy of markets with the perceptions of local key informants. Local people in rural or urban areas can be an invaluable source of information about the hierarchical classification of market areas and market types, and about market schedules and functions. U L Ukwu used this approach in studying and classifying markets in eastern Nigeria, describing how 'in every locality the principal markets

are known by common repute and are usually ranked by persons interviewed in much the same order...Responses to questionnaires on market visiting habits also revealed the fact that certain markets stand well above others in the extent of their service area.'

Skinner's hierarchical classification system fitted well in the study that economic geographer Wayne McKim (1972) made of periodic markets in north-eastern Ghana (see Figure 3.7 and Table 3.2), with many minor markets forming the base of a hierarchical pyramid and, in this case, with a single regional market at the top.

Not all marketing systems fit Skinner's hierarchical model as neatly, but it is through a process of systematic analysis that 'anomalous' cases are recognized, raising useful questions and insights into why they do not fit an expected pattern. As a result, anthropologist Carol A Smith (1985) found that regional markets in Guatemala were 'anomalous' (see Table 3.3) and did not fit the type of hierarchy shown in Table 3.2, with a higher number of central and intermediate level markets than expected.

Systematic analysis of marketplaces can therefore lead to useful questions about their social and cultural features which may otherwise have not been asked. As Smith (1985) points out in a very useful paper describing the methods she used to analyse regional market systems:

Table 3.2 *Market types in north-eastern Ghana and Guatemala classified on Skinner's (1964)*
hierarchical system

Market type	Ghana	Guatemala	Size	Frequency	Species sold
Regional	1	1			
Central	3	15	↑	↑	↑
Intermediate	10	26			
Standard	20	32			
Minor	34	78			

Sources: McKim (1972), Smith (1985), Skinner (1964)

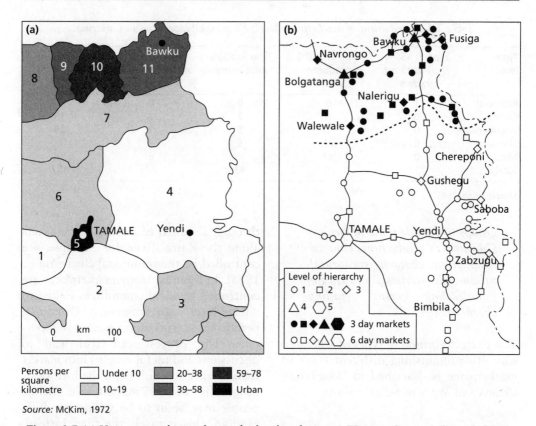

Persons per square kilometre: Under 10 | 20–38 | 59–78 | 10–19 | 39–58 | Urban

Source: McKim, 1972

Figure 3.7 *(a) Human population density by local authority: 1 Western Gonja; 2 Eastern Gonja; 3 Namumba; 4 Eastern Dagomba; 5 Tamale; 6 Western Dagomba; 7 South Mamprusi; 8 Builsa; 9 Kasani; 10 Frafra; 11 Kusasi. (b) Location of markets in the same area showing how most markets are located in high population density areas. The regional market (level 5) is in Tamale and the central markets (level 4) are in Bolgatanga, Bawku and Yendi*

'The measures I used for discriminating among marketplaces were simple ones, each of which reduced a great deal of information to a few crucial elements. The first and most basic measure was that of size or level in the marketing hierarchy. But the information contained in this measure, while important and necessary for all aspects of the analysis, was not sufficient to account for either the layout or the functioning of Guatemala's market economy. To achieve the latter result, I also had to consider the seller composition of marketplaces.

This measure involved only a simple trichotomization (division into three) of sellers by their functions, which could be used to categorize market centres by dominant seller type (leading to four basic marketplace types), on the first step; and an even simpler dichotomization (division into two) of the commodity movement, which could be used to characterize market centres by wholesale function (leading to two wholesale market types), on the second step. But while simple, this procedure divided market centres into two

Table 3.3 *Distribution of marketplace levels by marketplace types in Guatemala*

Type level	Type 1: >50% long-distance traders	Type 2: >50% producer-sellers	Type 3: >50% middlemen	Type 4: <50% of any seller type	Total
Regional	1	0	0	0	1
Central	0	6	2	7	15
Intermediate	0	12	5	9	26
Standard	0	21	6	5	32
Minor	0	42	30	6	78
Totals	1	81	43	27	152

Source: Smith, 1985

groups that made sense in terms of Guatemala's production character-istics, ethnic characteristics, rural–urban characteristics and trading (wholesaling versus retailing) characteristics.'

This characterization of types of seller as a way of distinguishing different types of marketplace is described in 'Marketing Chains and Types of Seller' below.

Marketplace micro-geography: politics and use of space

Categorizing how markets are organized in time and across landscapes or within urban areas provides a useful basis for planning surveys within markets. When you are working within each marketplace, it can be helpful to discern patterns of where people are located and why.

It is also important to start by finding out who is in charge of the marketplace. Even in the most informal and apparently chaotic marketplaces, there is often formal control and pattern in the location of sellers. In common with any ethnobotani-cal research, detailed market surveys can rarely be done efficiently without local permission.

As centres of economic activity and village life, markets are often controlled by local government or traditional leadership

through a system of fees. Barter markets along the Zaire River, for example, are controlled by the traditional chief (Ankei, 1985). In Uganda, many marketplaces are controlled by local committees linked to village-level government. Obtaining permission to work in the market is impor-tant. The process can also lead to discussions and useful insights into market fees, market schedules and the history or geography of the marketplace. While people may seem to be selling goods at random, this is rarely the case. Instead, they are located in different parts of the marketplace for a variety of reasons. Sellers may be located according to whether people can afford permanent stalls or not, on the basis of where they come from, or what they are selling. They may also be located to avoid social conflict. If beer is sold in markets (and this may be forbidden in some areas), then beer sellers are located in a place where patrons are least likely to disrupt the rest of the market.

Less obviously, people selling tradi-tional medicines may also be located on the periphery of the market to avoid social disruption resulting from 'bodily pollution' caused by proximity to supernaturally potent medicines.

Travelling sellers from the same district and cultural background frequently also sit together, although this may not be obvious to the outsider. These patterns give impor-

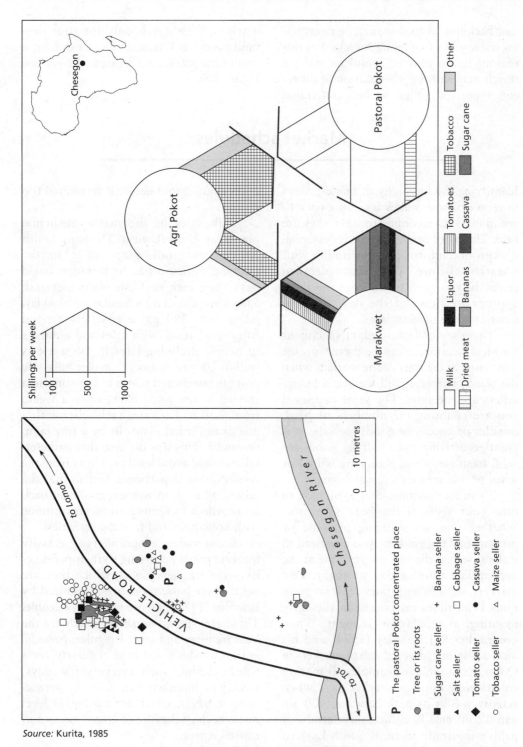

Source: Kurita, 1985

Figure 3.8 *Location of sellers and interchange of goods between different cultural groups with different systems of land use at a small market in Chesegon, Kenya*

tant background to designing or interpreting the results of sampling surveys. For this reason, it can also be useful to make a sketch map showing the location of different types of seller within individual markets, even if it is only for your own field notes, as Kazauaki Kurita did for a small rural market at Chesegon, Kenya (see Figure 3.8).

Market schedules

Identifying the hierarchy of market areas in terms of size makes it a lot easier to group markets according to when they are held. Timing of markets provides essential background information for timing your research. Before you start detailed research, you need to find out the most appropriate times of the day, week or month to visit marketplaces.

If you are collecting plant specimens for identification, it can be useful to time your visits at the start of the market, when the plant material is still fresh and before sellers are too busy. The same applies if you are counting the numbers of bags, bundles or bottles of goods for sale. It is pointless arriving when half the goods are sold, fresh medicinal plants are wilted or when people are on their way home.

If you are counting sellers, you have to time your visits at the peak sale time. Whether you are studying periodic or permanent daily markets, you also need to make sure that the surveys are done at the appropriate time of day or night. Few markets are all-day affairs with no peak time. Peak times may occur in the early morning, at midday or at night. When geographer R J Bromley (1974) and his local assistants surveyed urban markets in Quito, Ecuador, for example, all market counts were done on market days when activity was at its peak between 9.00 am and 12.00 am. In a long-term study of palm-wine trade in rural South-Eastern Africa, sales peaked around 10.00 am so that the palm wine could be transported, diluted and resold before it fermented too much.

Bulk sales of the major medicinal plants at Umlazi, near Durban, South Africa, also took place early in the morning so that urban herb traders could have their pick of fresh plant material. Sales also peaked on a Sunday or Monday, when over 300 gatherer-sellers arrived from rural areas, with sales and numbers of people declining later in the week as well as later each day. A smaller bulk-sale point for medicinal plants in the same area started in the pitch dark, once a week, from 4.30 to 7.00 am, each seller with a pile of medicinal plants lit by a tiny lamp or candle. This was done so that gatherer-sellers could avoid legal problems from the conservation department and so that the sellers, all of them women, could get back home, often to remote areas, to continue with household and farming activities.

Economic geographers classify markets partly according to their periodicity – the frequency with which they are held. Three basic types are recognized by Bromley (1971) and are widely applicable. These are: *special markets*, which are the least frequent and most irregular; *periodic markets*, which are held regularly on a fixed schedule such as every few days, weekly or monthly; and *daily (or permanent) markets*, which are the higher level markets characteristic of larger towns and urban centres.

Periodicity of markets depends upon whether traditional or Western calendars

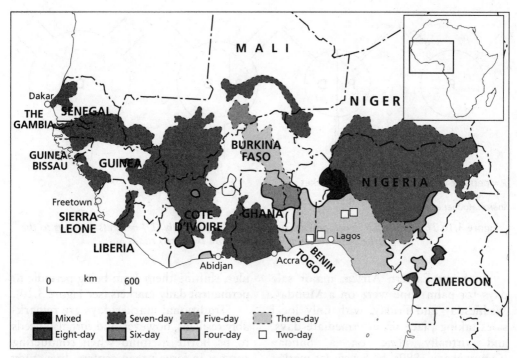

Source: Hill and Smith, 1972

Figure 3.9 *Seven-day market schedules are common in West Africa*

are used. Some parts of the world, such as southern China or West Africa, which have historically high human population densities, centralized political structures and concentrated settlements, also have a long history of well-developed long-distance trade. In these cases, market schedules can be based on ancient traditional calendars such as lunar or solar cycles. In southern China, for example, Skinner (1964) found that market cycles were based on the lunar *hsün* ('decade') which averaged 9.8 days and on solar or lunar fortnights, in addition to other schedules. At the time his study was conducted, market schedules were most commonly based on the lunar *hsün* or a 12-day (duodenary) cycle on a fixed sequence of twelve *chih* ('branches'). These then determine the marketing schedule (and the timing of research in markets). The duodenary cycle, for

example, would be a regular system leading to 3-day, 6-day or 12-day weeks. William Skinner also found that marketing cycles, in turn, were characteristic of particular regions of southern China. Duodenary cycles were limited to the upper drainage basins of the Hsi and Hung River systems, while schedules of markets along downstream plains and deltas followed lunar (*hsün*) cycles.

By contrast, the market schedules of many African countries have been influenced by the calendar introduced during the colonial period, based on a 7-day week (with a day off on Sunday). In a study of 154 markets in Uganda, for example, geographer Charles Good (1975) found that 81 per cent of markets occurred every 14 days, 16 per cent every 7 days and 3 per cent every 28 days, with 14-day markets attended by the most people and having the widest range of goods.

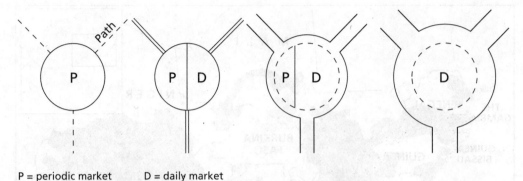

P = periodic market   D = daily market

Source: Hodder and Lee, 1974

Figure 3.10 *The sequential development from periodic (P) to daily (D) markets as paths to the marketplace develop into tracks and then into roads*

In South-Eastern Africa, major sale days for palm wine were on a Monday, Wednesday and Friday, with only local sales taking place on intermediate days, and virtually none on a Sunday (Cunningham, 1990a, b). Seven-day market schedules are also common in West Africa (see Figure 3.9), with Islamic limitations on market activity on religious days and main market activity on other days of the week (Hill and Smith, 1972). Markets in East Africa are similarly influenced by the seven-day week or may take place every 7, 14 or 28 days. A seven-day schedule introduced by Belgian colonists is also still followed in barter markets in Zaire, with only the trace of a traditional market cycle remaining. Anthropologist Yuji Ankei (1985), in a detailed study of barter markets along the Zaire River (see Figure 3.3), found that the majority of markets were held every 7 or 14 days, with only one following a traditional four-day cycle. It is these schedules that are followed by the itinerant traders or travelling merchants described further on in this chapter.

As human populations grow, and demand becomes more concentrated, so market schedules are compressed. Improved transport networks and higher numbers of people 'shrink' market sched-

ules, shifting them from being **periodic** to **permanent daily markets** (see Figure 3.10).

Traditional market days are remarkably resilient, however, and this also needs to be borne in mind when conducting surveys in large urban centres. In a study of periodic markets in South Korea, Siyoung Park (1981) found that the numbers of people in daily, permanent markets increased several times on a five-day schedule. This trend is also a feature of urban markets in Lagos, Nigeria (Sada et al, 1978).

Seasonal schedules and annual trends of plant products and harvesters

You also need to be aware of the seasonal bias that can result from short-term surveys of marketplaces, and ideally you should visit markets at regular weekly or monthly intervals during the year. The link with fruiting times of wild fruits is obvious, but seasonality also applies to the timing and sale of items such as fresh wild spinach, wild mushrooms or insects. In their study of the Mercado de Sonora in Mexico City, for example, ethnobotanists Bob Bye and Edelmira Linares (1985) found that while some cultivated edible

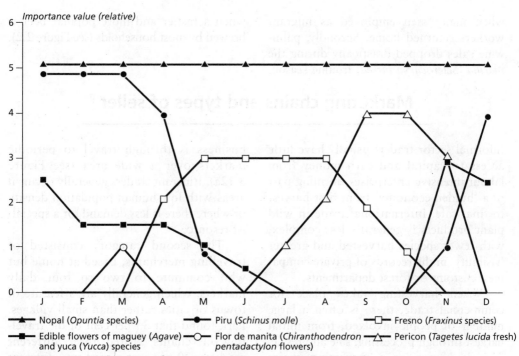

Importance value (relative)

- —▲— Nopal (*Opuntia* species)
- —●— Piru (*Schinus molle*)
- —□— Fresno (*Fraxinus* species)
- —■— Edible flowers of maguey (*Agave*) and yuca (*Yucca*) species
- —○— Flor de manita (*Chiranthodendron pentadactylon* flowers)
- —△— Pericon (*Tagetes lucida* fresh)

Note: The importance value is relative and ranges from 0 (absent) to 5 (abundant).
Source: modified from Bye and Linares, 1985

Figure 3.11 *Changes in the importance of some plant species sold in Mercado de Sonora, Mexico City, over a year*

species such as 'nopal' (*Opuntia* spp) were available throughout the year, others, such as the aromatic food additive 'pericon' (*Tagetes lucida*), were only seasonally available, while *Yucca* and *Agave* flowers appeared in the market for only a few weeks (see Figure 3.11).

To avoid this problem, Peruvian botanist Rodolfo Vasquez visited the Iquitos market virtually every week for nine years (Vasquez and Gentry, 1989), making valuable records of species sold and price fluctuations. If his team had not done this they would have missed recording some of the most important wild-collected fruits, which appeared on the market between June and October.

Seasonal differences may also occur for less obvious reasons than growing season. Sales of the popular traditional medicines *Alepidea amatymbica* and

Siphonochilus aethiopicus declined sharply at the wholesale marketplaces I surveyed in Durban, South Africa, in spring and summer. This was due to a taboo against collecting these species during the growing season, reinforced by the belief that breaking the taboo would result in lightning striking the household.

Conversely, sales of bulbous species such as *Scilla natalensis* and *Eucomis autumnalis* in South Africa increased in summer when plants could be readily located and dug up from mountain grasslands; but occurrence in markets declined sharply in the winter dry season when the leaves of these species died or were burned off in fires. Social issues also affected palm-wine sales in the region. Firstly, there was a higher consumption of palm wine at Christmas time, not only because of the hot summer days but because it was a time when many men employed as migrant workers returned home. Secondly, palm-wine sales dropped drastically during the *marula* (*Sclerocarya birrea*) fruiting season, when a tastier and more popular beer is brewed by most households (see Figure 2.2).

Marketing chains and types of seller

Informal sector traders usually have little access to capital and earn money from labour-intensive enterprises, forming part of a 'hidden economy' from first harvest to final sale. International trade in wild plant products is generally less complex, with fewer species harvested and greater 'visibility' in the records of private companies, customs or forest departments.

When harvesting takes place for commercial trade, there is often a large number of people involved, from initial harvest through processing, sale and resale. This is known as a **marketing chain**. Different types of seller feature at different parts of the marketing chain, from initial bulk gathering of plants from the wild, through to processing, sale and resale.

As mentioned earlier, the extent of demand for goods influences the size and timing of markets, and these factors in turn influence the types of seller at markets. Several economic geographers and anthropologists have categorized the marketplace, using types of sellers as indicators. This method has mainly been applied in studies of agrarian societies. The principles and approaches can also be applied, however, in studies of wild plant harvest, sale and resale.

Siyoung Park (1981), in a study of periodic rural markets in South Korea, distinguished three main types of seller, representing a transition from mobile to sedentary traders. Firstly, there were **itinerant traders**, who move from one small market to another, returning home at the end of the market cycle. This is not an easy life, but one of the few ways in which itinerant traders are able to stay in business is through travel to periodic markets over a wide area (see Figure 3.12a). Itinerant traders generally occur in areas with low human population density or where there is less demand for a specialist resource.

The second category consisted of **travelling merchants**, based at home but who commute to two to four daily markets, which generally are a feature of towns or cities rather than small villages. Park found that 35 per cent of the travelling merchants visited three different markets, 30 per cent visited two different markets, 19 per cent visited four different markets and only 16 per cent visited a different market each day of the five-day market week.

The third category comprised **permanent sellers**, who travel from home to permanent stalls at the market (see Figure 3.12b), and who are a feature of larger marketplaces rather than smaller ones.

In her analysis of regional market systems in Guatemala, Carol Smith (1985) first categorized marketplaces according to the quantity and variety of goods being sold. She then recognized three categories of trader, each of whom deals with commodities in different ways. The first category, at the start of the marketing chain, comprised **producer-sellers**, who sold local goods, mainly food items, most of which they grew themselves (rather than buying them from other markets). The second category comprised **middlemen** (and women) who sold goods that had been produced elsewhere; and the third category consisted of the **long-distance traders**.

Figure 3.12 *Patterns of market visits, with African medicinal plant sales as an example. (a) An itinerant trader – a herbalist selling at village level, Malawi. (b) Permanent market seller at Owino herbal market, Kampala, Uganda. (c) Breaking down bulk medicinal plant supplies collected by women at a market in Bouake, Côte d'Ivoire. (d) A permanent herb trader's shop (next to doctor's quarters!) in Pietermaritzburg, South Africa*

She then went on to categorize marketplaces according to the proportions of different traders represented within them, using these three types of trader indicators. Markets with many producer-sellers indicated markets in an area of local exchange, or where there was bulking of goods redistribution upwards along the marketing chain. Marketplaces dominated by local middlemen generally sold goods for local use or distribution down the marketing chain, while marketplaces dominated by long-distance traders indicated places where there was whole-sale exchange among these traders. On this basis, Smith distinguished four types of market:

- type 1: markets with >50 per cent long-distance traders;
- type 2: markets with >50 per cent producer-sellers;
- type 3: markets with >50 per cent middlemen;
- type 4: markets where there were sellers of all sorts, and where no category of trader was dominant.

This facilitated the grouping of market-places into two functional types:

- **bulking centres**, which are mainly rural marketplaces of types 1 and 2, supplied by producer-sellers or long-distance traders;
- **bulk-breaking (or dispersing) centres**, which receive goods from bulking centres and disperse them from there, characterized by types 3 or 4 market-places; bulk-breaking is the term used to describe the division of the commodity into smaller amounts.

By bringing together both economic and ethnographic components, this systematic classification enabled Smith to develop several hypotheses about marketplace specialization in the Guatemalan study area, illustrating the close relationship between the role of Indian or 'Ladino' Guatemalans in the economy.

The principles behind this systematic analysis of regional marketing systems are certainly applicable to the harvesting of wild plants, and they also need to be more widely applied in ethnobotanical surveys of market networks. Several categories of seller are evident in the African traditional medicine trade – for example, in market-places of different size or centrality.

Firstly, there are the middlemen, repre-sented by itinerant traders doing a circuit of several periodic markets (see Figure 3.12a). Next would be categories of permanent seller, who visit a single marketplace. Rural people (often women) regularly supply large regional or central markets as bulk-supply wholesalers (see Figure 3.12c). There are also two types of permanent retail seller: specialist sellers in central markets, and permanent traders with large storage space who work in retail and bulk-breaking in regional markets (see Figure 3.12d).

Marketing chains and wild plant resources

Although hierarchical classification of markets by size and centrality, or of marketplaces by function and seller type, is useful, in the case of ethnobotanical surveys – which have a focus on wild plants instead of on all products sold – we are faced with a greater level of complex-ity on at least two levels.

Firstly, for wild or managed species, particularly those traded to regional or central markets, the marketing chains may be complex and very long. The marketing chain from harvest to final use of *sal* (*Shorea robusta*) leaves harvested from woodland in West Bengal, India, to make plates is a good example of how long such

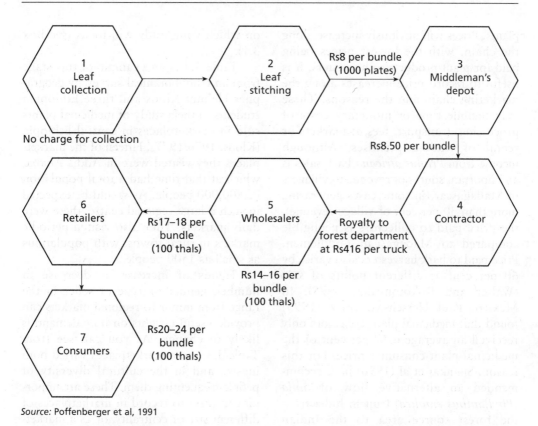

Source: Poffenberger et al, 1991

Figure 3.13 *A marketing chain in the sale of plates made from* sal *(Shorea robusta) leaves harvested from woodland in West Bengal, India*

a chain can be (see Figure 3.13).

Secondly, although species entering commercial trade represent a 'short list' of a far greater diversity of species used in rural areas, the number of species involved in species-specific harvest is far greater than an economic geographer or anthropologist would encounter in studying the sale of clothing, manufactured goods or agricultural crops. In their study of edible fruits sold in the marketplaces of Iquitos in the Peruvian Amazon, for example, Vasquez and Gentry (1990) recorded over 57 wild-collected fruit species being sold. In Germany, Lange and Schippmann (1997) have documented 1543 medicinal plant species comprising 854 genera in 223 families in the import or export trade. In South Africa, 400 to 500 species are sold

for traditional medicines (Cunningham, 1990; Williams, 1996), and in north-west China alone, Pei-Sheigji, Li Yanhui and Yin Shuze (1990) recorded 574 medicinal plant species traded in local markets. By contrast, the considerably fewer species sold for building material, thatch, palm wine, woodcarving and fuelwood or charcoal make analysis easier.

The complexity of marketing chains is important to keep in mind when recording prices for wild plant resources being sold, or when classifying markets on the basis of the types of sellers within them. The people you see selling wild plant resources may be way down the chain of sale and resale, influencing your records of the prices, gender of sellers, quantities sold or information on where they obtained the plants. Prices will obviously increase along the chain, with the lowest prices being paid for plant products to harvesters. It is useful to record price increases along the marketing chain and the reasons. These may include time or monetary costs of processing, transport, fees at markets or rental of trading premises. Although income from *Prunus africana* bark sales is an important source of revenue to villagers in Madagascar (in some cases generating more than 30 per cent of village revenue), the price paid to collectors is negligible compared to Madagascan middlemen. Price paid to bark harvesters also varies by 60 per cent at different points of sale (Walter and Rokotonirina, 1995). In Mexico, Paul Hersch-Martinez (1995) found that medicinal plant collectors only received an average 6.17 per cent of the medicinal plant consumer price. For this reason, Shankar et al (1996) have recommended an alternative flow of *amla* (*Phyllanthus emblica*) fruit in India from the forest source area to the Indian consumer, improving economic benefits to the Soliga people involved as a means of improving household income while reducing overharvesting of fruits.

Market vendors: number, gender and change

From the mapping exercise and initial visits, you should have a good idea about which markets have the largest number of sellers, and which are selling plants wholesale or are retail centres. Unless the markets are very large, you may also be able to count or estimate the total number of vendors in each marketplace. With local assistance you should be able to get an idea of the cultural and socio-economic status of people visiting the market to buy the categories of wild plants (such as fuelwood, building poles, crafts, charcoal, wild fruits, wild greens, medicinal plants)

on which your study will focus (see Box 3.1).

Table 3.4 is an example of this stage from an ethnobotanical survey by geographer Helmut Kloos and three Ethiopian students in their study of medicinal plants sold in marketplaces in central Ethiopia (Kloos, 1976/1977). Fifteen of the marketplaces they visited were in Addis Ababa, which at that time had a total population of 800,000 people. As would be expected in such a large regional centre, these were daily markets. They also visited periodic markets in rural towns, with populations as small as 1500 people.

Trends of increase or decrease in number, gender or type of seller in the range from **minor** to **regional** markets can provide useful insights on how demand is likely to change. As you can see from Table 3.4, these marketplaces varied both in size and in the cultural diversity of people frequenting them. These are important features to record in marketplaces of different size or centrality, or as a marketplace grows or shrinks in size over time. It can also be useful during a marketplace survey to group sellers in appropriate categories, as Park and Smith did in their studies in South Korea and Guatemala (see 'Marketing Chains and Types of Seller'). Record whether people selling wild plant resources are **permanent sellers, itinerant traders** or **travelling merchants**. Are they selling only one category of wild plant resource or are they selling wild plants amongst other items?

In addition to socio-economic status, sellers frequently differ by ethnicity and gender. Helmut Kloos (1976/1977) noted that the majority (95 per cent) of the people selling medicinal plants at Ethiopian markets were women, most of them Gurage rather than Amhara women, due to the low social status of *kosso* (*Hagenia abyssinica*, Rosaceae) sellers in traditional Amhara society.

Table 3.4 *The top 10 medicinal plants sold in the markets in Ethiopia, showing number of sellers in 3 of the 15 markets sampled, including the total sellers/species for all markets, showing the percentage of sellers of the 4 most popular species in the 3 main markets*

| Plant species | Three markets in Addis Ababa | | | Total (% of total) |
	Merkato	Kirgos	Selassie	
Hagenia abyssinica	115	33	18	229 (72%)
Embelia schimperi	101	26	14	219 (64%)
Glinus lotoides	113	28	16	194 (73%)
Silene macroselene	115	20	11	180 (85%)
Echinops sp	112	17	8	178
Withania somnifera	109	19	10	162
Lepidum sativum	105	15	6	160
Thymus serrulatus	95	14	12	155
'dingetenya'	104	14	7	140
Myrsine africana	87	9	3	115

Source: derived from Kloos, 1973

Similarly, large numbers of women sell herbal medicines in the large regional markets of Africa, such as in Abidjan, Côte d'Ivoire, or in South Africa. One of the main reasons for this is that men stop non-specialist herbal medicine sales when it becomes an increasingly marginal economic activity, persisting only as sellers of traditional medicines from animals, an activity often closed to women. It is useful to record trends of increase in number, changes in gender or type of sellers as one goes from minor to regional markets. This provides useful insights into how demand and marketing networks are changing.

In many developing countries, urban growth has been particularly rapid since the 1950s. This has been accompanied by changes in the number, gender and types of sellers at marketplaces. In 1929 in Durban, South Africa, for example, there were only two herbal traders and most people selling herbal medicines at the eMatsheni market were men. By 1987, Durban was a regional market for medicinal plants, with more than 100 herbal traders supplied by over 300 people commercially harvesting medicinal plants from the wild. Virtually all of these harvester-sellers were women. By 1991 their numbers had increased to over 500 due to rising unemployment and rural poverty.

Inventory and frequency of plants on sale

In ethnobotanical surveys of marketplaces aimed at identifying plant species under threat, the question is not just 'what is being sold?' but also, 'which species are being depleted by commercial trade?' If different species populations are being depleted, the next question is: 'how can different species be prioritized?' This last question is introduced here and is then covered in Chapters 4 to 6. Information

on the uses of wild-collected species which are (or were) commonly being sold can provide important insights into the social issues which need to be addressed as part of the solution to overexploitation of wild stocks. Conversely, such insights also indicate the social benefits from plants that will no longer be available if overexploitation occurs. The medicinal plant species most frequently recorded by Kloos

(1976/1977, see Table 3.4), for example, are mainly used to treat internal parasite infestations (*Hagenia abyssinica* ('*kosso*'); *Embelia schimperi* ('*enkoko*'); *Glinus lotoides* ('*metere*'); *Croton macrostachys* ('*bisanna*'); *Myrsine africana* ('*kechemo*')). This reflects the social circumstances (diet, housing density, sanitation), and links plant conservation to primary health care issues.

Demand is most likely to exceed renewable supplies of species which are destructively harvested and which are slow growing; reproduction of these species is limited, while their habitat requirements are very specific. The shortlist of commercially harvested species can be further prioritized on the basis of this information, selecting commercially harvested species with limited geographical distribution that are most likely to be subjected to destructive harvesting (see Box 3.2). Marketplace surveys add to this information, enabling rapid assessments that include species from a wide geographical area, and highlight species which should be the focus of monitoring programmes.

In addition to knowing which species are sold, it is also important to glean information from traders on the sources, habitat and price per local unit (for later conversion to a price/kg basis) of priority species. This information can be analysed in different ways to study flow patterns from source areas to urban sales points, frequency of sales for different species or whether the species sold are from wild, managed or domesticated plant populations. Information on source areas (and areas not being harvested) is useful for deciding on the best places to set up plots to assess harvesting impact or to monitor the effects of harvesting on indicator species. Usually, this would be carried out through carefully located sample surveys to enable comparison of impacts on indicator species where: there was protec-

tion from human impact (for example in core conservation areas); harvesting was unregulated; and where managed harvest took place, if this occurred at all (see Chapters 5 and 6). Whether this information is gathered during the inventory of species on sale or not can only be decided on a case-by-case basis. In some cases, it is possible to record information about the uses of commercially harvested species. In others, such as collection of information on medicinal plant species, it can be highly sensitive and would best be left until a later period, or obtained from other published studies.

In her survey of crop plants sold in Guatemala, Carol Smith used systematic marketplace surveys to record the species on sale, and then arranged them into hierarchical levels which reflected their relative demand (Smith, 1985). The same can apply to wild plant species, with one complication: sometimes the most popular species no longer appear in markets because they have been overexploited. For this reason, it is as important to determine which species are in demand but are no longer sold, and to distinguish these from those currently being sold. It is useful to ask vendors to free list species which they consider **most expensive**, are becoming **increasingly difficult to obtain** and where **substitution** of one species with another is occurring, and why.

Helmut Kloos (1976/77) and his coworkers, in their study of medicinal plants in Ethiopian markets (see Table 3.4), counted the number of sellers who were selling different species in each market, recording the total number of people selling each species for all markets. Their data also illustrate a lesson which is widely applicable for people who have limited time and funds and need to focus market survey effort. All species sold within all markets surveyed were recorded within just four main markets, and the

Box 3.2 Ethnobotanical Surveys of Markets

Ethnobotanical surveys of markets are the first steps in identifying species which are a conservation or resource management priority. They also are useful in identifying popular, higher-priced species which have the potential for agroforestry production or which are already managed or domesticated by local farmers and which may escape notice in social surveys. It is important that local values and views of resource scarcity and conservation priority are not overshadowed by categories developed for international application (see steps 5 and 6 below). Identifying the 'most valued, most vulnerable' subset of species at the local level and at a national or international level provides an opportunity to stimulate resource management action at two levels: one local, the other national/international. In some cases these will overlap.

Step 1: Identify Species in Commercial or Highest Demand

An important focus is species used in high volume locally (building poles, fuelwood) or in smaller volumes in highly species-specific trade (crafts, medicines, edible plants) (see Chapter 2 for more on local values and volumes). The identification of species in trade can be done at 'both ends': in source areas and in sites where they are used (or on sale). Correct identification is best performed in source areas. It is extremely important that this is done through collection and expert identification of good voucher specimens (see Chapters 5 and 6). If working from ethnobotanical studies of markets that are linked to informal trade networks, it is useful to survey the largest (regional and central) markets which carry the widest range of species; then work 'upstream' to source areas identified on the basis of discussions with commercial collectors and traders in order to collect fresh voucher specimens (see Chapters 2 and 6). In the case of **international export trade**, this could be from listings of exporting companies or from customs data and phytosanitary certificates.

Step 2: Prepare a Shortlist of Species

The shortlist should include species which are:

- destructively harvested (bark, roots, bulbs, stems, wood, whole plants);
- slow growing (separation on the basis of life form can be useful);
- most popular and/or most expensive, or sold in greatest number (small plants) and/or volume, in local marketplaces;
- considered to have become, or be in the process of becoming, scarce by market traders or commercial collectors. Species substitution (often due to scarcity) can be a useful 'flag' in this case.

Step 3: Identify Species that May Require Special Conservation Effort

Conservation biologist Reed Noss (1990) has suggested five categories of species that may need special attention.

- **Ecological indicator species:** such species signal the impact of events that will affect other species with similar habitat requirements. Afro-alpine plants such as giant lobelias and giant senecios, which will be affected by global warming, are a good example.
- **Keystone species:** these species play a pivotal role in the community or ecosystem (such as fig species whose fruits support many primate, bird and invertebrate species, but which are exploited on a large scale for making drums and beer brewing troughs in Uganda).

- **Umbrella species:** these species have large area requirements; if given enough protection, they will enable the conservation of many other species in the same area. The plant equivalents of eagles and large mammalian carnivores would be dioecious tropical tree species which occur at low densities and require large areas of forest to maintain viable populations.
- **Flagship species:** these consist of popular, charismatic species which are symbolic of the need for conservation and stimulate conservation initiatives. Several medicinal plants, such as the Madagascan rosy periwinkle (*Catharanthus roseus*) have been used as 'flagships'. Culturally important species can also be 'flagships'.
- **Vulnerable species:** these comprise rare species with low reproductive ability and low genetic variation. This category would include species that are prioritized by other steps 4 to 6, which are particularly vulnerable to human impacts.

Step 4: Shortlist Species Further on the Basis of Commonness or Rarity

This is based on species' characters of geographic distribution, habitat requirements and local population size. From an international (and often local) perspective, the highest priority would be given to a species with narrow geographical distribution, a restricted habitat and small population size.

Table 3.5 *Rabinowitz's seven forms of rarity*

Geographic range	Large		Small	
Habitat specificity	Wide	Narrow	Wide	Narrow
Local population size				
Large, dominant somewhere	Locally abundant in several habitats over a large geographic area	Locally abundant in a specific habitat over a small geographic area	Locally abundant in several habitats over a small geographic area	Locally abundant in a specific habitat over a large geographic area
Small, non-dominant	Constantly sparse in several habitats over a large geographic area	Constantly sparse in a specific habitat over a large geographic area	Constantly sparse in several habitats over a small geographic area	Constantly sparse in a specific habitat over a small geographic area

Source: Rabinowitz et al, 1986; Pitman et al, 1999

Step 5: Set Priorities on the Basis of Phylogenetic Distinctiveness

Within the resulting shortlist, the highest priority should be given to the following species (in descending order).

- species in a monotypic family (highest priority);
- species in a monotypic genus;
- species in a segregate genus, subgenus or section of a medium to large genus;
- species in a small genus (two to five species);
- species in a medium to large genus;
- species which are part of a species complex;
- infraspecific taxon in a medium-size to large genus (lowest priority).

Step 6: Prioritize Species According to IUCN Categories of Threat

In common with step 5 above, these priorities were developed for application on a global scale, such as judging the extinction risk of the whole species. In many cases, this will differ from the local perspective of resource users. It is important that local, national and international perspectives are taken into account.

most commonly sold species in these markets were usually sold through all the markets surveyed.

With hindsight, the lesson is that if you are making an inventory of species sold and do not have the opportunity of visiting all marketplaces in a region, but are able to visit a few markets regularly, then select large (regional or central) markets rather than smaller ones. Size and number of marketplaces in developing countries is generally a function of city size. Cities are also more likely to have more culturally diverse populations, drawn in from many rural communities. Diversity of species sold decreases with decreasing size of marketing area. The most species are sold in **regional** markets, fewer in **central** markets, still fewer in **intermediate** markets, yet fewer in **standard** markets and least in **minor** markets.

This also depends upon the importance placed on certain categories of plant use in large urban areas. Regional and central markets, which bring together a wide array of species from a large area, are therefore important sites for an inventory of which species enter commercial trade. Alternatively, surveys of smaller rural periodic marketplaces in more remote (and often more resource-rich sites) near to conservation areas can provide an important 'early warning system' for local resources which may need to be monitored for the impact of an emerging commercial trade.

Data can then be compared with information from historical records, discussions, participatory (PRA, RRA) surveys and individual interviews, indexing methods (see Chapter 2), or social survey data – for example, on major health problems in the study area. Data from markets on frequency of sale can also be compared to species preference data from social surveys or quantitative ethnobotanical methods that link plant-disease combinations (Johns,

Kokwaro and Kimanani, 1990; see also Chapter 2), or compared to statistical data on health, housing or the availability of alternative energy sources to fuelwood or charcoal. In Ghana, for example, where 107 woody plant species have been recorded as used for chewing sticks in dental care, one may wonder which species should be short listed for monitoring. Interview surveys with a sample of 887 people showed that just six species (known by four local names) accounted for 86 per cent of all chewing sticks used for dental care and the bulk of commercial sales (Adu-Tutu et al, 1979).

Although you will initially record the prices for which different species are sold on the basis of local units (see Chapter 2), it is important that this is converted to a price per dry mass, as unit sizes can vary. Prices for products sold in markets are useful for several reasons. Firstly, they are useful for assessing economic returns regionally, according to different people along the marketing chain or the economic viability of cultivation. Secondly, price reflects resource supply in relation to demand. Records of price changes over time can 'flag' increasing scarcity. Locally common species are rarely sold in local marketplaces unless it is bulk sale for processing or retail elsewhere.

When a popular species is scarce, due to geographical distribution or overexploitation, then trade occurs from resource-rich areas to the places where there is demand, but little or no supply. As scarcity increases, so does the price. When alternatives are not available, the higher the price, the greater the incentive to go further and further afield for a scarce species. Improved roads and cheaper transport reduce this cost. As a result, internal marketing systems change in two ways, each shortening the marketing chain. Firstly, cheaper transport enables rural people to get to larger centres to sell their products. Secondly, better roads improve the access that outsiders have to more remote plant resources. Outsiders frequently have more buying power than local people in remote, resource-rich areas. If this takes place and resource tenure starts to break down, then this hastens the scramble for resources in high demand.

When scarcity results in higher prices, this can stimulate a shift from high-density, resource-rich patches to low-density, less accessible or marginal areas where resource densities are lower. Where alternatives are available, this continues until *price capping* occurs: in this instance, prices reach a point where alternatives are cheaper. For highly species-specific uses, such as traditional medicinal plants, prices continue to rise because only that species will suffice in a traditional remedy, for symbolic or medical purposes. This stimulates a trade over very long distances. In between these situations is one in which there is a ripple effect, where overexploitation of one species results in a shift in harvesting to other species.

Knowing which species are sold and, of these, which are most commonly traded is useful, but it is also important to know the source of these species by habitat and by location. In their study of the Santa Catarina del Monte market in Mexico, for example, Bob Bye and Elemira Linares (1985) found that of the 114 species sold, 28 species were gathered from wild habitat, 52 species gathered from anthropogenic vegetation types, 32 species were domesticated and 2 species were non-domesticated species in cultivation. Of the 1560 species identified in trade in Germany, 70 to 90 per cent are primarily harvested from the wild (Lange, 1997). In KwaZulu/Natal, South Africa, over 99 per cent of the 400 medicinal plant species are wild harvested (Cunningham, 1988).

Ethnobotanical surveys of markets can also go beyond grouping species as to whether they are wild collected, managed or domesticated, to focus on genotypic variation within species and local preferences for particular qualities represented by this variation. The widest variation is displayed by domesticated indigenous species in markets, some of them little known as crop plants outside that region. In West Africa, for example, agroforesters Roger Leakey and David Ladipo (1996) surveyed local markets in Cameroon to get the vendors' opinions on what fruit qualities were preferred by people buying fruit of the 'bush plum' (*Dacryodes edulis*), an indigenous tree species which has been domesticated in West Africa as a tree crop. Apart from the useful information, this cost-effective, short survey provided information on preferred qualities of pulp-to-seed ratio, flavour and cooking qualities; their analysis of fresh fruit mass and pulp–seed ratio shows the extent of variation which can occur through domestication by local farmers (see Figure 3.14).

Volumes sold; sources of supply and demand

Before you spend a considerable amount of time and money quantifying the amount of material sold, you need to be certain that this is going to result in the answers you need. In some cases it may be more cost effective to select the major source areas on the basis of social surveys, such as participatory rural appraisal (PRA) or interview methods, and to use these as a basis for carrying out damage assessments of harvest impacts on populations of indicator species; this will avoid spending a large amount of time and resources quantifying the amount of plant material sold.

If the objective of your study is to determine the value of wild plants in trade, or to establish the amount of an alternative supply that must be provided to take

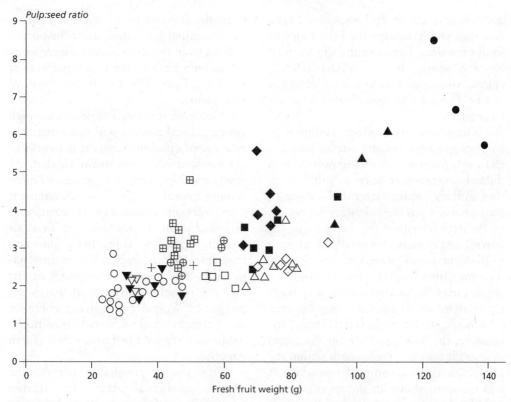

Note: Different symbols represent different fruit lots. Symbols in bold are fruits being sold for more than 500 CFA francs/kg.
Source: Leakey and Ladipo, 1996

Figure 3.14 *Genetic variation in* Dacryodes edulis *(Burseraceae) fruits from a survey of market stalls in Yaounde, Cameroon*

the pressure off wild stocks, then it may be necessary to quantify the volume of plant material sold. In this case, you need to carefully pick the marketplaces and sale points where this is done.

If you are measuring volume sold or harvested, it is important to monitor and identify this at the start of the chain. In Southern Africa, for example, sale of fermented palm sap involved a marketing chain which began with the initial tapping by local men, moved to primary sales by women, transport by entrepreneurs, and finally to resale at households outside the palm savanna zone. At this point, in order to make a profit, the women who resold the palm wine doubled the volume by diluting

it with water and adding sugar. Monitoring volume sold at this stage without understanding the process involved would obviously provide a gross overestimate.

Do not be too ambitious. Instead, focus on the species or resource category sold in the most volume or which is most vulnerable. It is usually best to do this at wholesale or 'bulk-breaking' centres where 'units' of sale are larger, such as large sacks of fruit, medicinal plants or charcoal, truckloads of fuelwood or containers of undiluted palm sap.

Are the 'units' in which plant products are sold consistent within or between markets of the same type? If not, your end result may yield unreliable data, after considerable effort and expense. Make sure that you have identified the range of local unit sizes, have community support for the work, have selected reliable enumerators and that you have designed and field tested any appropriate forms (see Chapter 2).

Where the wild plant resource is harvested in high volume (rattan bundles, charcoal, fuelwood, building poles), or is difficult to transport (such as palm wine), then bulking centres are usually close to the resource areas were they are harvested.

Where transport is easier, due to harvest and demand for smaller quantities of plant material (traditional medicines, weaving fibre, edible fruits), bulking centres may be located a long way from the source habitat through long-distance bulk trade. In South-Eastern Africa, for example, the bulking centre for the palm-wine trade was at a cross-roads within the *Hyphaene* palm savanna, from where it was transported outside the palm savanna zone by women who earned money from dilution and resale of palm wine (see Figure 3.2).

The distance that wild plant resources are transported also depends upon the perishable nature of the plant product. The rapid fermentation of palm wine, for example, meant that it was only transported 60 to 70 km from source to final sale. A similar constraint is placed on the harvesting and sale of perishable fruits or of freshly gathered medicinal leaves or stems, affecting the distance that these products are transported. 'Perishability' also increases the risk that wholesale harvester-sellers face in selling harvested material before it deteriorates.

By contrast, bark, roots and bulbs are generally far less perishable. For this reason, dried bark, roots or bulbs, or dried bundles of whole plants, are a common feature of the long-distance trade across vegetation zones. In West Africa, for example, dried roots of *Entada abyssinica*, locally called *terenefou*, are transported 800km from the dry savanna source areas of Burkina Faso to the urban markets of Abidjan, Côte d'Ivoire, in the tropical forest zone.

However, if prices and profits are high enough, local traders will make remarkable use of efficient transport networks to get perishable species to the market. As road networks extend into more and more remote rural areas, so commercial harvesters or middlemen flow in, and favoured plant species flow out. Even air freight is used to transport edible and medicinal plants, regionally or internationally: 'bush plums' (*Dacryodes edulis*) and *eru* (*Gnetum africanum*) leaves are bought by West Africans living in France or Belgium and Chinese traditional medicines are sold in Europe and North America.

Due to its perishable nature, the African medicinal plant *khat* (*Catha edulis*) is a good example. Remarkably, for a product in long-distance trade, the young leaves of *Catha edulis* need to be chewed while still fresh for maximum effect – and for this reason, the price of *khat* rapidly drops with time. As a result, the trade has to be highly organized to get leaves from the farm to the end-user as soon as possible. Even at the height of the recent conflict in Somalia, light aircraft filled with carefully packed bundles of *khat* would fly into Mogadishu from Nairobi's Wilson Airport and the bundles would be whisked away to the Mogadishu market in Somalia. In Kenya, most *khat* is grown in Meru district just north of Mount Kenya. Packed into fast motor cars with dare-devil drivers, the *khat* is then driven to Wilson Airport outside Nairobi as fast as possible, packed into a light aircraft and flown to Mogadishu. It is packed into vehicles again and driven to the Mogadishu market for sale.

International air transport is also the reason why expatriate Yemeni or Somali communities as far afield as Australia, Holland, Italy, England, Canada or the US are able to buy *khat* leaves to chew (Beekhuis, 1997). A recent survey amongst 70 Somali people living in Liverpool, UK, for example, found that 43 per cent of men had used *khat*, with 39 per cent chewing it on a daily basis.

In the *Catha edulis* case, the high-value leaves led to this species being cultivated hundreds of years ago. In other cases, trade leads to an unsustainably high impact on some species, particularly when supplies of slow-growing, destructively harvested species have been diminished by habitat degradation. Evidence for unsustainable harvest comes from the observations of local people, including gatherers and traders. Rural communities in many parts of Africa, Asia, Central Europe and the Americas are increasingly concerned about losing self-sufficiency as their local wild populations of favoured, popular species are dug up, bagged and transported to far-away regional markets.

In addition, many medicinal species have multiple uses, some of which have a far greater impact than harvesting for medicinal purposes. From detailed studies in Belem markets, in the Brazilian Amazon, Patricia Shanley and Leda Luz (in press) showed that, in addition to the 9000kg of *Tabebuia* bark sold for medicinal purposes, over 5500m^3 of *Tabebuia* timber were exported annually from Belem. The important questions are: what impact is this is having on species? How can harvesting impacts be measured? What are the options for sustainable use? The following three chapters set out to answer these questions.

Chapter 4

Measuring Individual Plants and Assessing Harvesting Impacts

Introduction

The social survey methods and ethno-botanical work in local markets described in Chapters 2 and 3 are the first steps towards understanding patterns of **demand** for particular plant species. The next three chapters are a 'nested progression' covering methods for studying the **supply** of plants which are a focus of that demand.

Although it is important to consider harvesting impacts on plants at the larger spatial scales of plant populations (see Chapter 5) and landscapes (see Chapter 6), we also need to understand how individual plants respond to harvesting. Usually, we see and measure things at the individual plant level first. When you walk through forest, savanna or grassland with local harvesters, it is likely that you would see signs of harvesting: stumps of cut trees, debarked trees or signs of root or tuber removal for food or medicine. You may know which species have been harvested, or if not, would collect good-quality herbarium specimens to enable identification. But this is just a first step. You may also know how much is harvested (see Chapter 3); but what size are the harvested

plants (or plant parts) and how much harvestable material is there? From market and social surveys or field observation, you may know what range of products has been, or is likely to be, harvested from the plant; but how long does it take to reach harvestable size? How does size or age relate to production of leaves, bark or other non-timber products? What effect does harvesting these non-timber products have on individual plants? All of these are important questions from a resource management viewpoint.

This chapter deals with the methods which can be used to answer these questions. Chapter 5 then puts harvesting into a plant population dynamics perspective. The methods described in this chapter are linked to a 'bird's eye view' of vegetation dynamics, maps and aerial photographs in Chapter 6, which deals with the interplay between plant population dynamics and disturbance. These community and landscape-scale factors provide the crucial context for understanding plant harvesting at the population and individual plant levels.

Necessary Equipment

The great thing about applied ethnobotany is that you can do good-quality field work without buying a lot of expensive equipment. The main skills are in understanding what you see in the field or hear from local resource users, and in knowing the key measurements necessary for a particular study. In the methods described below, a great deal of very useful data can be collected using the following:

- a regular tape measure or a 3m diameter (dbh) tape or forestry callipers;
- a can of paint for marking measured stems;
- aluminium tags for marking plants;
- aluminium nails;
- measuring scales, with size depending upon what you need to measure, ranging from 100g or 1kg balances to 5kg, 25kg or even larger hanging scales;
- Swedish bark gauge or a Vernier calliper;
- a *panga* or machete;
- field notebooks, graph paper, ruler, pencils;
- plant presses and specimen labels;
- a hand lens.

In some cases you may need more expensive equipment such as a global positioning system (GPS), a direct reading hypsometer (also known as a clinometer) for measuring tree height, a Swedish increment borer (used to extract wood from trees to determine age), or a battery operated electronic balance for measuring fresh bark or leaf mass. Only under exceptional circumstances would you require the very expensive equipment sometimes used in commercial forestry research, such a Relaskop, which is used for optical measurement of tree diameters and heights, or an infra-red gas analyser to measure photosynthetic rates. You would also need equipment for setting up plots as described in Chapter 5. I have tried to avoid describing methods that are not available to most field workers. In a few cases, however, I explain how to section perennial corms or tree stems in order to age trees. I also mention the use of an electronic balance (fresh bark mass, leaf mass), leaf area meter and the spherical crown densiometer, which is used to measure tree or shrub canopy closure.

Measuring diameter, height and bark thickness

With their historic focus on commercial timber, foresters have used systematic methods to obtain measurements for tree diameter, height, volume, and cross-sectional area, and many well-established methods are available (Philip, 1994). The same does not apply to non-timber products or harvesting foliage, bark, resins or roots from trees. Nor does it apply to vines, lianas or deadwood. Until recently,

for example, many foresters considered lianas a nuisance that suppressed timber tree production, and were more interested in systematically removing lianas than measuring them or assessing their value to local people. In the past, most foresters also had little interest in standing dead trees or fallen logs. Conservation biologists see their ecological importance and local people value deadwood for fuel and prize lianas as multipurpose binding material. As a result of these changing views, some methods used to measure non-timber products or to assess harvesting impacts on plants are relatively new.

Measuring individual plants and dividing them into size classes according to diameter or length is an important aspect of collecting inventory data, estimating yields or developing population matrix models or survivorship curves (see Chapter 5). Use of stem diameter or length size classes can also be related back to records of size-class selection by local harvesters collected during household surveys, in markets or from bundles of harvested plant material (see Chapter 2). Bark thickness also relates to stem diameter, increasing with tree size. Measurements of stem diameter (or length) are made on the basic assumption that stem diameter (trees, bulbs or corms) or stem height (palms, tree ferns) reflect plant age. Size is often only poorly correlated with age, so this assumption must be treated with caution (see Chapter 5). A 2-metre tall sapling, for example, may be 5 years or 50 years old, depending upon growing conditions. Methods of ageing plants are therefore very important (see 'Methods for Ageing Plants' below).

One of the reasons for using stem diameter or height classes is that accurately ageing plants is difficult for most species, particularly in the tropics and subtropics. Tree stems, bulbs and corms generally get thicker as these plants grow older, and diameters are therefore used as the most appropriate measure for grouping them into size classes. Most palms and tree ferns have an apical meristem on an unbranched stem, growing upwards (longer) as they grow older, rather than increasing in diameter. Rattan palms, for example, show a great increase in length for very little increase in stem diameter. For these reasons, *stem length* rather than stem diameter is a more accurate measure for assessing the population structure of palms, cycads, grass trees and tree ferns.

Diameter: stems, bulbs and corms

Diameter measurements of trees are conventionally taken at a set height of 1.3m ('breast height') and this is expressed either as diameter at breast height (dbh) or circumference (girth at breast height) (gbh). This is the most commonly used tree measurement in forest inventory work, and will vary according to the shape and growth form of trees (see Figure 4.1). When you need to calculate tree volume, then diameter measurements are taken at regular intervals along the trunk, so that tree-trunk volume calculations are made for each trunk subsection as a way of minimizing error as the trunk tapers (see 'Stem Mass and Volume' below). Basal diameter and dbh measurements can either be done with a forestry 'diameter tape' which enables the dbh to be read directly from a girth measurement, with forestry callipers, or with a standard tape measure, later converting from circumference (girth).

Diameter at breast height (dbh) is the key measurement used to calculate basal area (ba), the area occupied by a cross-section of the stem, usually expressed as m^2 per ha. This is used to get an estimate of stand biomass of different tree species within a known area. As an alternative to climbing trees to make these diameter measurements, two expensive optical instruments, either the Spiegel Relaskop or Tele-Relaskop invented by Walter Bitterlich, are used by foresters to accurately measure tree diameter when light conditions are good and there is a clear view of the tree trunk. It is also possible to measure tree height, distance and assess basal area using a Relaskop. In permanent sample plots, the increase in

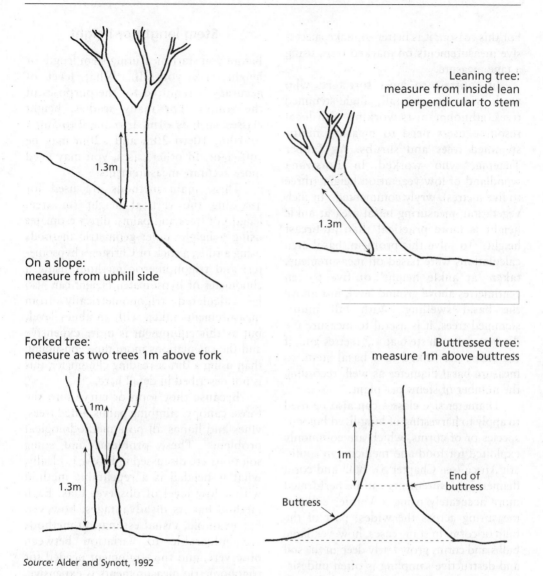

Leaning tree:
measure from inside lean
perpendicular to stem

1.3m

On a slope:
measure from uphill side

Forked tree:
measure as two trees 1m above fork

1m

1.3m

Buttressed tree:
measure 1m above buttress

1m

End of
buttress

Buttress

Source: Alder and Synott, 1992

Figure 4.1 *Standard measurements of diameter at breast height (dbh) or of girth at breast height (gbh) in trees that are leaning or strangely shaped*

tree diameter (dbh) is usually measured on successive intervals with a tape measure.

Increases and seasonal changes in tree girth can be measured using a Vernier girth band, usually made from steel or aluminium (Hall, 1944; Alder and Synnott, 1992). Girth bands can be made locally at little cost using the metal bands found on packing cases, which are then marked using a template so that accurate reading to an accuracy of 0.1mm can be made. This process is described by Liming (1957). Girth bands are not suitable for trees smaller than 7cm in diameter as they do not allow enough room for the spring and scale on the girth band. Limits on the number of girth bands can lead to poor sample size and a false sense of accuracy.

For this reason, it is better to make successive measurements on marked trees using a tape measure.

In contrast to most foresters, who work primarily with tall, single-stemmed trees, ethnobotanists working with local resource users need to measure multi-stemmed trees and shrubs. As Tauber Tietema, who worked in Botswana woodland of low vegetation height (three to five metres), wryly commented, 'In such vegetation, measuring basal area at ankle height is more practical than at breast height.' To solve this problem, basal area calculations were based on measurements taken 'at ankle height' of five to ten centimetres above ground level, just above the basal swelling. With tall multi-stemmed trees, it is useful to measure the diameter of each stem at 1.3 metres and, if the stems are linked to a basal stem, to measure basal diameter as well, recording the number of stems per plant.

Diameter size classes can also be used to apply to harvesting of long-lived bulbous species or of corms, which are commonly exploited for food and medicine in southern Africa (see Chapter 5). Bulb and corm diameter measurements can be performed more accurately using a Vernier calliper, measuring across the widest part of the bulb or corm. In some cases, however, large bulbs and corms grow fairly deep in the soil and destructive sampling is often undesirable, particularly where rare species are concerned. If destructive sampling is likely, it may be necessary to harvest a subsample to measure bulb depth, diameter and fresh bulb mass. With some bulbs, corms and tubers there is also the opportunity to age plants by counting leaf scales (some Amaryllidaceae and Liliaceae) or to count epidermal sheath layers which accumulate around stem tubers (some Droseraceae); these measurements can be related back to fresh mass bulb or diameter (see 'Ageing Palms, Tree Ferns and Grass Trees' below).

Stem length or height

Before you start measuring stem length or height, ask yourself: 'What level of accuracy is required for the purposes of the study?' For many studies, height classes, such as <1m, 1 to 2m, 2 to 5m, 5 to 10m, 10 to 20m and >20m may be sufficient. In other cases, you may need more accurate measurements.

Three main methods are used for assessing the vertical height (or stem length) of trees and palms: direct estimates using a height pole; geometric methods using a ruler, a stick or Christen's hypsometer; and trigonometric methods using a clinometer or hypsometer. Height can also be calculated trigonometrically from measurements taken with an abney level, but as this equipment is more expensive and the calculations more time consuming than using a direct-reading clinometer, this is not described in detail here.

Because they loop or curve into the forest canopy, climbing palms, tilted trees, vines and lianas all pose methodological problems. These problems and some solutions are discussed in Box 4.1. Ideally, what is needed is a repeatable method with a low level of observer bias. Each method has its disadvantages, however. For example, visual estimation methods are vulnerable to variation between observers, and the equipment needed for trigonometric measurements is expensive. In a comparison of height measurement methods, however, Mary Stockdale (1994) found that the ruler method was as accurate as any other in measuring straight rattan palm stems and that it was the most accurate method for estimating the length of curved or looped rattan stems (see Box 4.1).

Direct estimation

This uses a measured pole clearly marked at 0.5m intervals and usually 3 to 4m long.

This is held vertically at the base of the tree, enabling an observer standing far enough away to see the base and the top of the stem. The number of pole lengths is then counted by eye to estimate the height of the tree.

Geometric methods

The most commonly used of these is the ruler method. This uses cheaper equipment but is more difficult to learn than the clinometer method. The ruler method needs at least two people to carry out measurements. One person stands at the base of the tree stem holding a pole or ranging rod which is marked into 1-, 2- and 3-metre intervals. A second person stands far enough away from the tree so that they can see the top and bottom of the tree at a distance where regular intervals on the ruler (such as every 3, 6 and 9cm) correspond to the 1-, 2- and 3-metre intervals on the pole. Using the ruler as a guide for scale, the height of the tree is read off from a distance against the ruler, converting the known 1-metre intervals on the scale against the tree into an estimate of tree height.

Trigonometric methods using clinometers (or hypsometers)

Examples are different models of Suunto clinometers, and Haga and Blume-Liess hypsometers. Clinometers (and diameter tapes) are available from companies which supply the forestry industry. There are two basic types of clinometer. Direct-reading clinometers incorporate a prism and enable quicker measurements to be made, but are more expensive. As their name implies, tree height can be read off the instrument directly. With more basic clinometers, tree height has to be calculated. Tree heights are determined on the same principle with both types of clinometer, taking measurements from a set distance (usually 15m or 20m) away from each tree, so that there is an imaginary triangle between the person doing the measurement and the tree (see Figure 4.2). The first step is to make sure you are the set distance away from the stem (at least 15m). In dense forest, it is often impossible to get a line of sight 15m or 20m away from the tree. The alternative is to pick the best vantage point, measure the distance to the tree and angles to the base and top of the tree and then calculate height. If you are working in tropical forest, you will realize that foresters who work in plantations have it easy: they rarely have to cut a trail for a sight line to the base of each tree!

You also need to take slope into account. Measurements are always taken from eye level. In most cases you will find that your eye level is slightly higher or lower than the base of the tree and this has to be taken into account. If you are on level ground, you need to add your height to the reading given to tree-top height. If you are on a slope below the tree base, you need to perform the following calculation. Sight onto the tree base and take a reading (eg 2.5m); then take a reading to the tree top (eg 15m); subtract the two to get tree height (stem length) (12.5m). If you are standing on a slope above the tree base, go through the same calculation but add, rather than subtract, the two readings.

With palms you need to decide and clearly state in your methods which sighting you used in measuring length: the top of the stem or the total length including the leaves. As this second measurement is influenced by leaf harvesting, or will be less relevant to studies of palm-stem harvesting, it is best to sight to the top of the stem and not include the leaves above this point. Again, it is much easier to take slope into account with a direct-reading clinometer (see Figures 4.2 b and c); but this has to be calculated trigonometrically

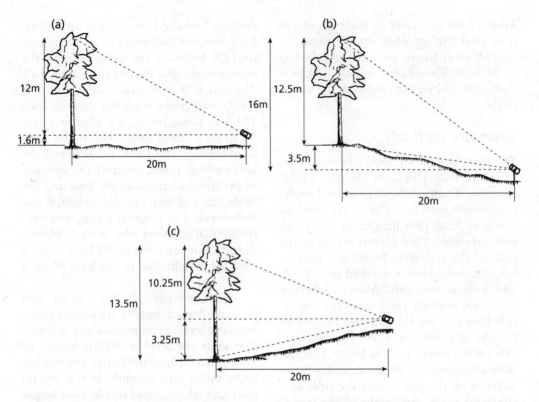

Figure 4.2 *Use of a clinometer to measure tree height. (a) On level ground one simply adds the observer's height (here 1.6m) to the tree height. (b) and (c) The reading obtained is from the observer's eye level, so on sloping ground suitable adjustments need to be made*

with basic clinometer models. If you encounter a tree with a broken tip, you should note that the stem is broken, record the height of the break and, based on trees of a similar size for this species, estimate the height the tree would have been before the tip broke off.

Measuring biomass and volume

Ethnobotanists are interested in measuring a far greater diversity of plant resources than traditional foresters, whose main interest has been measuring 'timber height' – the length of the tree bole being the main source of sawn timber. In general, however, the tree bole represents only roughly 30 per cent of the biomass of a tree.

Ethnobotanists involved in resource management are not only interested in tree stems, but also in measuring the many harvested products from the remaining 70 per cent of dry mass, including roots (30 to 55 per cent), twigs and leaves (about 10 per cent) or branches (about 15 to 30 per cent), as well as exudates and bark. In some cases all the above-ground or below-ground biomass is measured so that correlations can be made between shoot:root ratios or between fresh tree biomass and other tree (or shrub) dimensions, such as stem diameter, basal area or canopy diameter.

Regression equations derived from correlations between total biomass and factors such as stem basal area or stem height are useful tools to estimate biomass,

Box 4.1 Lengths of 'Awkward Customers': Climbing Palms and Tilting Trees

Clinometers are easily used by foresters who have the luxury of working in plantations or coniferous forests, where most trees are straight. Working in tropical forests and savanna is more challenging, particularly if we encounter tilted trees or are interested in non-timber plant products such as climbing palms (rattans) or lianas that curve or twist as they climb into the forest canopy. Each of these cases will be dealt with separately. In each scenario, the methodological dilemma results from two factors. Firstly, there is a need to avoid destructive harvesting. In the past, most studies that measured rattans resulted in pulling them out of the canopy. This is time consuming and destructive; and if you are pulling an ant-associated rattan such as *Calamus deeratus*, you are also likely to get covered in angry, biting ants! Particularly if you are working in a national park or on scarce resources valued by local people, it is important to minimize destructive harvesting. Secondly, it is also crucial to use a method for measuring length of these 'awkward customers' in an accurate, repeatable way that minimizes the bias between field workers using that method.

Working in Brunei, forest researcher Mary Stockdale (1994) carried out a very interesting test of the accuracy of four different methods for measuring rattan palm lengths. She compared visual estimates of length with the ruler method, the clinometer method and length estimation based on internode counts. The internode method counts the number of internodes by eye (or with binoculars) and multiplies by the mean internode length (based on five randomly selected, measured internodes for each stem).

In order to get around the problem of rattan stems curving into the forest canopy, a three-metre pole was held vertically so that its tip touched the rattan stem (Stockdale, 1994). This formed an important reference point for the ruler and clinometer methods. Electrician's tape was used to mark a point three metres below where the marker pole touched the stem, dividing the rattan stem into two sections: **ground length**, from the root collar to the tape, and **above-ground length**, from the tape to the base of the petiole of the top-most leaf of the stem (see Figure 4.3a). If the stems were very crooked, observers had to imagine where the top would have reached if the stem had been straight. Visual and ruler methods both followed similar procedures to those described above for straight stems. With the clinometer method, the angles were measured to the top of the stem (θ_{top}) and base of the height pole (θ_{base}). The next step was to measure the distance (X) from the observer's eyes to the base of the rattan stem using a tape measure. To calculate the horizontal distance from the observer's eyes to the stem, Stockdale used the formula:

$$D = X(\cos \theta_{base})$$

The above-ground length (L) was then calculated using the formula:

$$L = D(\tan \theta_{top} + \tan\theta_{base})$$

In assessing the accuracy of these four methods, Stockdale also took into account how long it took to take measurements and factors that commonly affect height measurements, such as variation between observers performing the measurements, topography and light levels in the forest. Her results were surprising and encouraging to field workers who cannot afford a clinometer. Contrary to Philip's (1994) report that geometric methods such as the ruler method are less accurate than trigonometric methods using a clinometer, the ruler method was the most accurate and quickest for measuring curved or looped stems. The internode counting method was the least accurate (15.3 per cent mean error) and also the most time consuming. The only disadvantage was that the ruler method took longer to learn. However, the field assistant in the experiment who found it most difficult to learn the ruler method was as accurate with the ruler method as with a clinometer. The main reason for the lower accuracy of the clinometer method in measuring curved stems was that while the ruler method only needed one measurement, the calculation of length needed to measure two angles and the distance from the observer to the base of the stem.

When trees are leaning, the height is usually estimated (B'D) as an average of two readings, each taken from positions (A and C) opposite one another and exactly the same distance away from the base of the tree (Philip, 1994). A more accurate measurement of tree length (BD) can only be made if you measure the angle at which the tree is leaning (θ) and calculate the true length (BD) as:

$$BD = DB'/cos\theta$$

Another alternative for measuring crooked, forked or bent trees is to use a range-finding dendrometer (Grosenbaugh, 1991), but these are very expensive and unavailable to most field workers.

usually expressed in kilograms or tonnes per hectare. In this way, harvested quantities (see Chapter 2) can be compared against the standing stock (biomass). By contrast, with detailed work on a few forestry plantation species, a variety of different regression equations have been developed by researchers in natural subtropical woodlands in Asia and Africa. Examples of different regressions are biomass regressed against stem basal area in Southern African savanna (Rutherford, 1982; Tietema, 1993), against stem circumference in dry tropical forest in India (Singh and Singh, 1991) and against stem diameter in Somalia (Bird and Shepherd, 1989).

Although different methods are used to measure biomass or volume, fresh mass of plant material is commonly standardized to an oven-dry mass equivalent (dried at 80°C until no more mass is lost), since there is a significant seasonal variation in the amount of moisture in fresh (or even air-dried) plant material. The ratio of fresh

mass:oven-dry mass is based on subsamples of plant material – sample discs of stems and branches or of bark, roots, leaves or browse (stems/leaves) – as you cannot expect to fit large quantities of plant material into the drying oven!

Leaf measurements

The type of leaf measurements you choose depends upon the aim of the study and the type of leaf resource being harvested. If selective harvesting of leaves takes place, then you may combine counts of the number of harvested (or harvestable) leaves (see 'Harvesting Vegetative Structures' below) with measurements of **leaf, leaflet, culm length** or **petiole width**. These are usually made to assess leaf size-class selection, primarily for long-lived leaves harvested for fibre (Agavaceae, Cyperaceae, Juncaceae, Palmae). With Cyperaceae and Juncaceae, the whole culm is usually measured. With palms, this depends upon what harvesters use, and the

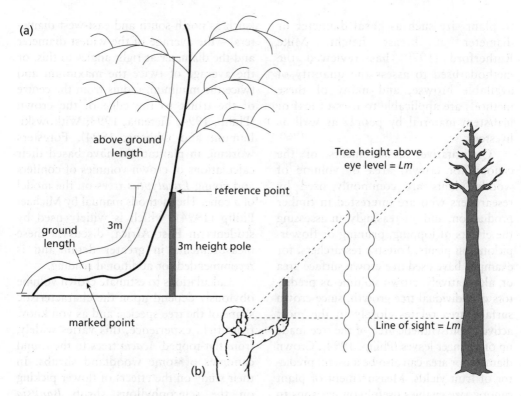

Sources: (a) Stockdale and Power, 1994; (b) Philip, 1994

Figure 4.3 *(a) Dividing the rattan stem into two sections: ground length, from the root collar to the tape, and above-ground length, from the tape to the base of the petiole of the topmost leaf of the stem. (b) The isosceles triangle method of measuring tree height*

correlation between palm stem size and leaf or leaflet size. Palm leaflet length has been commonly used in studies of *Hyphaene* palms in Southern Africa (Cunningham, 1988; Cunningham and Milton, 1987), but in her work on the palm *Sabal uresana* in Sonora, Mexico, Elaine Joyal found that petiole width provided a statistically significant correlation with palm size class and this was used instead of leaf length (Joyal, 1996).

Foliage mass, on the other hand, is used as a measure of the quantity of leaves harvested for livestock fodder (in kilograms) or as edible greens (in grams). This is often done on the basis of local units such as bundles (see Chapter 2), usually measured as fresh ('green') mass.

This is then converted to dry weight equivalents on the basis of fresh mass samples which are oven dried and reweighed.

A third method of measuring leaves is **specific leaf area** (SLA) – the ratio of leaf area to dry leaf mass. Measurements of SLA provide useful insights into the biology of plants and are discussed in Chapter 5.

Measuring the plant canopy: biomass, volume, area, density and crown position

A common direct measure of foliage (or forage) mass is to clip and weigh foliage to get fresh mass and then to obtain oven-dry mass, relating total amount measured to plant size such as basal diameter or diameter at breast height. Mike Rutherford (1979) has reviewed the methods used to assess the quantity of available browse, and many of these methods are applicable to uses of leaf or leaf/stem material by people as well as livestock.

Quantitative measurements of the canopy (or crown) area or volume of woody plants are commonly used by researchers who are interested in timber production, and, increasingly, in assessing the effects of lopping, pruning or flower-picking on plants. Forestry researchers, for example, have used tree-crown surface area or, alternatively, crown volume as predictors of individual tree growth, since crown surface area relates closely to the most active photosynthetic area of the tree made up of younger leaves (Philip, 1994). Crown diameter or area can also be a useful predictor of fruit yields. Measurement of plant canopy size enables useful comparisons to be made between harvested and unharvested populations of trees or shrubs as an indicator of available browse or the effects of plants lopped for forage. It has also been used in studying the effects of commercial flower picking on Proteaceae in Australia (*Banksia*) or South Africa (*Protea, Leucodendron*).

Foresters interested in timber production most commonly measure crown diameter, crown depth or clear bole length (to the lowest live branch or lowest complete whorl of branches). While shrubs are short enough for direct measurements of crown height and depth, a hypsometer is often used to take these measurements for tall trees. Crown diameter (width) is used to calculate the crown (canopy) area. The crown diameter measurement used in this calculation is commonly the average of two crown diameter measurements taken at right angles, either taken at random or in a predetermined direction

(such as north-south and east-west diameters) – the average of the widest diameter and the diameter at right angles to this, or the average of twice the maximum and twice the minimum radius from the centre of the trunk to the edge of the crown (Philip, 1994; Tietema, 1993; Witkowski, Lamont and Obbens, 1994). Foresters working in plantations have based their calculations of crown volumes of conifers and young *Eucalyptus* trees on the model of a cone. The methods manual by Michael Philip (1994), which is widely used by students in East Africa, discusses these measurements in greater detail and is recommended for additional reading.

Calculations to estimate crown volume obviously depend upon the characteristic shape of the tree species; and as you know from field experience, this varies widely, from flat-topped *Acacia* trees to the round canopies of some woodland shrubs. In their study on the effects of flower picking on the sclerophyllous shrub *Banksia hookeriana* (Proteaceae), for example, Witkowski et al (1994) randomly selected *Banksia* shrubs in each of six sites and calculated canopy area and canopy volume using the formulae:

$$\text{Canopy area} = \pi \frac{W_1}{2} \frac{W_2}{2} = 0.7854 W_1 W_2$$

$$\text{Canopy volume} = \frac{4}{3} \pi \frac{W_1}{2} \frac{W_2}{2} \frac{H}{2} = 0.5236 W_1 W_2 H$$

where W_1 was the widest canopy diameter; W_2 the perpendicular diameter to this; and H the canopy height.

In addition, they measured the openness of each shrub's canopy using a forest (or spherical crown) densiometer. A densiometer is an instrument that determines forest canopy density, used by foresters in forest thinning operations or to assess light requirements for forest regeneration. Densiometers have a convex or concave mirror reflector covered by grid squares, marking out an overhead plot. Placing it under the canopy and counting the number of grid squares shaded gives a measure of the percentage shading. The results of their study showed that *Banksia* shrubs which had not been harvested had a significantly greater canopy area (1.59 times), canopy volume (1.78 times) and were taller (1.1 times) than shrubs in sites where flower picking had taken place (Witkowski, Lamont and Obbens, 1994). In addition, seed storage and seed production per individual plant were 57 per cent and 50 per cent lower respectively in the harvested plants: an issue that will be discussed in the next chapter, dealing with this issue at a plant-population level.

Access to light is a crucial factor which needs to be taken into account if you are measuring plant growth in forests (such as stem diameter increments in terms of growth rates or palm leaf production rates). If you do not have a densiometer to measure forest overstorey density or a lux meter for measuring light intensity, you can use Dawkins's field classification of tree crown position (Dawkins, 1958) which he developed in Uganda. The Dawkins crown classification system, which has also been used in West Africa and South-East Asia, rates tree crown position according to the following scale:

5 = emergent: crown plan fully exposed to overhead light and free from lateral competition (this is defined as being exposed to overhead light at least within the 90° cone of an imaginary inverted cone with its point touching the base of the tree crown;

4 = full overhead light: crown plan fully exposed to light from above (vertically) but next to tree crowns of equal or greater height within the 90° cone;

3 = some overhead light: crown plan partly exposed to overhead light, but partly shaded by other crowns;

2 = some side light: crown plan fully shaded from above, but exposed to some direct light from the side, coming through a gap or past the edge of the overhead canopy;

1 = no direct light: crown completely shaded from above and from the sides.

Although this is subjective, it has shown to be a method giving consistent results (Wyatt-Smith and Vincent, 1962). In addition, a study of indigenous tropical hardwood growth rates in forest in Ghana found that Dawkins's classification of crown position also correlates well with tree increment (Alder and Synott, 1992). It is also a useful field method for studying forest palm-leaf production rates, since palm-leaf production rates vary considerably with shading (see 'Ageing Palms, Tree Ferns and Grass Trees' below, and Martinez-Ramos, 1985).

Flower, fruit and seed production

The simplest method of measuring the number of flowers or fruits per plant is by direct counting. This is a suitable method for plants which produce relatively few large flowers, such as the Proteaceae, or large fruits such as palms, but becomes impractical with very tall trees, or when short plants produce huge quantities of small fruits. When direct counts are impractical, small, circular fruit traps (usually 0.5m² – 79.8cm diameter to 1m² – 112.8cm diameter) or square plots (1 x 1m square) are commonly used to subsample fruit fall from trees. Each trap or plot has to be numbered. Circular traps consist of netting which is fixed loosely across a wire frame placed on wooden 'legs' 0.5 to 1m off the ground. Square plot traps are easier to make with a wooden frame. The netting needs to sag (about 30cm deep in the centre of the trap). If it is too tight, the fruits may bounce out!

This method assumes that most of the fruits fall under the tree crown and does not take fruit removal by birds or other animals into account. As Charles Peters (1996) points out in his review of methods for assessing fruit production, measurement of what is left after frugivores have had their fill is not necessarily a disadvantage for an ethnobotanical study of fruit yield since it gives a realistic estimate of what would be available for harvest. However, they still need to be visited every few days before fruits rot and to limit animals taking fruit from the sample plots or traps.

The first step in sampling fruit fall is to estimate the 'shadow' of the tree crown: the area it would cover on the ground. This is a lot easier in savanna than in tropical forest, where the tree crowns overlap. This is measured, drawn on graph paper and the area calculated. As fruit fall under trees is seldom even, it is best to place the fruit traps or plots within four quadrants around each tree. These are established by dividing the 'crown shadow' into four, with lines drawn at right angles to each other extending out from the tree trunk. Fruit traps or plots are placed in a stratified random design within each quadrant. Either a constant proportion of the crown area can be sampled or a constant number of traps can be placed under each tree regardless of crown area. Both methods have disadvantages. A constant number of traps results in more intensive sampling of small trees than large ones. Varying the number of traps with differences in crown area complicates some statistical tests as sample sizes will vary. Based on his studies of measuring fruit yields, Charles Peters (1996) suggests that if a fixed sampling percentage is needed,

then you should use enough fruit traps or plots to cover 10 per cent of the total crown area, and if a constant number of traps is used then you need 8 to 12 traps or plots per tree. As you would need to sample about five to ten fruiting trees in a range of stem diameter classes (for trees) or stem-height (in the case of palms) size classes, you need to choose carefully which species you study, as this amounts to a lot of work.

Methods for estimating annual fruit and seed production from trees have been reviewed by Green and Johnson (1994) and by Peters (1996), both of which are recommended reading.

Bark: thickness and mass versus tree diameter

By contrast with the low diversity of plantation trees harvested for bark, such as cinnamon (*Cinnamomom verum*, *C. aromaticum*), black wattle (*Acacia mearnsii*) and cork oak (*Quercus suber*), local communities harvest bark from tens of thousands of tree and shrub species for many purposes (medicine, fibre, fish poisons, spices). Bark harvesting is often selective for particular stem size classes or bark quality. Inner bark fibre for binding purposes is stripped from young *Brachystegia* (Leguminosae) saplings which have smooth bark, rather than older trees with rougher, thicker bark.

In Southern Africa, most herbalists preferred to harvest thick bark from older trees, as this was considered more potent. In Uganda, Maud Kamatenesi found that herbalists were even more selective. Not only did they select mature *Rytigynia kigeziensis* (Rubiaceae) trees, but they preferred trees with small yellow-green leaves growing close to or on top of hills, rather than in valleys.

Seasonal factors can also be a factor in the timing of bark removal as this is often easier during the growing season. A good example is the seasonal removal of bark from *Brachystegia* trees for making bee hives in the *miombo* woodland of South-Central Africa. Other factors can also influence tree selection. In Zambia, for example, beekeepers cut small test blocks from *miombo* woodland trees prior to bark removal, selecting for 10 to 60 per cent (mean = 34 per cent) of *Brachystegia*, *Julbernardia* and *Cryptocephalum* trees with cross-grained inner bark (Clauss, 1992). Measuring bark thickness enables us to correlate the tree diameter (dbh) with bark thickness for individual plants and to determine potential bark yields. It is also an important link to records collected in ethnobotanical surveys of local markets (see Chapter 3). Bark varies considerably from species to species in its thickness and texture. Between and within species, bark thickness also varies with tree size or age, rate of growth, genotype and location of the tree. In Southern Africa, for example, *Rauvolfia caffra* trees growing at the coast have a very different outer bark texture from those growing in upland sites.

Bark thickness

This can be measured in two ways which differ in cost and in their impact on the tree: either using a bark gauge or a Vernier calliper. Bark measurements should be taken at breast height (1.3m), with four separate measurements taken around the trunk to get a mean bark thickness per tree. Bark gauges (Swedish and Finnish types) are available from suppliers of forestry equipment. The bark gauge has an inner 'chisel' which is pushed through the bark to the surface of the wood (see Figure 4.4). As the thin shank of the gauge is pushed in, the base plate of the gauge is pushed outwards, enabling a measurement of bark thickness (in mm). This method minimizes bark damage, an important

factor when dealing with rare trees such as *Faurea macnaughtonii*, which are susceptible to fungal attack. If a bark gauge is unobtainable, then the more destructive method of cutting out a small block of bark from four points at breast height (1.3m) can be done to get a mean measurement of bark thickness. Bark thickness can be measured using a Vernier calliper. If you do this, you need to avoid large bark slashes which damage the tree. You also need to avoid inaccurate measurements which might occur when layers splay out as a result of cutting with a blunt knife or *panga* (machete). Alternatively, carefully use a sharp chisel to push through the bark in the same way that a bark gauge would be used, marking the bark thickness and measuring it directly once the chisel blade is pulled out.

Bark mass per tree

It is important to take accurate measurements of bark thickness, particularly if you are calculating bark mass for each tree. In a single species, trees with the same height and diameter but with different bark thickness will have very different bark yields. In general, if height and dbh are constant, a 1mm difference in bark thickness will cause an increase or decrease of about 10 per cent in bark mass (Schonau, 1973).

In most trees, bark mass per tree increases with increasing dbh and tree height (Schonau, 1982; Kamatenesi, 1997). As few data are available for wild species, bark yields from cultivated trees such as black wattle are very useful in placing cultivation and bark production into perspective as an alternative to overexploitation of wild stocks. Based on studies of over 1300 trees, Schonau (1972) developed a multiple regression for *Acacia mearnsii* of bark mass on dbh, height, bark thickness:

Figure 4.4 *A Swedish bark gauge being used to measure the thickness of* Prunus africana *bark*

$$log\ BM = 1.87253\ (log\ D) = 0.72118\ (log\ H) + 0.152919\ (BT) - 0.11767\ (BT \times log\ D) + 0.037728\ (BT \times log\ H) - 2.04586$$

where BM = total fresh bark mass per tree to a stem tip diameter of 5cm underbark in kg; D = dbh in cm; H = total height in m; and BT = bark thickness at breast height in mm.

Although based on *Acacia mearnsii*, this equation has also proved useful in calculating single tree bark mass in other species (*Rytigynia kigeziensis, Prunus africana*). Although fresh bark mass has been used by Schonau (1972), a forester who has done extensive work on *Acacia mearnsii* bark yields – since he found fresh bark mass a more useful independent variable than oven-dry bark mass – use of fresh bark mass is usually fraught with problems. For two reasons, it is more prudent to convert fresh mass to oven-dry bark mass. Firstly, the moisture content of bark generally varies seasonally and between sites. Secondly, oven-dry bark mass provides a standard against which to compare the price per kilogram of oven-dried bark (not air-dried) samples from local markets, which is very useful if you want to compare different bark (or root or leaf) prices per kilogram of different species. In *Acacia mearnsii*, bark moisture content varied between 48 to 52 per cent, with a mean of 50 per cent (Schonau, 1973); in *Prunus africana* (42 to 50 per cent) and in *Rytigynia kigeziensis* it averaged 59 per cent (Kamatenesi, 1997). Fresh bark mass should be measured as soon as possible in the field using either a mechanical O'Haus

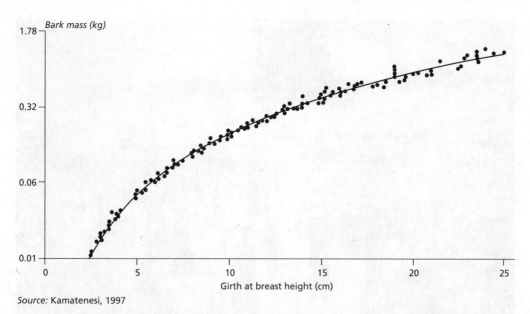

Source: Kamatenesi, 1997

Figure 4.5 *The relationship between* Rytigynia kigeziensis *diameter (dbh) and bark mass available from tree stem (up to 2m)*

balance or a battery-operated electronic balance. Each sample should be carefully labelled. The bark samples were then dried at 80°C until dry in a laboratory oven and reweighed to determine the range and mean moisture content.

A good example of the practical value of these data is provided by part of a study from the multiple-use management programme in Bwindi-Impenetrable National Park, Uganda. In this case, Maud Kamatenesi's study aimed to determine the bark mass available from the medicinal shrub *Rytigynia kigeziensis* (see Figure 4.5). These data were then compared with tree densities within multiple-use zones, and with the quantities local herbalists expected to be able to harvest.

Stem mass and volume

For many years, ethnobotanists interested in wood consumption for fuel, building or carving have been weighing bundles of fuelwood, or individual tree stems cut for

building purposes, using 5 to 50kg hanging scales. Unless you can chop trees into sections and weigh them, wood volume has to be calculated for large trees which are too heavy to lift. If logs have been harvested for woodcarving or use for housing or fencing, you will not want to offend anyone by cutting them up! Instead, calculate the volume of wood on the basis of diameter and height measurements.

In Namibia, for example, Antii Erkkila and Harri Siiskonen (1992) calculated the volume of *Colophospermum mopane* and *Combretum* stems used for traditional Owambo home construction (see Figure 4.6). Using measurements of the height and diameter of the poles, they calculated that the 21,599 poles used to make Mr Lazarus Uugwanga's homestead would have a combined volume of 69.5m³. With an additional 20 per cent of this to account for debarking and wood loss when shaping the poles (13.9m³), and the assumption that an additional 10 per cent of this was trimmed off after felling, the

Source: Duggan-Cronin collection, reproduced with permission from McGregor Museum, Kimberley, South Africa

Figure 4.6 *With complex palisade fences, traditional Owambo housing used a spectacular amount of wood*

result was that 91.7m³ of wood were used to construct the homestead. Fortunately, they could take measurements directly. The only highly accurate way of measuring volume of wood is with a xylometer. This measures how much water is displaced when the tree trunk (or whatever item is being measured) is fully lowered into the xylometer tank. This equipment is generally not available for the field researcher, so unless you can improvise and use a water tank instead of a xylometer, the next best option is to find the volume by direct measurement.

Due to their interest in assessing timber volumes, the most detailed approaches to measuring the volume of tree stems have been developed by foresters on the assumption that different parts of the tree stem are similar to geometric shapes. The simplest example is the main branch-free trunk, which is assumed to be a truncated cone on a cubical parabloid. To avoid the bias caused by slight tapering, it is important to make a series of diameter measurements along the length of the trunk. The best way to do this with a felled tree is to mark off sections with chalk and measure the diameter at 1m to 2m intervals. The volumes are calculated for each subsection and summed to get the total volume of the trunk. It is important to take a series of measurements along the trunk to avoid overestimating timber volume. Even then, you can expect an overestimate due to irregularity of the tree stem and bark.

To date, many ethnobotanical studies on the use of timber for building purposes, such as Christine Liengme's (1983) study of wood use in Gazankulu, South Africa, have estimated wood volumes assuming that the poles or logs are cylindrical. Other geometric shapes used in forestry to calculate tree volume are the cone, cubic parabolic and quadratic parabolic. Detailed information on these calculations are given in Michael Philip's (1994) manual on measuring trees. Volumes of logs are usually estimated using Huber's formula, which works well for logs which are cylindrical or shaped like a quadratic parabolic which has had its upper portion cut off parallel to the base. Because Huber's formula underestimates volume in logs that taper sharply, it is best to base your calculations on short, measured sections as described above. Huber's formula is:

$$volume \ (v) = \frac{\pi L d^2_m}{4}$$

where d_m = diameter of the log at mid length; and L = log length.

In some cases you may want to compare data on wood volumes (in m^3) with data on wood mass (in kg). To do this, you need to know the density of the wood being used (in kg/m^3). Be aware that this varies within trees, depending upon whether wood is from the top or base of the tree or from heartwood or sapwood. For example, if you have calculated that a *mukwa* (*Pterocarpus angolensis*) stem felled by a woodcarver has a volume of 1.9 m^3, and you know that the wood density is 650 kg/m^3, then the estimated wood mass before carving would be 1235kg.

Assessing the quantity of deadwood per tree is an important issue in studies of fuelwood availability, yet much of the deadwood that local people collect comprises crooked smaller branches for which accurate volume calculations are impractical. For this reason, weighing deadwood is a more practical option. In addition to assessing the quantity of deadwood per tree, you also need to weigh the woody 'litter' that has fallen onto the ground.

As part of his study on fuelwood availability in Southern African savanna, Charlie Shackleton (1993) first assessed deadwood availability and the effects of wood harvesting on individual trees of different species. He then used these data to determine standing deadwood biomass per hectare and the deadwood yield per hectare per year for harvested and unharvested sites (see Chapter 5). In addition to the standard approaches of recording the species, stem circumference and height of each tree or shrub, he visually estimated of the amount of deadwood as a proportion of the whole tree and the proportion of wood chopped from the tree. He also recorded whether chopped trees had resprouted (coppiced), were dead, or were alive but had not resprouted. Repeating these measurements for trees and shrubs within randomly selected plots showed that only 6 per cent of stems showed signs of severe chopping (>50 per cent removal). This suggested that when wood was cut from standing trees, chopping was severe, since almost 90 per cent of chopped trees had more than 50 per cent of biomass removed. Harvesting also focused on larger trees, with 36 per cent of trees with stems more than 16cm in circumference having lost over 50 per cent of woody biomass. However, the data he collected on whether resprouting had taken place or not illustrated the resilience of most trees, as 77 per cent had resprouted and, of the remainder, 19 per cent were dead and 4 per cent were alive but had not resprouted (Shackleton, 1993).

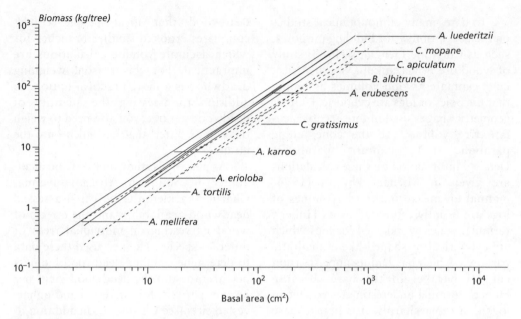

Source: Tietema, 1993

Figure 4.7 *A comparison of the stem basal area/weight regression lines for ten Southern African savanna tree species. Solid lines = Acacia species, dotted lines = Boscia albitrunca,* Colophospermum mopane, Combretum apiculatum, Croton gratissimus

Whole plant biomass

As long as you have an accurate balance, weighing smaller plants is straightforward. Whole trees, however, pose a logistic challenge! For this reason, there are relatively few studies outside of forestry plantation research which have correlated the dimensions of trees and shrubs covered earlier in this chapter, such as canopy diameter or dbh, with total above-ground tree biomass. This information is very useful for studies of fuelwood availability or harvesting impacts in the field, or through the interpretation of aerial photographs. For these reasons, Tauber Tietema (1993) carried out a study in Botswana which measured total biomass of 14 tree species, correlating the results with crown area, stem basal area and height. Trees were selected to get a representative sample of different size classes,

and biomass was measured with a spring balance mounted in a crane fitted onto a vehicle. Tree height and crown diameter were measured before each tree was cut. With multi-stemmed trees, each stem was weighed individually. Tree mass most closely correlated with stem basal area (see Figure 4.7), but correlations between tree mass and tree height or crown basal area were less significant. When he compared the single regression curve combined for all trees in his sample with similar work on tree species from Africa, India and Europe, Tauber Tietema found that to a large extent this described the relationship between basal area and tree mass for these species as well.

What measurements of biomass, volume or diameter do not tell you is how long the plants took to grow. This crucial issue in resource management is covered in the next section.

Methods for ageing plants

Potentially, information on the age of harvested plants is a key to many issues in resource management. It also leads to a better understanding of plant life histories. In many cases, however, the age-determination key is missing or does not quite fit, particularly with tropical and subtropical plants. There are exceptions, however, and more and more tropical trees are being aged using tree rings (Jacoby, 1989). Reasons for difficulties in ageing some tree species are the variation in growth rates of the same species in the same site or between populations, indistinct or non-existent annual growth rings, leaf scars or nodes. These are discussed in more detail below. Wherever possible, it is important to make comparisons with plants of known age or with plants which have been marked at specific times, so that 'annual' rings and growth can be cross-checked to see if they really are annual or not. Where it is possible to age perennial plants, however, this provides valuable information for resource users, managers and researchers in predicting yields.

Slow-growing, slowly reproducing plants are known to be vulnerable to overexploitation, yet we rarely know how old individual plants are or how long they live. This information is not only of great interest in developing resource management programmes, but is of value to local resource users, who often underestimate the age of slow-growing (and therefore vulnerable) plant species, and who are often amazed to find out that the tree they are carving or using for building is three or four times older than they are! Being able to age individual plants is also of great value in developing matrix models of plant populations by providing accurate information on recruitment, the time

taken to shift from one size class or stage to another, and on plant life spans (see Chapter 5). Although some methods of ageing plants (particularly dendrochronology) require laboratory work, this is possible for some field workers and so is included here. The following basic steps are generally involved.

- Select plant species that have potential for ageing and are important from a resource management perspective. This could be done on the basis of previous studies or through the two steps below. Although annual rings of some tree species can be seen with the naked eye (macroscopically), these can be deceptive and microscopic identification should be performed to avoid errors where growth rings are indistinct (Lilly, 1977).
- Cross-check with plants of known age (usually from known date of planting of bulbs – Ruiters, McKenzie and Raitt, 1989), corms (Werner, 1978; Levins and Kerstner, 1978) or trees where the cambium has been marked at known annual intervals by hammering successive nails into the trunk to mark the cambium (Shiokura, 1989; Grundy, 1995); and cross-check with trees that are marked by climatic extremes (drought, cold) of known date.
- Age trees based on cores taken from the trunk using a Swedish increment corer or from cross-sections of stems, where rings are counted in sanded, polished wood or stained corm cross-sections (Werner, 1978); or examine leaf-base counts from longitudinal sections of bulbs (Ruiters, McKenzie and Raitt, 1989). Destructive sampling

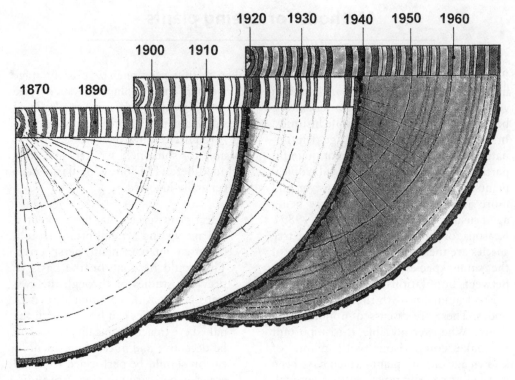

1870   1890   1900   1910   1920   1930   1940   1950   1960

Figure 4.8 *Diagrammatic representation of three tree stems where the distinctive growth rings indicating specific years have been matched for the periods 1900–1910 and 1920–1930*

should be avoided whenever possible. There is an extensive literature on non-destructive sampling methods for wood samples (see, for example, Swart, 1980).

- Take site differences into account; if you are ageing plants from different sites, be aware that differences between sites and populations will need to be assessed before extrapolating data from one site to another.

Counting tree rings

Ageing trees by counting tree rings (dendrochronology), seen in stem cross-sections, was substantially developed early this century by A E Douglass (1914, 1936). Douglass made the fundamental discovery that information on past climatic variation was reflected in tree-ring patterns and that these could be matched between trees. He used this method to build up a time series (chronology) by matching successively older tree rings (see Figure 4.8). This pioneering work was developed further by H C Fritts (1971), who identified six principles for minimizing non-climatic influences that obscured ring-width variations due to climatic variation. Computer sequences of these tree rings can be developed to cover very long periods, and very long, accurate chronologies have been constructed. The longest of these is based on *Pinus longaeva*, a species in which individual trees live to 2000 years. This enabled the development of a chronology extending back 8000 years, and was so accurate it was used to recalibrate the radio-carbon time scale (Ferguson, 1970; Lilly, 1977).

Most dendrochronological work has taken place in temperate Europe, North America and Asia. In some cases, this is done by counting rings in cut cross-sections of tree trunks. A less destructive method is to use an increment borer. These are T-shaped tools comprising the handle and a borer bit, 4.3 to 12mm in diameter, which is screwed into the tree trunk to extract a core of wood. Thicker (12mm diameter) cores are often used for quantitative analysis, but taking cores from hardwood trees can be very difficult. For two reasons, ageing trees is not as simple in tropical and subtropical areas. Firstly, temperate gymnosperms are particularly suited to tree-ring dating. Although oak (*Quercus*) and ash (*Fraxinus*) trees are easy to age using tree rings, some angiosperm wood is more complex and difficult to age. Secondly, dendrochronologists select trees from arid or very cold sites which show marked variation in tree-ring thickness. They avoid studying trees that grow in sites with enough water throughout the year, as their tree rings are likely to be uniformly wide with little variation between rings. They also avoid trees that grow densely together, since competition between trees obscures changes in growth rings due to climatic change. These conditions are more difficult to find in well-watered, warm tropical areas, dominated by angiosperms with less seasonal growth than in cool temperate areas.

Although it has been widely accepted that growth rings are not a reliable method of ageing many tropical and subtropical tree species, surveys of woody plants from southern Africa (Lilly, 1977), southern Australia (Schweingruber, 1992) and the tropics (Jacoby, 1989) show that many species have potential for ageing based on tree-rings. Based on an examination of 108 Southern African tree species, for example, five species were considered promising for dendrochronological work (*Albizia forbe-*

sii and *Burkea africana* (Leguminosae), *Ekebergia capensis* (Meliaceae), *Zanthoxylum davyi* and *Vepris undulata* (Rutaceae)). More recent studies in Southern Africa have also shown that several species which Lilly (1977) gave a very poor rating for dendrochronological work, such as *Acacia karroo*, produce rings which do correlate with age (Gourlay and Barnes, 1994; Prior and Gasson, 1990). One reason for this is the marked dry-season leaf fall and wet-season flushing common in deciduous woodlands in Southern Africa and probably also in other subtropical areas. In addition, trees which produce annual rings, but are less suited to dendrochronological work, can still be very useful for resource managers in determining stem age, estimating annual increments and developing practical cutting rotations. A good example is Isla Grundy's (1994) study of *Brachystegia spiciformis* in Zimbabwe, a tree species widely used for building poles. Her studies of growth rings showed that this species set down annual rings which were very useful in developing local woodland management based on coppice rotations.

Counting scars: trees and reiteration

Long-lived species which experience annual leaf flushes will also show visible scars in smooth-barked (usually younger) stems. These scars can be used as a field method for estimating stem age. Many subtropical and tropical tree species in areas with highly seasonal rainfall are deciduous, losing their leaves during the dry season (or the longer of two dry seasons in equatorial areas with bimodal rainfall). A new flush of leaves is produced at the start of the wet season (for instance, in several *Acacia*, *Brachystegia* and *Erythrina* species). The period of dormancy is long enough to induce an anatomical change evident as a wrinkled 'bud-scar' on tree stems and branches where the new season's growth starts. An annual flush of leaves and consequent scarring is also evident in evergreen trees such as *Podocarpus* and *Afrocarpus* in Afromontane forest. In addition to its value in ageing younger (less than 30- to 40-year-old) shade-tolerant reseeders such as *Podocarpus* (often harvested as building poles due to its straight growth form), this is a good method for showing students how poorly diameter (dbh) and age correlate between trees in forest canopy gaps or shade. When long-term growth records are not available, it is useful to count past seasons' flower heads in serotinous species and to examine bud scars marking annual iteration; this can help to develop realistic transition matrix models and to assess the probability of saplings and young trees in making the transition from one size class (stage) to the next (see Chapter 5).

The concept of 'reiteration', the replication of part the tree's basic architectural structure with the addition of new 'modules', is the basis for the **plant architectural models** developed by Francis Hallé and R A Oldeman (1970) (see Chapter 5, and Bell, 1998). In some tree species, the scars formed at the end of each growing season during this process can remain visible for years (or even decades) until obscured when rough bark develops on the stem. This is evident on trees with growth from a single meristem (monopodial) and those with sympodial growth (successive lateral meristems). This offers the opportunity for ageing younger (10- to 40-year-old) tree stems in the field by counting the number of scars. In the Cape Floral Kingdom (*fynbos* – fine leaved shrublands) many serotinous shrub species in the Proteaceae and Bruniaceae also mark this reiteration with annual or biennial flowering. Since the flower heads are retained on the plants, these can be counted to give field estimates of age as long as you know the phenology of the species you are studying.

Ageing palms, tree ferns and grass trees

Since palm and tree-fern stems are harvested for building purposes, grass-tree and tree-fern wood for lathe-turned bowls and many cycad species for horticultural use, ageing provides useful insights for conservation management and population studies. This ageing method has also been used to assess habitat disturbance history based on ageing palms affected by tree falls in tropical forest in Mexico (Martinez-Ramos et al, 1988) and the fire frequency of vegetation in south-western Australia (Lamont and Downes, 1979) (see Chapter 6).

Many tree ferns, cycads and arborescent (tree-like) monocotyledons, such as Australian grass trees (Xanthorrhoeaceae) and palms, have a single stem with a single growing shoot (apical meristem) at the tip. This type of architecture (Corner's model; see Chapter 5) offers the opportunity for age estimates based on leaf scars (in palms, tree ferns and cycads) or the depressions and ridges left by annual growth flushes (grass trees). Palms and many tree ferns produce leaves singly in regular acropetal order (developing from below upwards) from a single growing shoot (apical meristem) at the end of their stems. These leaves live for a few years, die and in many cases drop off and leave distinct leaf scars on the stem (see Figure 4.9). Leaf number is therefore a useful marker of growth events. Counting leaf scars has been widely used in short-term population studies to age individual palms (Bullock, 1980; Enright and Watson, 1992; Sarukhan et al, 1984; Tomlinson, 1963; Pinard, 1993). Knowing that tree ferns, such as *Cyathea* (Cyatheaceae) and

Leptopteris (Osmundaceae), produce a single growth flush of new leaves each season enabled James Ash to derive age estimates and population models from counting the scars left by leaf (or stipe) scars on tree-fern trunks (Ash, 1986, 1987; see Figure 4.10c). In Australia, Byron Lamont and Susan Downes (1979) used annual fluctuations in the diameter of the stems of grass trees (*Xanthorrea* and *Kingia*) to age the stems (see Figures 4.10a and b). With *Xanthorrea* plants living up to 350 years and *Kingia* up to 650 years, this was a very useful tool for studying frequency of flowering and of incidence of fire. They found, for example, that some grass trees were at least 200 years old before they flowered for the first time, and that fire frequencies prior to European settlement were far lower than the two- to four-year frequency previously suggested.

Age estimations, as one step in developing a population matrix model (see Chapter 5) can be useful in putting the harvesting of palm or tree-fern stems into perspective. Working in Sian Ka'an Biosphere reserve in Yucatan, Mexico, Ingrid Olmsted and Elena Alvarez-Buyulla (1995) used leaf scars to estimate the age and growth rates of *Thrinax radiata* ('chit') and *Coccothrinax readii* (nakax) palms harvested to make lobster traps and houses. Over 480 adult *Coccothrinax* palms are used by Mayan fishermen to build a single hut. Ageing clearly demonstrated the slow growth rates and consequent vulnerability of these two species. To get to just 3 metres high took *Thrinax* palms between 31 and 55 years, with adult palms living 100 to 145 years. *Coccothrinax readii* palms were even slower growing, taking 63 years to get 3 metres high and living over 145 years. The steps generally used in this method comprise the following.

Figure 4.9 *The stem of the nikau palm (*Rhopalostylis sapida*) in coastal forest, New Zealand, a species whose population dynamics have been well studied by Enright and Watson (1992) using counts of the frond scars clearly visible on the stem*

- Assess the number of palm or tree-fern leaves produced each year. There are two methods, depending upon how leaves are shed from the palm (Tomlinson, 1963). With arecoid palms that have 'self-cleaning' trunks – cleanly shedding their dead leaves (see Figure 4.9) – a painted mark is made directly below the tubular base of the oldest leaf. Before you do this, you may need to rub off the waxy coating so that the paint sticks to the palm stem. Alternatively, with palms that retain

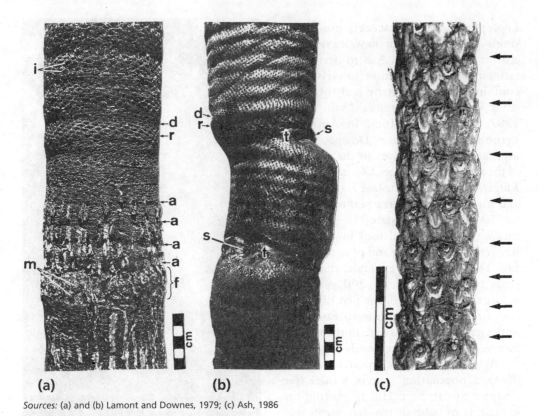

(a)　　　　　　　　　(b)　　　　　　　　　(c)

Sources: (a) and (b) Lamont and Downes, 1979; (c) Ash, 1986

Figure 4.10 *Grass trees and tree ferns. (a) Surface features of a* Kingia australis *stem after removal of the leaf bases, showing rings of aerial roots (cut back to their bases). The depression (d) and ridge (r) of an annual flush of vertical growth, the remnants of aborted (i) and mature (m) inflorescences and of fire-response flowering (f) are also shown. (b)* Xanthorrea preissii *stem showing the depression (d) and ridge (r), indicating annual vertical growth. The remnant of spikes (s) and the associated ring of smooth tissue (t) are also shown. Background scale for grass-tree stems in centimetres. (c) Stem of the Fijian forest tree fern* Leptopteris wilkesiana *with arrows indicating annual bands corresponding to growth flushes*

their leaves on the trunk for many years (or to use a consistent method for both categories of palm), you can tie an aluminium or plastic tag to the petiole of the most recently fully emerged leaf. Mark a sample of all stem size classes (ideally, 30 stems per size class) over a number of years (two to four years) to measure leaf production rates. Annual counts are made of the number of leaves produced per stem each year to get the mean number of leaves produced by each size class per year. The same tagged leaves can also be used

to assess palm-leaf life spans, which are relevant to leaf resource management.
- Count the number of leaf scars on each palm or tree-fern stem. Direct counts are made of the number of leaf scars for each height segment.
- Take the length of the seedling and establishment phases into account (when no stem is visible), so that this can be included in the age estimate. The seedling phase comprises the duration when the embryo emerges from the seed and becomes independent of the food reserves in the seed

endosperm by putting out the first roots and leaves. The establishment phase can be a long period of early development when the seedling diameter grows downward to form a stem base at, or below, ground level before growing upwards. In their study of the palm *Sabal palmetto*, for example, Kelly McPherson and Kimberlyn Williams (1996) found that the minimum length of the establishment phase was 14 years and the fastest-growing 1 per cent, 10 per cent and 50 per cent of plants would respectively take 33, 42 and 59 years to develop an above-ground trunk. The time this takes will also vary depending on whether the palm is produced from seed (a genet), which takes longer, or by clonal sprouting (a ramet) from lateral buds on the parent plant, which is quicker since the establishment growth phase is much shorter.

Working in Chico Mendes Extractive Reserve, Brazil, Michelle Pinard (1993) used leaf scars and known leaf-production rates to age palm stems in her study of the impact of stem harvesting on *Iriartea deltoidea* palms. She measured palm-stem heights and counted leaf scars on palm stems that were 5 to 10m high, which had consistent, longer internodes. Leaf-scar counts were also made on a sample of fallen palms greater than 10m long, as internode lengths were shorter in upper-stem sections of these tall stems. The number of leaf scars was then estimated on the basis of the mean number of scars per metre using two different mean numbers of leaf scars per metre: one for stems less than 10m and the other for stems greater than 10m high.

Although this method has proved useful in short-term demographic (population) studies of palms, it should be used with care as it can lead to incorrect age estimates in palm species with variable growth rates (Oyama, 1993). Problems with this method include the following. Firstly, it assumes that there is little variation in growth rate of the palm species. This is not always the case. As a result, you need to study leaf-production rates for different palm size classes (seedlings, saplings, juveniles and adult size classes) in different habitats within your study area. Robin Chazdon, for example, was able to use this method to age *cana de danta* (*Geonoma congesta*) palms in Costa Rica, as variation in rates of leaf production and leaf drop (abscission) was statistically insignificant. Over a three-year period, marked *Geonoma congesta* palms in a range of size classes produced an average of 10.1 new leaves, and abscised 9.7 leaves (Chazdon, 1992). In other cases, there is variation in palm or tree-fern leaf production and growth rates, resulting in plants of the same height having very different numbers of leaf scars (see Figure 4.11) (Ash, 1987; Oyama, 1993). Palms growing in forest gaps in Veracruz, Mexico, for example, were found to produce twice the number of leaves and fruits relative to palms in the same size class as palms in shady 'mature' forest (Martinez-Ramos, 1985). Dawkins's classification system for tree crown position (see early section on 'Measuring the Plant Canopy') is a useful field method for developing an understanding of the effects of shading on leaf production rates.

Secondly, young palms with underground stems and short internodes pose a problem, as the leaf scars cannot be seen and seedlings vary in the time that they take to form a trunk. Thirdly, leaf scars may be difficult to detect on older palms, leading to an underestimate of the age of older stems. Scars are difficult to count towards the top of very tall palms, so counts are often done from a subsample of fallen or felled adult palms.

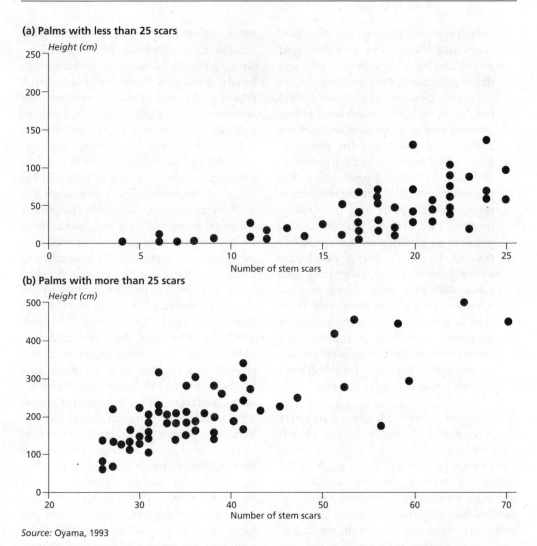

(a) Palms with less than 25 scars

Height (cm)

Number of stem scars

(b) Palms with more than 25 scars

Height (cm)

Number of stem scars

Source: Oyama, 1993

Figure 4.11 *The relationship between the number of leaf scars and height of* Chamaedorea tepejilote *palm stems (n = 148 palms) in Mexico showing stems with (a) fewer than 25 scars and (b) more than 25 scars*

Ageing bulbs, corms and stem tubers

Many plants use store nutrients, but some have specially adapted below-ground roots or stems. These are classified as bulbs, corms, stem tubers or root tubers on the basis of their structure. A **bulb** is really a large bud, with swollen modified leaves or 'scales', attached to a small, compressed stem which bears adventitious roots. Food is stored in the thickened scale leaves. Onions (*Allium* spp) and many other plants in the Liliaceae are familiar examples. **Corms** look similar to bulbs but consist mainly of compressed stem tissue, with much thinner scale leaves and the bulk of storage within the compressed stem. Many plants in the Iridaceae, such as *Watsonia* and *Gladiolus*, have corms. The potato, a swollen, starch-filled underground stem, is a familiar **stem tuber**. These differ from **root tubers**, such as sweet potatoes (*Ipomoea*), which are swollen storage roots. Relatively few studies have been conducted on ageing underground storage organs; but this is a very important tool in developing sustainable harvesting rates of a large group of plant species of great importance for food or medicine. Many geophytes are surprisingly long lived and some are vulnerable to overexploitation. Although all three of the methods discussed below require destructive sampling (which should obviously be avoided with rare species), they are useful in ageing subsamples of individuals in a population or for assessing the age of plants that have already been harvested.

Leaf-base counts

In some bulbous species, new scale leaves are produced seasonally from the centre of the bulb, while formation of new adventitious roots each season depletes bulb reserves of the outer scale leaves. Bulbs usually increase in diameter with age. These two factors offer an opportunity for ageing individual bulbs and studying bulb population dynamics. For reliability, it is crucial that any ageing is cross-checked on the basis of leaf production rates, bulb mass and flowering patterns with known age populations. One of the main reasons for this is that the number of leaves, rosettes of leaves or flowers produced by the same bulb species per year may vary between populations or seasons. If this is the case, then ageing may not be possible. Even if the bulbous species you want to age is known to produce just one leaf a year, or to flower once a year, this can be deceptive. There are two reasons for this. Firstly, many geophytes in the Amaryllidaceae, Liliaceae and Iridaceae family only flower when they reach 'critical bulb mass' (Rees,

1969; Ruiters et al, 1993). Secondly, leaf production rates in some Amaryllidaceae and Liliaceae can be at one constant rate for up to ten years in pre-reproductive plants, then double to another constant rate when the bulbs reach reproductive maturity (Ruiters et al, 1993; Kawano et al, 1982). These have to be taken into account when ageing bulbs. If not, major over- or underestimates of bulb age will result.

Cornelius Ruiters et al's (1993) study of bulbs of the medicinal plant *Haemanthus pubescens* (Amaryllidaceae) in coastal *fynbos* in South Africa is a good example of how ageing can be performed on the basis of leaf-base counts (see Figure 4.12a) and a thorough knowledge of bulb biology.

On the basis of studies of marked plants and of bulb mass, Ruiters and his coworkers knew that individuals were ten years or older when they flowered. They also knew that juvenile (pre-reproductive) plants (one to nine years old) produced one leaf per year, while reproductively mature plants (ten years or older) produced two leaves per year. This enabled them to avoid errors in ageing plants on the basis of leaf-base counts since they knew that the first nine leaf bases each represented a year, but after that two leaf bases were produced per year, from year ten onwards. A similar pattern of leaf production in juvenile and reproductively mature corms has also been recorded in *Erythronium japonicum* (Liliaceae), a genus whose corms are used medicinally and as a source of edible starch (Kawano et al, 1982).

Annual rings in perennial corms

The corms of many well-known horticultural plants such as cyclamen (Primulaceae), crocus and gladiola (Iridaceae) are short lived, producing a new corm after flowering while the previous season's corm decays. Some corms are perennial, however, with old leaf bases and storage tissues staying within an outer layer called a tunic. Very few studies have been conducted on ageing perennial corms. Although the example given below uses microscopic methods similar to tree-ring counts rather than a macroscopic method which may be more practical for a field biologist, I am including it here since this method could be important in ageing some of the wide range of perennial corms harvested for medicinal purposes. Some species of *Liatris*, such as the Kansas gayfeather (*L. spicata*), are used medicinally. In studies of transverse sections of known-age *Liatris aspera* corms, Patricia Werner (1978) showed that annual markers could be found in the xylem tissue in the vascular bundles if the corm was carefully sectioned and stained with safronin and fast green, two dyes commonly used in laboratory work.

There is, however a cautionary note. Patricia Werner's microscopic ageing method followed up on an earlier study by Harold Kerstner, which showed that cross-sections of juvenile (less than four-year-old) corms had pigmented rings visible to the naked eye which conformed to known ages of the individuals. These consisted of sclerenchymatous tissue. In her follow-up study, Patricia Werner showed that even with young corms, the number of rings depended upon where the cross-section was taken. In one case, a three-year-old corm had 16 rings near the centre, 9 rings at the apex and 10 at the base. This problem, as well as differences between sites and plant populations, needs to be borne in mind if the annual ring-count method is used (Werner, 1978; Levin and Kerstner, 1978). Despite the complex structure of older corms, this method offers a great opportunity to ethno-botanists interested in resource management. Key requirements to check the reliability of this method for any species you are investigating is to assess known age, marked plants and the differences between sites and populations.

Counting spent remains of annual corms and stem tubers

After initially starting from seed, many corm-producing species and some species with stem tubers, clonally (vegetatively) produce a new 'daughter' tuber or corm each season. In many cases, the fibrous remains of the past season's corm or stem tuber remain in the soil. These clonal successions of 'daughters' may proceed for ten years or more. Flowering may not take place in the first few years after recruitment from seed. As the years since germination increase, so successive daughter corms or tubers are generally heavier, deeper in the soil and, once at a flowering stage, produce more fruits per plant. These factors are important to take into account when studying harvesting and its impact on plant populations. For this reason, the innovative methods used by John Pate and Kingsley Dixon (1982) in ageing three West Australian geophytes – *Philydrella pygmaea* corms, and two tuberous sundew (Drosera) species, *D. bulbosa* and *D. erythrorhiza* – offer an opportunity for more widespread application to other harvested species. Tuberous *Drosera* species, for example, were gathered as a food source by Aboriginal people in south-western Australia (Hammond, 1933). Many plant species with seasonally clonal corms are locally traded for medicinal purposes (Cunningham, 1993) and at least three *Drosera* species are in international trade for medicinal purposes (Lange and Schippmann, 1997). Careful investigation of hundreds of *Drosera* plants showed that in the two tuberous sundew species, the

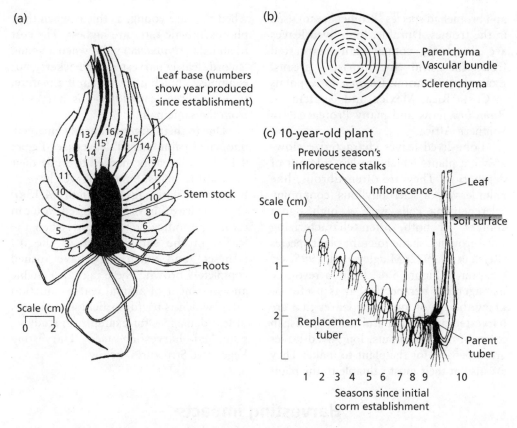

(a)

Leaf base (numbers
show year produced
since establishment)

Stem stock

Roots

Scale (cm)
0   2

(b)

Parenchyma
Vascular bundle
Sclerenchyma

(c) 10-year-old plant

Previous season's
inflorescence stalks

Inflorescence

Leaf

Scale (cm)

Soil surface

Replacement
tuber

Parent
tuber

1 2 3 4 5 6 7 8 9   10

Seasons since initial
corm establishment

Sources: (a) Ruiters et al, 1993; (b) Werner, 1978; (c) Pate and Dixon, 1982

Figure 4.12 *Ageing methods for bulbs and corms. (a) Median longitudinal section of a 16-year-old* Haemanthus pubescens *(Amaryllidaceae) bulb with numbered leaf bases to show how the bulb was aged. (b) Idealized transverse section of a perennial corm of* Liatris aspera *(Compositae) showing the location of the collateral vascular bundles which can be used to determine the age of individual corms. (c) Ten-year-old corm of* Philydrella pygmaea *(Philydraceae) showing the lateral accumulation of spent corms, which can be dissected and counted to assess the years since an individual plant was recruited as a seedling*

replacement ('daughter') tuber formed on the inner side of the previous season's stem tuber. As each tuber is surrounded by a persistent outer skin (epidermal sheath), Pate and Dixon were able to count the number of epidermal sheaths to assess the age of each plant. In *Drosera bulbosa*, this internal replacement continued for up to 17 years, and in *Drosera erythrorhiza*, for up to 60 years on lateritic soils, but only to 15 years or so in sandy soils.

Leaf life spans

In contrast to most edible greens with their soft, short-lived and tasty leaves, wild plants selected for durable qualities have a high lignin or fibre content (as a defence against herbivory and mechanical damage), and often have low rates of leaf production and long-lived leaves. Examples would be leaf selection for weaving fibre, such as many palms (Arecaceae), agave species (Agavaceae), and bromeliad species (Bromeliaceae) used in the tropics. Durable, long-lived leaves are also being commercially harvested from the wild for florists' greens. Examples are various *Chamaedorea* palms in Costa Rica, Mexico and Guatemala, *Rumohra* ferns and many Proteaceae in Southern Africa.

Long-lived leaves characterize slow-growing plants which are less tolerant of defoliation. They are often fibrous, like palm leaves, or sclerophyllous (containing sclerenchyma cells with a high lignin content) or both, often characterizing slow-growing, shade-tolerant plant species (Reich et al, 1992; Midgley et al, 1995; see Chapter 5, Figure 5.4). From a resource management perspective, it is useful to know the age of long-lived leaves that are harvested and their natural life spans. In terms of nutrient inputs, long-lived leaves are expensive for the plant to make. They are also at their most valuable to the plant when they are young, as this is when their photosynthetic rates are highest. The cost to an ilala (*Hyphaene*) palm when a young 'sword' leaf is harvested for basketry, for example, is much greater than if a mature, two- to three-year-old leaf is harvested from the same palm.

Due to their large size, newly emerged, unopened palm 'sword' leaves (see Figure 4.13c) can be easily marked to study their natural life spans. Smaller leaves have to be marked with tags (see Figure 4.13a). Once the leaves have been tagged, you can return periodically to record when the leaves in the sample start to die off (senesce) and when they have turned completely brown. These tags also enable an assessment of annual leaf-production rates, which is useful in field assessments of leaf damage – for example, in studying palm-leaf harvesting (see 'Harvesting Vegetative Structures' below).

Harvesting impacts

The effect of harvesting on individual plants will obviously vary according to what part of the plant is used – indeed, sometimes the whole plant is removed, making it very difficult to measure impacts unless harvesting occurred within a permanent plot (see Chapter 5). Harvesting impact on a plant also depends upon the frequency and intensity of harvest. Harvesting of leaves, fruits or flowers clearly has far less impact on individual plants than does damage to roots, bark, stems, or removal of the whole plant.

Whether recording damage to individual plants or plant populations, it is useful to have a systematic way of measuring individual plants, and field methods for assessing the intensity and frequency of harvest. This depends upon the funding and time you have available, as well as on plant population biology and growth form. In some cases, you may be guided by methods used by other researchers, while in other cases you may need to develop assessment methods yourself. It is also useful to learn from experimental studies that have measured the impact of harvesting on individual plants. In this section, I describe different field rating systems and the results of harvesting experiments (defoliation, debarking and bark regeneration, stem cutting and resprouting) which enable a better evaluation of the consequences of harvesting on individual plants. Although dealt with separately, it is important to bear in mind the direct links between harvesting the vegetative parts of the plant (stems, bark,

Sources: (a) and (b) S J Milton; (c) and (d) author

Figure 4.13 *(a) Seven-weeks fern (*Rumohra adiantiformis*) with metal tag, micrometer in front of the sampling grid. (b) Information provided by harvesters on season, size class and area harvested is very useful in designing defoliation experiments. (c) Mokola palm (*Hyphaene petersiana*) marked with paint. (d) Lawrence Mbatha and Sam Ncube taking a monthly measurement of lala palm (*Hyphaene coriacea*) leaf growth*

roots, buds and leaves). Frequent and/or intense harvests of any of these vegetative structures will deplete the plants' carbohydrate reserves or disrupt water and nutrient flows.

Harvesting reproductive structures (flowers, fruits and seeds)

When you see wild-collected fruits, flowers or seeds in baskets at a marketplace, you may first assume that these were harvested with no impact on the individual plant. At first sight, harvesting of fruits, flowers or seeds may seem to be as close as people can get to sustainable harvest. Do not be too quick to make this assumption. Although harvesting of flowers or fruits generally has a low impact on individual plants, destructive harvesting – ironically of the most favoured species – has been recorded in many cases, with cutting of branches or even felling plants to collect flowers, fruits or seeds.

If neither pruning nor felling take place, then the main concern for sustainable harvesting of reproductive parts is at a species-population level (see Chapter 5) rather than concern for individual plants. The mental 'alarm bells' of the resource manager should go off loudest when the fruits of dioecious and monocarpic (hapaxanthic) reseeders are commercially traded. In this section, I discuss factors that lead to destructive harvesting of fruits, flowers or seeds, and methods for measuring the impact of this at the individual plant level.

To a certain extent, the 'behavioural bottleneck', as Rodolfo Vasquez and Al Gentry (1989) called the felling of trees for their fruits for commercial trade, is predictable on the basis of **fruiting phenology**, whether plants are **dioecious** or **monoecious**, on **fruit accessibility**, on **demand** for the fruits and on **tree tenure**. All of these should be noted in the field.

The first three of these are biological factors and are discussed below. Commercial sale of fruits or flowers is a good indicator of which fruits or flowers are in highest demand (see Chapter 3). The majority of destructively harvested flowers or fruits enter commercial trade, but some are collected only for home consumption. In the Peruvian Amazon, for example, the seeds of *hambre huayo* (*Gnetum leyboldii* and *Gnetum nodiflorum*) vines were not recorded sold in Iquitos market, but the vines were down-pulled out of the forest to collect the edible seeds (Vasquez and Gentry, 1989). From a plant biology perspective, it is useful to record the following as predictive factors of destructive harvest of fruits.

Fruiting phenology

The timing of fruit release is a major influence on harvesting method. If fruits fall and can be collected from the ground, then harvesting impacts are likely to be low. If the plants are tall and the fruits therefore difficult to reach, then felling for favoured fruits is likely. For this reason, you need to check whether the fruits are:

- shed as soon as they are ripe (or sometimes just before, so that final ripening takes place on the ground), such as in Brazil nut (*Bertholletia excelsa* – Lecythidaceae) or marula (*Sclerocarya birrea* – Anacardiaceae) trees;
- slowly released over a period of weeks or even months, the rest of the fruits displayed to potential dispersal agents (birds, primates) in the canopy, something common with many palm species;
- serotinous, where seeds are held for 1 to 30 years in canopy seed stores, a reproductive strategy recorded for at least 530 species in 40 genera of woody

plants (Lamont et al, 1991), most commonly in the Bruniaceae, Ericaceae, Myrtaceae, Pinaceae and Proteaceae; when serotinous species are harvested for flowers or fruits, stems (with foliage) are often cut as well, with the added impact of removing new, long-lived and metabolically active leaves.

This issue is clearly illustrated in Oliver Phillips's (1993) survey of fruit accessibility and local harvesting methods for over 30 species of preferred edible fruit-bearing trees in the Peruvian Amazon. Where l0 per cent or fewer of edible fruits fell onto the ground and fruit access height was between 8 and 23 metres, then trees were felled.

Dioecious, monoecious or hermaphroditic?

Dioecious species bear male and female flowers on separate plants. Monoecious plants have male and female flowers on different parts of the same plant. Hermaphroditic plants have flowers with both stamens and carpels. Dioecy is common amongst long-lived perennial plants, many of which produce large, edible fruits (such as the Anacardiaceae and Palmae family). This has important implications for fruit and flower harvesting at the individual plant and population levels. At the individual plant level, when destructive harvest of fruits (eg Palmae) or flowers (eg Proteaceae, Bruniaceae) takes place in dioecious species, it is obviously selective of female plants. At a plant population level, overexploitation of female plants can totally disrupt breeding systems. In addition, plant species harvested for flowers, particularly those in the Bruniaceae and Proteaceae, are susceptible to fungal infection.

Access height

Are fruits accessible or out of reach of human harvesters? Tall plants bearing popular but inaccessible fruits are likely to get felled or, if vines or lianas, pulled out of the forest canopy. It is a good idea to record how harvesting behaviour is influenced by access height. In a study in the Amazon, for example, Oliver Phillips (1993) recorded fruiting phenology, access height and divided harvesting methods into five categories: *Ground* = collect felled fruits from the ground; *Picked* = fruits picked by hand; *Pole* = fruits knocked (or pulled) down with a hooked pole; *Climb* = tree climbed and fruits cut or shaken off; and *Cut* = whole tree cut down for fruits. In my experience, these are widely applicable in Asia and Africa as well.

Direct assessment of nutrient depletion or susceptibility to fungal attack requires field experiments backed up by laboratory work. In short-term surveys, these indirect impacts can be assessed in terms of crown die-back or death (see Figure 4.14). Field researchers have also used a rating system in short-term assessments of the effects of picking serotinous flowers or fruits, which requires cutting branch stems as well. In a study of the effects of foliage removal on multi-stemmed, 1m to 3m tall *Brunia albiflora* (Bruniaceae) plants, Tony Rebelo and Pat Holmes (1988) rated plants according to plucking intensity on a six-point scale:

1   dead with no evidence of plucking (*K*);
2   killed by harsh plucking (*D*);
3   alive, but harshly plucked (>90 per cent of the estimated original foliage removed);
4   alive and heavily plucked (>50 per cent and <90 per cent of the estimated original foliage removed);
5   alive and lightly plucked (<50 per cent of estimated original foliage removed);
6   alive and not plucked (*U*).

In addition, in each population of *Brunia*

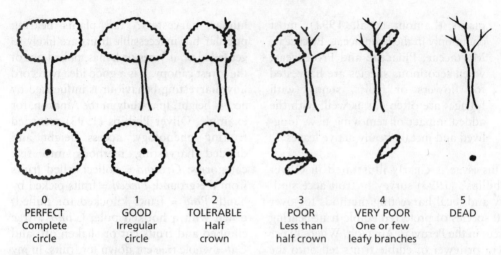

0	1	2	3	4	5
PERFECT	GOOD	TOLERABLE	POOR	VERY POOR	DEAD
Complete	Irregular	Half	Less than	One or few	
circle	circle	crown	half crown	leafy branches	

Definition of crown ratings
0 = Perfect: excellent size and development, wide, symmetrical and generally circular in plan.
1 = Good: slightly asymmetrical with some dead branch tips ('silviculturally satisfactory' to foresters).
2 = Tolerable: markedly asymmetrical, some dieback.
3 = Poor: extensive die-back, leaves form less than half original crown size.
4 = Very poor: badly damaged, unlikely to survive.
5 = Dead.

Figure 4.14 *Although used by Dawkins (1958) to rate tree-crown condition, due to various reasons, including competition, crown ratings also reflect tree health generally, for instance as a secondary response to bark or root use*

albiflora, they recorded **plant height** and **stem diameter** at 30cm above ground level, and the number of individual seed heads (infructescences) produced in that year, for all plants in a series of one-metre wide random transects. Knowing that grouped flower heads (conflorescences) are produced on main vertical stems of *Brunia albiflora* plants every alternate year during April and May, and that these are retained on the plant for at least four to six years, they were also able to estimate when the harvesting of seed heads had taken place.

More detailed studies on flower harvesting in the Proteaceae in South Africa (*Protea*, *Leucodendron*) (Mustart and Cowling, 1992) and Australia (*Banksia*) (Witkowski, Lamont and Obbens, 1994) have both shown the extent to which commercial flower picking results in a decline in plant canopy volume and seed production, affecting both individual plants and plant populations (see Chapter 5).

Harvesting plant exudates (gums, resins and latexes)

Latex is a rubbery exudate tapped from the bark of trees and lianas in the Apocynaceae (*Dyera*, *Couma*, *Landolphia*), Euphorbiaceae (*Euphorbia*), Moraceae (*Ficus*), Sapotaceae (*Manilkara*, *Palaquium*) and other plant families. Gums are water-soluble exudates, primarily from woody plants in the Leguminosae (*Acacia*, *Astragalus*) and Sterculiaceae (*Sterculia*). Resins are divided into two groups, both tapped from tree bark. There are hard resins, such as copal from trees in the Araucariaceae (*Agathis*) and damar from Dipterocarpaceae (*Shorea*, *Hopea*, *Vatica*), and soft resins (or balsams), such as benzoin from *Styrax* (Styracaceae) and copaiba from *Copaifera* (Fabaceae). Most commercially traded gums, resins and latexes are produced from deliberately damaging tree or shrub bark. Exceptions

(a)

(b)

Diameter growth (%)

—○— No tapping
—□— Normal tapping
—△— Heavy tapping

Years

Source: Dijkman (1951) in Peters, 1994

Figure 4.15 *(a) Methods of latex tapping from the rubber tree (*Hevea brasiliensis*). (b) Comparison of plantation rubber tree growth rates under two different tapping regimes compared against untapped trees*

are gums and resins produced from tapping roots (asafoetida from several *Ferula* species Umbelliferae and gum tragacanth from several *Astragalus* species) or fruits (East Indian dragon's blood resin from the fruits of several rattan palm *Daemonorops* species). Resin and latex exude from existing resin canals in the bark and wood. In gum-producing species, the gum ducts only form after the bark is slashed (lysigenous ducts).

Despite low exudate yields, commercial trade is amazingly high. In 1993, for example, Sudan exported 11,410 tonnes of gum arabic from *Acacia senegal*, Indonesia 13,285 tonnes of jelutong latex from hill jelutong, *Dyera costulata*, and swamp jelutong, *D. lowii*, trees (Apocynaceae), and India 1443 tonnes of karaya gum from *Sterculia urens* and *S. villosa* (Sterculiaceae). Given that exudate yields are relatively low – *Acacia* yields 250 grams per tree per season, *Dyera* yields 3.5kg of

coagulated latex per tree per month, and *Sterculia* yields 1 to 5 kg per tree per season – the number of trees involved in commercial exudate tapping is considerable.

In common with the fruit harvesting example in the previous section, it is easy to assume that plant exudates can be sustainably harvested. This is certainly possible, offering the opportunity to tap trees by periodically making cuts in the bark to maintain a flow of exudate. In this way, trees and shrubs are maintained in steppe, savanna or forest, thus generating a commercial resource without felling. However, tapped plants do pay a high physiological price when nutrient-rich exudates are removed, growing much slower and sometimes not fruiting at all (see Figure 4.15b). In cases where communal or private ownership is established for exudate producing plants, then sustainable harvesting generally takes place. Strict tenure is established in parts of Somalia, for example,

131

where *Boswellia* (Burseraceae) shrubs are tapped for frankincense (gum olibanum), with *Boswellia* stands belonging to extended family groups (Coppen, 1995). Other cases where tenurial rights are established for exudate production are examples from Sudan (gum arabic from *Acacia senegal*) and southern Sumatra where the damar gardens (*kebun damar*) of *Shorea javanica* are a model of tropical agroforestry.

Unfortunately, cases of destructive harvesting for exudate are common. The classic example is a *Ferula* species known as 'silphion', tapped for an aromatic, medicinal gum for trade from North Africa to the Roman Empire, and providing one of the earliest examples of plant extinction through overexploitation. Other cases are more recent. Industrial companies established in Mozambique and South Africa in the late 19th and early 20th centuries to extract latex from *Landolphia kirkii* liana stems all collapsed, overexploiting a resource which had been sustainably harvested for its fruits for centuries (Cunningham, 1985). In Indian savanna, mukul trees (*Commiphora wightii*) and the source of karaya gum (*Sterculia urens*) have also been heavily exploited.

The methods that can be used to measure harvesting impacts vary according to the tapping method and the time available. The impact of the least damaging form of tapping is best measured through long-term comparative studies of tree growth rates under different tapping frequencies and intensities. In South-East Asia, for example, high frequency tapping reduced the growth rates of rubber trees (*Hevea brasiliensis*) by up to 50 per cent over a five-year period (see Figure 4.15b).

A similar approach could be taken in a long-term comparison of growth increments of tapped and untapped tropical forest trees, such as *Garcinia xanthochymus* (Guttiferae), tapped for an orange latex (gamboge) in order to dye Buddhist robes in South-East Asia, and *Copaifera* species (Leguminosae), tapped for resin in Central America and South America. *Copaifera* trees are tapped for oleo-resins in Brazil and Colombia by boring into the trunk to tap resin-filled cavities. Indirect measurements of oleo-resin yields show that although first tapping yields are high (up to 3 litres), these progressively decline over a 3.5-year period (Alencar, 1982). The effects of this process on tree growth or fruit production have not been studied.

Harvesting vegetative structures (leaves, roots, bark, stems)

Leaf harvesting

It is useful to think of the impact of leaf harvesting in terms of plant growth rates and life spans (see earlier section on 'Leaf life spans'). At one extreme is the use of edible wild greens and, at the other, leaves harvested for fibrous and long-lasting qualities. Collection of edible leafy greens ('spinaches') is generally selective for the young leaves of crop plants such as Curcurbitaceae or fast-growing plant species in recently disturbed sites (Amaranthaceae, Capparaceae, Tiliaceae), or leaves from annual or biennial aboveground stems and leaves that are produced from a perennial tuberous root, such as in some Cucurbitaceae and Acanthaceae. Edible leaves are generally gathered from fast-growing species from early successional stages, often in nutrient-rich sites such as agricultural fields, alluvial terraces along river banks, forest margins or canopy gaps, roadsides, or old livestock pens.

Long-lived leaves characterize long-lived, slow-growing plants (see Chapter 5). These plants invest more in physical or chemical defences. Harvesting leaves for their fibrous qualities (basketry, thatching, twine) involves leaf gathering from plants with long-leaf life spans and slower

growth rates, typically from later successional stages. Two methods can be used to
assess the impact of defoliation on plants.
Ideally, both should be used, the first as a
quicker 'reality check' and the other as a
controlled experiment to assess plant
response to harvesting in a rural situation
where intensive management outside of an
experiment may well be unlikely. The two
methods are listed below.

Retrospective counts of harvested leaves

Plants such as palms and ferns which
produce large leaves are ideal for undertaking an initial 'first approximation' of
defoliation rates based on a knowledge of
annual leaf-production rates from tagged
leaves on plants in different size classes
(see Figure 4.13). It is important to be
aware that young palm seedlings (genets)
or sprouts (ramets) may have differently
shaped 'sword' leaves compared to older
plants. Harvesters generally harvest larger
leaves from older palms, however, rather
than seedling leaves, since in most cases
long leaflets are preferred for basketry or
building. Once the seedling stage is passed,
palms generally bear bigger leaves as they
get older, with a relationship between
leaflet size class (see Figure 4.16a) and
stem size class. In some cases, however,
petiole width can provide a statistically
significant correlation with palm-leaf size
class, and this has been used instead of leaf
length (Joyal, 1996).

Unless you are working with palms
which show no difference in leaf production rate with increase in stem size, you
need to take the increased annual leaf-
production rate into account to avoid
biased results in a retrospective assessment
of the number of leaves harvested per year.
In his study of the vegetable ivory palm
(*Phytelephas seemannii*) in Colombia, for
example, Rodrigo Bernal (1998) developed a regression equation to calculate

annual leaf-production rate (y), based on
stem length (x), where $y = 5.8 + 0.0065x$
as a way of avoiding the inaccuracy of
using average annual leaf-production rates
for plants of all sizes.

If you look at the youngest emerging
shoot in the centre (apex) of a palm stem,
you will notice that leaves are produced in
a radial sequence. The youngest shoot is
just emerging, a newly emerged 'sword
leaf' is next to it, and next to that a fully
opened leaf, and so on. Let us assume, for
example, that the stem size class you are
looking at produces five leaves per year. If
you count five leaves 'backwards' from the
most recently emerged 'sword leaf', this
would represent the annual leaf production over the past year. This is shown
diagramatically in Figure 4.16b. You
should also record the number of leaves
that have been harvested, browsed by
cattle or damaged in some other way.
Browsing by animals is recognizable due
to the jagged defoliation pattern compared
to the clean cut from harvesting of the
leaves with a *panga* or sharp knife (see
Figure 4.16c and d).

Repeating this process for many stems
in a sample population enables you to
assess relatively quickly the proportion of
annual leaf-production cut by local
harvesters and the size-class selection for
particular plants, leaf sizes or leaf ages. It
also provides good insight into the
complexity of multiple-use of the same
plants. The same palm, for example, might
be used for its young leaves (weaving), old
leaves (housing), grazing by livestock or
cut for palm hearts. A disadvantage is that
this is not a long-term experiment which
enables the response of plants to defoliation to be compared against a control. You
also need to bear in mind that the effects
of defoliation on individual stems of clonal
ramets is more complicated than on single
plants grown from seed. Clonal plants can
partially compensate for loss of leaf area

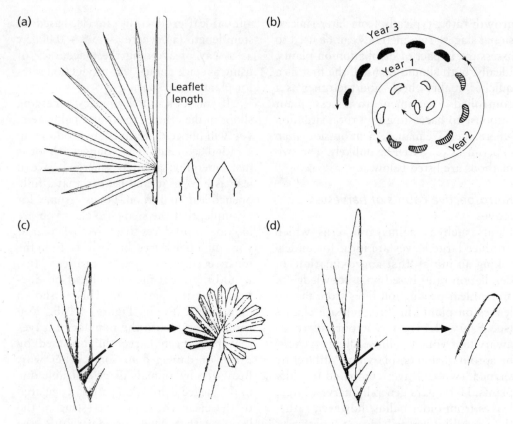

Figure 4.16 *(a) Measurement of leaflet length in* Hyphaene *palms, showing point of measurement where the leaf base is oblique or 'normal'. (b) Diagrammatic representation of 'retrospective' leaf counts viewing the palm stem apex from above for a palm producing five leaves per year. (c) and (d) A straight cut across the petiole of the young 'sword' leaf or across the unopened leaf is clearly visible in retrospective leaf counts even two to three years later, and is also distinguishable from the jagged browsing of palm leaves by livestock*

by reallocating nutrients from one part of the clone to another.

Simulated defoliation

This is applicable to any plant and has been applied to woody plants, grasses and palms. A typical case would be to select 20 to 30 plants for a control treatment with no (0 per cent) defoliation, and the same number in increasing, successive levels of annual defoliation. These are commonly 25 per cent, 50 per cent and 100 per cent defoliation (Oyama and Mendoza, 1990; Ratsirarson et al, 1996) or 30 per cent, 60 per cent and 100 per cent defoliation (Mendoza et al, 1987). A good example is the well-designed study by Ana Mendoza and her colleagues on the effects of defoliation on the palm *Astrocaryum mexicanum* (Mendoza et al, 1987). In their study, they used three different defoliation rates for palms in four stages (seedlings, juveniles, immature and mature) over a four-year period. The effects of defoliation were measured in terms of changes in the rate of leaf production, fruit production, palm survival and the probability of reproducing. Furthermore, it is possible to compare the effects of defoliation on male versus female palms, as Ken Oyama and Ana Mendoza (1990) did with the dioecious palm, *Chamaedorea tepejilote*. If you are uncertain about experimental design, it is important that you consult a statistician. Useful text books on experimental design and statistical techniques are by Maxwell and Delany (1989), Sokal and Rohlf (1987) and Zar (1998).

An advantage of the experimental defoliation method is that you are able to assess the response of different size classes of plants to different levels of defoliation. A disadvantage is that defoliation experiments take a considerable amount of time and effort if they are carried out properly. Defoliation treatments need to be continued for several years – for example, to avoid being misled by short-term 'compensatory growth' of leaves in the first year or two, which gives the impression that high rates of defoliation merely stimulate leaf or fruit production.

The effects of defoliation are strongly influenced by factors such as plant physiology, the intensity and frequency of harvest, and habitat. Woody plants show great variation in their tolerance to pruning (Lay, 1965; Trlica et al, 1977). Tolerance of defoliation also depends upon whether defoliation takes place when total non-structural carbohydrate reserves in the root and stem are low (Menke and Trlica, 1981). Plant species palatable to animals appear to be more tolerant of leaf removal. Defoliation of long-lived large leaves from plants can have a high impact on the plant, particularly if leaf removal takes place shortly after the leaf has matured. At high (greater than 50 per cent) defoliation levels, this frequently results in subsequent depression of leaf productivity. Slow-growing ferns, for example, are vulnerable to defoliation. Milton (1987), in a study on the effects of harvesting several fern genera (*Blechnum*, *Polystichum* and *Rumohra*), which are harvested from Afromontane forest in Southern Africa, found that defoliation resulted in smaller frond size and but no change in frond production rate. Even after five years, seven-weeks ferns (*Rumohra adiantiformis*) had not recovered from defoliation for florists' greenery (Milton, 1991).

Bark harvesting

Bark, produced by a thin layer of cambium cells, surrounds the xylem tissues that transport water and nutrients to and from the roots and leaves. Bark protects plants against fire, fungal and insect attack, and bark removal can therefore have serious consequences for the plant. Bark harvesting is often highly selective for family, genera or species, based on particular bark qualities. Many species in the Bombacaceae, Malvaceae, Moraceae, Sterculiaceae, Thymeleaceae, Tiliaceae and Urticaceae, for example, are used to make twine for trapping, fishing, weaving or home construction. Bark is often rich in secondary plant chemicals, and many species in the Apocynaceae, Euphorbiaceae and Loganiaceae, for instance, are widely used for traditional medicines. Similarly, the Ebenaceae (*Diospyros*, *Euclea*) are a rich source of phenolic compounds used as dyes. For this reason, species-specific bark removal takes place for medicinal purposes or dyes.

Bark damage may remain visible for many years, enabling field assessments of the extent of damage to species populations due to bark removal. Figure 4.17 shows a simple seven-point scale for rating debarking damage on tree trunks. This can be combined with diameter (dbh) measurements to assess bark damage within a tree population. It is important to record factors that influence the intensity of bark removal, such as the following.

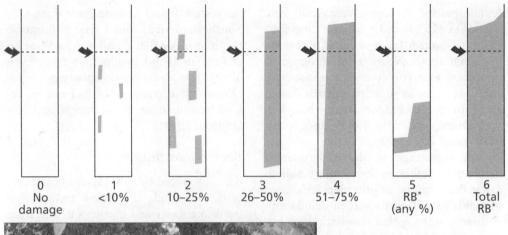

0	1	2	3	4	5	6
No damage	<10%	10–25%	26–50%	51–75%	RB* (any %)	Total RB*

Definition of bark damage ratings

0 = No damage

1 = Small patches removed (<10% of trunk bark) (usually by traditional healers for local use)

2 = Larger patches removed (10–25% trunk bark). Usually scarce species in high local demand or small-scale, emerging commercial trade

3 = Large strips (26–50% of trunk bark), generally from popular, open-access species in commercial trade

4 = Extensive bark removal (51–75% of trunk bark), popular species in large-scale commercial trade, easy and open access

5 = Ringbarking or girdling, where bark is completely removed around the trunk. This leads to death of many tree species, regardless of level of girdling

6 = Complete girdling, all trunk bark removed. At this stage trees or large branches may be felled or trees climbed to maximize bark removal

Figure 4.17 *A seven-point scale used for bark damage ratings. The photograph shows a harvester removing medicinal bark from an Afromontane forest tree*

- What is the purpose for which the bark is removed? For example, traditional healers harvesting bark for their own use, rather than for commercial purposes, generally only require small quantities of bark. In contrast, bark twine production requires long strips of bark and large slabs of bark are needed for making bee hives, canoes, cloth and aboriginal bark paintings.

- Is the outer or inner bark removed and is the cambium exposed? Cork, used for flooring and bottle stoppers, is produced from the outer bark of the cork oak (*Quercus suber*), enabling bark removal on a rotational basis from the same trees. By contrast, the Australian black wattle (*Acacia mearnsii*), which is cultivated for its tannin-rich bark for the leather tanning industry, and the cinnamon tree (*Cinnamomum zeylanicum*), which is grown for its spicy bark, are both killed if bark is removed from the main trunk. For this reason, black wattle trees are used for fuelwood after being stripped of bark, the next generation growing up from seed, while cinnamon trees are grown on a coppice rotation, based on a succession of individual stems that are felled and stripped of bark.

- From what part of the plant is the bark removed (trunk, main branches, secondary branches)? Depending upon the tree species and bark quality, bark for twine may be removed from secondary branches rather than the main branches or tree trunk. Bark from thinner branches of the hippo fig (*Ficus trichopoda*), for example, is a source of strong twine that is easier to strip and roll into twine than bark from the trunk or main branches.

Research participants from the local community will often know the reason why bark has been removed. Be careful not to confuse casual bark slashes encountered along paths through forest or woodland with bark removed for other purposes, or with bark removed by animals. In many cases, careful inspection of the tree trunk or remaining bark will show teeth marks of bark-eating rodents such as porcupines, or tusk marks where elephants have removed bark. Similarly, cut marks from a machete or removal of more regularly shaped blocks of bark often distinguish bark removal by people.

Although many people believe that most tree species regenerate their bark after it has been damaged, this is not a common response to bark removal. The effects of bark removal on the plant depend upon **plant physiology**, **bark chemistry** and **exudates**, and the **intensity** and **frequency** of bark removal as well as **season**, **habitat** and **microclimate**. In the field, you will notice that a tree's ability to withstand bark removal varies with different plant families, species and even between individual plants. Many Proteaceae and Podocarpaceae are highly susceptible to fungal infection or attack by wood-boring insects. The endemic Afromontane forest tree *Faurea macnaughtonii* (see Figure 4.18b) is one such example. In Australia, the cinnamon fungus (*Phytophthora cinnamoni*) poses a major conservation threat to many endemic Proteaceae. On the other hand, plants in some families, such as the Euphorbiaceae, Moraceae and Canellaceae, show a marked resilience to bark removal, in part because the cambium is protected by exudates after bark removal, enabling bark to regenerate outwards from the scarred area rather than inwards from the sides of the wound. The African baobab (*Adansonia digitata*) is very unusual (and resilient) to bark damage, with parenchyma cells right through the old wood forming a callus-like tissue that seals off the wound and produces new bark (Fischer, 1981).

Source: (c) and (d) with permission from Robin Guy

Figure 4.18 *(a) Resilience to bark removal due to bark regeneration by secondary xylem: baobab trees* (Adansonia digitata) *debarked for twine in Malawi. (b) Vulnerability to removal of even a small patch (five-centimetre long slash), showing fungal infection after small-scale bark removal in the Afromontane endemic canopy tree* Faurea macnaughtonii. *(c) Complete girdling of* Brachystegia *trees is a common seasonal practice in miombo woodland through much of Eastern and South-Central Africa. (d) Dead* Brachystegia *– ironically, also the major source of honey to bees and beekeepers*

Frequency of bark removal is also an important factor, but very few studies have been performed on the long-term effects of periodic bark removal from tree species that regenerate bark after it has been removed. There is no doubt, however, that the stress of bark removal, which results in loss of nutrients and moisture, fungal infection or insect attack, even if it does not kill the tree, reduces the tree's growth rate and life span. Discussions with bark harvesters can also yield useful insights into whether repeated bark removal occurs and how harvesters feel that this influences bark quality. In Uganda, Natal figs (*Ficus natalensis*) may be debarked as many as 30 or 40 times within the life of a single tree (Picton and Mack, 1989), with harvesters considering that bark qualities were improved by harvesting, due to production of thinner, flexible bark.

Bark regrowth also varies with **site differences**, **season** and **microclimate**. Trunk-bark regrowth in windswept, drier sites is often poor compared with regrowth on trees in shady, moist sites protected from wind. A common East African example of sustainable bark harvesting based on bark regrowth and production is from *Ficus natalensis*, often planted in fields as a boundary marker and bark source. The process of bark removal and regeneration, described by Picton and Mack (1989), illustrates local knowledge of the importance of microclimate and of protecting the trunk from desiccation after bark removal:

> 'The bark itself is easily removed. First the outer surface is scraped off, usually with a knife; then circular incisions are made at the upper and lower levels of the main trunk and a single vertical incision is run down between the two. A tool made from a sharpened section of a banana leaf spine, or in some cases a section of the fruit-bearing stem of the banana, is worked in behind the exposed layer of bark which is carefully peeled away in a cylindrical strip. The average dimensions for such a strip would be about 12 feet by 2 feet. This process of stripping the bark does not damage the tree as the whole of the exposed trunk is immediately swathed in a bandage of banana leaves to protect it from exposure to the sun and the wind. After about a week the tree has already regenerated sufficiently for this protective covering to be removed. Any subsequent damage to the newly forming bark may be treated by the application of a poultice of sheep's dung.'

In common with the less damaging effects of defoliation, it is likely that two other factors, **season** or **phenological stage**, influence the impact of bark removal, although few data are available on how bark harvesting is influenced by these factors. It is likely, however, that bark removal during spring or summer would have a higher impact on the tree. Knowledge of the time when it is easiest to debark *Brachystegia* trees, for example, is widespread amongst beekeepers throughout the miombo (*Brachystegia* and *Julbernardia*) woodlands of Central and Southern Africa, although it is unlikely that *Brachystegia* trees would survive debarking in any season. In species such as *Ficus natalensis*, the easiest time to debark the tree, when the bark is looser during spring or summer, may in fact be the worst time for the tree itself.

Figure 4.19 *One of the problems of damage assessment and monitoring that illustrates the need for permanent plots: after a ten-year history of root removal for dyeing basketry, these stunted* Euclea divinorum *shrubs, pointed out by local research participant Julius Rivero, have been completely uprooted, obscuring any future signs that they were ever there*

Underground ethnobotany: roots, tubers, bulbs and corms

Nutrients and secondary plant chemicals are often concentrated in roots and bark. For this reason, selected species are harvested for use as medicine or food. Selection also depends upon **size** and/or **age**, **shape**, **chemistry** (medicinal plants, traditional dyes, fish poisons or food), **structure** (qualities such as fibrous root bark for twine or 'corky' root qualities for fishing floats) or **function** (as in well-developed underground storage organs for food or medicines). Assessing the extent of harvesting of underground plant parts is difficult for two reasons. Firstly, removal of bulbs, corms, tubers or tap roots often means that the whole plant is dug out. At most, the only sign that there was a plant may be a hole in the ground, which in many cases will fill in with soil or be obscured by regrowth of other vegetation. Secondly, even when more obvious lateral or tap-root removal has occurred, with signs of digging around the base of the stem, partial root removal is also difficult to assess as holes dug at an earlier stage may have filled in, obscuring the true extent of root damage.

When root harvesting is recent, it is possible to use a field rating scale for root damage. In many cases, however, this is not as useful as the rating system for bark damage, since root damage is often obscured when the holes from which roots were removed fill in with soil – for example, when trees fall over after lateral root removal or when shrubs are entirely removed (see Figure 4.19). Nevertheless, where root removal is recent, it is possible to rate damage to trees and shrubs using

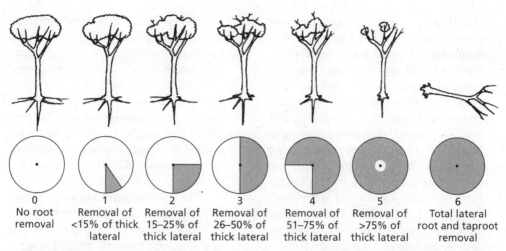

Figure 4.20 *A seven-point scale used for rating root harvesting damage. This is not as widely applicable as the bark damage scale, but is useful where recent destructive harvesting has taken place when a 'frontier' population has rapidly been exposed to high intensity or frequency of harvesting and where the soil shows clear signs of uprooting*

the rating systems shown in Figure 4.20. **Basal diameter (bd)** or **diameter at breast height (dbh)** should be recorded for each plant. Unless root removal is recent and clearly visible, however, this approach is likely to lead to an underestimate of damage to both individual plants and of overall damage to the species population, as dead trees or shrubs killed by earlier root damage may not be found.

Where damage is older, tree-crown death or complete tree die-off can take place after root removal, and it is useful to have a parallel assessment rating root damage (see Figure 4.20) and crown condition as a result of uprooting damage (see Figure 4.14).

Roots serve several important functions in most plants. They anchor the plant in the soil, or on host plants in the case of epiphytes or parasites, and they also absorb water and minerals. Foods produced in the leaves through photosynthesis move through the phloem tissue to be stored in the roots. Although the roots of many tropical and temperate plant species are harvested by herbalists, craft

workers or fishermen for use as medicines, dyes, fibres or fish poisons, experimental work on the effects of root removal has been limited to studies on temperate and deciduous fruit crops, such as apples and peaches. One example is **root pruning**, an old-fashioned technique used to manipulate the growth rate and leaf and fruit production of trees. As roots are not only storage organs, but also a place where some growth hormones are produced before being moved through the plant to the shoots and leaves, the effects of root harvesting can be very damaging to the plant. The impact of root damage depends on the following.

• **Type of roots harvested:** which roots are removed? Unless infection occurs, many trees and shrubs appear to survive removal of some lateral roots. Tap-root removal, however, has a high impact on most plants. Unless vegetative reproduction takes place, bulb or corm harvesting generally represents removal of the whole plant. Vegetative reproduction, through formation of

141

clonal populations in a variety of ways, is an important factor that can buffer the effects of root exploitation.

- **Plant physiology:** resilience to root removal varies with species. For example, damage to roots can stimulate regeneration in some plants, but lead to fungal infection in others. Members of the Proteaceae and Lauraceae family, in particular, are susceptible to infection by the fungus *Phytophthora cinnamoni* after root damage. There is little known about the more subtle effects of root pruning, such as an increase in secondary infections through root damage.

- **Rooting depth and distance:** rooting depth, and the distance that roots spread, influence both how easily roots are removed and the extent to which root removal affects the anchorage of the plant. Roots, bulbs or other underground plant parts near to the soil surface are clearly easier to remove, and these will be selected unless there is an incentive to remove more deeply rooted plants. Harvesting often focuses on lateral roots, rather than on tap roots, and on younger, more shallow-rooted corms, bulbs or tubers.

- **Intensity and frequency of damage:** this depends not only upon the type of roots which are harvested, but on how often root removal takes place, and on what proportion of the roots is removed. Just as plants need to maintain a certain leaf area for food production through photosynthesis, they also need to maintain enough root surface area for absorption of water and nutrients, as well as for anchorage and food storage. Field observation of lateral root removal for dyes, chewing sticks or traditional medicines shows die-off of trees when most lateral roots are removed. This is not an uncommon situation where

there is commercial demand for these resources, leading to local extinction through uprooting – for example, with *Berchemia discolor* and *Euclea divinorum* trees uprooted for dyes for commercial basketry production in Botswana (Cunningham and Milton, 1987; Cunningham, 1988), and with several *Garcinia* species (*G. mannii*, *G. epunctata*, *G. afzelii*) used for chewing sticks in West Africa.

The interactions between a low level of root removal on leaf, flower or fruit production are less obvious and less well known, although some possible effects can be inferred from fruit crops. Root pruning in apple trees reduces fruit yield, growth and leaf production (Schupp, 1992). In apple orchards, this is sometimes used to reduce fruit drop and to improve the colour and quality of the remaining fruits.

Field assessment: tree canopy (crown) health

During field work, you may have seen trees or shrubs showing die-back of the crown due to age, bark or root removal, or secondary factors such as fungal infection as a result of bark or root damage. This can be assessed quantitatively or visually, as foresters do when using the system of 'pre-emptive mortality' used by Amin Seydack and his colleagues (Seydack et al, 1995a, b) in Afromontane forest in South Africa, which marks trees for harvesting shortly before they would die anyway. The crown health rating is a visual rating method used by foresters (Philip, 1994; see Figure 4.14). It is also a useful indirect indicator of the effect of bark or root harvest on what were once healthy trees. The crown health rating method can be used together with direct ratings of bark or root damage described earlier in this chapter.

Stem harvesting

Tree, climber or shrub species and populations vary in their vulnerability to stem removal. Important questions to ask in the field are: is the species characteristically single stemmed or multi-stemmed? What are the selection criteria, if any? Do plants regenerate after stem cutting or not? Does this vary between sites or with stem age or diameter? Does the species have multiple uses and do these uses affect recruitment by exploiting different stem size classes within the same population?

Where stem harvesting occurs, resprouting adds resilience to the individual plant and plant population, so it is important to consider the importance of seeds or sprouts (vegetative shoots) in the regeneration of harvested plants. Regeneration after stem harvesting can be from seed or by sprouting (or both). Stem removal of single-stemmed plants can reduce reproductive output of the species population, but this is less often the case with multi-stemmed plants where several stems remain due to selective harvesting or where rapid resprouting occurs. By working with knowledgeable local people, it is also possible and useful to identify cut stumps to species level and to record how they were cut (with an axe, saw, chainsaw), the height of cut, the response to cutting (number and size of sprouts), and additional impacts affecting recovery (such as browsing by livestock or wildlife). In addition, measure basal diameters to determine the structure of sample populations before harvesting occurred.

Most trees resprout to some extent, some very vigorously, some only weakly, and a few, such as various *Podocarpus* and *Raphia* species, not at all. The ability to resprout is also affected by stump size. Many tree species which resprout vigorously when the stumps are small do not resprout from the large stumps of mature trees.

Growth rates after resprouting are a key factor in determining rotation times if coppice rotations are proposed as a management strategy. The ability to sprout in response to cutting does not automatically infer an advantage to harvested individuals or populations over reseeders. Dirk Muir (1990), for example, who worked with Zulu woodcutters in Hlatikulu forest, South Africa, compared two tree species with very different responses to stem removal for local building purposes. The first species, *umphatawenkosi* (*Strychnos usambarensis*, Loganiaceae) regenerated very well (79 per cent of cut stems) and the second, *idlabatega* (*Chionanthus foveolatus*, Oleaceae), regenerated poorly, with only 24 per cent of cut stems resprouting. Populations of both species were resilient to harvesting, however, presumably due to rapid seed regeneration in *C. foveolatus*.

Although quantitative studies of the standing stock of a plant resource or of the effects of harvesting start at the individual plant level, they are usefully put in perspective at the plant population level through studies of harvesting impacts and yields. This synthesis is the goal of the next chapter.

Chapter 5

Opportunities and Constraints on Sustainable Harvest: Plant Populations

Introduction

Although the response of individual plants to harvesting impacts provides useful information (see Chapter 4), it is crucial to avoid getting sidetracked when witnessing destructive harvest at the individual plant level. Harvesting has to be seen from the perspective of plant population dynamics, and harvested plant populations in turn need to be viewed in terms of their abundance, distribution and how they are influenced by disturbance at the landscape level (see Chapter 6). A seemingly low impact use, such as harvesting of fruits, for example, may have a high long-term effect on populations of that species, either because of long-term impact on seedling recruitment or because fruit collection involves tree felling. On the other hand, even if harvesting bark, roots, or stems kills some individual plants, it may have little impact on the populations of fast-growing, fast-reproducing species.

Harvesting of sweet-thorn (*Acacia karroo*) bark is a good example. At the individual plant level, local people commonly girdle trees for bark for making rope, which may kill the tree (see Figure 5.1). At a species population level, however, subsistence requirements for bark twine are easily met, as dying *Acacia karroo* trees are replaced by young, fast-growing plants from a soil seed bank. In addition, human and livestock impacts on the landscape favour *Acacia* populations, as intense grazing and exclusion of fire favour these trees and reduce competition from grasses. This is clearly seen in Figure 5.2, where *Acacia* populations have encroached upon what was open woodland outside a protected area, compared to the protected area itself, where open woodland has been maintained through controlled burning and lower levels of grazing.

Chapter 4 discussed methods for measuring plant size, age and the impacts of harvesting on individual plants. This chapter first discusses the biological factors that influence the resilience or sensitivity of plant populations of different species to harvesting and how this sensitivity should guide decisions on what species to monitor, including where and how. It then describes methods used to assess what is available (standing stock), harvesting impacts and yields at the plant population level. The necessary equipment, in addition to the items listed in Chapter 4, includes: measuring tapes (ideally a 30m or 50m tape marked in cm), calipers, field data sheets, pencils, flagging

Figure 5.1 *Good or bad, sustainable or not? For these* Acacia *trees, impact is high. They will not recover from bark removal for twine. This impact also needs to be seen, however, against a background of species population biology, where high growth rates and recruitment from a soil seed bank provide resilience against the death of debarked trees*

tape and a compass. If you are going to establish permanent plots, you will also need aluminium tree tags, 7cm long aluminium nails, hammers, cable ties, and bright paint (blue or yellow). Aerial photographs and, if available, large-scale vegetation maps are also useful. If you decide to develop population projection matrix models, you will also need a desk-top or lap-top computer and an appropriate spreadsheet programme.

Plant populations and practical constraints: selecting species

When choosing which species will be the focus of density, yield or harvesting-impact studies, two important factors need to be taken into account. Firstly, is harvesting considered from the perspective of local livelihoods or conservation – species loss through overexploitation benefits neither local people nor conservation in the long

145

Figure 5.2 Acacia *population dynamics: high recruitment and high tree growth rates – coupled with a habitat factor of disturbance due to removal of grass cover, with high cattle numbers and exclusion from fire – result in a high density and number of* Acacia *trees outside (left) compared to inside (right) a protected area (Mkuze Game Reserve, Natal, South Africa)*

term. Unrestricted access to a valued but vulnerable species may provide a high initial harvest, but this will merely be a temporary 'bonanza' followed by loss of local self-sufficiency and higher effort or prices to get the species elsewhere. When conservation becomes the focus of high-impact harvesting, overexploitation also undermines the primary goal of any protected area: the maintenance of habitat and species diversity.

Secondly, the assessments of standing crop, plant densities, yields or harvesting impacts can be expensive and time consuming. While participatory rural appraisal (PRA) methods provide useful background information for studies of plant population dynamics, there are no 'quick fixes'. At the same time, while there is no substitute for quantitative studies of plant population dynamics as a basis for

making decisions for conservation or resource management, these data can take decades to collect. Recruitment of young plants and mortality rates of plant populations, for example, are generally derived from long-term census data on marked plant populations in permanent sample plots (PSPs). The dilemma many field workers face is that decisions on resource management are often urgently required, yet hundreds of species are harvested, with little or no published data on their growth rates, biomass or demography. Good examples are the hundreds of medicinal plant species sold at markets in South Africa (500 species) or Brazil (600 species), including every plant life form, from herbs to forest trees. We therefore need to use whatever 'short cuts' we can, including conceptual 'filters' for choosing priority species.

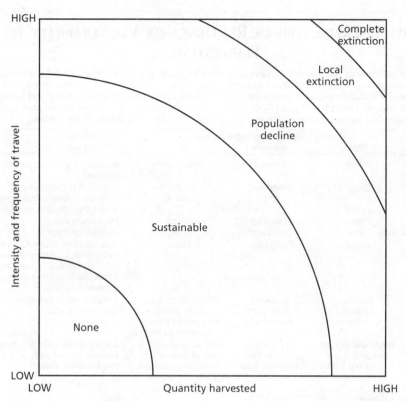

Source: modified from Bennett, 1992

Figure 5.3 *The effects of harvesting on a plant population depend upon what part of the plant is harvested and on the quantity, intensity and frequency of harvesting. Most harvesting has some effect, but local extinction is infrequent and extinction of the harvested species even rarer. When extinction occurs, it is usually a product of habitat destruction coupled with commercial harvesting of restricted range species*

'Filters' for choosing priority species for monitoring

Whether you are walking through a market or on a forest trail, knowing the scientific names of the species you encounter is undoubtedly important (see Chapter 2). It is also useful to think of grouping plants together in alternative ways, and several of these have been covered already. Harvested plant species can be grouped according to demand – for example, the quantity harvested (see Chapter 2) – or according to whether they are used for subsistence or commercial purposes (see Chapter 3). They can also be grouped in relation to the part

of the plant which is harvested, or by harvesting intensity and frequency (see Chapter 4). We know, for example, that species in low demand or species harvested at a low frequency and intensity are of less concern compared to species where bark or roots are in high demand (see Chapter 3), and that a shift from subsistence to commercial trade often results in an influx of harvesters, breakdown of local tenure systems and an increased intensity and frequency of harvesting (see Chapter 7). We also know that the likelihood of overexploitation and population decline increases with how much is harvested and

BOX 5.1 PREDICTORS OF RESILIENCE OR VULNERABILITY TO HARVESTING

Predictors of resilience or vulnerability to harvesting based on geographic distribution, habitat specificity, local population size, growth rates, part of the plant used, variety of uses and reproductive biology. These need to be linked to social and economic factors (commercial versus. subsistence use) (see Chapters 2 and 3) and strength of local land or resource tenure systems (see Chapter 7). An additional 'flag' from an international plant conservation perspective (but not relevant to village-level harvesters) would be phylogenetic distinctiveness.

	Opportunity for sustainable harvest			Predictors and
Criteria	High	Medium	Low	information sources
Geographic distribution	Wide	Limited	Restricted	Herbarium and distribution records[1]
Habitat specificity	Broad	Restricted	Highly specific	Life-form (eg widespread ruderals (therophytes), clonal sprouters, nitrogen fixing or not)
Local population sizes	Often large	Large to medium	Everywhere small	Herbarium and distribution records
Growth rates	Rapid	Fairly rapid	Slow	Tree seedling Relative Growth Rates (RGRs) and Specific Leaf Area (SLA) ratios,[2,3] data on productivity, growth rates and biomass production
General resource group	Leaves, flowers, fruits	Exudates, deadwood phloem sap	Whole plant, bark, roots, apical meristems (non-sprouting palms)	Case studies of resource resilience or crash
Single versus multiple use	Single use or non-competing use species (eg fruits, leaves)	Few uses, low conflict between uses	Multiple,conflicting uses of several size classes (eg different stem size classes, bark and roots)	Local market and household surveys, impact and regeneration studies
Reproductive biology[4]				
Pollination	Wind and other abiotic pollination. Many viable seeds or asexual reproduction (clonal sprouters)	Common biotic pollinators (insects, birds)	Highly specific pollinator mutualisms (eg temperate shrublands of SW Australia and South Africa (specific flies, bees, beetles, butterflies) or bats/nectar feeding birds in tropical rainforests)	Pollination ecology and study of the mutualism between plants and pollinators or dispersers[5]
Dispersal	Wind, water (or other) abiotic dispersal	Common, generalist biotic dispersers (small birds, small mammals)	Reseeders/weak resprouters, dispersal by large (frequently overhunted) mammals or large birds	Ecological studies of dispersal, local knowledge of animal/bird feeding behaviour
Costs and complexity: monitoring and management	Vegetation dominated by few (1–3) species. High plant biomass and production (eg grassland or swamp dominated by Poaceae, Cyperaceae or Juncaceae or 'oligarchic' forest (eg palm dominated))	Savanna or woodland with low diversity (less than 10 tree species >10cm dbh/ha) or grassland with low medicinal geophyte diversity	High diversity (>50 spp/ha) low biomass/species, long plant lifespans, high impact harvest (bark, roots, stems, timber, whole plants)	Time required per ha for adequate monitoring and management of sustainable harvest
Phylogenetic distinctiveness	Species in large genera (eg *Euphorbia*, *Astragalus*)	Species in medium to large genera	Species in monotypic families and monotypic genera	Taxonomic reviews[6]

Notes: 1 Rabinowitz, Cairns and Dillon, 1986; 2 Reich, Walters and Ellsworth, 1992; 3 Midgely, Everard and van Wyk, 1995; 4 Peters, 1994; 5 Bond, 1994; 6 Mabberley, 1987

BOX 5.2 VULNERABILITY OR RESILIENCE TO HARVESTING

Although harvesting of different plant parts can be grouped into lower-impact (leaves, flowers, fruits) and higher-impact uses (bark, roots, stems, whole plant), each of these can be subdivided according to the biology of the plant species concerned. While tapping of exudates or harvesting deadwood can be classed as lower impact uses, this varies so much according to harvesting method (eg selective cutting versus felling the entire tree) that these are excluded here.

| Criteria | Opportunity for sustainable harvest[1] | | | Predictors |
	High	Medium	Low	
Lower impact				
Leaves	Rapid leaf growth and production rates. Deciduous	Slow leaf production rates, long leaf lifespans. Evergreen	Very slow leaf production rates, very long leaf lifespans and few leaves (1–10 leaves/yr)	Leaf-life spans, Specific Leaf Area (SLA) ratios
Fruits/flowers	Many small flowers or fruits produced annually	Medium size flowers or fruits, periodic (1–2 yr) and abundant	Few, large flowers/ fruits, serotinous or mast-fruiting dioecious and/or recalcitrant	Fruit size, serotiny, seedling bank versus soil seed bank of orthodox seeds, dioecy versus monoecy
Higher impact				
Bark	Sap protects cambium rapid bark regeneration (eg some Moraceae)	Good regeneration in favourable sites (eg *Warburgia* (Canellaceae) *Adansonia* (Bombacaceae)	Cambium dies in area where bark is removed, sensitivity to fungal or insect attack (eg Proteaceae, Podocarpaceae)	Field observation, impact assessments in sites with high harvest levels
Stems	Vigorous resprouters, small size classes used (= rapid rotation times) or stems of large Poaceae (eg bamboo)	Resprouters, small/medium size classes cut	Reseeders, no/weak resprouts, hapaxanthic, dioecious, large individuals cut	Reproductive biology, growth rates, impact assessment in high impact sites
Roots	High production rates, sap production seals wounds. Sexual reproduction (from seed) common as well as being clonal resprouters	Intermediate	Low root production rates, sensitive to fungal attack. Slow growing resprouters that rarely reproduce from seed are very vulnerable	Field observation, impact assessment in high harvest level sites. Reproductive biology and growth rates are useful predictors
Whole plants	Common, fast growing ruderals (eg Asteraceae, Acanthaceae, Amaranthaceae, Poaceae, Chenopodiaceae)	Intermediate (eg some Cyperaceae and Fabaceae)	Long-lived, slow growing, hapaxanthic species with long times to reproductive maturity	Life-form, reproductive biology, plant architecture,[2] growth rates

Notes: 1 modified from Peters, 1994; 2 Halle and Oldeman, 1970

the intensity and frequency of harvest. These simple categorizations, summarized in Figure 5.3, help prioritize species for studies of density, regeneration rate, yield or harvesting impact at a plant population level.

Think of this as a series of 'filters' which help to sift out species that are likely to be resilient or more vulnerable to overharvesting. In Box 5.1, for example, plant resources are grouped according to

their potential for sustainable harvest, from high potential (leaves, flowers, fruits) to low potential (bark, roots or the whole plant).

Each of these coarse filters can be subdivided again on the basis of functional ecological attributes and field observation (see Box 5.2).

Despite the coarseness of these filters, thinking about plant species in this way is a useful process towards a 'first approximation' of plant species where there is a high or low opportunity for sustainable harvest. The next sections describe the theoretical background to some of these 'filters'. Readers who are not directly concerned with these issues may prefer to go directly to the next section: 'Costs and Complexity: Inventory, Management and Monitoring'.

Bridging gaps in knowledge: life forms, plant architecture and reproductive strategies

Developing an ecological perspective that cuts across taxonomic boundaries at a species level is a useful tool for grouping harvested plant species and setting priorities for detailed studies of density, yield or harvesting impacts. In almost any society, people classify plants according to their growth form – for example, as trees, shrubs, vines, lianas, epiphytes or grasses. For centuries, botanists and ecologists have developed classification systems based on plant attributes that group plants into different categories. Several of these may already be familiar to you, such as plant life form (Raunkiaer, 1934), plant architecture (Hallé and Oldeman, 1970), leaf characteristics (Reich et al, 1992), reproductive strategies (reseeders versus resprouters) or seed characteristics (orthodox versus 'recalcitrant' seeds) In forests, it is possible to identify 'guilds' of plants based on successional stage (early pioneer, late secondary, primary forest species), or to group plant species according to their light requirements, such as shade-tolerant versus light-demanding species, or 'gap' versus 'non-gap' species. As you walk through grassland, savanna or along a forest trail, coming out of deep shade and dappled light into sun-filled gaps edged with vines and large-leaved shrubs and young trees, it is a useful exercise to think about how the plant species you see fit into these categories and how different 'guilds' of species are influenced by disturbance, such as fire, drought, disease, tree falls or clearing of habitat.

These classifications get away from the detail of species-level identifications and enable plants to be sorted into functional ecological groups; they give a better insight into plant population dynamics and improve our ability to predict the impact of harvesting. For this reason, they are described here for field researchers who want background information on why these 'ecological filters' are useful.

Plant life forms

In the early 1900s, the Danish botanist Christian Raunkiaer categorized plants into 'life forms' (Raunkiaer, 1934). This widely accepted classification system grouped different vascular plants according to the height of mature individuals, the type of shoot systems (such as woody or herbaceous, climbing or self-supporting, and whether plants were found in water or on land). Raunkiaer also took into account the form and location of the buds or storage structures, such as bulbs, corms, rhizomes or tubers, which enable perennial plant species to persist from one season to the next. Although he used rather cumbersome names for different life forms, thinking about plants in terms of life-form categories is useful in establishing basic resource-management principles, since these represent a sequence from large trees ('mega-phanerophytes') and shrubs ('micro-phanerophytes') through to annual herbs ('therophytes'). This helps to bridge the gap in knowledge about plant population dynamics, enabling a first approximation of categories of vulnerability to destructive harvesting. Large trees ('mega-phanerophytes') commercially harvested for their medicinal bark, for example, represent a vulnerable category when there is selection for thick bark from large (old) plants which have a long period to reproductive maturity, a low ratio of production to biomass and specialized habitat requirements.

Plant architectural models

In trying to predict different impacts on the vast range of plant species harvested, one of the ways of simplifying things is to group the species according to their growth pattern and form. Plant architectural models were developed through pioneering studies by French botanists Francis Hallé and Roelf Oldeman (1970). Adrian Bell's recent book (1998) is an excellent illustrated guide to plant architectural models. Architectural models began with studies of tropical trees as a system for explaining their structure and growth, but has been expanded to include temperate and tropical shrubs, lianas and herbs. Architectural models can provide a useful predictive tool for studies on harvesting in several ways:

- They provide a theoretical basis for understanding different levels of sensitivity to stem harvesting or harvesting of apical meristem – the tissue involved in stem growth (such as harvesting palm-hearts).

- Plant species are chosen whose architecture and rhythmic growth patterns enable age estimates in a range of very different plant families, such as those in 'Corner's model' – for instance, palms, tree ferns and grass trees (Xanthorrhoeaceae), whose architecture lends itself to field assessments of leaf production and leaf harvesting rates, assessments of how stem harvesting impacts branching (see Chapter 4), past disturbance events by fire (Lamont and Downes, 1979) or tree falls (Martinez-Ramos et al, 1988).

- Tree stems are aged based on scars that are visible from modular stem growth. In developing architectural models, great interest was shown in 'iteration', the repeated process of stem growth and branching as trees matured from saplings to maturity ('Massart's model'; Podocarpaceae and some Araucariaceae; see Chapter 4).

Resprouters, reseeders and resilience

The way in which plants reproduce is an important issue in conservation and resource management. Categorizing plant species in terms of where they are on the continuum from 'reseeders' (which regenerate primarily from seed) to 'resprouters' (which reproduce clonally through the production of new shoots) gives better insight into the potential for sustained yield harvest or regeneration studies (see Box 5.3).

An investment of time and effort in monitoring the impact of fruit harvesting may be very appropriate in tall tropical forest, for example, where many canopy trees regenerate from seed (Peters, 1994). A similar focus on regeneration from seed would not be a priority in short subtropical thicket or forest in southern Africa, where all common canopy species (with

Box 5.3 Characteristics Across a Continuum: Long-lived Reseeders versus Resprouters

Reseeders

- Reseeders regenerate from seed, some maintaining canopy seed banks ('serotiny').
- Examples are common in the Proteaceae, Pinaceae, Ericacae and Podocarpaceae families.
- Reseeders are single stemmed, not multi-stemmed. Examine smaller shrubs closely. Some reseeders are single stemmed, but branch off close to the ground, giving the incorrect impression that they are multi-stemmed reseeders.
- They do not resprout when the stem is cut.
- They usually are self-pollinated or have diverse pollinators. If there are exceptions dependent upon specialist pollinators or seed dispersers, then they are vulnerable to extinction.
- Their seeds often germinate faster than those of resprouters.
- They produce abundant seedlings (a large 'seedling bank').
- They have higher stem growth rates than resprouters, since they allocate nutrient resources into growing upwards, rather than into underground storage organs. As a result, reseeder species in a particular vegetation type tend to be taller than resprouters.
- Most reseeders are short lived compared to clonal resprouters.
- They often are habitat specialists (wetlands, moist montane sites, cool temperate forests).
- Their annual reproductive output is generally higher than in resprouting species.

Resprouters

- Resprouters maintain 'bud banks' rather than seed banks, regenerating clonally by sprouting rather than from seeds.
- They are often multi-stemmed, some shedding stems as they get older.
- They produce new stems from buds which are above or below ground level (basal or upper trunk sprouting).
- Resprouters' cut stems show obvious signs of resprouting (but be careful: resprouting vigour declines with tree size or age).
- Resprouters may have large, underground storage organs (rhizomes, tubers, ligno-tubers) or lateral runners (eg many forest lianas).
- Recruitment from seed is infrequent and irregular.
- They may be pollinator-limited, but can still maintain long-lived clonal populations consisting of a genetically identical clonal organism (the **genet**), which is made up of **ramets**, sprouted from buds, each of which has the potential to grow and reproduce as an independent, individual plant.
- Few seedlings occur in the population; most small plants are ramets.
- Resprouters grow more slowly than reseeders, since they have to put resources into underground storage organs and into production and protection of buds.
- Resprouters are usually generalists, found in a wide variety of habitats, rather than habitat specialists.

Note: Recommended reading on this subject includes the following texts: Bond (1994); Harper (1977); Kruger, Midgley and Cowling (1997); Lamont et al (1991); Midgley (1996); Sakai et al (1997); Schutte et al (1995).

the exception of tall succulent species such as *Aloe* and *Euphorbia*) reproduce by sprouting, and the few seedlings bear no relation to frequency of those species in the forest or thicket canopy (Midgley and Cowling, 1993; van Wyk et al, 1996).

Plants that reproduce solely from seed follow a very risky lifestyle, particularly if they have very specific pollinators or seed dispersers. In most cases, however, this risky lifestyle is rare, and reseeders usually have generalist pollinators or are wind pollinated (Bond, 1994). Unlike animals, where small populations are particularly vulnerable to extinction, small population size in plants is less closely linked to local extinction because so many plants can resprout. Plants that are able to persist through resprouting are far less dependent upon new recruits from seed. The rare South African fynbos shrub, *Ixianthes retziodes* (Scrophulariaceae), is a good example, still persisting through resprouting despite the extinction of its pollinator, an oil-collecting bee (Steiner, 1993). Root harvesting of plants which depend upon resprouting for reproduction must be 'flagged' as a potential threat.

Reseeders either build up seed stores in the soil or through canopy seed storage. Canopy seed storage where mature seeds are held for some time before they are released is termed serotiny. Unlike resprouters, reseeders typically do not survive disturbance events, such as fire, but recruit from seed. Many Proteaceae, for example, wait for a fire to pass through and stimulate seed release. As reseeder populations can be seed limited, special care has to be taken in harvesting their flowers, fruits and seeds, particularly in species producing few, large seeds. Since many reseeders in the Proteaceae, Bruniaceae (*Brunea*) and Ericaceae families produce spectacular flowers, they are harvested for a massive cut-flower industry. Much of this harvesting is still from wild populations. For this reason, controlled harvesting of flowers and seed heads of reseeders is a very real management issue in South Africa and Australia (see also Chapter 4).

Although reseeders produce greater numbers of vigorous seedlings and are therefore more likely to recover from localized overutilization of saplings, they are vulnerable to overexploitation of the large trees which produce the most seeds. This is clearly seen in the predictable overexploitation and slow recovery of *Podocarpus* and *Afrocarpus* (Podocarpaceae) populations after logging in Africa. Palms that generate primarily from seed rather than by resprouting are also vulnerable to population declines through stem use. The South-East Asian rattan palm, *Calamus manan*, is a good example. Single stemmed, and growing up to 171 metres long (twice the height of a California redwood), they were once widespread in Malaysia and Indonesia and very abundant in west-central Sumatra (Dransfield, 1974; Siebert, 1991). By the late 1980s, only a few thousand mature individuals were left (Dransfield, 1987), many populations having been eliminated by overexploitation. The most vulnerable reseeders of all are commercially harvested, relatively long-lived monocarpic (or hapaxanthic) palms and trees. The term 'monocarpic' refers to their strategy of flowering once, setting seed, and then dying. If mature stems are cut prior to setting seed, then the plant's entire investment in reproduction is lost.

Rather than build up a seed bank as reseeders do, resprouters develop a 'bud bank' and respond to damage by producing new stems from these buds. In some instances all the above-ground stems are removed during disturbance, for example by fire, herbivores, humans or hurricanes. Most woody plants in tropical and subtropical savanna, woodland and short forests are resprouters, and many tropical and subtropical palms survive through resprouting in the hurricane-prone monsoonal tropics. In fire-prone systems such as African and Australian grasslands, savannas and woodland, many resprouters have large roots, rhizomes or specialized lignotubers (James, 1984; Hansen, Pate and Hansen, 1991). These store starch and nutrients, and after disturbance such as fire, produce new stems from dormant buds.

Resprouters are not only found in frequently disturbed vegetation types, however. Large-scale disturbance due to fire, hurricanes or mass damage by large mammals such as elephants are rare events in temperate and many tropical forests, yet many trees in these forests are resprouters (van Wyk et al, 1996; Sakai, Sakai and Akiyama, 1997). Although resilient to stem damage, resprouters are poor colonizers if overutilization causes local population declines. Root harvesting, for example, for dye or medicinal purposes, has serious implications for their survival because resprouters often produce few viable seeds or seedlings. Once the parent plant has died through root removal, re-establishment from seed will be a rare event. Another factor is that the seedlings of resprouters grow very slowly because some resources are allocated to storage products, protection, dormant buds and a number of stems.

Light and leaves, gaps and growth rates

One of the commonest ways in which forest trees are grouped is according to their light requirements, such as shade-tolerant versus light-demanding species or 'gap' versus 'non-gap' species. Also common is to group plants on the basis of successional stage (eg early pioneer, late secondary, primary forest species). A classic example of similar looking trees which occupy similar positions in a forest is the large-leaved pioneer *Musanga* (tropi-cal Africa) and *Cecropia* (tropical Latin America) (see Figure 5.4a). At the other extreme are shade-tolerant, slow-growing species such as *Podocarpus* (see Figure 5.4b). These groups of forest plants have particular ecological characteristics in common (see Table 5.1), many of which influence the opportunity for sustainable harvesting, as summarized in Box 5.1.

As you become more familiar with the species in your study area, it is useful to think about the harvested species in terms of their ecological characteristics. You may also find anomalies to the three basic categories in Table 5.1. The *Brachylaena huillensis* trees which support the bulk of the Kenyan woodcarving industry are one anomalous example: light-demanding, regenerating from small wind-blown seeds in canopy gaps and with weak resprouting ability, one would expect from this habit and from the plant family (the Compositae) that they would be fast growing with light timber and a short life span. On the contrary, the beautiful golden timber is dense, the growth rate slow and the trees very long lived, taking 100 years just to reach 40cm in diameter and living for over 200 years.

From field observation, it is clear that light-demanding 'pioneer' trees often have large, thin, short-lived leaves, and that shade-tolerant forest trees often have thick leathery leaves with longer leaf life spans. The leaves of pioneer species are also commonly eaten by insects, mammals or people, while the leaves of many shade-tolerant species are often unpalatable and rarely eaten. In some cases, field observation is not enough and quantitative methods for studying leaf characteristics are used. One method that has been used for its predictive value in plant population biology is **specific leaf area** (SLA), the ratio of leaf area to oven-dry leaf mass. Measurements of SLA have been rarely used in applied ethnobotany, but have

Figure 5.4 *(a)* Musanga *(left) and* Cecropia *(right), large-leaved, light-demanding, fast-growing pioneer trees with short leaf life-spans (often less then one year) and high specific leaf areas, occupy ecologically similar positions in tropical forest in Africa and South America. Here photographed in Cameroon, where* Cecropia *has become an invasive species. (b)* Podocarpus, *at the other extreme, is a shade-tolerant, long-lived tree with a long leaf life-span (four to five years) and a low specific leaf area*

important predictive value for resource management for individual plants, plant populations (see Chapter 5) and disturbance. There is a significant correlation, for example, between SLA and leaf life span, relative growth rate, photosynthetic rate and leaf nitrogen content (Reich et al, 1992; Midgley, 1995). Fast-growing trees generally have thin, short-lived leaves and high SLA values. Slow-growing trees have thick (often sclerophyllous), long-lived leaves, slow growth rates and low SLA values (see Figure 5.5).

To date, SLA measurements have apparently only been applied to plants with small- to medium-sized leaves. For broad surveys, leaf area is measured for a sample

number of leaves (usually six to ten) collected from well lit branches (generally in gaps or ecotones) of each tree species being investigated. SLA is calculated by measuring the area of fresh leaves (cm^2) and dividing this by oven-dry leaf mass (g) (Midgley et al, 1995). This is done for all the leaves in the sample in order to get a mean for each species. Leaf area can be measured with an electronic leaf area meter. As a field exercise, leaf area can also be measured by tracing the outline of a leaf onto graph paper, counting the squares and converting this to area (cm^2). Leaf mass has to be measured with an accurate balance.

A rapid way of getting an approximate index of shade-tolerance is to collect infor-

Table 5.1 *The basic ecological characteristics of early pioneer, late secondary and primary tropical forest species*

Character	Early pioneer	Late secondary	Primary
Distribution	very wide	very wide	usually restricted; many endemics
Seed dormancy	well-developed	slight to moderate	none
Seed or fruit size	small	small to intermediate	large
Seed dispersal	birds, bats, wind	mainly wind, but also mammals	mammals, birds
Shade tolerance	very intolerant	intolerant	seedlings very tolerant, later intolerant
Gap size required	large	intermediate	small
Seedling abundance	very scarce	usually scarce	abundant
Growth rate	very fast	fast	slow to very slow
Wood density	light	light to medium	very hard
Life span	10 to 25 years	40 to 100 years, sometimes more	100+ years

Source: Peters, 1994

mation on specific leaf area (SLA) (Midgley, van Wyk and Everard, 1995). To determine SLA, fully expanded young sun leaves must be collected and pressed. They must then be dried and weighed. The area of each leaf must be determined (using a leaf-area meter, graph paper or gravimetrically). SLA is then the leaf mass divided by area. Evergreen trees in the family Podocarpaceae (white pines or yellow wood trees) typically have very low SLA values. By contrast, fast-growing deciduous species have larger, lighter leaves and much larger SLA values. Studies in South America have also shown that SLA values are closely linked to leaf life span (Reich et al, 1991; Reich, Walters and Ellsworth, 1992). Trees with low SLA values are shade-tolerant species and have long leaf life spans. *Podocarpus* leaves, for example, live for four to five years. Trees with high SLA values are shade intolerant with short-lived leaves and fast growth rates, typically occurring in canopy gaps. In a survey of over 100 tree species in southern Africa, the highest SLA values were found in deciduous legumes (*Erythrina*, *Acacia* and *Erythrophleum*), with short (less than one year) leaf life spans. Other leaf attributes, besides high SLA and short leaf life span, which indicate fast growth rates and shade intolerance, are if the leaf is compound, if the leaf is large and if the leaf has high levels of nitrogen (most of which are in photosynthetic enzymes) (Midgley, van Wyk and Everard, 1995). At the scale of different forest types, the southern Africa survey of SLA values grouped trees into those with low SLA values (Afromontane forests) and high SLA values (subtropical coastal forests on sands).

Costs and complexity: inventory, management and monitoring

Once you have decided on a group of priority species, you need to map the area available for harvesting, perhaps with aerial photographs, and use this as a basis for sampling populations of the selected species. Sampling can be fairly quick and

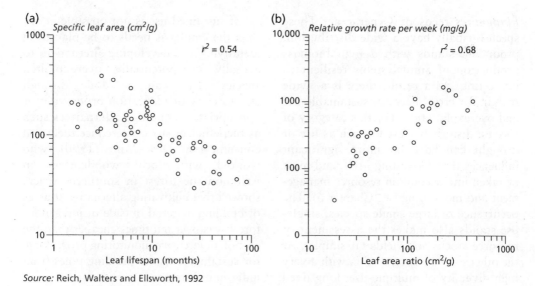

Source: Reich, Walters and Ellsworth, 1992

Figure 5.5 *(a) Specific leaf area in relation to leaf life span. (b) Relative growth rate of young plants for a range of species from different ecosystems*

straightforward or very time consuming, depending upon the diversity of the vegetation and biology of the species involved. What is often underestimated are the costs of monitoring programmes. The complexity and costs of inventory, management and monitoring all increase rapidly with an increase in the diversity of species and uses, number of users, quantity harvested and number of harvesters per unit area. When time and funds are limited, before you design a sampling or monitoring system you need to ask yourself several questions, such as:

- What is the overall objective (eg maintaining biodiversity or catchment values)?
- What question(s) are you trying to answer?
- How precise do you want to be (eg statistical precision to 5 per cent, 10 per cent, etc)?
- Who will do the work, and what training needs are there before this can start?
- What is the control (ie compared to what – for example, comparisons

along harvesting gradients)?
- Who will analyse the data?
- Who will act on the results (and who will translate these into a suitable format for decision makers)?
- What is the spatial and temporal scale (ie time and rate of change; how big and where)?
- What other factors are also affecting the same resource (and how can these be distinguished from what you are monitoring)?
- How long will it be before decisions regarding management options can be made?

It is not worth spending a huge amount of time and resources on relatively unimportant questions. Monitoring systems that do not take these factors into account are literally designed to fail as they will be unsustainable in terms of either funds, time, technology or personnel requirements.

The simplest situation is with dense stands dominated by a single species with one main use such as *Cymbopogon* thatching grass, or wetlands dominated by

Phragmites reeds or Cyperaceae. These species usually have a wide distribution, producing stands with a high biomass production of annual stems resilient to harvesting. As a result, there is a 'wide margin for error' between sustainable use and overexploitation. For this category of species, disturbance events such as fire or drought can have far more significant influences than harvesting itself, and must be taken into account in resource management and monitoring (see Chapter 6). The occurrence of large single-species, single-use stands also makes the assessment of resource stocks and yields far simpler. At the other extreme is vegetation with a very high diversity of multiple-use, long-lived species. This poses a particularly complex case which can be expensive in terms of time and funds for thorough inventory and monitoring. Sustainable harvest of timber from Afromontane forest, which has a relatively low species diversity compared to tropical forest in South-East Asia or Amazonia, provides a good example. With just a single product (timber) and few species involved, a team of one forester and two staff selecting trees greater than 30cm dbh for logging is only able to cover 5ha per day (Seydack et al, 1995). Costs also increase rapidly with an increase in species diversity and a decrease in the diameter size class of trees that need to be monitored.

The most attention, therefore, needs to be given to species which are in high demand, slow growing and habitat-specific, and which are harvested at a high frequency and intensity. An **adaptive management** approach should be taken to this category of species, with harvest levels based on yield studies and where harvesting impacts and regeneration are monitored and the results used to make harvest adjustments. Figure 5.6 shows a flow chart for sustainable harvest of non-timber resources from tropical moist forest which uses this approach.

If sustained use is not possible at all, then the emphasis needs to be placed on identifying and developing alternatives to actually or potentially overexploited species. This can be done through agroforestry or plantation production or appropriate technology alternatives such as fuel-efficient stoves to reduce fuelwood consumption. Dirk Muir (1990), who worked with local woodcutters in Afromontane forest in southern Africa, showed that cultivating alternative sources of building material outside of indigenous forest was over ten times cheaper than the cost of an intensive monitoring programme for sustainable use of building poles from indigenous forest.

Insight into impacts: studying harvesting effects on plant populations

Ideally, the effects of harvesting need to be studied on the same sample population over time through establishment and subsequent resurvey of permanent plots. In many cases, you will find that there was no previous interest in 'your' focal species and consequently no permanent plots for comparative work. One reason for this is that ethnobotanists often focus on locally important species such as medicinal plants or lianas in which there has been little national or international interest. Another reason is that, despite their importance, permanent plots are still rare in much of the tropics. Under these circumstances, two methods can be used to get insight into the effect of harvesting without having to wait for decades for results from permanent plots.

Firstly, in cases where more spectacular, long-lived large plants such as palms, cycads, cacti or *Pachypodium* species are harvested from open habitats (desert, grasslands, savanna), it is possible that you may be able to use **matched photographs** or

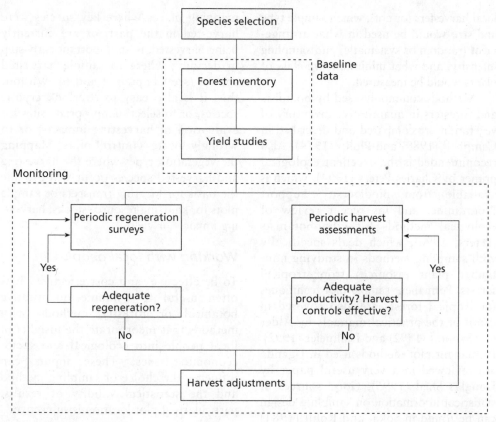

Source: from Peters, 1994

Figure 5.6 *A flow chart showing an adaptive management approach to sustainable harvest of non-timber resources from tropical moist forest*

fixed point photographs as a monitoring tool (see Figure 5.11). For most harvested species, particularly in forests, the use of matched photographs will not be an option. A second and far more widely applicable method is to measure the size classes of harvested populations. The measurements of plants from sample populations are then grouped into different **size classes** to indicate the **population structure** of the harvested species and to get insight into regeneration patterns. A useful way of doing this is within plots at different points along a **gradient** from places where harvesting impacts are high to where they are low (or absent). Each of these methods is described in the sections that follow. Later

in the chapter, a third method, **population matrix modelling**, is discussed. This is inappropriate for field workers who do not have access to a computer, but can be a useful tool to understand harvesting impacts. Before this is done, however, it is important to decide where to sample and what sampling method to use.

Vegetation sampling: where and what method?

Having decided on which species will be the focus of a detailed inventory, monitoring programme or study on harvesting impacts, you need to decide on where the study area will be **located**, whether you will work with local harvesters (or not), which sample type and size would be used in what arrangement (random or systematic) and sampling intensity, and what minimum size class of plants would be measured.

Methods commonly used by botanists and foresters in quantitative inventory of vegetation are compared and described in Campbell (1989) and Philip (1974). Also recommended is the excellent ecological primer by Charles Peters (1994), which is available from Biodiversity Support Programme, and his recent review of ecological methods for ethnobotanists (Peters, 1996), which deals specifically with sampling methods in studying non-timber plant resources from tropical forests. Permanent sample plot techniques for tropical forests are also covered in detail in the practical manuals by Alder and Synnott (1992) and Dallmeier (1992). Permanent plot methods used in Uganda are reviewed in a very useful paper by Douglas Sheil (1995). Good sources of statistical information on sampling design can be found in Sokal and Rohlf (1981) and Zar (1998). With these references readily available, sampling methods will only briefly be described here. What is dealt with in more detail are practical ways of identifying priority species and sites, and rating harvesting damage to determine the effects of harvesting on sampled populations using these techniques.

Location of study sites

Many factors influence where people harvest: topography, location of paths, roads or tenure, or the density of favoured species or favoured size classes within a species population. You need to take this into account before locating any plots or transects. Local harvesters' knowledge is an important step in this process and the use of participatory mapping methods in mapping places where key species were harvested in the past, or are currently being harvested, is an important early step in deciding where to sample harvested species (see Chapters 2 and 6). Without this, it is also easy to overlook cryptic species, or to select inappropriate sites for evaluation of harvesting impacts, or to wrongly locate 'control' plots. Mapping the vegetation types where the harvesting and harvested species occur will provide the basis for locating transects or sample plots for studying resource stocks, harvesting impacts or yields.

Working with local people

To be effective (and cost effective), it is often useful to combine quantitative botanical or forestry methods with methods that incorporate the insights of local people into ecological and socio-economic issues. These inputs can influence the choice of sampling method and the statistical validity of results, particularly if plot location is subjective.

If local resource users are involved in resource inventories or in monitoring impacts, then it can be worthwhile to use transects rather than plots (see Figure 5.7). Local resource users with low or no numeracy or literacy skills can become frustrated by plot-based samples when focal species are not measured because they occur outside of the plot boundaries. In these circumstances, whether sample plots are systematic or random, some local people feel that they 'waste time' (due to the time required to set up the plots) or 'were not accurate' (as trees were missed out, outside the plots). For these reasons, belt transects would be more productive under these circumstances. The limitation that this places on statistical analysis due to lack of random plots is often repaid by the insights of local resource users during joint field work. Issues such as size-class selection can be linked to the practical field assessments of stem and leaf harvesting, root removal, bark damage or tree crown condition described in Chapter 4.

Local resource users can also add to the quality of the data collected by identifying cut stumps which have died, what implements were used for felling, why felling took place, or which animals have browsed back resprouting stems. The quality of the information derived from joint resource assessments with local harvesters therefore adds predictive value on likely impacts of harvesting. This is not only useful information for resource management purposes, but can add to and sometimes be cross-checked against information from 'informant consensus' and 'inventory-interview' methods described in Chapter 2. Field work with resource users in plots or walking through the forest or savanna is also an opportunity to get insights into local people's views of vegetation dynamics. You will find that local people in a wide variety of environments have an excellent knowledge of the causes of disturbance, routinely identifying trees that have died due to lightning strikes, elephant damage, fire, fungal infection and so on. In some cases, for example in post-fire or agricultural succession, they are also able to estimate the time elapsed since this has occurred.

Type of sample unit

The most commonly used types of samples are the following.

Square, rectangular or circular plots
Choice of plot shape depends upon the objectives of the survey and concerns about the influence of plot perimeter ('edge') effects per unit area sampled (see Peters, 1996). Rectangular plots (and belt transects) have the most edge, and circular plots the least edge. A large amount of

edge usually means that more habitats are covered, with inventory results more representative of the study area. One problem is that a long plot edge means a greater chance of error in deciding whether plants on the border of the plot are 'in' or 'out', which can soon lead to biased results. For this reason, it is essential that plot boundaries are carefully measured. For trees directly on the borderline, an unbiased rule can be decided on beforehand. For example, trees located directly on the border of two edges of the plot would be considered 'in' and those on the other two edges 'out'.

Belt transects
Belt transects sample vegetation on either side of a transect line (see Figure 5.7a). Transects are also a commonly used method for assessing harvestable plant resources – for example, in narrow transects at right angles to forest paths. The size of plots or length of transect lines will depend upon the size and abundance of the species and individuals you are sampling. Belt or line transects cover a wider spectrum of microhabitats and can show subtle changes in the density or structure of sample populations compared to quadrats or circular plots. An advantage of using transects when conducting resource assessments with local resource users is that in some cases they considered belt transects more useful compared to quadrat methods, which they felt 'missed out' plants in the spaces between plots. Transects have two main disadvantages. however. Firstly, since transect lines are long and narrow and cover a range of microhabitats, they are inefficient as a method of characterizing diverse vegetation types or varied vegetation (Campbell, 1989). A second problem is that even if a transect is as long as one kilometre, it still only represents a sample size of one; therefore, it generally is better to have more short transects than a few

very long ones. In diverse vegetation types, one solution is to break transects up into homogeneous units, such as a series of 100m x 5m transects.

Point-centred quarter (PCQ)

The PCQ method enables sampling of microhabitats, determining patterns of species distribution from analyses of associated plants within patches (near-neighbour analysis). This method is often considered very efficient in characterizing vegetation. It also minimizes damage to the forest understorey. The main disadvantages are, firstly, that unlike quadrats or belt transects, the PCQ method does not cover an exact area each time, so that species richness cannot be related to area sampled. Secondly, since only four trees are sampled per sampling interval, this makes the method rather labour intensive if large sample sizes are required (Campbell, 1989).

Arrangement of samples

Sample units can be arranged systematically at regular intervals (see Figures 5.7 a and b), or randomly within the entire study area (see Figure 5.7c), or in a stratified random sample within different habitats of the study area (see Figure 5.7d). The choice of sampling design will strongly influence the statistical validity of your results and how long it takes to establish (or relocate) the sampling units. Random selection is done to avoid bias. In practice, this can be performed through drawing lots, pulling numbers out of a hat or, ideally, using random number tables, which are available as appendices to many statistical textbooks – such as Fischer and Yates's (1945) *Statistical Tables for Biological, Agricultural and Medical Research*, which has been reprinted many times.

Part of a random number table is given below as an example. Assume, for example, that you have drawn a grid over the aerial photograph or map of the vegetation you want to sample and need to select 20 sample units at random from the total of 81 numbered sampling units located in the grid. Start by randomly selecting a number in the table of random numbers by blindly touching the page with a pencil.

Once this is done, there is no need to continue at random as the numbers are already in random order. Instead, proceed systematically along the row or down the column; when that row (or column) is finished, continue with the next one. In this case, since you have a choice of 81 sampling units, include all numbers from 00–80 (counting 81 as 00) and reject all numbers between 81–99. Any number drawn twice is also rejected. If the first number the pencil touched was 30, and the next ones were 77, 40, 44, 22, 78, 84 and 26, for example, 84 would be rejected and the others included, continuing until 20 sample units are selected. You then need to locate these sample units, measure and sample them.

Random plots are preferable from the point of view of statistical analysis, but may be very time consuming to locate in rough, forested terrain. Systematic sampling may be quicker since plots or transects are easier to relocate, but because sampling is not random, it does not allow for any statistical assessment of precision or sampling error (Peters, 1996). In systematic plot sampling, the first plot may be selected at random, but all the rest follow a set spacing. This would be acceptable if the plants being sampled were located at random; but in the natural world, plants are rarely spaced independently of each another. For these reasons, the use of regular (non-random) samples should be avoided whenever possible.

If plots are located on sloping ground, then there has to be a correction for slope,

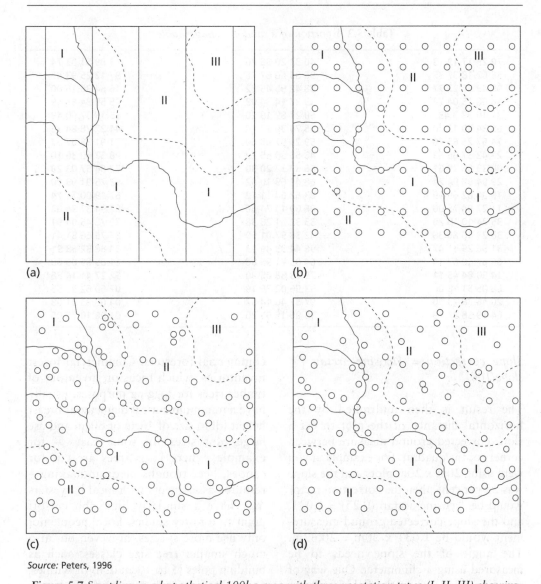

Source: Peters, 1996

Figure 5.7 *Sampling in a hypothetical 100ha area with three vegetation types (I, II, III) showing contour lines (dotted lines) and a river (black line). (a) Systematic transect samples. If these were 10m wide and 1000m long, separated by 200m, they would give a sample intensity of 5 per cent. (b) Systematic plot sampling. If circular plots 12.62m in diameter (each with a sample area of 500m²) are used, then 100 plots would give a sample intensity of 5 per cent. (c) Simple random sample, with plots located at random through the whole area (note that only two plots fell within vegetation type III). (d) Stratified random sample where the number of plots allocated to each vegetation type is based on the percentage of the total area represented by that type. This method located seven plots in vegetation type III*

as the distance between two points measured along a slope is always greater than the corresponding horizontal distance. The formula used to calculate this correction (Durr et al, 1988) is:

Table 5.2 *A portion of a random number table*

70 29 17 12 13	40 33 20 38 26	13 89 51 03 74
56 62 18 37 35	96 83 50 87 75	97 12 25 93 47
99 49 57 22 77	88 42 95 45 72	16 64 36 16 00
16 08 15 04 72	33 27 14 34 09	45 59 34 68 49
31 16 93 3 43	50 27 89 19 20	15 15 37 00 49
68 34 30 13 70	55 74 30 77 40	44 22 78 84 26
74 57 25 65 76	59 29 97 68 60	71 91 38 67 54
27 42 37 86 53	48 55 90 65 72	96 57 69 36 10
00 39 68 29 61	66 37 32 20 30	77 84 57 03 29
29 94 98 94 24	68 49 69 10 82	53 75 91 93 30
16 90 82 66 59	83 62 64 11 12	67 19 00 71 74
11 27 94 75 06	06 09 19 74 66	02 94 37 34 02
35 24 10 16 20	33 32 51 26 38	79 78 45 04 91
38 23 16 86 38	42 38 97 01 50	87 75 66 81 41
31 96 25 91 47	96 44 33 49 13	34 86 82 53 91
66 67 40 67 14	64 05 71 95 86	11 05 65 09 68
14 90 84 45 11	75 73 88 05 90	52 27 41 14 86
68 05 51 18 00	33 96 02 75 19	07 60 62 93 55
20 46 78 73 90	97 51 40 14 02	04 02 33 31 08
64 19 58 97 79	15 06 15 93 20	01 90 10 75 06

Slope correction = 1/cosine arctan (% slope/100)

The result is then multiplied by the horizontal distance of the plot to get a slope-corrected ground measure between corners of the quadrat. For example, if you were using 20m x 20m plots and the slope was 25 per cent, then the correction factor would be 1 cosine arctan (0.25) = 1.031, and the slope-corrected ground measurement would be 1.031 x 20m = 20.62m. The angle of the slope needs to be measured using a clinometer. One way of speeding things up in the field is first to develop a slope correction table which gives correction factors for the plot size you are using for a range of slope angles. An example of a table of slope corrections for different slopes and horizontal distances is given below.

Plot size, sampling intensity and minimum size class

Quantitative ethnobotanical surveys are often more detailed than those used by commercial foresters. Commercial forest inventories, which focus on inventory of timber trees for logging purposes, usually have a minimum cut-off diameter at breast height (dbh) size of 40cm or 60cm and use large plot sizes. In some cases – for example, where large trees are cut for canoes, beer troughs or drum-making – resource assessments with local harvesters may have a similarly high dbh cut-off point to forestry studies. Local people not only use more species, however, but also much smaller tree size classes, such as building poles (5 to 10cm dbh) or withies, and stakes or weaving material which may be less than one cm in diameter. Dawkins (1958), who worked in Ugandan forests, calculated that if the minimum size of trees measured in a 1ha plot in tropical forest is 40cm, then a single forestry working party would take about 5 hours to mark and measure the trees in the plot (excluding marking the access line or plot boundaries). With each 10cm reduction in size limit, working time doubles, so that even with two working groups, measurement to

Table 5.3 *Slope corrections for different distances on slopes of varying steepness*

Slope (%)	Horizontal distance (m)				
	5	10	15	20	25
10	5.02	10.05	15.07	20.10	25.12
15	5.06	10.11	15.17	20.22	25.28
20	5.10	10.20	15.30	20.40	25.50
25	5.15	10.31	15.46	20.62	25.77
30	5.22	10.44	15.66	20.88	26.10
35	5.30	10.59	15.89	21.19	26.49
40	5.39	10.77	16.16	21.54	26.93
45	5.48	10.97	16.45	21.93	27.41
50	5.59	11.18	16.77	22.36	27.95
55	5.71	11.41	17.12	22.83	28.35
60	5.83	11.66	17.49	23.32	29.15
65	5.96	11.93	17.89	23.85	29.82
70	6.10	12.21	18.31	24.41	30.52
75	6.25	12.50	18.75	25.00	31.25
80	6.40	12.81	19.21	25.61	32.02

Note: Slopes in excess of 80 per cent are not shown. The values in the table show the distance along a slope that must be measured to obtain the horizontal distance indicated by the column heading.
Source: Peters, 1996

a 10cm minimum size would take about 3 days (Dawkins, 1958).

The size of plots needs to vary according to the size of the plants being sampled. For statistical analysis, more small plots are preferable to few large plots: but with small plots there is a greater chance of error in terms of estimating plant density. Due to the level of detail required and the consequent cumulative time per plot, it can be useful to use a system of tiered plots to subsample smaller diameter size classes (Alder and Synnott, 1992) (see Figure 5.8). It is important to spend an equal amount of time sampling each of the size classes of interest. For example, if in a series of nested plots there are 1000 seedlings in $100m^2$ but 10 big trees in $1000m^2$, decrease the former and increase the latter. Also bear in mind that if your plots are too small, you may get many plots without the plants in which you are interested.

Sample intensities of 5 to 10 per cent of the study area are common in forestry surveys. There are statistical formulae for calculating how many sample units are needed to achieve a given level of precision, but these require a random sampling design (Philip, 1994; Peters, 1996), which can pose practical problems in ethnobotanical work.

Comparisons along harvesting gradients

Where no base-line data are available from permanent plots, it is useful to compare harvesting impacts over a gradient from heavily harvested to unharvested populations at the resource-rich 'frontier'. Firstly, an unharvested 'frontier' site is where populations of plant species in high demand have been protected from harvesting, such as places protected from exploitation under customary law or in remote areas away from transport routes – where harvester population densities are low – or in protected areas. Secondly, sites where high-intensity harvesting takes place are sites of high harvester density, easy access or focal points of commercial harvesting. It may also be useful to select an intermediate site between these two extremes.

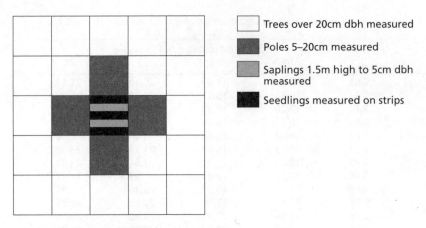

☐	Trees over 20cm dbh measured
■	Poles 5–20cm measured
▨	Saplings 1.5m high to 5cm dbh measured
■	Seedlings measured on strips

Source: Alder and Synnott, 1992

Figure 5.8 *Possible arrangement of tiered subplots for measuring below 5cm and 20cm diameter at breast height (dbh) thresholds on a 1ha plot*

Studies in comparable sites along a gradient from high to low harvesting impacts can provide insight into different levels of resilience or sensitivity to harvesting.

The simplest case is to compare two species size-class distributions at different sites representing different harvesting intensities or frequencies. This is where the simple methods described in Chapter 4 for measuring plant size or rating damage are useful. You also need to be confident that valid comparisons can be made between sites in terms of structure and density of sample populations, soil type and aspect. This is far easier in low-diversity vegetation such as wetlands or palm forest, or savanna-dominated areas on flat sites. Comparisons become more and more difficult with increasing complexity of sites in terms of species diversity, disturbance patterns, soils and topography (see Chapter 6).

Studying harvesting impacts along a gradient will enable you to assess the effects of harvesting on resource supply. It also enables harvested species to be grouped in terms of their resilience or vulnerability to harvesting. This can provide very useful insights into opportunities or constraints on sustainable harvest and may further prioritize which species require more intensive monitoring or management. Assessing the response of different species along gradients from high to low disturbance in South African savanna enabled ecologist Charlie Shackleton and his colleagues (1994) to group woody plant species according to their response to disturbance (harvesting, trampling, grazing) into four groups: **invasive species**, which increased in density with increased disturbance; **tolerant** species; an **intermediate** group; and **sensitive species**, whose density declined under high levels of disturbance.

The resilience or vulnerability of different plant species populations to a high frequency or intensity of harvesting is a direct reflection of their regeneration characteristics and growth rates. The extent to which resprouter tree species can persist was shown by ecologist Tauber Tietema's study of high and low harvesting impact sites in mopane (*Colophospermum mopane*) woodland, a tree species highly favoured in southern Africa for building poles and fuelwood (Tietema et al, 1991).

The method Tietema used was to count the density of coppice stems in plots along a transect, starting close to Morwa village in south-eastern Botswana. Near the village, there were over 2700 mopane coppice stems per hectare, but a kilometre away, fewer than 200 coppice stems per hectare (see Figure 5.9b). What drastically changed due to cutting of this vigorous resprouter was the structure of the mopane woodland, from fewer tall trees to short multi-stemmed resprouts (see Figure 5.9a). This can be clearly shown by assessing population structure.

Harvest of whole plants: herbs, bulbs, corms and tubers

In her classic book about the !Kung-San people in the Kalahari desert, anthropologist Lorna Marshall (1976) describes how two !Kung-San women, Di!ai and !Ungka, selected edible tubers:

'They set out while the morning was still cool and walked briskly for about 50 minutes. They each began by picking about 2 pounds of n≠a berries from a clump of bushes near the area, eating berries as they picked. They then went to the part of the area where they knew they would find /ga [Coccinia rehmannii], n≠wara [Trochomeria debilis], /dobi [vine, scientific name unknown], and !ama [Ceropegia tentaculata]. That day Di!ai found 34 roots; 34 times she sat down, dug a root, stood up, picked up her son, walked on to look for another root to dig. She dug 17 /ga [C. rehmannii], 9 /dobi, 2 n≠wara [Trochomeria debilis], 4 !ama [Ceropegia multiflora], 1 /ama [Ceropegia pygmaea], 1 !gau [Cyperus sp]. Of these roots, 1 /ga [C. rehmannii] was too immature to take, 2 /ga, 4 /dobi, and the /ama [C. pygmaea] were thrown away after they were dug because they were too old, bitter and pithy. One n≠wara [T. debilis] and 2 /dobi were so deep in the ground Di!ai abandoned them in the holes after struggling with each of them for 10 or 15 minutes. This left 23 roots for Di!ai to carry back to the encampment, 14 /ga, 3 /dobi, 1 n≠wara, 1 !gau, and 4 !ama.'

This useful account of a foraging expedition gives a good idea of the effort that goes into food gathering, the species and quantities gathered and the selection criteria used in collecting edible tubers. It also illustrates a dilemma faced by ethnobotanists interested in measuring the effects of harvesting on harvested populations where whole plants are removed and little evidence remains after harvest, or where harvesting has been going on for so long that the remains of harvested plants (cut stumps, debarked trees) have rotted away. For smaller woody plants and herbaceous or bulbous species, the only evidence that remains is local knowledge of where these species used to occur and the increasing time it takes harvesters to collect the same quantity of those species. In these cases, it is useful to set up permanent plots at the 'resource-rich frontier' and follow what happens as harvesting increases over time.

By contrast with the tuber removal for water or food described by Lorna Marshall (1976), commercial harvesters of bulbs, tubers, corms and rhizomes for the traditional medicine trade generally select the largest (oldest) individuals from multiple-aged populations to obtain the thick bark and large bulbs, tubers or roots that have highest economic value. In order to obtain the most bark, bulbs or roots per unit time, gatherers also appear to select for dense stands. Once the plants have

(b)

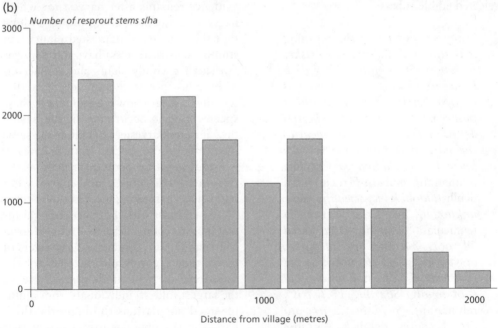

Source: (b) Tietema et al, 1991

Figure 5.9 *(a) Mopane (*Colophospermum mopane*) trees outside a village in Botswana showing multiple stems resprouting from the stumps of trees felled for building poles and fuel wood. (b) Change in density of mopane coppice (resprout) stems in relation to distance from Morwa village near Mochudi in south-eastern Botswana*

been removed, there is little sign that they were there at all. In these cases, it may be desirable to set up permanent plots in sites selected on the basis of discussions with resource users or predictions on where harvesting intensity and frequency are likely to focus in the future. The size of plots would depend upon the plant size and its population density. Permanent plots in forests would clearly be larger than those for bulbous species in grasslands, and small plants at low population density would require more replicate plots.

If local harvesting patterns and practices are not affected by the presence of outsiders, then this can be a good opportunity to record information on species and size-class selection of underground roots and tubers. You may also have the opportunity of measuring the sizes of bulbs, corms or tubers after harvest, at markets, in herb wholesaler shops or in bags confiscated by forestry or conservation authorities. Patrick Nantel and his colleagues (1996), for example, measured bulb size and mass in samples of edible wild leek bulbs which had been confiscated from illegal collectors in Quebec, Canada (see 'Population Modelling Using Transition Matrices' below), using this as one of the sources of information to develop matrix population models to assess the impact of harvesting. In other cases, it may be possible to return to the site where gathering has taken place and to assess the proportion of the population that has been harvested.

Although harvesting of corms, bulbs or tubers usually means that the whole plant is removed, the impact of destructive harvesting at a plant population level depends upon bulb, corm or tuber size-class selection. Few data are available for size-class distributions of wild populations of species harvested for bulbs or roots; however, bulb or ligno-tuber diameter can be a useful measure of population size-class distributions in sample populations

in a similar way to foresters' use of diameter at breast height (dbh) for studying tree populations (see Chapter 4 and Figures 5.10 and 5.12).

Large plants produce larger quantities of seed than smaller plants. As geophytes grow older, they also grow deeper in the soil (see Figure 5.10). This results in better protection from fire and drought (Beadle, 1940; Weaver and Albertson, 1943), enabling geophytes and ligno-tuberous species to thrive and have a competitive advantage in savanna and fire-maintained grasslands. Soil temperatures are high on the surface during a fire, but decline rapidly with depth (Beadle, 1940). Larger, deeper-rooted geophytic plants have greater stored moisture, and are rooted within cooler and possibly moister subsurface soil where they are able to reach water reserves untapped by shallow-rooted grasses.

The size class of geophytes that are harvested and the proportion of the population removed have an important influence on recruitment of young plants and the ability of the species population to survive fires or drought. In Africa, harvesting of geophytes for medicinal purposes or for moisture or food provides examples of two extremes. The toxicity, starch or water reserves of geophytes that provide protection against herbivores, drought and fire may also attract harvest by people rather than protect these species. Local people who gather medicinal plants from the wild for commercial trade in traditional medicines generally select the largest individuals from within each population, since these are most favoured for sale in urban medicinal plant markets. Smaller individuals are usually less favoured. As a result, there often is a progressive decline over time in bulb or corm diameter of heavily exploited species, such as the Liliaceous medicinal bulbs *Eucomis autumnalis*, *Bowiea volubilis* and *Scilla*

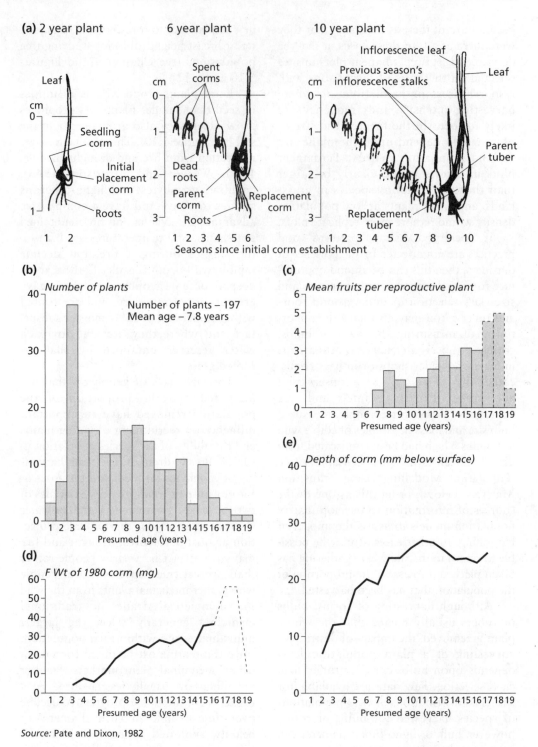

Source: Pate and Dixon, 1982

Figure 5.10 *The increase in reproductive output, age and depth of corms of the west Australian geophyte* Philydrella pygmaea *(Philydraceae)*

natalensis in South Africa. Selective harvesting of large medicinal bulbs or corms can seriously affect recruitment from seed and the resilience of the population against random events such as fire, drought or landslides which can damage plant populations (termed stochastic events by ecologists) (Chapter 6). By contrast, hunter-gatherers who dig tubers for food or water may avoid the largest tubers in a population because they are too deeply rooted, pithy or bitter.

At the other extreme to these small herbaceous or bulbous plants are some spectacularly large plant species. These species offer the opportunity of using matched photographs of the same plant population in the absence of base-line data from long-term plots. This is described in the next section.

Matched and fixed-point photographs

Matching historical photographs with recent ones can be used to study changes in the abundance of large, long-lived plants as a result of habitat destruction or harvesting. In South Africa, for example, 'long-term' studies of cycad populations are only available for a few species and only span 20 years or less. For this reason, John Donaldson (in press) used matched photographs as a method to study changes on South African cycad numbers over time. By searching through specialist collections, publications and through appeals to the general public, he obtained 210 photographs taken between 1906 and 1986 and relocated 92 of the sites where the historical photographs were taken. He then carefully examined the site to identify new plants or to see what had happened to the plants identified in the older photographs.

Before each site was rephotographed, the position of the camera was recorded with a global positioning system (GPS) and

marked with a metal stake. Donaldson then supplemented records from relocated sites with information from written reports and interviews with local farmers and conservation officials. Analysis of these data showed that illegal collection of individual plants for horticultural purposes was the main reason for a decline or disappearance of cycads (60 per cent of sites), compared to decline as a result of natural death (20 per cent of sites), habitat destruction (12 per cent of sites) and cycad bark removal for traditional medicinal purposes (5 per cent of sites).

The advantages of using historical photographs are that they provide ways of assessing long-term changes in the number of selectively harvested species such as cycads, cacti or palms when little or no baseline data exist. Such photographs can cover a far longer time span in which to assess vegetation change (from at least 1880 onwards) than is available from aerial photographs (generally from 1930 onwards). Taking fixed-point photographs as part of a supplementary baseline study is also a relatively inexpensive method which can be applied for selected species as a way of monitoring species-selective harvesting of adult plants (see Figure 5.11). Disadvantages are, firstly, that historical photographs usually focus on adult plants, with limited information provided on the recruitment or survival of juvenile plants. Secondly, the method is only applicable to large, long-lived spectacular species in sites which have been photographed in the past and is more appropriate to relatively open vegetation types rather than to thickets or forests. Thirdly, because it requires resampling of the same site, the method assumes that cycad populations are static and does not provide information on new populations that may have developed nearby. Despite these disadvantages, this method can provide a useful record of changes in the

Source: Donaldson, in press

Figure 5.11 *An example of a matched pair of photographs showing decline in a population of* Encephalartos frederici-guiliemi *from the time of the original photograph, taken by R A Dyer in 1946, to the matched photograph taken by De Wet Bösenberg in 1996. The decline was due to exploitation for traditional medicine and for horticultural purposes*

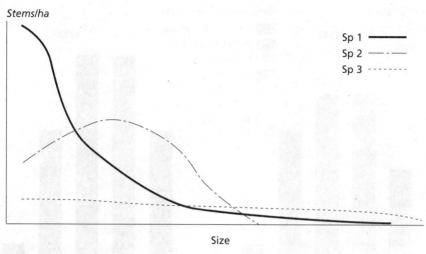

Source: Geldenhuys, 1992

Figure 5.12 *Generalized models showing how 'typical' tree diameter (dbh) size-class distributions are usually considered to indicate whether a species population is expanding, stable or declining. Species 1 shows the typical reverse J-shaped or negative exponential curve indicative of continuous recruitment of young stems. Curves shown by species 2 (bell-shaped) and species 3 (flat) both show low numbers of seedlings but different numbers of saplings due to differences in reproductive strategies and site requirements, such as canopy gaps*

number and survival of adult plants which could be applicable to long-lived, large plants such as palms, tree ferns, *Pachypodiums*, aloes and cacti.

Size-class distributions, survivorship and population structure

Information on how a plant population is regenerating provides valuable data for resource management purposes and is widely used in planning for sustainable management of uneven-aged, mixed-species forests. By contrast with life tables for animal populations, which are usually based on age, studies of plant populations are generally based on size-class distributions. These take plants within a sample population and group them into size classes based on stem diameter (trees, bulbs) or stem length (palms, tree ferns). These size-class distributions are a way of showing

plant population structure and indicating the chance of plants in one size class to survive into the next size class. They are used as a tool for understanding plant population dynamics, most commonly for trees.

Three ideal types of size-class distribution are usually recognized for trees in uneven-aged, mixed-species forests (see Figure 5.12). The assumption is made that size-class distributions give an indication of size-specific mortality and therefore the status of the population. The reverse J-shaped (or negative exponential) curve is considered to indicate species **tolerant** of **shade** or **competition** from other species. Recruitment is continuous and populations are expanding under these circumstances. The second size-class distribution is for a species with equal amounts of regeneration to mature individuals. A **bell-shaped curve** or a **unimodal (flat) curve** indicates **shade-intolerant** or **competition-intolerant** species

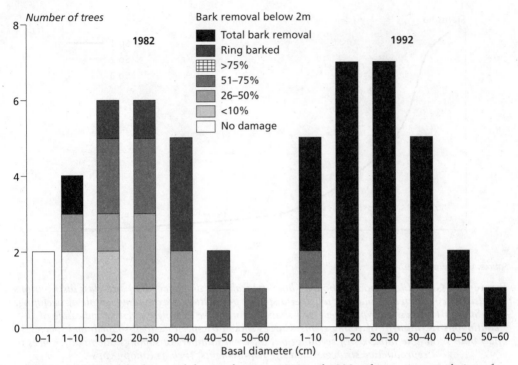

Figure 5.13 *The debarking and demise, between 1982 and 1992, of an entire population of* Berchemia discolor *trees due to bark harvesting for basketry dye. These occurred scattered on termitaria over a 10ha area in what had been a favoured dye harvesting area. As this species is widespread in southern Africa, bark overexploitation posed more of a problem for basket makers in the form of loss of local self-sufficiency than as a species conservation issue*

or **low numbers of seeds** due to an unusual reproductive strategy. Species with the third size-class distribution shown in Figure 5.12 may be pioneer species which regenerate in canopy gaps or other disturbed sites, represented either by large canopy trees or dense stands of seedlings in gaps. The flat curve, showing small numbers of seedlings which decline through sapling and adult stages, may be due to levels of light, competition or irregular reproduction. Be cautious in making these assumptions, however (see Chapter 6, Figure 6.8). Remember that in practice you will encounter curves that are far from the ideal curves shown in Figure 5.12, including multi-modal curves which may show survival or reproduction in different cohorts.

These different distribution levels suggest different sensitivities to harvesting.

Shade- or competition-intolerant species showing a **flat curve** are often much more vulnerable to overexploitation when young seedlings or saplings are harvested than species exhibiting a **reverse J-shaped curve**. Species with size-class distributions following a flat curve indicate the scarcity and great importance of young plants for recruitment. Cutting many young stems for building purposes, for example, limits recruitment of these species into future size classes, particularly if regeneration from sprouting is weak or if resprouts are killed by browsing mammals. The reverse J-shaped curve, on the other hand, is indicative of a high mortality of stems in smaller size classes. Harvesting some of these individuals may have little impact on population structure, since some would die anyway.

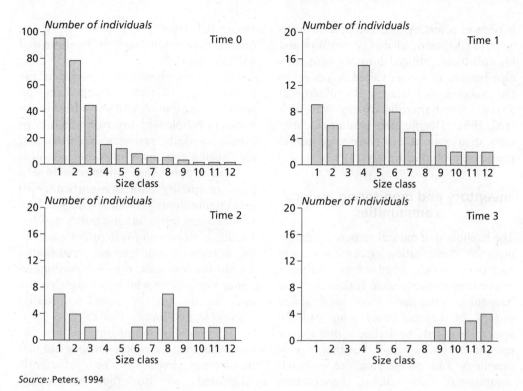

Source: Peters, 1994

Figure 5.14 *A hypothetical example of long-term change in the population structure experienced by a tropical forest tree species due to intensive harvesting of fruits, showing changes in the number and population structure of trees in the harvested population at 30-year intervals. Size class intervals are 10cm*

Use of size-class distributions is a practical field method for recording assessments of harvesting impacts and for illustrating the response of plant populations to harvesting. Figure 5.13, for example, shows the impact of commercial harvesting of bark for basketry dye on the same *Berchemia discolor* tree population over an 11-year period, and the resultant die-off of trees in what had formerly been a favoured harvesting area. Changing population structure indicated by size-class distribution may also be used as a field measure of subtle effects, such as the intensive harvesting of large fruits from reseeder species (see Figure 5.14).

The use of survivorship curves has two main weaknesses, however. The first is the assumption that the tree stem diameter (or palm height) always reflects plant age. This is not always the case and can be a dangerous assumption (see Chapter 4). Growth of understorey trees, for example, can be suppressed when the young trees are in shade. Alternatively, tree growth rates are faster when gaps form in the forest canopy. In addition, a few individual trees within an initially even-aged stand, such as in a disturbed site or canopy gap, may grow faster than others, eventually dominating the gap (Harper, 1977). The second assumption is that the shape of the survivorship curve reflects harvesting impact alone, rather than a combination of vegetation disturbance dynamics in addition to harvesting. It is crucial that disturbance dynamics are taken into account, in order to prevent misinterpretation of data on size-class distributions of plants. A good example of this is given in Chapter 6, where G F van Wyk and his colleagues noticed how the size-class distributions of species varied according to the successional stage of subtropical lowland forest after disturbance (van Wyk et al, 1996). Despite these weaknesses, size-class distributions are considered useful predictive tools (Geldenhuys, 1992).

Inventory and monitoring by local communities

The likelihood of natural resource management or conservation occurring in any society increases when people value a resource or resource area, realize that it is becoming scarce and have local social groups or organizations who can do something to halt the decline in that area or resource (see Chapter 7). For this reason, inventory and monitoring are essential components in any conservation programme, including community-based natural resource management programmes.

While local knowledge assessed by participatory rural appraisal (PRA) or interview methods is useful in illustrating general trends in resource availability, it is no substitute for quantitative data. Where key resources are concerned, more rigorous methods need to be used. In the Brazilian Amazon, for example, ethnobotanist Patricia Shanley worked with local villagers to obtain estimates of the density and fruit yields of forest trees well known to people whose families had lived in the forest for generations. Estimates of fruit yields varied over tenfold, and local estimates of tree abundance were highly inaccurate. A very knowledgeable local hunter, for example, estimated that 1000 mature piquia (*Caryocar villosum*) trees occurred in their 1500ha forest, at densities up to 20 trees per hectare. In contrast, their tree census found just 149 mature *Caryocar villosum* trees in this same forest,

about 0.1 trees per hectare. In short, quantitative studies have to be done and will take time.

In regions where trained personnel are scarce and detailed information on resource distribution and use is held in the minds of people with low or no literacy or numeracy skills, resource inventory and monitoring systems need to be accessible to local people. The challenge is how to produce quality data of significance to local (community) resource managers, as well as to professionals and policy makers. Ideally, a monitoring system designed for use in resource management programmes should use low-cost, robust, low-maintenance equipment which is simple to use and locally (or at most nationally) repairable, and locally available.

If periodic monitoring is to be sustained, then the people carrying out that monitoring need to be sufficiently motivated to do the monitoring. Appropriate equipment and training on their own are not enough. For this reason, a clear distinction has to be made between monitoring performed by local people employed to work in national parks as patrol rangers, forest guards or trackers, and monitoring by resource users from the local community who are not employed to undertake formal resource monitoring. Where local resource users are involved in resource monitoring, then they must have a personal incentive. Resource users are usually busy with other day-to-day activities, such as tending children, farming, and collecting fuelwood. For this reason, however 'user-friendly' the monitoring systems are, they need to be relevant and limited to very few species (or resources) which are important to the people doing the monitoring – such as food, fuel or water resources – and, ideally, fun to do. There also has to be a good reason for local people to go beyond the way in which they informally monitor gathered resources:

that is, through noting a changing 'catch per unit effort' – in fishing terms – since resource users spend more (or less) time to collect the same resource. Examples of key resources in which local people may have an interest in monitoring in a more formal way are major food resources or the main indigenous plant species with commercial value which are nearing complete extinction (see Figure 5.3).

Biological inventory and monitoring of a wide range of plant and animal resources by local people is becoming more widespread. In the Brazilian Amazon, for example, Marli Mattos, Daniel Nepstad and Ima Vielra (1992) trained local people on how to assess the size classes, harvestable volumes and values of timber on their land, and have produced an illustrated handbook in Portuguese so that these methods are locally accessible. In forests as far apart as the Peruvian Amazon, West Kalimantan, Indonesia and the Gulf province of Papua New Guinea, ethnobotanist Charles Peters has trained local resource users to monitor the regeneration of tropical tree species (such as *Spondias mombin* and *Shorea* species, which produce respectively *uvos* and *illipe* nuts) which are favoured sources of large, commercially collected edible fruits (Peters, 1996b). Villager-level monitoring also extends to marine resources. In the Verata area of Fiji, for example, local villagers chose to count and measure saltwater cockles (*kaikoso*), which are a favoured food, and compare the results in harvested and non-harvested *tabu* sites (areas traditionally closed to harvesting) (Biodiversity Support Programme, 1998). These initiatives have produced encouraging results. John Parks, the Biodiversity Support Programme (BSP) officer associated with this example, points out how:

'The government officials saw that the village residents were perfectly capable of doing a fairly sophisti-cated level of quantitative monitoring and that such efforts could clearly complement policy level actions...they were amazed at the ability of the Verata people to monitor their resources and explain the results. Some admitted they thought such skills could only be developed through formal university education.'

Nevertheless, methods used for monitoring by people with no literacy or numeracy, but who have a good knowledge of the resources in question, have to be carefully developed.

Interfacing different worlds: local skills and field computers

Can local people, with low or no literacy or numeracy but detailed knowledge of natural history and their local landscape, use computers in inventory and monitoring? One school of thought promotes the view that computers should not attempt to replace humans, but rather enhance human skills and expertise. This approach differs fundamentally from the artificial intelligence (AI) school of thought, which attempts to develop computers that replicate (and therefore potentially replace) human skills. Examples include computers that can play chess better than humans do, or robots that replace humans in the workplace. An interesting example where local skills and field computers are linked together is the Cybertracker system (http://www.icon.co.za/~ctracker), developed by computer scientist Lindsay Steventon and tracking expert Louis Liebenberg.

A pilot study using the Cybertracker system was employed in the Karoo National Park, South Africa, to monitor wildlife (see Figure 5.15a). The objective was to enhance the unique skills of expert

177

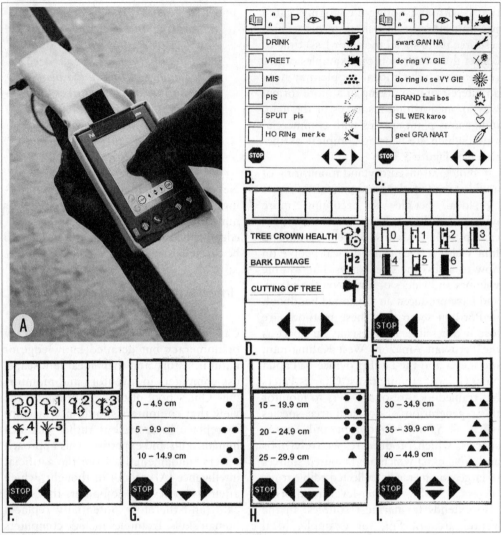

Source: (a) and (c) Liebenberg and Steveton, 1998

Figure 5.15 *The palm-pilot field computer (a) used by low/no literacy trackers in the Karoo National Park, South Africa, for recording animals, with (b) a focus on black rhino activity and (c) feeding records by species indicated by different icons, with observations classed according to whether these were from tracks or direct observation (Liebenberg and Steveton, 1998). A similar system (d) has been developed for local community monitoring of harvesting impacts on trees, using (e) visual rating systems for bark harvest or (f) tree crown health example, where (g, h, i) icons based on one to five dots, triangles, squares and diamonds can be used to represent tree diameter size classes (eg 0–4.9cm); these icons are on the pilot field computer and a ruler (or tape measure)*

wildlife trackers with no literacy and numeracy, and it provides an example of this new school of thought in computer science. Two trackers, Karel Benadie and James Minye, both employees of the conservation department, have been testing the field computer on an ongoing basis. Although they cannot read or write, they have used the field computer to record their observations in the field and download the data onto the national park's personal computer (PC) by themselves. The data collected in the Karoo National Park are very detailed and comprise, for example, the home ranges or feeding behaviour of rhino, showing the change in plant species favoured as browse, and shifting from the rainy season through to the dry season. In addition, the researchers have been recording tracks of rare or nocturnal species that are not normally monitored, making it possible to observe species that would not otherwise be noticed at all. Initial field tests indicate that a tracker can generate more than 100 observations in one day. The highest number so far has been 266 observations in one day, and 473 observations over a 3-day period. The approach which should be taken in communal areas is very different, with fewer observations recorded each day on one or two key species.

Due to the potential advantages of this system, we recently tested the Cybertracker system in community-based monitoring of wild plants rather than animals, and compared it with more standard methods for measuring and assessing harvesting impact. The species chosen for this monitoring experiment was the bird plum (*Berchemia discolor*) tree, whose bark provides the major source of dye for commercial basketry production in Botswana, Namibia and Zimbabwe. The challenge is to develop practical methods which basket makers can use, and which do not put knowledgeable basket makers with low literacy skills at a disadvantage. One of the easiest ways of doing this is to use pictures illustrating rating systems which represent harvesting impacts. In this case, icons for tree-diameter size classes, tree crown health, tree crown size and bark-damage rating systems (see Chapter 4) were transferred to a hand-held (palm-

pilot) computer in a similar way to the icons used for monitoring animals (see Figure 5.15). Tree diameters were measured using a ruler which uses symbols to indicate different tree-stem diameter size classes instead of numbered measurements. These symbols ('icons') consisted of one to five dots, triangles, squares and diamonds to represent 0–4.9cm, 5.0–9.9cm, 10.0–14.9cm size classes, etc. These icons are also on the palm-pilot field computer so that they are linked to dbh measurements made with the icons on the ruler (or tape measure). Using the touch-sensitive screen, people can point to the appropriate icon to take them to different screens and then press stop (which is like a street stop sign) to complete the record; a global positioning system (GPS) reading can be made at the same time.

Advantages of the palm-pilot field computer that are apparent from the Karoo National Park case include the following. It is quick and easy to use, including use by people with low/no literacy; automatic GPS readings can be taken for every observation; it stimulates interest in monitoring; it enables quick and easy data processing and storage; it provides easy retrieval of large amounts of data and data analysis for vast areas over long time periods. With these advantages, the Cybertracker system provides the opportunity for resource users, national park patrol rangers or forest guards to record their observations easily. At the same time, it enables observations to be stored in a database for subsequent analysis. This means that the collective observations of a large number of local people (resource users, patrol rangers, wildlife trackers) can be analysed over large areas and long periods of time, even after many of the trackers are no longer working in the area. Long-term trends can then be established.

Disadvantages compared to collecting data in written (paper-based) format include the relatively high cost and the need for technical support and regular access to electrical power – 'paper data collection sheets don't need batteries', as Zimbabwean basket makers said, in a wry comment on the use of palm-pilot field computers. It also requires access to a desk-top or lap-top computer so that data can be transferred from the palm-pilots for storage, mapping or processing. For this reason, the system is most appropriate to conservation programmes or rural development projects with an equipped office. The main disadvantage of the Cybertracker field computer system in the short term is the cost of the computer equipment. However, the cost of hand-held computers is expected to decrease rapidly in the near future.

The cost of this equipment also needs to be compared with the cost of monitoring systems which require much higher levels of professional staff time, often in situations where there are few professional staff, many of whom have other commitments. Aerial census of wildlife, for example, costs about US$200 per hour. Intensive monitoring of plant resources can also be expensive. Training local people, including those working in protected areas, to use the palm-pilot system enables patrol rangers to record a range of issues in the course of normal patrols, such as the occurrence of traps, broken fences and pit-sawing activity, or to focus on monitoring rare animal or key plant species. Far more local staff can be involved in the process for the same cost as a single qualified professional person. If implemented, the resulting employment opportunities will provide an additional benefit for protected areas or community-based conservation programmes.

Yields: supply versus demand

In trying to reach a balance between demand and resource supply, we need to know how much of a resource is produced within a specific area. The methods described in Chapter 4 for measuring plant size (diameter, length), volume, age, stem or foliage biomass, and bark volume, or for directly counting annual leaf or fruit production, are useful tools in this process.

In even-aged stands of fast-growing species with annual above-ground production, such as thatching grass or reeds, an estimate of annual yield can be a relatively simple task, particularly when there is just a single use, or where harvest impacts do not conflict with one another. In most cases, however, yield assessment is more complex, requiring measurement of yields of products from marked plants in different size classes, as well as plant density and size-class data from inventories to extrapolate annual yields to an area basis (eg tonnes/ha/year). In addition to a variation in yield according to plant size class, yields often vary from year to year with site differences. For this reason, yields need to be measured over several years. Yield curves can then be developed to predict estimated annual production of harvested products according to plant size class or of yields on a standing biomass per area basis (see Figure 5.16). This information is of great practical value in making resource management decisions. Involving local harvesters in yield assessments, for example, can lead to a greater awareness of the limits to resource yields compared to demand. This, in turn, can lead to development (or reassessment) of local rules which set limits on who or how many people will

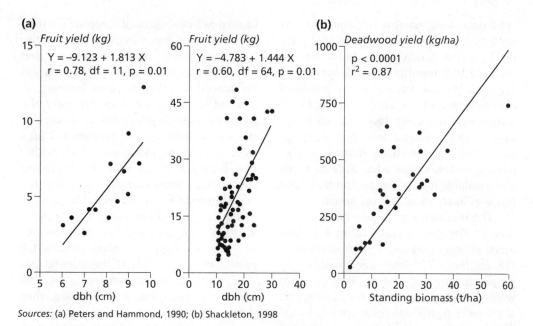

Sources: (a) Peters and Hammond, 1990; (b) Shackleton, 1998

Figure 5.16 *(a) Edible fruit yield related to tree diameter size. (b) Deadwood yield for fuel related to tree standing biomass in semi-arid savanna, southern Africa*

harvest from a set area and on harvesting methods (Chapter 7), or a reassessment of local decisions on land-use options.

Ecologist Charlie Shackleton, for example, set up long-term experiments to assess the production of deadwood used for fuel in semi-arid southern African savanna. In the first study, he marked 9500 trees in 51 sites to monitor annual mortality rates of trees. In the second study he monitored annual fuelwood production in 28 plots within three rainfall zones. Tree mortality was 3.6 ± 0.6 per cent in the first year and 5.2 ± 0.7 per cent in the second year. As expected from the reverse J-shaped population curve (which characterizes many savanna tree species), more small-sized stems died than large ones. Taking into account the preference of fuelwood harvesters for stems over 10cm in circumference, he used allometric equations developed for southern African savanna (Rutherford, 1979) to calculate that these mortality rates represented fuelwood

production rates of 216 ± 61 kg/ha in the first year and 418 ± 92 kg/ha in the second year. Deadwood production estimates from cleared plots provided similar results, with yields of 378 ± 53kg/ha in the most arid site (480mm/year), 270 ± 48 kg/ha in the semi-arid site (670 mm/year), and 438 ± 69 kg/ha in the mesic savanna site (870mm/year). He found a strong statistical relationship between standing biomass and annual yield of dead fuelwood, which was summarized as: deadwood yield (kg/ha = a x standing biomass (t/ha), where a varied in different years between 16.7 ($r^2 = 0.87$; p < 0.00001) and 17.7 ($r^2 = 0.56$; p < 0.0001) (Shackleton, 1998; see Figure 5.16b).

The simplest case is with dense stands of common, single-use species which have a perennial root stock but annual above-ground production (some Poaceae and Cyperaceae; see Box 5.1). In the early 1980s, for example, I worked with local enumerators who had recorded how many bundles of *Phragmites* reeds were being cut from a long, narrow wetland that was soon to be fenced within a national park on the South Africa/Mozambique border. Over 19,000 bundles of reeds were sold per year. We also knew that the height of the reeds was a key factor and that if reed stands were too short (less than 3m high), they were unsuitable for harvesting for local building purposes. What we also needed to know was what area of reeds was available for harvesting and how long this was likely to meet local needs.

The first step was to map out the total area of *Phragmites* reeds using 1:10,000 aerial photographs (orthophotos). Most of the reedbeds (296ha) were within the proposed conservation area, 38ha of which were short and unsuitable for cutting and 80ha were near elephant watering holes. This left 135ha available for harvesting just inside the boundary of the proposed conservation area, in addition to 43ha outside the boundary. Other published data showed that reed yields were 500 bundles/ha, so we could work out total yield for the wetland and compare this against the estimated local demand for the building material. Assuming that building preferences remained constant, and there was a block rotation so that each block was rested for a year then cut the following year, the 178ha of reedbed available for harvesting would sustain local demand for reeds (which was increasing at 4.37 per cent per year) for a further 36 years (Cunningham, 1985).

Things get more complex when disturbance affects yields. A good example is botanist Sheona Shackleton's (1990) study of *Cymbopogon validus* thatch grass production in Mkambati Game Reserve, South Africa, which was a major source of thatch for local Pondo and Xhosa people, most of whom travelled 10 to 40km to cut thatch. Starting off with the same steps of studying demand based on local units (standard head-load bundles of thatch

known as *isithunga*) and mapping the total area of *Cymbopogon* thatch grass, she also had to take into account that *Cymbopogon* thatch grass production was influenced by the biennial burning of selected blocks of the reserve as part of a fire management programme. To do this she worked with local harvesters in 20m x 20m sample plots in grass stands with a post-burn age of one year, two years and sites such as forest margins which had not been burned for even longer. The bundles of thatch yielded per plot were counted, air dried, and then weighed. Extrapolated to a hectare basis, *Cymbopogon* thatch grass yields were only 97 bundles/ha one year after a burn, increasing to 200 bundles/ha two years after burning, then decreasing to 150 bundles/ha thereafter.

Single-species, single-use stands with an annual above-ground production of harvested product such as the above two examples enable yields (in bundles/ha or kg/ha) to be related to area. Yields from multiple-use species become more complex when one type of harvest influences another. A classic case is the coppice management system which was practised in Europe for thousands of years to produce three products: sticks and fuelwood from younger resprouts (from underwood or coppice), timber from standard trees growing amongst the underwood, and pasture for deer or livestock from grasses, sedges and herbaceous plants (Peterken, 1993). Coppice was cut on a block rotation (usually 5 to 25 years) and each area was divided into blocks (or coupes) depending upon the rotation time. If a species required a ten-year coppice rotation, for example, then there would be ten coupes, with one coupe cut each year. Tall upright trees (termed standards) were grown on a multiple of the coppice rotation, with timber trees usually produced in less than 100 years. If a standard rotation was 50 years, for example, then one fifth of the trees in the coupe would be felled at the same time that the coppice was cut. If 15 trees were cut for timber, then the same number (or more) of saplings were conserved to grow into tall trees. Each coupe was usually closed to grazing for four to seven years until the resprouts had grown enough to avoid being damaged by deer or domestic animals.

Different uses and interacting impacts were taken into account in developing management recommendations for ilala palm (*Hyphaene coriacea*) savanna. In this case, livestock grazing, palm-sap tapping, edible palm-heart harvesting, leaf harvesting for basketry fibre and the infestation of tapped palm stems by edible palm weevil larvae were all involved, but needed to be quantified. Three potentially conflicting palm uses were of limited significance in this case, since harvesting of palm-hearts and cattle browse of palm leaves were negligible and only 0.3 per cent (3 stems) of 902 tapped stems were affected by beetle larvae. Palm-sap tapping can influence palm-leaf production rates, however, so we worked with palm-wine tappers and marked palms to assess annual leaf production. Sap yields from separate batches of a known number of tapped palms were measured daily over a 12-month period to determine sap yields (see Chapter 2). Sap yields were very low compared to other palms, ranging from an average of 4.4 litres/palm (n = 90 palms) to 14.5 litres/palm (n = 18 palms), due to the small size of available palms.

Although tapping had a negative effect on individual palm stems (ramets), only 3.7 per cent (7 stems) of 155 marked *Hyphaene* palms (genets) died after tapping, 13.8 per cent (26 stems) regrew from the same apical meristem, and the majority sprouted new branch stems that would be tapped again after 6 to 8 years (Cunningham, 1990a, b). Over hundreds

of years, this has changed the structure of palm savanna from one dominated by tall palms with few stems to one with short, multi-stemmed palms. This change is associated with decreased sap yields per palm, but it also stimulated a multi-stemmed growth pattern, thus increasing leaf yields per hectare per year. Leaf yields and palm-leaf size class increased with palm size. Palms in the 80 to 99cm leaf size class, for example, produced 3.15 ± 0.45 leaves/stem/year while those in the 100 to 119cm leaf size class produced 3.79 ± 0.59 leaves/stem/year. Using this as a basis for 'retrospective counts' to estimate leaf harvesting rates (see Chapter 4), harvesting rates were very low, ranging from no leaf harvesting to a maximum of 8 per cent of annual leaf production in palm populations at four sample sites. Based on the conservative recommendation that every third leaf could be cut (30 per cent of annual leaf production) and a palm density of 91.4 palms/ha (483.6 stems/ha), there was a massive unharvested surplus of leaves suitable for basketry in the 17,600ha of palm savanna in this part of South Africa (Cunningham, 1988). In contrast, palm-sap tapping was nearing its limit, as the average palm-wine tapper used 712 palms (902 stems) per year, producing over 4800 litres of palm wine per year, but requiring 4200 to 5600 palms to continue tapping on a sustainable basis. Based on annual palm sap yields (4800 litres/year) and total regional palm-wine sales (980,000 litres/year), I estimated that 200 full-time tappers were involved. Each commercial palm-wine tapper taps an average of 4200 to 5600 palms per year. On this basis, the 1.63 million palms that are estimated from palm-density data to be in the area under commercial palm-wine tapping would support a maximum of 300 to 400 palm-wine tappers.

If neither the data nor the time for long-term monitoring are available, then it may still be possible to use other published data to answer the demand versus supply question. This is possible, for example, in low diversity woodlands such as miombo (*Brachystegia/Julbernardia*) and mopane (*Colophospermum mopane*) woodlands in southern Africa, or *sal* (*Shorea robusta*) forest in India. In Zimbabwe, for example, Isla Grundy and her colleagues (1993) wanted to know whether the level of wood use for building purposes by 155 households in the Mutanda communal area was sustainable. They knew from their studies of construction-timber use that average annual consumption of timber by the 155 households was 1400 tonnes/year. Most of this was from *Colophospermum mopane* trees, with average household consumption of 3.4 tonnes per household per year,

an annual requirement of 527 tonnes per year.

From vegetation mapping they knew that harvesting was from an area of 6000ha of woodland, about 1300ha of which was *Colophospermum mopane*. They were fortunate that an earlier study had studied biomass production in Zimbabwean miombo woodland (1m³ per ha per year) and that data were available on air-dry mass (750kg per 1m³). On this basis, the household construction-timber consumption of 1400 tonnes per year was well within the sustainable yield of 4500 tonnes per year from the 6000ha woodland area, based on a yield of 0.75 tonnes per ha per year. The household need for 527 tonnes of mopane wood was also within the yield of 850 tonnes per year from the 1300ha of mopane woodland.

Population modelling using transition matrices

Models can be useful tools for examining why plant populations change. Matrix projection models were introduced over 50 years ago to study organisms classified by age (Leslie, 1945) and later developed to describe the population growth of organisms grouped by stage (rather than age) (Lefkovitch, 1965). Over the past 20 years, population matrix models classifying plants by stage (or size) have gained acceptance as a useful tool in understanding plant population dynamics and the impact of harvesting. These models require more sophisticated analysis than the size-class distributions described earlier in 'Size-Class Distributions, Survivorship and Population Structure' and are a step beyond this manual's focus on applied field-based methods. However, with the increased availability of lap-top computers, they are briefly outlined here.

For those interested in more detail, the following references are suggested in Further Reading at the end of this book: Caswell (1979); Enright and Watson (1992); Desmet, Shackleton and Robinson (1996) and Bernal (1998).

Population matrix models take advantage of the fact that the life cycle of any plant species can be divided into a few (generally five to seven) stage classes and the associated probability of moving from one stage class to the next. In the case of forest species, for example, the stage classes might be: seeds, seedlings (less than 0.5m high), saplings, juveniles and adults. Additional study may show that 10 per cent of seeds become seedlings and an average adult produces 250 seeds. The opportunity to age plants using methods described in Chapter 4 can lead to more accurate models. These data can conveniently be put into a tabular matrix format. A further advantage is that by multiplying the probability matrix by the present state of a population, a picture can be obtained of what future generations may look like (assuming probabilities do not change with time). In particular, the matrix can give some idea of whether the population is growing or declining, and whether the proportions of each class are likely to change with time.

Like any method, matrix population models have advantages and disadvantages (Desmet et al, 1996). Advantages are that matrix models can easily be manipulated to examine the life histories of harvested plant species over time as a tool in answering 'what if' questions about the short-term responses of plant populations to harvesting. Resource managers commonly ask, for example: 'What would happen if 80 per cent of seed production is collected? What if uncontrolled harvesting removes 60 per cent of individuals in a particular size class? What will the population be like in 100 years' time if we start with a total population of 400 plants, with 10 per cent of bulbs harvested and only large bulbs taken?'

Mathematical background to matrix modelling

The mathematical background to the transition matrices given here is taken from Desmet et al (1996) and is based on their study of harvesting mukwa (*Pterocarpus angolensis*) in South Africa.

The general form of the population matrix (Lefkovitch, 1965) is:

$$An(t) = n(t + 1)$$

where $n(t)$ is the population vector (in the form of a matrix of a single column of numbers) whose components, $n_i(t)$, describe the size-class distribution of the sample population at the present time (t). A is a square matrix, the **population projection** or **transition matrix**, with i rows and j columns, which describes the number of offspring produced to each stage that survive time period t, the proportion of individuals that remain in that stage and those that survive and enter the next stage. Multiplying the present size-class distribution by a matrix of transition probabilities gives the expected population size-class distribution after one time period has passed, $n(t + 1)$.

The transition matrix contains values for the stage-specific fecundity (F) on the first row of the matrix; values for the probability of surviving and remaining in the same stage per time period (R) on the diagonal; and the probability of surviving and growing into the next stage class or any other stage class per time period (G) on the subdiagonal or any other cell in the 4×4 matrix not occupied by F and R values. In this way, the elements of matrix A characterize the properties of a population by taking into account its fecundity, mortality and growth rates for each stage in its life history. These variables cannot be arbitrary. They must be relevant to the organism concerned. The simplest state variable is the number of individuals in the population – clearly an impractical task for very large populations and an important one for small threatened ones.

A population can be projected into the future for any number of time periods, k:

$$n(t + k) = A^k n(t)$$

In a constant environment, as the value of k increases, the predicted size distribution of the population approaches stability, such that the proportion of individuals in each size class becomes constant. This is known as the stable-stage distribution (SSD) and can be calculated algebraically as the dominant right-hand eigenvector

(w) of the transition matrix corresponding to λ defined by (Crouse et al, 1987):

$$Aw = \lambda w$$

where λ is the dominant eigenvalue of the matrix.

The SSD describes the population structure as it would develop if the transition probabilities were constant through time. Comparisons of the SSD with observed initial size-class distribution (ISD), described by $n(t - 0)$, will show whether the population is in balance, with measured rates of growth, survival and fecundity. Differences between the two distributions may indicate past variations in, for example, recruitment, growth or mortality. Discrepancies between observed and predicted size-class distributions are most likely to arise from estimation errors where rates for growth, survival and fecundity are measured over short periods or are poorly known.

Once the population-stage distribution has stabilized, the rate of population change from one time period to the next must also be stable for both the individual size classes and the population as a whole. This rate can be described as:

$$\lambda = n(k)/n(k - 1)$$

where λ is the finite rate of natural increase, and $n(k)$ denotes the projected distribution vector k time periods into the future, such that a stable stage distribution has been reached. The value of k required to reach this may vary markedly and depends very much upon how close the ISD is to the SSD. Solved for algebraically, λ is the dominant eigenvalue (not vector, as for SSD) of the transition matrix.

The finite rate of increase, λ, has a value of 1.0 when the total population remains constant through time; is greater than 1.0 when the population is increas-ing; and is less than 1.0 when the population is declining. It is related to the intrinsic rate of natural increase, r, such that:

$$r = ln\lambda$$

where ln is the natural logarithm.

Estimates of λ and SSD provide insights into the current status of species populations under a given set of environmental conditions (Hartshorn, 1975). These population parameters can be used to compare separate sample populations for which transition matrices have been derived – for example, along an environmental gradient.

It must be remembered that the SSD is the dominant right-hand eigenvector and λ the dominant eigenvalue of the transition matrix. They are, therefore, entirely independent of the ISD. For any starting population vector, the values of SSD and λ will always be the same, provided the transition matrix is unchanged.

There are a number of different methods whereby one can calculate these two population parameters. The obvious method is to use a computer-based mathematical package capable of working with matrices and performing eigen-analyses. Another approach is to use a computer programme specifically developed for ecologists to deal with matrix population models. For most biologists, the simplest approach is to use a spreadsheet. This approach does involve some knowledge of matrix multiplication, so that one can enter as formulae the actual matrix multiplication implied by the general Lefkovitch equation (see previous page). These values can be copied down the spreadsheet for however many time periods one wants to iterate the model. Naturally, care must be taken when entering and copying the formulae so that the $n(f)$ value referred to is in the previous row, namely, $n(t - 1)$, and the transition matrix value is locked, thus referring to the same transition probability for each time period or iteration. Therefore, each row would contain a successive population vector $n(t = 0, 1, 2, 3...x)$, where x represents the maximum number of time periods.

For example, a spreadsheet for a 4 x 4 transition matrix would probably have the following format. In column A are values from 0 to x to keep track of time (t); in columns B to E are the values for $n_1(t)$, $n_2(t)$, $n_3(t)$, and $n_4(t)$, respectively; in row 1 are the observed numbers in each stage class (ISD); in row 2 are the first matrix multiplication formulae. The transition matrix could be anywhere else in the spreadsheet. Equation 4, the finite rate of increase, can be entered in column F, where n in the formula represents the sum of columns B to E.

Following the value of λ through time, one will notice that it will eventually stabilize. This is time k. At this point, the value for λ is similar to that which would be derived if performing a formal eigenanalysis and can therefore be referred to as the dominant eigenvalue of the transition matrix. Similarly, we have reached the SSD, which can be calculated by converting the population vector at $t = k$ to a vector of proportions summing to 1.

Desmet et al (1996) sound a note of caution here about decimal places. They found that λ is sensitive to seemingly insignificant decimal places in the values of the transition matrix and that working to an accuracy of four places will suffice. Researchers will also notice that with the spreadsheet method, λ never really stabilizes. As t increases, λ is constantly changing, but at a decimal accuracy beyond that required for a simple population model. Desmet et al also suggest another useful population parameter that can be calculated for a transition matrix: the reproductive vector. This is the relative contribution of a given stage class to future population growth (Enright and Watson, 1991). As with SSD, the reproductive vector is only valid once the stable distribution has been reached because only then is the structure of the population constant in time. It is calculated algebraically as the dominant left-hand eigenvector (v) of the transition matrix defined by (Crouse et al, 1987):

$$v^1 A = \lambda v^1$$

In Desmet et al's spreadsheet model, the calculation is performed simply by transposing the transition matrix. At time k, instead of being left with a vector representing the SSD, one now has the reproductive vector. The time to stability (k) will not have changed, nor will the value of λ.

The one major downfall of matrix population models is that the prediction of future population size is generally of little relevance. If this is your goal, then Desmet et al (1996) suggest you start searching for a different modelling approach now! In most matrices, mean rates for fecundity, survival and growth are used. More importantly, deterministic and/or stochastic functions or factors are not implicit in the transition matrix and there are also no population-regulation mechanisms or feedback loops. Generally, one tends to find that when the model is iterated, if λ is greater than 1.0, the population grows exponentially, or, if λ is less than 1.0, the population declines exponentially.

One use of matrix models lies in being able to examine the behaviour of the transition matrix and population vector elements over time (Enright and Watson, 1991). The added advantage of this approach is that it quantitatively predicts the behaviour of an ideal population, and provides a means to determine actual direction of change in a particular population at a particular time, and how this change might respond to changes in fecundity, growth or mortality (Caswell, 1989). These types of quantitative analysis are only possible when one is confident that the derived transition matrix for a sample population is an accurate reflection of reality. Such transition matrices require detailed long-term population life-history data, a luxury for most organisms studied.

Are matrix models of any use if we cannot predict future population sizes or states? The answer is most definitely yes. Generally, we are interested in short-term responses of organisms to some form of perturbation, whether human or otherwise. We are interested in the 'what if' questions. What if there is no recruitment next year? What if poaching eliminates 50 per cent of the individuals in a certain size class? This is where matrix models come into their own by providing a simple, easily manipulated, approach to prising open the life history of the organism concerned.

The intuitive approach would be to perform a sensitivity analysis on the population matrix, in order to test how sensitive the population growth is to variations in fecundity, growth and survival; this is performed by simulating changes in the parameters and then determining calculation λ of the new matrix. By simulating the same proportional change for each stage successively, one can compare the relative effect on the different life-history stages (Crouse et al, 1987).

One disadvantage of simulation experiments of this sort is that the results are dependent upon the chosen perturbation of the original matrix. Secondly, for large matrices, the process is very tedious. Analytical methods avoid these difficulties by calculating the sensitivity of λ to changes in life-cycle parameters. Here we are interested in the proportional sensitivity or elasticity of λ – that is, the proportional change in λ caused by proportional change

in one of the life-cycle parameters. These proportional sensitivities can be calculated, given the SSD (w) and the reproductive vector (v). The proportional sensitivity (for elasticity) of λ to a change in each matrix element a_{ij} is given by:

$$e_{ij} = \frac{a_{ij}}{\lambda} \left(\frac{v_j w_i}{<vw>} \right)$$

where $< >$ denotes the scalar product and v is a row vector with j columns, and w a column vector with i rows (Crouse et al, 1987).

Elasticity analysis provides an index of the relative contribution of each transition matrix element to the value of λ (Enright and Watson, 1991). The elasticities of λ with respect to fecundity, growth and survival sum to 1.0. Therefore, the relative contribution of the matrix elements can be compared both between elements of the same matrix or other matrices representing different sample populations or organisms. The larger the value e for an element of the transition matrix, the greater that element's influence on the value of λ. Thus, one can isolate those matrix elements most sensitive to change. When analysing a population matrix, the best approach would be, firstly, to perform an elasticity analysis to isolate those matrix elements or life-history processes most sensitive to change, followed by traditional sensitivity analysis or scenario testing ('what if' questions) centred on these elements.

Analysis of data in matrices is usually done using commercially available computer spreadsheet programmes, such as Microsoft Excel, Borland QUATTRO-PRO, Mathcad 3.1 (Mathsoft Inc, Cambridge, Massachusetts), or programmes developed for stage-based modelling such as RAMAS/Stage Software (Exeter Software, Setauket, New York).

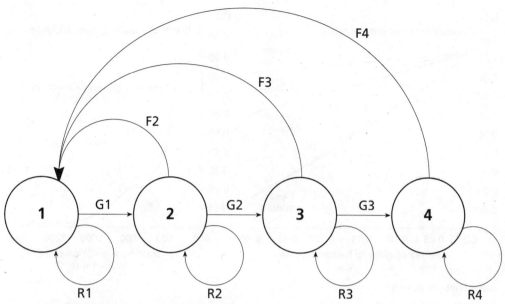

Source: Desmet, Shackleton and Robinson, 1996

Figure 5.17 *A life-stage graph for* mukwa *(Pterocarpus angolensis), a southern African savanna tree species commonly harvested for woodcarving and timber. The arrows show all possible life-history transitions. F represents fecundity (the number of offspring), R the probability of remaining in the same size class, and G the probability of progressing to the next size class within the specified time period of the model (in this case, one year or one complete growth season)*

Models

In their study, Paul Desmet and colleagues used a simple four-stage model to represent all possible transitions an individual plant could make in any of the stage classes in one time period (see Figure 5.17). In terms of the future of the *mukwa* population, they concluded that if the current harvesting rate of 5.6 per cent per annum is maintained (1.1 stems per ha per year or a total of 373 stems for the entire study area), then after 20 years the number of trees removed will decline to 0.56 stems per ha per year (187 stems in total), and after 40 years to 0.29 stems per ha per year (98 stems in total). On the basis of these projected declines, they concluded that the harvesting intensity they encountered was unsustainable. At a 25 per cent reduction in the harvesting rate, to 0.825

stems per ha per year (276 stems in total), the population will be exhausted in 35 years, and at a 50 per cent reduction (0.55 stems per ha per year – a total of 184 stems), the harvested population will be exhausted in 60 years.

Based on this modelling exercise, they suggest that when trying to isolate elements of the matrix most sensitive to change, the best approach is first to identify the parts of the plant life history most sensitive to change and only then to follow this with 'what if' questions, testing different harvesting scenarios (sensitivity analysis) (Desmet et al, 1996). Elasticity or sensitivity analyses help to point out which are the critical phases for maintaining growing populations. They also help to identify the most sensitive phases of the plant life cycle and which phases should, therefore, be avoided for utilization. In the case of *Pterocarpus*

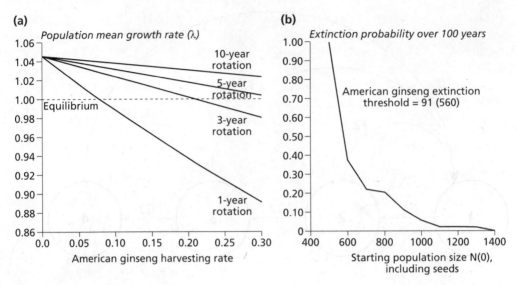

Source: Nantel et al, 1996

Figure 5.18 *(a) Decline of the mean growth rate (λ) of an American ginseng (*Panax quinquefolium*) population under different harvesting rotations. Mean population growth rates (λ) were computed from 200-year stochastic projections using four transition matrices. (b) The larger the population, the lower the chance of extinction: extinction probability over 100 years for American ginseng as a function of starting population size*

angolensis trees, the most important requirement for population survival was the continued presence of mature, reproductive trees in the population.

Simulating different 'what if' situations using matrix models has the advantage of stimulating counter-intuitive answers and prompting questions otherwise not anticipated. A disadvantage is that realistic population projections require long-term population life-history data: something that is rarely available for most harvested plant species. Another disadvantage is that random disturbance events such as fire, drought or landslides are not accounted for by simple transition matrices, nor are there population-regulation mechanisms or feedback loops. Matrix modelling of fire-prone populations is complicated, for example, because transition probabilities change as the result of a fire (Bond and van Wilgen, 1989).

Two exceptions to more simple transi-

tion matrices are the models Patrick Nantel and his colleagues (1996) developed when studying the viability of American ginseng (*Panax quinquefolium*) and wild leek (*Allium tricoccum*) harvesting in Canada, and Elena Alvarez-Buylla's (1994) matrix models for the tropical forest pioneer tree *Cecropia obtusifolia* (Moraceae). Both can be used to assess the effects of different harvesting regimes and are briefly described here. Both studies are recommended reading for those interested in more detail on matrix modelling.

Patrick Nantel et al (1996) estimated the extinction thresholds (the population size below which no population increase is possible) and minimum viable populations (MVPs) of wild leek and American ginseng using transition matrices with different harvesting rates, different harvest rotation times and seasonal variations in growing conditions. Due to lack of relevant data, their population projections did not take random catastrophes into account. For their model of wild leek harvesting, they modelled two harvesting strategies based on analysis of confiscated bulbs: 'choosy' harvesters, who selected large bulbs, and 'busy' harvesters who took many more bulbs across a wide size-class range. Simulated harvests used a random sequence of matrices and were run on a time horizon of 200 years. This provided a basis for suggesting that the sustainable harvest rate of 15.8 per cent, under the assumption of a favourable, unchanging environment, should be reduced to a far more conservative 5 per cent if harvests were to be sustainable. In addition, using an extinction threshold of 91 plants (560, including seeds) gave an estimated MVP for American ginseng of 172 plants (1068, including seeds; see Figure 5.18). A population of this size would have a 4 per cent chance of going extinct in 100 years – yet only a dozen American ginseng populations in Canada have more than 170 plants. This is a good example of how stochastic events need to be taken into account as they can significantly reduce sustainable harvest levels.

In her study, Elena Alvarez-Buylla (1994) developed four separate models which incorporated different combinations of density-dependence and habitat disturbance resulting from canopy gap formation, and applied these to *Cecropia obtusifolia*, a canopy-gap dependent tree species which is widespread in Central and South America. This modelling approach enabled her to test situations where harvesting was, or was not, linked to forest disturbance. Where harvesting was linked to gap formation (as one would expect when the harvested trees are felled), she found that *Cecropia obtusifolia* populations would be expected to reach maximum population levels since *Cecropia* needs canopy gaps in which to regenerate.

Different responses of different species to disturbance and stochastic events is a critical factor to take into account in applied ethnobotany. Random events such as landslides, wind throws or fires, which can cause catastrophic damage to populations of some species, may also provide the conditions under which other species regenerate. This is an important factor to take into account in resource management, and is the focus of the next chapter.

Chapter 6

Landscapes and Ecosystems: Patterns, Processes and Plant Use

Introduction

Most landscapes have been influenced by natural disturbances. Disturbance by people – for example, by burning, farming or the effects of livestock – has also played a role. As a result, vegetation patterns reflect complex interactions between physical factors such as topography, rainfall and geology with biological and socio-economic factors. Rate of loss, fragmentation, dynamics and degree of protection of vegetation are also taken into account in conservation programmes. It is equally important to recognize the great differences within and between forest, savanna and desert systems in terms of patterns of disturbance, plant use and our perceptions of these in the development of resource management or conservation programmes. It is widely recognized now that protected areas have to be seen in the context of the surrounding landscape and land use.

This chapter emphasizes how patterns of harvesting relate to vegetation dynamics and disturbance, and what methods can be used to take this into account in developing conservation and resource management plans. To make sure that you 'see the wood for the trees' in developing such programmes, it is essential to view harvesting in the context of wider spatial scales and longer time scales. This is best done by working from the 'top downwards', starting at the landscape level, moving to the community-ecosystem level and eventually looking at the species-population and genetic levels (Noss, 1990; see Figure 6.1). The 'mental maps' which harvesters have of the past or present distribution, or seasonality, of plant resources can provide useful insights into processes of vegetation change. Participatory methods discussed in Chapter 2, such as mapping, transect walks and time lines with knowledgeable local people which can be combined with use of aerial photographs or satellite images, are a useful step in this process.

In addition to starting with this 'bird's eye view', it is important to understand how and why plant populations change over long time scales. Landscape ecology is a well-established field of study, influenced by geography and the biological sciences, which has emphasized the dynamic nature of natural processes (Turner, 1989). The close association between climate, soils, vegetation and land forms makes landscape classification a useful tool in understanding and setting priorities for land and resource

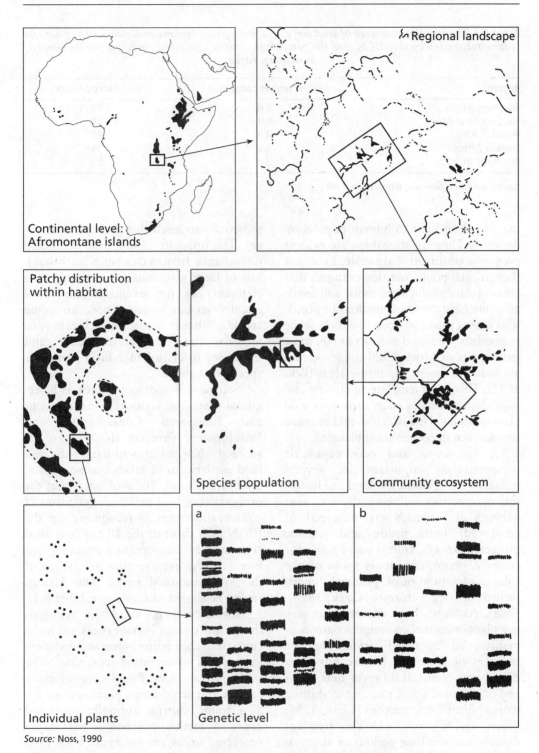

Continental level: Afromontane islands

Regional landscape

Patchy distribution within habitat

Species population

Community ecosystem

Individual plants

Genetic level

a

b

Source: Noss, 1990

Figure 6.1 *Levels of detail will vary with spatial scale in a hierarchy from a global or continental level to that of species levels and genetic levels within a population*

193

Table 6.1 *The overall percentage of land surface in five African regions under all forms of conservation recognized by the IUCN, and the percentage of these conserved areas that are designated as national parks*

Region	% of region conserved	% in national parks
Southern Africa	8.4	74
South-central Africa	9.1	39
Western Africa	4.2	63
Eastern Africa	6.6	39
Northern Africa	3.3	53

Source: Siegfried, Benn and Gelderblom, 1998

use, based on links to human population densities. These relationships are evident even at a continent-wide scale. Ecologist Richard Bell points out, for example, that areas of Africa which are moist and fertile generally have dense populations of people who grow crops and keep livestock, while pastoralists are found in low rainfall, more fertile parts of Africa. Cultivating societies are found in moist, less fertile areas (Bell, 1982). This basic template of climate and soils also determines many aspects of wild plant and animal use which should be taken into account in conservation planning.

A landscape and ecosystem-scale perspective is important for several reasons. Firstly, landscape-level and historical perspectives influence the way that habitats and species are managed or conserved, both inside and outside protected areas. Thirty years ago, for example, people commonly spoke of 'the balance of nature' or of 'primary', 'undisturbed' or 'virgin' forests (Clark, 1996). Today, ecologists have realized that very few plant or animal communities are in an undisturbed 'balanced' state. The life histories of most species are linked to disturbance events at different time scales and of different sizes, forming a 'shifting mosaic' of dynamic patches (Clark, 1996; Pickett and White, 1985). Very frequent disturbance over long periods or at excessively large spatial scales can certainly reduce biodiversity and plant productivity,

sometimes to levels that go beyond recovery. The opposite is also true. Reducing disturbance frequencies (such as through loss of large mammals – for example, the elephant) or fire exclusion can have equally serious consequences for some species. What is needed in each case is to identify the appropriate scale and frequency of disturbance for a particular species or habitat.

Secondly, if approaches such as bioregional planning, ecosystem management and Integrated Conservation and Development Projects (ICDPs) are to succeed, then patterns of harvesting and land use have to be taken into account at a landscape level. The problem is that the proportion of land area under all forms of conservation that is recognized by the IUCN falls short of the 10 per cent ideal suggested by conservation agencies (see Box 1.1). An even smaller percentage of this is in national parks. The African region is a good example (see Table 6.1).

If viable populations of large mammals that require large home ranges are to be conserved, then buffer zones and corridors linking core conservation areas have to be taken into account. Populations of many rare or restricted-range plant species are also found outside formally protected areas. A further problem is that many protected areas are far apart from each other, requiring long, linking corridors. In their landscape-level analysis of African

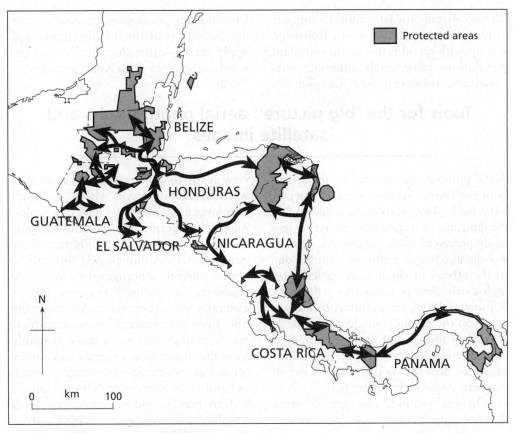

Source: Miller, 1996

Figure 6.2 *The proposed Central American Biological Corridor*

protected areas, conservation biologist Roy Siegfried and others (1998) found that the average distance between protected areas in Eastern Africa was greater than 290km², and in Northern Africa a massive 2396 km². In many cases, therefore, the system of corridors and buffer zones linking core conservation areas covers vast areas of land which are occupied by rural farmers or pastoralists. Examples are the Wildlands Project in North America, the Central American Biological Corridor (see Figure 6.2) and the Greater Serengeti Ecosystem in East Africa (Miller, 1996; Mann and Plummer, 1993).

In terms of harvesting plants, a decline in the area covered by vegetation types

with characteristic species associations is highly significant to conservation and resource management programmes. Firstly, this clearly represents a decline in available vegetation or key species that would have been used by local people. Secondly, it means that the remaining blocks of vegetation become the focus for more frequent and intensive harvesting of high value species.

Thirdly, a landscape-level perspective on patterns of harvesting or processes of vegetation disturbance can influence how quantitative sampling is planned and how its results are interpreted (see Chapter 5). We usually first notice the effects of harvesting at the individual plant level (see

195

Chapter 4) and only later consider impacts at the plant-population level, following this up with quantitative studies of plant populations using small sampling units (quadrats, transects) (see Chapter 5).

Unfortunately, ecologists frequently 'scale up' the results of small-scale studies and apply them – often uncritically – to the whole study area (MacNally and Quinn, 1998).

Tools for the 'big picture': aerial photographs and satellite images

Aerial photographs or satellite images are both extremely useful in any inventory of harvested plant resources, and enable recognition of vegetation patterns less easily perceived from the ground. Loss of woodland cover in northern Namibia due to the effects of small-scale agriculture, high cattle densities and tree felling for housing and fuel, for example, is difficult to see on the ground, but clearly visible in a Landsat image, and may be compared with the less densely populated, better vegetated area across the border fence in southern Angola (see Figure 6.3).

On the ground, one gets a more detailed perspective of a cultural landscape influenced by increasing numbers of livestock and people and changes in their distribution. Additional influences are the 'traditional' Owambo architectural style with its spectacular wood requirements (see Chapter 4), and woodland clearance for millet fields. 'Ground-truthing' in the field also gives the opportunity to recognize where and why some tree species are conserved by local people in small areas (graveyards) or over large areas (for edible fruits and shade). A major reason for maintaining woody cover in this area has been the 'traditional' conservation of favoured edible fruit-bearing trees (particularly *Sclerocarya birrea*, *Berchemia discolor*, *Diospyros mespiliformis*, *Ficus sycamorus* and the palm *Hyphaene petersiana*) as part of the food production system.

This process of getting a bird's eye view leads to a better understanding of which vegetation occurs where (and why) over large areas and fairly long time scales. Aerial photographs are available for some parts of Africa from the 1930s and 1940s (see Box 6.1). Although it is difficult to obtain aerial photographs in some countries for security reasons, this is generally the exception rather than the rule. Even in economically poor countries, aerial photographs are usually available from the department of lands and survey (or its equivalent). Satellite imagery – such as Landsat, Système pour l'Observation de la Terre (SPOT) and Advanced Very High Resolution Radiometer (AVHRR) from NOAA-AVHRR weather satellites – covers much larger areas than aerial photographs but has been available for less time. Landsat data for southern and south-central Africa from the early 1970s, for example, can be bought from the US National Landsat Archive (Eros Data Centre, Sioux Falls, South Dakota, US), and NOAA-AVHRR data have been available for Africa since 1981. Major providers of satellite imagery are the National Aeronautics and Space Administration (NASA) in the US and the Centre National d'Études Spatiales (CNES) in France. One of the problems for field researchers is the high cost of high-resolution satellite data. In most cases, however, aerial photographs, which are available at comparatively low cost, are more appropriate for most applied ethnobotanical field work.

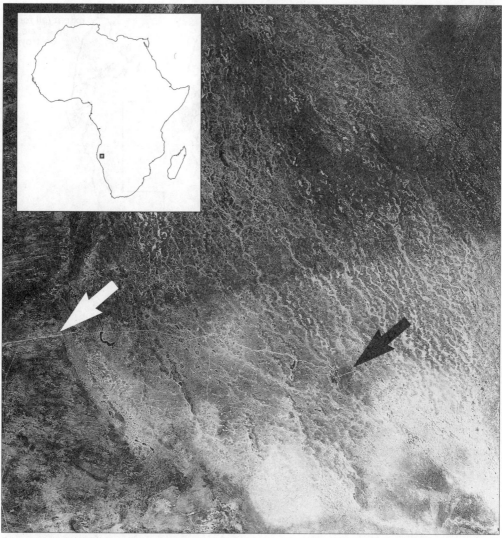

Source: NASA, in Marsh and Seely (1992)

Figure 6.3 *Landsat image showing differences in vegetation cover between southern Angola (north) and northern Namibia due to higher numbers of cattle and people, with consequent impact on woodland and perennial grasses in Namibia as a result of the impacts of grazing and clearing woodland for millet fields. The white arrow shows the line of the international border and the black arrow a fenced site at Ongongo Agricultural College*

Satellite imagery can be extremely useful for understanding land-use patterns at a landscape scale and as a planning (and predictive) tool for conservation and rural development work. Two good examples are firstly, use of the daily NOAA-AVHRR data by the International Geosphere-Biosphere Programme's (IGBP) miombo network to understand burning patterns in miombo woodland. Secondly, Danish ornithologist Jon Fjeldså and his colleagues used ten years' daily NOAA-AVHRR data to recognize tropical African montane forests with ecoclimatic stability

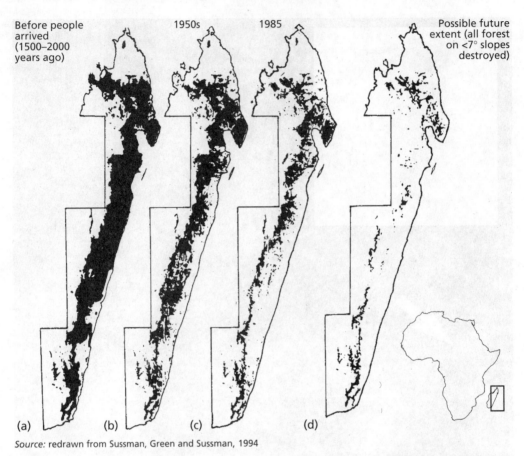

Before people arrived (1500–2000 years ago)

1950s

1985

Possible future extent (all forest on <7° slopes destroyed)

(a) (b) (c) (d)

Source: redrawn from Sussman, Green and Sussman, 1994

Figure 6.4 *The deforestation history of eastern Madagascar, derived from aerial photographs and satellite images. (a) Estimated original extent of forest. (b) Forest extent in 1950. (c) Forest extent in 1985. (d) Computer-generated map predicting the possible future extent of rainforest in eastern Madagascar if all forest on slopes <7° were to be cleared*

as an indicator of 'museum' sites with concentrations of evolutionarily 'old' species, and less stable sites which were 'hot spots' of 'new' species (Fjeldså et al, 1997). These data have an important predictive value for conservation and land management at the ecosystem and landscape level.

Anthropologist Robert Sussman and his colleagues (1994) combined ethnographic studies with maps generated from Landsat images at 1:1,000,000 scale, a vegetation map prepared from 1949/1950 aerial photographs and a map showing

slope (called a digital terrain model) to map the deforestation rate, and to understand why it had occurred and where it was likely to take place in the future (see Figure 6.4). One of their main conclusions was that if forest conservation is to be successful, conservation agencies have to work outside of core conservation areas as well, focusing effort in cooperating with local people at 'deforestation fronts', which were identified from this mapping process. In making comparisons between different photographs or satellite image series, it is essential to remember that this

Figure 6.5 *(a) High resource value, high-diversity Afromontane forest within a protected area (Bwindi-Impenetrable Forest, Uganda) that provides habitat for half the world's mountain gorilla population and is considered to be a Pleistocene forest refugium. Highly dynamic forest on steep slopes due to natural disturbance through canopy gaps created by tree falls, yet with good tree cover, altered to (b) agricultural fields with a few remnant Agauria salicifolia trees retained for fuel wood. The boundary of the protected area is on the crest of the ridge. As shown in Figure 3.3, this clearing has taken place since 1954. What does this represent in terms of local availability of fuel wood, building timber, medicinal plants (roots, bark)? What does it represent for local availability of annual or biennial 'weedy' species used as edible greens or medicines (leaves, whole plants) and favoured by disturbance?*

can only be done if the different images are brought to the same scale. One way of doing this is with a zoom stereoscope (see Box 6.1).

The scarcity or abundance of particular vegetation types that are classified according to biogeographic units stands out even at a continental scale; depending on the focus of the study, one can work from a broad scale towards increasing levels of detail (see Figure 6.1), with different methods appropriate at each spatial scale. The seminal paper by conservation biologist Reed Noss (1990) is recommended reading on hierarchical approaches to understanding biodiversity.

Periodic assessment of the extent and rate of loss (or expansion) of habitat at a landscape level using aerial photographs or satellite images can be a cost-effective way to monitor the success or failure of conservation programmes, but it does not give the full picture. Forest, grassland or woodland cover may not change at all – but underneath the canopy, populations of high-value, vulnerable species can be disappearing due to overexploitation. For this reason, monitoring at a large spatial scale needs to be combined with monitoring of a few high-value 'indicator' species

Box 6.1 Aerial Photographs for Vegetation Interpretation

Aerial photographs used for the production of base maps are taken vertically from a fixed-wing aircraft, using special vertical air cameras along a series of set flight paths. In the past, most aerial photographs were taken with black-and-white panchromatic film (see figure below), with black-and-white infra-red film used for some vegetation studies. More recently, a range of colour film types are employed.

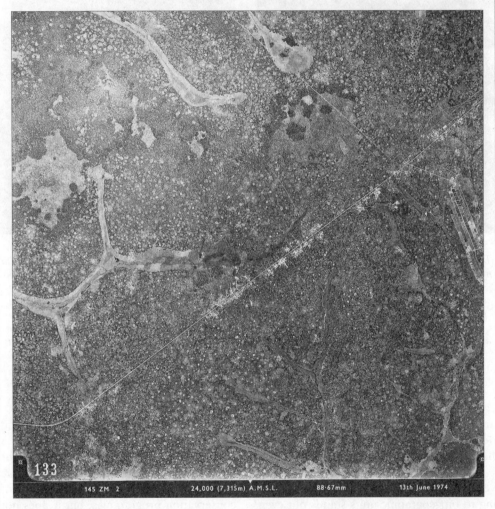

145 ZM 2   24,000 (7,315m) A.M.S.L.   88·67mm   13th June 1974

Miombo (Brachystegia and Julbernadia) woodland in Zambia, showing elongate dambo wetlands, the circular patterns created by characteristic chitemene agriculture, where trees are pollarded and burned to fertilize agricultural fields. More recent settlements are adjacent to the road. Margin of photograph shows date, altitude and series number

In order to locate the photographs you are using within a base map, it is important to refer to the original flight plan. The scale of aerial photographs taken for the production of base maps can vary considerably. In studying long-term changes in savanna trees, for example, Viljoen (1988) used aerial photographs which varied from 1:20,000 for the 1940 series, 1:30,000 for the 1974 and 1977 series and 1:60,000 for the 1965 photographs of the same area in different years. For comparisons to be made, these had to be optically enlarged to the same scale using a zoom stereoscope. This enabled Viljoen to compare tree densities determined from aerial photographs over a 5560 km^2 area and compare these with data on elephant numbers in the same area (Viljoen, 1988). Similar analyses could be done comparing anthropogenic effects in savanna woodlands.

Each photograph is taken so that it overlaps with the next one. Overlap is usually 60 per cent to allow for stereoscope use. A stereoscope is a relatively simple optical tool, with a pair of lenses on a stand which, when placed over a pair of photographs in the same flight series and the correct distance apart, gives a three dimensional appearance. This makes recognition of patterns within vegetation much easier, facilitating vegetation mapping. In combination with checking in the field, including insights provided through participatory ground mapping exercises by local people, characteristic species associations can be marked out on the photograph and then traced to produce a vegetation map. Aerial photographs are also useful in recognizing relict forest patches traditionally conserved for their use as burial sites and settlement patterns, and trends or plant species associations with geological features such as deep sands, limestone outcrops or termitaria.

Although aerial photographs on a scale of 1:20,000–1:60,000 are very useful for mapping vegetation types, and have been used for monitoring populations of large savanna trees, the scale is generally too large for more detailed vegetation surveys, where a scale of 1:1200–1:4500 is usually preferred. Photographs on this scale also enable finer detail of disturbance or unusual vegetation patterns to be recognized, unless tree canopies are close together, obscuring understorey species. Photographs on this scale are rarely commercially available in developing countries. In special cases where there is the opportunity to take photographs at this scale, you need to ensure that you have made the correct preparations and have the correct film and equipment. This is described by Connah and Jones (1983). You also need to decide what scale you require. This is determined by the equation:

$$scale = \frac{lens\ focal\ length}{flying\ height\ above\ the\ ground}$$

You may find the reference by Burnside (1979) helpful. When using aerial photographs in the field, be sure to keep them flat, and protect them from moisture or dust. It is often convenient to place the photographs in a plastic sleeve and keep them clipped to a board. Be conscious that use of aerial photographs or maps may be viewed with suspicion by local militia or police in some countries. You need to take local advice on how to avoid this problem.

at a population level (see Chapter 5) to give a comprehensive picture.

The broad perspective given by aerial photographs or satellite imagery nevertheless gives an important background to information collected from local people (discussions, interview surveys, PRA methods) or botanical surveys (transects, plots) at different spatial scales. In Uganda, for example, the majority of formerly forested areas have been cleared for small-scale agriculture by the high density (150–350 people/km^2) of local farmers; the remaining forests are found mainly within forest reserves or national parks. Penny Scott (1993), for example, compared 1954 and 1990 aerial photographs to show how much forest had been cleared outside Bwindi-Impenetrable National Park – the highest biodiversity site in East Africa. The loss of forest and replacement by farmland evident from the comparison of these aerial photographs gives a clear indication of the declining availability of all wild plant resources of old-growth vegetation (see Figure 6.5a) and the expansion of fields and weedy species (see Figure 6.5b).

The reverse can also occur. Working in the forest-savanna transition zone of Guinea, West Africa, where there is a much lower density of people (10–50 people/km^2), social anthropologists James Fairhead and Melissa Leach (1996) compared aerial photographs from the early 1950s and recent SPOT images to show that 'islands' of forest, and thickets within the savanna, had increased substantially, not decreased. Combined with historical records and the knowledge of local people, they showed how people have created these forest islands in the savanna and that, counter-intuitively, forest area has in this case increased with human population growth.

Distribution, degree of threat and disturbance

How much is out there? Is a harvested species common or rare, and why? Balancing supply and demand is an important part of resource management. Methods for assessing biomass or volume of specific products or yields at the individual plant and population levels have been covered in Chapters 4 and 5. Before getting involved in the detail at the plant population level, it is important to use records of the geographical distribution of a species as a 'first cut' in deciding which species should be the focus of more detailed work – and which are of less concern from a conservation or resource-management perspective. When species have restricted distributions, implying that there may be a limited supply, and are potentially threatened by overharvesting with high demand, it is equally important to know why those species are rare.

Distribution and degree of threat

In terms of geographical distribution, the commonness or rarity of a species is widely publicized as a global or national issue expressed in *Global Action* plans or *Red Data* books at a global or national scale. Distribution on a global scale and the focus on small populations of **endemic** species (species with limited distribution, often with restricted habitats) are both undoubtedly important. A variety of spatial scales must be taken into account, however, so that resource-management plans retain relevance at a local or regional level. A restricted-range endemic of global importance may be considered common and of little concern to villagers living adjacent to its only locality in the world. Conversely, a useful species which is widespread may be of great concern to local people because of destructive harvest coupled with a limited supply; yet the species may be of little conservation interest globally.

Let us assume that you have a list of harvested species for a particular area, based on ethnobotanical studies of markets (see Chapter 3), with their correct local and current scientific names. The next step is to use information from three main sources, listed below.

Published sources

Published sources include standard works on the flora of the region (eg *Flora of Tropical East Africa, Flora Zambesiaca*) or country (such as *Flore du Cameroun*); taxonomic monographs, checklists, revisions (eg *Legumes of Africa*, Lock, 1989); comprehensive field guides on a national scale (eg *Kenya Trees, Shrubs and Lianas*, Beentje, 1994) or on particular families (eg *A Field Guide to the Proteas of southern Africa*, Rebelo, 1995); *Red Data* lists (eg Hilton-Taylor, 1996) and conservation actions plans (eg for palms: Johnson, 1996, or cacti and other succulents: Oldfield, 1997).

Herbarium collections and computer databases

In contrast with species-poor temperate countries whose flora is extremely well known (such as Britain with its circa 1800 species and its many published field guides and several atlases), published records for many high-diversity tropical or subtropical countries may not be available; in this case you need to get distribution records from national, regional herbaria (eg the East African Herbarium) or herbaria which have large international collections and have specialized on plants from particular continents (such as the African collections at Royal Botanic Gardens, Kew, or the Missouri Botanical Gardens). This enables distribution records taken from many herbarium sheets to be mapped (see Figures 6.6a and b). This can be very time consuming. In addition, visits to international herbaria are impractical for most field workers. For these reasons, the increasing availability of electronic databases is very useful. Examples of these are: the threatened plants database developed at the World Conservation Monitoring Centre (WCMC), Cambridge; the International Legume Database and Information Service (ILDIS), coordinated through the Department of Biology, University of Southampton; or regional databases such as LEAP (*List of East African Plants*) covering Kenya, Ugandan and Tanzania, developed at the East African Herbarium, the Plants of Southern Africa Database and SARARES (Southern African RARES database).

Information from local people

Some small, unspectacular species are rarely collected by botanists, yet are well known to local people such as traders and harvesters, who can often provide information to supplement scanty published information or herbarium records – sometimes with embarrassing accuracy! In the mid 1980s, for example, I carried out a conservation assessment of commercially traded medicinal plants in KwaZulu-Natal province, South Africa, cofunded by conservation agencies, herbalists and herb traders. I went through the normal process of identifying voucher specimens collected in markets and with herbalists in the field. A year later, mid-way through the study, with most species identified and with herbarium and published distribution records, I disputed with herb traders their assertion that the parasitic plant *Hydnora africana* (*umavumbuka*, Hydnoraceae) occurred in the province. Thinking that herb traders were saying this because of conservation legislation against transporting some medicinal species across provincial boundaries, I confidently insisted that the specimens in the marketplace must have come from the adjacent provinces of eastern Cape or the Transvaal, where *Hydnora* had been recorded. A few months later, I realized how wrong I was: specimens were commonly being collected in several parts of KwaZulu-Natal by herbalists and

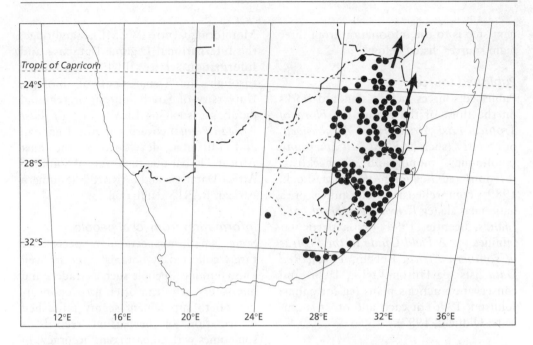

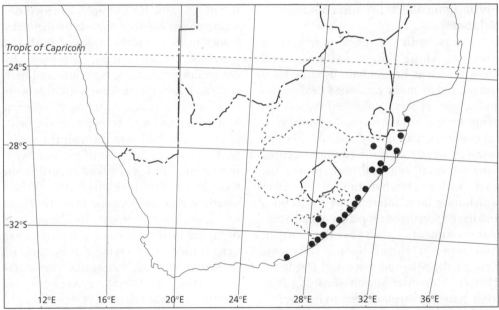

Figure 6.6 *Geographical distribution helps prioritize species in high demand that are likely to be in short supply, which could be the focus of more detailed work. These maps, prepared from herbarium records as part of a study on conservation of medicinal plants (Cunningham, 1988), show two traditional commercially traded medicinal species, both exploited for their woody tubers, both in high demand but with very different distributions. (a) Pentanisia prunelloides (icishamlilo, Rubiaceae), with a wide geographic distribution in South Africa (and occurring northwards to Tanzania), is found in large populations in grassland. (b) Of greater concern is the cycad Stangeria eriopus (imfingo, Stangeriaceae), a monotypic genus with a narrower distribution and smaller populations, which is endemic to coastal grassland and forest in south-eastern Africa*

commercial gatherers (but rarely by botanists).

Information from these sources can be used to grade species according to commonness or rarity. Although this can be done by one person, it may be subjective, so it is far better for a group of experts to assign species to different categories of commonness or rarity. In a medicinal plants survey carried out in the 1980s, for example, I assigned commercially traded medicinal plants to a five-point scale. In addition to grouping commercially traded medicinal plant species according to life form and which part of the plant was used, I also categorized each species into three basic groups (rare, uncommon or common) based on their geographical distribution. The second two categories (uncommon or common) were subdivided further according to whether they were 'uncommon but widespread' or 'uncommon and localized', or common species which were either 'widespread' or 'locally common'. These criteria were then used to prioritize species from the 400 medicinal species in commercial trade in that part of South Africa (Cunningham, 1988, 1991). A better system was used by Deborah Rabinowitz and her colleagues (1986) to examine commonness and rarity in the British flora on the basis of geographic distribution, habitat requirements and local population size. Highest conservation status is given to a species with narrow geographical distribution, a restricted habitat and small population size (see Box 3.1, step 4).

The geographical distribution of species changes as populations expand into new areas, or contract, with habitat loss and/or overexploitation. More than 3000 wild-collected *Stangeria eriopus* cycads have been recorded sold per month at the traditional medicine market in Durban, South Africa (Osborne et al, 1994). At that rate, it is likely that the distribution map shown in Figure 6.6b will shrink alarmingly over a decade. The extent of decline in populations of restricted-range species is used to assign species to the IUCN *Red List* categories to indicate the degree of threat to them (see Box 6.2). The old version of the IUCN *Red List* categories (Davis et al, 1986) was considered to be too subjective and has been modified (Mace et al, 1993; IUCN, 1994) so that a plant species can be rated as **Critically Endangered** (CR), **Endangered** (EN) or **Vulnerable** (VU), based on specific criteria which are identified within the following five main categories:

Criterion a

Proportion of the population loss: a reduction of at least 80 per cent for CR, 50 per cent for EN and 20 per cent for VU, observed, estimated, inferred or suspected over the last ten years or three generations (whichever is longer), or projected or suspected to be met within the next ten years or three generations.

Criterion b

Area occupied by the population: extent of occurrence estimated to be less than $100km^2$ for CR, $5000\ km^2$ for EN and $20,000\ km^2$ for VU, or area of occupancy estimated to be less than $10km^2$ for CR, $500\ km^2$ for EN and $2000\ km^2$ for VU. Estimates of severe fragmentation, continuing decline and extreme fluctuation are also considered.

Criterion c

Rates of population decline and fragmentation: fewer than 250 mature individuals for CR, 2500 for EN and 10,000 for VU. Estimates of continuing decline, severe fragmentation (minimum numbers within subpopulations) and all individuals existing in a single subpopulation are also considered.

Criterion d
Population size: fewer than 50 mature individuals for CR, 250 for EN and 1000 for VU. A VU taxon could also be characterized by an acute restriction in area of occupancy (less than 100 km^2) or number of locations (fewer than 5).

Criterion e
Probability of extinction in the wild: at least 50 per cent within ten years or three generations for CR, 20 per cent within 20 years or five generations for EN and 10 per cent within 100 years for VU.

In many cases, however, the information required on current population levels and rate of decline is not available for heavily harvested, restricted-range tropical species.

Nevertheless, this provides a globally accepted system for setting conservation priorities on a global scale. One way in which conservation priorities are being set in the face of information gaps are CAMP (Conservation Assessment and Management Plan) workshops. The CAMP workshops generally bring together 10 to 40 experts to evaluate the status of a chosen group of species within a country or region, and are designed to reduce bias and favour objective assessment of each species. Good examples of this are the CAMP workshops for endangered medicinal plants of South India, held recently in Bangalore, India. On the basis of ethnobotanical surveys of markets, market value, habitat availability, degree of trade and records from the *Red Data* book for Indian plants, the CAMP workshops held in Bangalore set conserva-

tion priorities for 256 medicinal plant species (Molur and Walker, 1996). In most cases, habitat loss is the major reason for population decline, but harvesting is superimposed on this as an increasingly significant factor.

The total loss of habitat, the rate of habitat loss, the number and size of blocks of vegetation that remain, and their degree of fragmentation, degradation and level of protection are important factors in setting conservation priorities to habitat types. As part of an exercise to set conservation priorities on a global scale, for example, Eric Dinerstein and his colleagues (1995) used five indicators of landscape integrity to classify ecoregions according to their conservation status, in the same way that the IUCN assigns conservation *Red List* categories to species (see Table 6.2).

An ecosystem approach to protected areas requires that sizable enough terrain is set aside to maintain viable ecosystems without outside interference and with minimal management input (Shafer, 1990). The problem is that many ecosystems have been transformed and have lost many of their large predators and herbivores. Maintaining smaller systems than this ideal requires more intensive management, including the need to understand why species are common or rare, and what conditions they need in order to regenerate. Plant species may be rare for several reasons. Firstly, the habitat of that species is only a small proportion of the landscape. Secondly, the factors needed for successful regeneration (such as fire-stimulated seed release, pollination or dispersal, or canopy-gap formation) occur infrequently and may not have occurred for some time. Thirdly, the species may have recently arrived in that landscape from another area. This requires an understanding of disturbance.

BOX 6.2 THE IUCN *RED LIST* CATEGORIES

Extinct (EX)

A taxon is *extinct* when there is no reasonable doubt that the last individual has died.

Extinct in the Wild (EW)

A taxon is *extinct in the wild* when it is known only to survive in cultivation, in captivity or as a naturalized population (or populations) well outside its past range. A taxon is presumed extinct in the wild when exhaustive surveys in known and/or expected habitat, at appropriate times (diurnal, seasonal, annual) throughout its historic range, have failed to record an individual. Surveys should be over a time frame appropriate to the taxon's life cycle and life form.

Critically Endangered (CR)

A taxon is *critically endangered* when it is facing an extremely high risk of extinction in the wild in the immediate future, as defined by any of Criteria a–e for CR species.

Endangered (EN)

A taxon is *endangered* when it is not *critically endangered* but is facing a very high risk of extinction in the wild in the near future, as defined by any of Criteria a–e for EN species.

Vulnerable (VU)

A taxon is *vulnerable* when it is not *critically endangered* or *endangered* but is facing a high risk of extinction in the wild in the medium-term future, as defined by any of Criteria a–e for VU species.

Lower Risk (LR)

A taxon is *lower risk* when it has been evaluated, but does not satisfy the criteria for any of the categories *critically endangered*, *endangered* or *vulnerable*. Taxa included in the lower risk category can be separated into three subcategories:

1   Conservation Dependent (CD)
These are taxa which are the focus of a continuing taxon-specific or habitat-specific conservation programme targeted towards the taxon in question, the cessation of which would result in the taxon qualifying for one of the threatened categories above within a period of five years.

2   Near Threatened (NT)
Taxa which do not qualify for *conservation dependent*, but which are close to qualifying for *vulnerable*.

3   Least Concern (LC)
Taxa which do not qualify for *conservation dependent* or *near threatened*.

Data Deficient (DD)

A taxon is *data deficient* when there is inadequate information to make a direct, or indirect, assessment of its risk of extinction based on its distribution and/or population status. A taxon in this category may be well studied, and its biology well known, but appropriate data on abundance and/or distribution are lacking. Data deficient is therefore not a category of threat or *lower risk*. Listing of taxa in this category indicates that more information is required and acknowledges the possibility that future research will show that threatened classification is appropriate. It is important to make positive use of whatever data are available. In many cases great care should be exercised in choosing between DD and threatened status. If the range of a taxon is suspected to be relatively circumscribed, and if a considerable period of time has elapsed since the last record of the taxon, threatened status may well be justified.

Not Evaluated (NE)

A taxon is not evaluated when it is has not yet been assessed against the criteria.

Sources: Mace et al, 1993; IUCN, 1994

Disturbance

The beginning of this chapter emphasized that the life histories of most species are linked to disturbance events (such as fire, hurricanes, droughts, landslides, disease or human-induced disturbance) at different time and spatial scales. These result in a 'shifting mosaic' of recovering patches of different ages. Some of these can be very extensive and others small, such as branch falls from trees or animals digging holes or building mounds (Hobbs and Mooney, 1991; Thorsten et al, 1997). Natural disturbance by fire is frequent in grassland, heathland, savanna and subtropical woodland, but rare in desert, tundra or forest. What is important is the appropriate scale, frequency and intensity of disturbance for a particular species or habitat.

Natural fires in moist savannas tend to occur once every 1 to 2 years, in dry savannas every 3 to 5 years or so, and every 15 to 20 years in the shrubby heathlands of Australia and South Africa. By contrast, fires are rare in moist tropical forest, but they do occur naturally during exceptionally dry periods (Geldenhuys, 1994; Hart, 1994). Teresa Hart and her colleagues' (1994) remarkable survey of charcoal found in soil pits in the Ituri forest of the Democratic Republic of Congo indicated 4 or 5 fires in the past 2000 years. This gives a valuable perspective on how this influences patterns of plant use. Fruits of the Caesalpinoid tree, *Gilbertiodendron dewevrei* (*mbau*), are gathered in large quantity by Mbuti hunter-gatherers where this slow-growing, shade-tolerant tree species dominates large areas of the Ituri forest today. Study of charcoal records representing 4000 years of vegetation history show that this species was either absent or very rare in the past (Hart et al, 1994): a great example of how contemporary vegetation patterns and use need to be placed in perspective.

Vegetation dynamics, harvesting and the population structure of component species are closely linked. Removal of long-lived bulb species in grassland, or debarking and die-off of forest trees, for example, can 'reset' small patches to earlier successional states, particularly when older

Table 6.2 *The matrix for integrating biological distinctiveness and conservation status of ecoregions to assign priorities for biodiversity conservation*

Biological distinctiveness	Final conservation status				
	Critical	Endangered	Vulnerable	Relatively stable	Relatively intact
Globally outstanding	I	I	I	I	II
Regionally outstanding	I	I	I	II	III
Bioregionally outstanding	II	II	III	III	IV
Locally important	III	III	IV	IV	IV

Note: The Roman numerals indicate biodiversity conservation priority classes:
Level I = Highest Priority at Regional Scale (shaded area)
Level II = High Priority at Regional Scale
Level III = Moderate Priority at Regional Scale
Level IV = Important at National Scale
Source: Dinerstein et al, 1995

plants are targeted. These events can also create openings for the germination and recruitment of other species, including invasive-introduced species.

Methods such as charcoal analysis used in the above example, or pollen analysis, are useful tools for understanding vegetation change over long time scales (see Chapter 1). Methods described in Chapter 4 for ageing plants or measuring plant size or biomass ratios can explain disturbance over shorter time scales. Fire frequencies, for example, have been studied in coniferous forest by cross-dating fire scars, and age of trees has been determined on the basis of tree rings (Wagener, 1961), or in the case of eucalyptus woodland using stem features of grass trees (Lamont and Downes, 1979), and in coastal heathlands using bulb leaf-base counts (Ruiters et al, 1993; see Figure 6.7). Ageing methods for palm stems bent by tree falls have also been used as a tool in understanding gap formation and disturbance in tropical forest (Martinez-Ramos et al, 1988).

It is essential that changes in plant population structure due to disturbance are also taken into account when assessing harvesting impacts on a species over time (see Chapter 5). Working in subtropical lowland forest in southern Africa, for example, van Wyk and colleagues (1996) noticed how species population structure, indicated by the number of stems within different size classes, varied according to forest successional stage after disturbance (see Figure 6.8).

A useful way of characterizing disturbance in forests is by thinking about different forest types in terms of the spatial scale of disturbance or 'grain'. On the basis of work in southern African forests, ecologist Jeremy Midgley has characterized African forests as 'fine-grained' or 'coarse-grained' in terms of the regeneration requirements of gap (shade-intolerant) and non-gap (shade-tolerant) species. 'Grain' refers to the spatial context of disturbance. Some simple ways he used to classify the idea of 'grain' were to:

- Investigate whether large and small stems of con-specifics (individuals of the same species) occur in small plots (such as $400m^2$-sized plots).

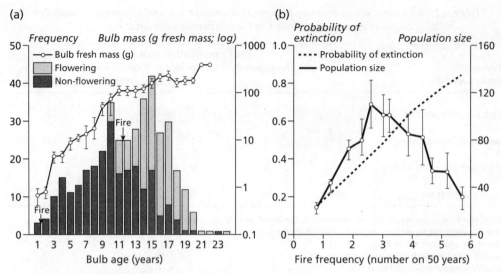

Source: (a) Ruiters et al, 1993; (b) Burgman and Lamont, 1992

Figure 6.7 *Fire frequency and survival. (a) Age distribution and bulb biomass of the medicinal plant* Haemanthus pubescens *in a single sample population (n = 783 bulbs). Flower number increases with bulb age and, like many 'fynbos' heathland species, flowering phenology appears to be synchronized to a fire frequency of 15 to 20 years. (b) The probability of extinction (dashed line) and mean and 95 per cent confidence limits for population size (solid line) as a function of fire frequency (number of fires in 50 years)*

- Investigate size-class distributions of dominant species. Those with inverse J-shaped distributions are likely to be from fine-grained systems.
- Use only canopy or potential canopy species to compare the overstorey composition with understorey trees in plots. In coarse-grained forests there is low similarity between canopy and understorey, suggesting radical compositional change with time.

On this basis, Jeremy Midgley et al (1995) characterized the relative shade-tolerance of tree species in Afromontane forests near Knysna, South Africa. Most of these exhibited reverse J-shaped curves, leading them to describe this forest type as having a 'fine grain' created by small canopy gaps formed by slowly dying trees. Most (70 per cent) of trees in the Knysna forest died standing, for example, and average gap size was small ($35m^2$) (Midgley, Cameron and Bond, 1995). In a fine-grained system, dominance by shade-tolerant species means that con-specific individuals of various sizes will be found close together. By contrast, Dave Everard (1992), working in subtropical coastal forest in South Africa, found that most species were shade-intolerant, with few seedlings or saplings in the understorey, suggesting a species composition characteristic of large-scale disturbance events – perhaps through large, infrequent cyclones, fire or disturbance by large mammals (eg elephants). However, since succession may take place over a scale of centuries, some short cuts are needed to gain insight into disturbance regimes and grain. One way of getting insight into tree life histories is to collect data on specific leaf area (see Box 5.2).

Thinking of forests in terms of 'grain', shade-tolerant or shade-intolerant species,

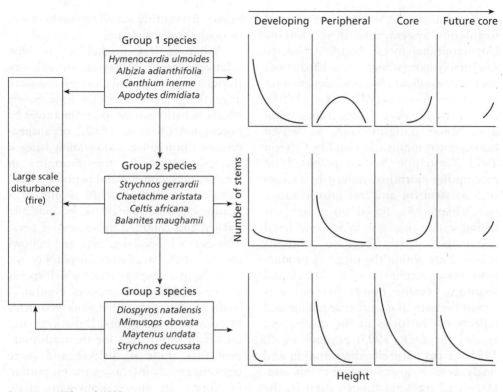

Source: van Wyk et al, 1996

Figure 6.8 *A conceptual model of the dynamics of a subtropical lowland forest in southern Africa (Dukuduku forest). Group 1 species refer to the developing forest species, group 2 species to peripheral forest species and group 3 species are typical core forest species*

or regeneration from seeding or resprouting, gives useful insights for protected area management and past history of natural or anthropogenic disturbance events. Fine-grained forests are in some ways the easiest for low-level utilization of stems because there is generally an abundance of recruits to replace harvested individuals. Coarse-grained systems are more complex in terms of stem harvesting. Early successional species may exist as single-aged cohorts and are likely to be replaced by more shade-tolerant species in the absence of a large-scale disturbance, such as a blow down or clear-felling. Coarse-grained systems can also influence the choice of natural forest logging systems and how these influence non-

timber forest products. In one of the few comparisons of the effects of different logging systems on production and reproduction of non-timber forest products, ethnobotanist Jan Salick (Salick, 1992; Salick et al, 1995) found that the Hartshorn Strip Clearcut System increased vine diversity, but significantly reduced palm density and diversity compared to a selective logging system (Hutchinson Liberation Silviculture). The Hartshorn Strip Clearcut System, for example, which was used by the Yanesha Forestry Cooperative in Peru, is geared to 'coarse-grain' forest (Hartshorn, 1989). Like the woodland coppice systems used in Europe for centuries, strip-rotation systems depend upon resprouting species.

By contrast, the Senility Criteria Yield Regulation System, used in the Knysna (Afromontane) forest, South Africa, to sustainably harvest high-value hardwoods (eg *Ocotea bullata*), has been designed for 'fine-grain' forest (Seydack et al, 1995). In order to minimize change from natural disturbance patterns and to lessen management inputs, the Senility Criteria Yield Regulation System is based on preempting mortality, judged by factors such as stem rot and tree crown health (see Chapter 4). Based on a ten-year felling cycle, this system is considered sustainable, firstly because amounts removed are within the range of productivity (basal increment) of the stand, and secondly, because timber harvesting is within the natural disturbance regime and reflects life histories of the component species (Seydack, 1995; Seydack et al, 1995). Trees naturally die standing and singly, as blow downs are rare in this area. Harvested trees are topped (that is, the crown is removed before the tree is chopped down), and abundant regeneration of most canopy species ensures replacement probabilities remain constant. Opening large gaps in 'fine-grain' forests can profoundly change regeneration patterns. One of the most serious legacies of the uncontrolled small-scale logging which took place in Bwindi-Impenetrable National Park, Uganda, during the Amin era is that this created large gaps in which regeneration is effectively 'frozen' by mono-dominant Acanthaceae or bracken (*Pteridium aquil-inum*), preventing seedling regeneration through intense shading.

What is less predictable is how relatively low-level habitat disturbance through species-selective exploitation can affect things at the landscape level. Subtle effects of bark damage to savanna trees by porcupines (Yeaton, 1988), or anthropogenic disturbance, can certainly cause a marked increase in tree mortality in combination with fire and periodic winds. Removal of bark patches results in a deadwood scar which is periodically burned and enlarged by successive fires. This causes lop-sided growth and hollowing out of the trees over 20 years or so, resulting in a chimney effect which speeds up the hollowing-out process, eventually leading to snapping of the weakened stems in periodic windstorms. Debarking and die-off of forest trees for the traditional medicines trade is quicker and more obvious, greatly increasing the proportion of forest in the canopy-gap phase (Cunningham, 1991). The question is whether it also has subtle effects. In the south-eastern US, small-scale die-off of individual trees due to lightning strikes may be spread to a landscape level by beetles. When conditions are favourable for the beetles (and stressful for trees), beetle damage to trees can spread from individual dead trees to become an epidemic where beetle-induced die-off creates large gaps in the forest (Rykiel et al, 1988). Does this occur in African forests? We do not know: but asking the right questions may help us find out.

Local knowledge, landscapes and mapping

Linking different mapping methods, such as aerial photograph analysis and participatory mapping, with local knowledge of resource preferences can help to predict or explain harvesting patterns within land types. Useful questions to bear in mind relate to resource abundance as well as to physical (paths, roads) and social (boundaries influencing tenure, territoriality) access to resources. Such questions include the following.

- How do local people classify land types? Are there seasonal differences in the use of particular land types? Do current land uses differ from those in the past, and why?
- How do these landscapes or vegetation types 'work' in terms of natural disturbance, the effects of livestock or people's use of fire or species-selective harvesting?
- How does disturbance influence species composition and density of favoured resources or other species?
- How is resource abundance influenced by land form or vegetation type?
- How do topographic features affect resource quality? Position in the landscape can affect resource qualities such as height or length (of reeds, thatch, weaving fibre or bamboo) or even the flavour and fruit size in the case of edible species (such as bitter fruits versus sweet fruits from individuals of the same tree species in swamp forest versus savanna).
- How are harvesting or human-induced disturbance affected by seasonality?
- Where is access influenced by land form or vegetation type, and where is it affected by social boundaries related to tenure or territoriality (see Chapter 7)?

These factors might initially be determined through 'walks in the woods' with resource users, informal discussions, interviews, participatory mapping, or whatever combination of interactive surveys is chosen as most appropriate. They can then be followed up with more detailed and longer-term work with resource users to confirm, refute or add more detail to information derived from mapping exercises. Fiona Walsh (1993), for example, working

with Martu people in the Western Desert, Australia, describes how men and women chose to forage in different land form units. Records of the time that Martu women spent foraging in different land forms reflect selection of species and resource richness within patches, with low species richness in the uplands and high species richness in burned sandplains or in wetland sites (see Figure 6.9). In contrast, men usually hunted opportunistically, frequently using vehicles to do so and consequently travelling longer distances; but they were more constrained to bush tracks.

At a finer level of detail, informal discussions and smaller-scale participatory mapping can be linked to quantitative surveys of vegetation at different stages after disturbance within these land forms, whether due to fire, rainfall or agricultural practice. In another study in the Great Sandy Desert, Western Australia, Fiona Walsh (1990) surveyed burned and unburned vegetation in different land form types in conjunction with field observations during foraging excursions with Martu women (see Figure 6.10a, b). The time that women spent foraging in different vegetation types was taken as an indication of which vegetation types were preferred, with burned sites generally preferred due to their high species diversity and resource richness. This approach can be applied to the harvesting of a wide variety of resources, whether food or medicinal plants, building timber or craftwork material.

Bear in mind, however, that selection of harvesting sites also occurs on smaller and more subtle scales of space and time. What we may have defined as a single vegetation type due to the obvious dominance of one or a few species may, in fact, contain a variety of subtle smaller patches within it. Selection may be based, for example, on stem or culm height

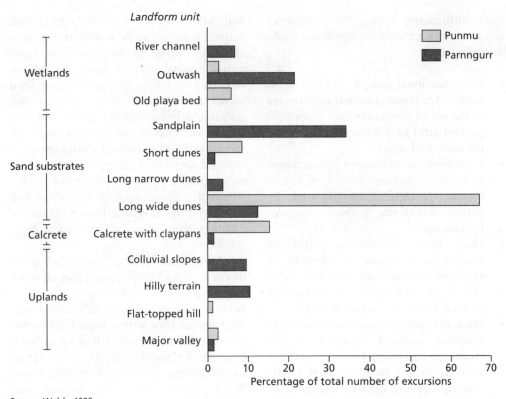

Landform unit

Source: Walsh, 1993

Figure 6.9 *Land form units traversed by women on foraging excursions from two different settlements (Punmu – 18 excursions; Parnngurr – 31 excursions) in the Great Sandy Desert, Western Australia*

within almost pure stands of single thatch, bamboo, sedge or reed species when harvesting for thatch, weaving fibre or for building purposes. Bamboo harvesting and dynamics are a good example. In 1955, as part of an early attempt to take local people's harvesting into account in tropical forest management, the Uganda Forest Department mapped the area under bamboo (*Synarundinaria alpina*) in what was then the Mgahinga Central Forest Reserve. In order to prevent 'overcutting' of bamboo, a series of four coupes (rotational management blocks) of equal size was demarcated. These were successively opened for cutting for one year, then closed for three years (Kingston, 1967). Eighty basket makers were registered by

the forest department. This rotational harvesting started in 1956 (coupe 1), rotating through to coupe 4 by 1960, and restarting in coupe 1 over again.

Apart from concerns that bamboo harvesting was destroying gorilla habitat and the ultimate closure of this area to bamboo harvesting, there was a fundamental flaw in the standard forestry approach to mapping and demarcating coupes: a lack of input from local harvesters. If this had been done, the distribution, size and seasonal use of the coupes would have been very different for three reasons. Firstly, bamboo harvesting for basketry and building poles is not evenly spread, but is concentrated at sites that are well known for their tall, flexible and long-internode

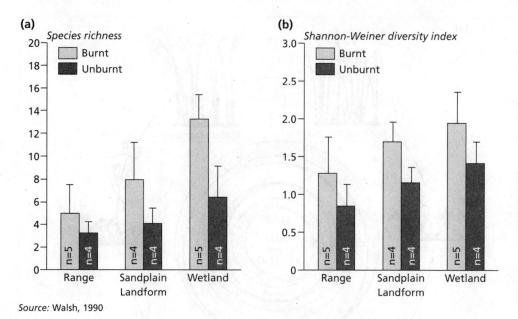

Source: Walsh, 1990

Figure 6.10 *(a) Species richness. (b) Diversity indices of food plants on major land form units in the Great Sandy Desert, Western Australia*

bamboo – usually moister sites with deeper soil. This is not an uncommon situation. In Indonesia, for example, Sundanese villagers prefer harvesting *Gigantochloa pseudoarundinacea* bamboo culms (stems) from hill slopes rather than from valleys, and for good reason. Comparison of bamboo culms showed that the tensile strength and specific gravity of bamboo from hill slopes were significantly higher than those in valleys (Soeprayitno et al, 1988). Secondly, the uprights (warp) of the basket weave (locally termed *inkingi*) can be collected throughout the year, but the more flexible weft material (*imitamu*) has to be collected seasonally before the bamboo stems are fully mature, but not when they are too young. Thirdly, bamboo stands themselves change over time in response to synchronous flowering and die-off and disturbance (fire) (see Figure 6.11).

Similarly, in savanna woodlands dominated either by mopane (*Colophospermum mopane*) or mogonono (*Terminalia sericea*) in southern Africa,

woodcutters wanting tall building poles may choose tall, even-aged stands that reflect soil type or post-fire regeneration. Within these patches, individual trees are selected for straightness, diameter size class and height. The use of ecotones between the vegetation types is another important factor. Walsh (1990), for example, records that ecotones between wetland and sandplain, or between the range and sandplain, were frequently chosen for resource harvesting when Martu women were moving between patches or temporary settlement sites.

Incorporating local knowledge into mapping

Use of geographic information systems (GIS) for computer-based mapping and programmes such as ARC/INFO have become standard practice in some countries but can be far less appropriate in others due to high costs. One way of describing GIS systems is as 'electronic

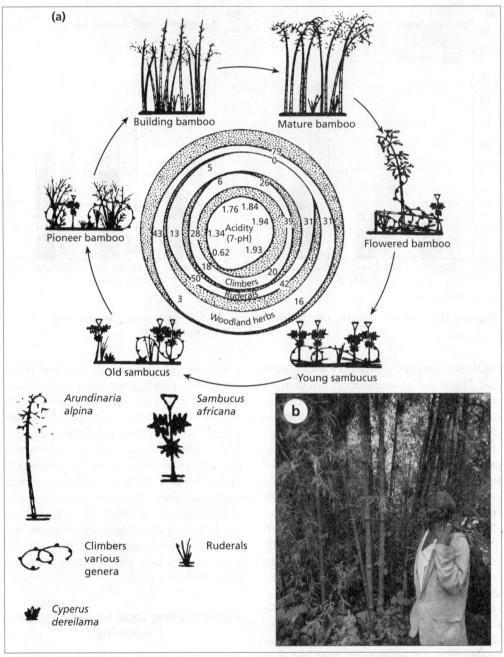

Source: (a) Agnew, 1985

Figure 6.11 *Patchy distribution of resources across landscapes and time scales must be taken into account in inventory, monitoring and management. (a) Diagrammatic representation of stages in* Synarundinaria alpina *succession in East African montane forest on the Aberdare Mountains, Kenya. The six stages do not exist for similar time periods. The course of change of acidity and percentage cover of three floristic elements are shown as concentric plots. (b) Local Abayanda-Twa plant expert Yakobo Bandusya at Mgahinga, Uganda, next to a patch of tall, long-internode* Synarundinaria alpina *bamboo used for basket weaving*

tracing paper', which provides a quick way of doing overlays of important variables such as vegetation change over time or of settlement patterns, roads and markets. Although more time consuming, these overlays can be done without high-tech equipment – for example, from aerial photographs as described in Box 6.1. What is less recognized amongst urban-oriented planners are the participatory approaches to mapping that have been successfully developed with many rural communities in Asia (Poffenberger et al, 1992), or the role that indigenous knowledge has played in soil mapping in Africa (Trapnell, 1953).

A key to the participatory mapping process is the production of maps which illustrate the spatial distribution of resources, of resource-flows or of landscape features of significance (see Box 6.3 and Chapter 2). As Poffenberger et al (1992) point out with specific reference to forest resources, in an approach which is just as relevant to mapping geological features, soil or vegetation types:

> 'Through interactive exercises with the community and observation, the research team can help create a picture of spatial resource use patterns by developing sketch maps, product flow maps and transects of resource use patterns. The main purpose of diagnostic sketch-mapping is to create a visual representation of the resource system which can easily be understood by both villagers and foresters.'

Resource mapping of landscapes familiar to local people can follow a series of steps for key resources and their dynamics in space and time. The extent to which this sequence is followed depends upon how much time and funding are available and what level of certainty and detail is required. If well done, participatory mapping is a good way of establishing common ground and for joint planning, which helps to identify regional landscape areas with outstanding biological and cultural significance – not from the perspective of formally trained planners, but from the viewpoint of the local communities themselves.

Participatory mapping needs as much care in recording local terminology for land types, habitats and localities as an ethnobotanist would take in recording vernacular names of plants. Local terminology for land types and localities is usually at a very fine scale. Despite this problem of scale, it can be extremely useful to 'translate' the 'mental maps' and patterns of resource use developed from discussions and ground maps onto topographic maps and, where possible, into more widely recognized terms for vegetation or land types.

A recent Australian example of participatory planning is the interaction between scientists and people of the Western Desert (Anangu) community in conservation planning in Uluru (Ayers Rock–Mount Olga) National Park, which has been jointly managed by the Anangu people and the Australian National Parks and Wildlife Service (ANPWS) since the granting of freehold title to the Aboriginal traditional owners in 1985 (Baker and Mutitjulu Community, 1992). As part of the process, Anangu classification of major landscape types was used in addition to internationally recognized (but in some cases, less precise) geographic terms for landscape units.

At a finer level of resolution, field work within habitats facilitates a better understanding of ecosystem dynamics amongst conservation biologists. This is particularly relevant in forest ecosystems, which are extremely complex in terms of

Box 6.3 Participatory Mapping Exercises: Resources at Landscape and Species Population Levels

Local participation in mapping has been developed and popularized, and is increasingly used to enable local people to share their experience as part of participatory rural appraisal (PRA) methods (Chambers, 1992). Participatory mapping exercises can be applied widely to natural resources management; but they also have weaknesses which should be avoided, where possible, through complementary use of aerial photographs or 'photo-maps' (local people mapping onto a transparent sheet placed over large-scale aerial photographs). A common problem with PRA mapping is the difficulty of establishing scale (and therefore transferring data onto other maps). In Nepal, for example, Richard Mather and his colleagues (1998) worked with villagers using large-scale (1:1250–1:2500) enlargements from 1:50,000 aerial photographs in conjunction with a GIS system to prepare management plans for community forests. They describe how the advantages of spatial accuracy, authenticity, consensus and trust through use of these 'photo-maps' were illustrated:

> '...when one woman, frustrated at trying to interpret a paper [PRA] map drawn by an earlier group, cast it aside and picked up an aerial photograph with words to the effect that: "This is real, let me see it." During the course of the evaluation it became more and more apparent that, in spite of all facilitation measures to the contrary, participatory maps largely represented the perceptions of one or two dominant people.'

Combining conventional PRA mapping with the use of aerial photographs provides a useful context in which to interact with local resource users and develop an understanding of natural resources from a local perspective. Mapping can apply to natural resources, whether mammals, insects, soils, reptiles or plants, in space as well as time. In northern Canada, for example, a map drawn for a project field worker by local hunters on northern Baffin Island illustrated the interaction between narwhals and killer whales, in their habitat at the margins of sea ice and open water. In this case, mapping enabled a greater understanding of how killer whale and narwhal behaviour related to the location and timing of spring ice break-up and land ice composition than discussions with local hunters would have done (Brody, 1976). Participatory mapping can include topics as diverse as vegetation mapping and maps by local beekeepers showing their knowledge of bee-hive location in relation to vegetation and topography.

Photo-mapping also has its disadvantages, however, particularly the difficulty of covering large areas (for example, in arid environments) and the cost of getting enlargements from 1:50,000 photographs. In these cases, thorough toponymic (local place name) surveys mapped onto standard 1:50,000 scale or smaller can provide common reference points that get round some of the problems of scale through providing common reference points. Alternatively, an innovative system linking local knowledge with user-friendly GIS technology also has the potential for resource mapping by local people over large areas. In this case, local trackers, who have no literacy but excellent field skills, have been using palm-pilot field computers designed with user-friendly icons by expert tracker Louis Liebenberg and computer scientist Lindsay Steventon to monitor wildlife such as rhino. In Zimbabwe, local basket makers are testing a modification of this system for monitoring the impact of *Berchemia discolor* bark dye use (see Chapter 5).

Suggestions for participatory mapping are listed below:

- Only undertake mapping exercises after permission is granted by the community to work in the area, and after you have established a good understanding of local vegetation and people–resource interactions. Mapping should ideally be preceded by 'walks in the woods' and informal discussions with knowledgeable local people, and possibly by market surveys. Aerial photographs and soil maps can be very useful at this stage.

- In any culture, and most of all in cultures with strong religious or symbolic attachment to the landscape, as in Aboriginal communities in Australia, mapping can only take place on the basis of an established position of trust with regard to intellectual property and sites of cultural sensitivity. The religious and spiritual dimension of landscapes to many indigenous peoples is widely acknowledged. So too are the varying perceptions of landscapes with gender and age. These factors alone provide a strong argument for a community-based research and planning process to enable community control over sensitive information, and for separate mapping exercises with men or women or specific user groups.

- Once key resources have been identified through community discussions (resource scarcity, importance), market surveys (high commercial demand) or community and international conservation concerns (overexploitation, endemic species), you need to consult key people within the community to select local experts on these issues. This will determine the type of map you will produce and what it will show (resource distribution, extraction routes, sale points).

- Choose a suitable place for ground mapping, where local people will feel relaxed to do the mapping exercise. Maps can be drawn in the sand or marked on harder soil or grassy sites. Have suitable markers available (stones, sticks, tins). You may need to bring along large sheets of paper, despite the fact that this constrains map scale and participation in the mapping process. In some places, for example, villagers have objected to drawing on the ground, affronted by the apparent assumption that they could not use pen and paper.

- Help people get started with the mapping exercise, but remember that it is their map, to be drawn on their initiative. Ground mapping often needs a lot of space. The first local person to put key points onto the ground map usually sets the scale of the map. In some cases, when marking is easy (such as drawing map lines in the sand with a stick), the map may end up 15m or 20m long. This can be an advantage, enabling resource users to walk over a 'conceptual landscape', marking and naming places and areas of resource richness.

- At the end of the mapping exercise, encourage someone to transcribe the map onto paper as a permanent record. Where culturally appropriate, add the names of the contributors.

life form and species diversity, where hardwood tree generation times are long and understanding of patch dynamics is limited.

On shorter time scales, traditional ecological knowledge can provide valuable insights into ecosystem functioning or habitat/species associations. Good examples are the Kayapo terminology for different forest types in Amazonia (Parker et al, 1983), and information from Anangu people on faunal habitat associations of reptiles in Uluru National Park, central Australia (Baker and Mutitjulu Community, 1992).

Local knowledge and spatial scale

The spatial scale of local knowledge varies according to social factors, such as mobility, and with biological factors. Knowledge of most resource users is usually focused within a 'home range' which will vary from large spatial scales (2000km^2 or more) among pastoralists and hunter-gatherer groups, to smaller scales among gatherers in tropical forests or more sedentary agricultural communities. The pastoralists and hunter-gatherers have great mobility as they 'track' resource patches in space and time that are created through natural events such as rainfall or by people through disturbances such as fire. In the semi-arid Kalahari sandveld in southern Africa, for example, small groups of part-time and full-time hunter-gatherer groups each ranged over an average area of 1500km^2 (Hitchcock, 1978). Within these 'home ranges', local ecological knowledge can be very detailed; knowledge may decrease with distance away from home ground.

In high rainfall areas, farmers' knowledge is much more localized, relating best to mapping scales of 1:10,000 or less. It is equally important, however, to take into account the more subtle influences on resource use at a much smaller scale, whether these relate to topography and settlement patterns (see Chapter 2) or clumped distribution of resources. For this reason, it is often useful to be aware that one is working within a set of hierarchies of scale and level of detail (see Figure 6.1).

Linking local knowledge to aerial photographs or, in some cases, to satellite images enables the localized knowledge of different adjacent communities to be linked into a 'patchwork' covering a wide area and range of ecological zones. In northern Australia, for example, O'Neill et al (1993) have used Landsat imagery and a geographic information system (GIS) to compare the effects of burning on eucalyptus woodlands on different land types over a 3-year period in a 995km^2-sized study area. This enabled a comparison of timing and size of burns by Aboriginal people with those by pastoral-ists, or 'hazard reduction' burns started by park rangers with aerial incendiaries. Local people, including Aboriginal people from the Marralam community and pastoralists, assisted in the interpretation and ageing of burns. Field information was essential in order to identify the ignition sources. Between 1988 and 1991, O'Neill et al concluded that, contrary to the widespread belief that burning by the Aboriginal community was destructive, impact was low and these perceptions unfounded when considered at a landscape level. In addition, the study suggested that lack of burning in eucalyptus woodland by Aboriginal people over the past 100 years has increased the chances of high-intensity, destructive fires in the late dry season across northern Australia. Indeed, efforts have been made in Kakadu National Park, northern Australia to re-establish, as far as possible, traditional practices of burning in order to create a richer patchwork of habitats, to the benefit of fire-dependent groups of plants and animals (Lewis, 1989).

Cultural views of landscape

The cultural context of mapping strongly influences how people interpret and understand landscape maps. Robert Rundstrom (1990), who analysed Inuit map-making, points out the importance of understanding the 'cultural filters' through which geographical information is organized and retains meaning. On one hand, participatory maps help to reveal links between people and the landscape. On another, interpretation of these maps is improved by an ethnographic understanding of these cultural links.

In the mapping process with local people, it is important to realize that landscapes and disturbance processes are viewed from very different perspectives both within and between cultures. In the same way that a 'walk in the woods' approach gives the opportunity to improve cross-cultural communication for researchers who are outsiders to the community, so it is important to record and cross-check local landscape classification systems.

Amongst formally trained researchers or planners, views of landscape are often clouded by orientation towards one academic discipline or another. Applied ecologists are primarily concerned with biological factors, while anthropologists or social scientists focus on cultural and socio-economic factors. Local resource users, on the other hand, may see landscapes or the resources within them through a different set of 'filters' which vary according to their age, gender, and specialization (herbalist, honey-hunter, master fisherman, midwife). Within the same human community, for example, a forest may appear to be a threatening habitat, or a resource-filled series of patchy habitats for hunting, trapping or harvesting timber. To African traditional healers, for example, as Victor Turner (1967) pointed out in his classic book on cognitive anthropology in Zambia, the same forest would be a 'forest of symbols'. Events such as rainfall, fire, cyclones or lightning, which create disturbance patterns and resource patchiness, all have strong cultural and symbolic meaning. Events which ecologists consider 'natural' may be thought to be under supernatural control. In many societies, for example, rainfall, lightning and storms are widely considered to be susceptible to the influence of shamans and symbolic medicines.

Only with careful understanding and sensitive discussion can ethnobiologists begin to bridge the gap between different interpretations of the same disturbance event or landscape. This empathy is worth the effort, since cross-cultural understanding can give crucial insight into people's attitudes as to how or why resources within patches should be conserved. This topic is discussed in Chapter 7.

Chapter 7

Conservation Behaviour, Boundaries and Beliefs

Introduction

In many ways, the term 'natural resource management' is misleading since it has more to do with 'people management' than with managing natural resources. There is no doubt that we need to prioritize the most valued or vulnerable species, or find out how much can be sustainably harvested (see Chapters 4–6). For good science to become good management, however, there needs to be wide social acceptance of management plans or regulations. Achieving this, in turn, requires an understanding of the social, economic, ethical, religious and political factors that either encourage resource conservation or lead to resource depletion. These are as important and as complex as the biological component discussed in Chapters 4 to 6. Background information on these factors can be gathered through local social surveys (see Chapter 2). There is also a close link with commercial trade, which brings in opportunistic 'outsiders' as well as income, as village economies shift from subsistence use and barter to links with external markets (see Chapter 3).

This chapter focuses on methods which can lead to a better understanding of tenure and boundaries, and resource-user characteristics which can form the basis for common ground between local communities and modern conservation practice. In particular, due to their complexity and significance in Africa, this chapter focuses on the interface between communal lands and land set aside for conservation by state governments. This relates directly to land and resource tenure (the rights and responsibilities under which land or resources are held) and the ways in which individuals or groups of people can use and control the area or resource, and the relations between state government (such as national parks authorities) and local people.

At first glance (particularly to most biologists), religion and social relationships have little to do with natural resource management or conservation. However, to local people and professionals in the social sciences, the links between conservation, religion, social issues and land and resource tenure are clear (see, for example, Nhira and Fortmann, 1993; Richards, 1996). Many national parks and forest reserves are recent. Seventy-six per cent of Central American protected areas, 65 per cent of those in the Caribbean and 38 per cent of those in South America were declared in the 1980s (McNeely, Harrison and Dingwall, 1994). Although the first African national park was proclaimed a century ago (1897), most have been established since the 1960s. Much of the land on which national parks have been created has a much longer human history, often with complex cultural links to the present. Anthropologist Parker Shipton (1994) eloquently describes this link between land and culture:

> '...*religion, ritual and cognition on one hand, and adaptation, sustenance, and production on the other, cannot be kept pure of each other. Land holding is at the centre of the confluence. Nothing evokes more varied symbolic connotations or more intricate legal philosophies. Nothing excites deeper passions or gives rise to more bloodshed than do disagreements about territory, boundaries or access to land resources. Nor is anything more likely to prevent misunderstandings across cultures, harmful to both humans, and their habitat, than are thoughtful definitions of land holdings in the first place.*'

This inevitably binds conservation (as one form of land use) to the social world of politics and religion – and, whether we like it or not, this has to be better understood if we are to achieve conservation and resource management objectives.

Earlier chapters of this manual were devoted to outlining ecological and scientific approaches to developing a functional classification of vegetation, as well as describing species' resilience or vulnerability to harvesting. This required using methods of analysis at a variety of spatial and time scales. The same applies to the analysis of factors that influence local resource management and conservation behaviour, with the additional element of communication that is central to human society. This chapter deals, firstly, with conservation behaviour and the 'ingredients' which are considered likely for successful community-based conservation. It then deals in more detail with the methods used to define some of those 'ingredients': in particular, methods used to identify tenure types, boundaries and the most significant stakeholders in resource management. In the process, since conservation organizations are generally staffed by people with a biological sciences background, the chapter will suggest relevant literature, giving theoretical background to these important practical issues in resource management.

Conservation and the ingredients for common property management

The protected area concept has broadened from strictly protected sites to protected areas within a bioregional or ecosystem framework. In most cases, this requires comanagement of resources within designated zones (buffer zones, multiple-use areas). This change in approach has increased the need for methods which lead to community-based conservation.

It is now widely recognized that legislation on its own is often ineffective. Conservation areas in private hands or under state control often face similar problems. Results from a postal survey of managers of private reserves, for example, listed poaching (81.3 per cent), lack of cooperation from government (71.95 per cent), budget deficiencies (56.3 per cent), political unrest (53.1 per cent), and community opposition to loss of access to the reserves' resources (43.8 per cent) as major problems (Langholz, 1996).

In many countries with high biological diversity but impoverished governments, centralized control of national parks, forest reserves or the natural resources within them by patrol rangers is often ineffective in preventing hunting in 'strictly' protected areas. Effective in-situ conservation for black rhino, for example, would cost US$400 per km² (Martin, 1994). Based on his experience in East Africa, for example, John Hall suggests that patrolling of forest reserves generally requires 2 forest guards per 500ha (or 4 guards per 10km²) (Hall, 1983). In most cases, neither this level of funding nor staffing are available. Even the most important forest conservation areas fail to meet this criterion. Bwindi-Impenetrable National Park, Uganda, for example, is a 330km² rugged, forested area world-renowned as the home of half the world's mountain gorilla population and the forest with the highest biodiversity in East Africa. Instead of the 130 patrol rangers considered necessary on the basis of John Hall's experience, Bwindi has 30 patrol rangers. Implementing a sustainable logging programme requires even more staff. In Afromontane forest in South Africa, which has a relatively low species diversity compared to tropical forests, and where only a single product (timber) and few species are involved, a marking team of one forester and two staff who only select trees greater than 30cm dbh is only able to cover 5ha per day (Seydack et al, 1995).

The challenge is to find appropriate and lasting solutions to conflicts over conservation land. Local participation through community-based conservation programmes within protected areas or in buffer zones around their margins has become widespread as one potential solution. Much of the success or failure of local participation in conservation programmes hinges on the social factors of relations, rights and responsibilities (see Figure 7.1). To avoid expensive failures, the design of Integrated Conservation and Development Projects (ICDPs) has to take local institutions, tenure and resource management systems into account. A first step towards this is to analyse the physical factors (bioclimatic, topographic) of the area, as well as the social factors (political organization and institutions, socio-economic, religious) covered in this chapter. Understanding people's conservation behaviour in terms of 'what they conserve, why, where, when and how' is also an important step towards consensus and reduced conflict with modern conservation objectives.

In theory, this seems straightforward; but in practice, defining relations, rights and responsibilities is far from simple. There has been too much generalization on a range of very diverse and dynamic situations. For every claim that 'rural people have sophisticated systems of natural resources management which have maintained biodiversity for thousands of years' (IIED, 1994), there are cases where local people have destroyed high-diversity habitat, or where the people living adjacent to protected areas are recent migrants. All of this is confusing to field researchers, rural development workers and protected area managers in trying to work out what should apply locally to the long-term benefit of both conservation and local communities. For this reason, we need to be able to look beyond the smoke screen of conservation politics and untangle the complex interplay of ecological, political, religious, economic and social undercurrents behind successful or failed examples of resource conservation.

Chapters 4 to 6 discussed biological factors that lead to resilience or vulnerabil-

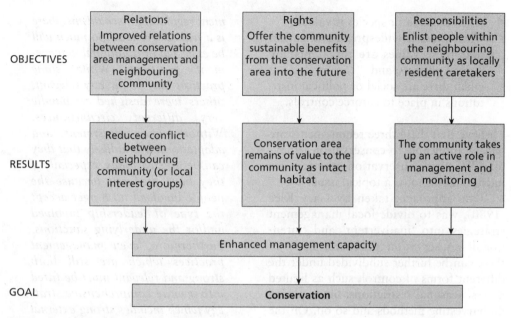

Source: adapted from Scott, 1995

Figure 7.1 *Much of the success or failure of local participation in conservation programmes hinges on the social factors of relations, rights and responsibilities*

ity of plant populations to overharvesting, methods for collecting data, and the role of this information in developing practical management plans. A parallel set of questions relates to human societies. Under what set of circumstances is conservation behaviour likely to take place without being imposed upon people by those from the outside? What makes people comply with customary controls, and what leads to their breaking down? How (and why) should we distinguish between intentional conservation practices by local communities, and ones that are merely the inadvertent end product of some other action?

Laws, whether an oral tradition of customary law, or written into national legislation, are only effective when just a small minority of the population are likely to break those laws. When most people disagree with regulations and disregard them, the costs of law enforcement become impossibly high. For this reason, control is only effective when the majority of people

choose to abide by resource conservation regulations. How long are these systems of customary conservation or resource tenure likely to last when conservation goals are based on long (ecological) time scales, and when cultural change is often rapid? Looking at a range of different situations from more remote to less remote areas, where population densities are higher, communities less homogeneous and commercial trade more prevalent, can lead to useful insights into this question.

Customary ('traditional') conservation practices

Are people conserving habitat or resources, or doing this for other purposes? Based on her work on traditional conservation practices in Oceania, geographer Margaret Chapman (1987) suggested that people traditionally conserve habitat or a resource when three conditions are fulfilled:

- when the area or species is valued;
- when there is widespread realization that these values are threatened by human impacts; and
- when there are social or political institutions in place to enforce controls.

I believe that these three requirements are widely applicable to conservation behaviour. Whether conservation practices are intentional or not is a topical issue.

One approach, taken by Gary Klee (1980), was to divide local management strategies into 'inadvertent' and 'intentional' conservation practices. Each of these can be further subdivided under the different forms of control, such as limited access, seasonal restrictions, limits placed on harvesting methods and so on. On the other hand, anthropologist Raymond Hames (1987) suggests that: 'Any persuasive account of conservation as a human adaptation requires a theory that shows that conservation is by design, and not a side effect of some other process, specifies the conditions under which conservation will evolve, and predicts how individuals will systematically regulate their behaviour to conserve resources.' To do this, researchers and resource managers need to test how resource users behave under conditions of resource scarcity or abundance as well as during socio-economic change. They also need to avoid a romantic view of customary ('traditional') conservation practices that raise expectations but lead to resource depletion. What Thayer Scudder and Thomas Conelly (1985) point out about management systems for traditional fisheries could also be said about some aspects of terrestrial community-based natural resource management (CBNRM) programmes:

'As fisheries managers search for other strategies to "shore up" or complement ineffective govern-ment regulatory mechanisms, there is a real danger that too much will be expected of traditional management practices. While some practices may be directly relevant, others were designed to handle very different circumstances. Without major adjustments and adaptations, it is unlikely that they can be utilized today, especially if they have died out because the people involved no longer accept the type of leadership involved and/or the underlying sanctions. Furthermore, even management practices which are still both strong and relevant must be fitted into a more comprehensive strategy which includes strong external support.'

Ingredients for community-based natural resource management

A useful analytical framework for field workers to use in sorting out the complex issues in predicting the likelihood of successful community-based conservation includes the design principles for common property resource management. The work of Elinor Ostrom (1990) on systems of self-governance and Robert Wade's (1987) study of village regulations on irrigation and grazing systems in South India are recommended reading on this subject. These 'design principles' for viable management of common property resources provide valuable guidelines in deciding where CBNRM programmes might succeed or fail.

This is no 'magic formula' for success, particularly when dealing with the added complexity of common property resource management: there are too many ecological, social, political and economic variables for this. What we have a responsibility to do, however, is to highlight

BOX 7.1 INGREDIENTS FOR SUCCESSFUL COMMUNITY-BASED NATURAL RESOURCE MANAGEMENT (CBNRM) PROGRAMMES

Conservation and resource management through decentralized control to local communities has been widely advocated in the past decade. The merits of local management of communal resources have also been rightly questioned, as the capacity of local institutions for resource management has been weakened by economic, political and religious change. Before decentralization is advocated, it is important to have a predictive understanding of where community-based conservation is likely to succeed or fail. Land-use factors have a strong influence on this (see the following section on 'Ecological Factors, Land Use, Tenure and Territoriality').

Boundaries

These include clear, accepted, controllable boundaries around the resource. They need to be defined and small enough to be controlled and monitored (see Figure 7.2e).

Tenure and Territoriality

Trust in long-term access increases the chances of sustainable management. Secure tenure is one part of this. Long-term tenure is a major incentive for successful resource management and conservation, whether the land or the resources themselves are privately or communally owned. Another part of this is that there should be local confidence of long-term access to resources, as agreed between the group which has legal tenure (such as national parks) and resource users within comanagement agreements (eg a memorandum of understanding). Based on his work in Nepal, Robert Fischer (1995) points out that formal tenure is less important than the confidence that agreements will be honoured.

Resource Predictability and Mobility

This includes predictability and low/no mobility. The greater the resource predictability in space or time, the greater the incentive for establishing property rights or managed use. Examples are the strong rights attached to long-lived perennial resources that provide a predictable resource in unpredictable environments, such as wild tree species that are sources of productive, favoured fruits or provide browse in arid/semi-arid environments (eg *Boscia* trees in East and Southern Africa), or the widespread private rights to bee hives or trees with wild hives (see Figure 7.2f). With mobile resources such as game animals or fish, private or common property rights apply to traps and trapping sites, rather than to the resource itself.

Relationship between Resources and the User Group

Resource value

The resource must be valuable to the group. As Marshall Murphree (1995) points out, 'effective management of natural resources is best achieved by giving the resource a focused value – to determine whether the benefit of managing a resource exceeds the cost, the resource must have value to the community.'

Resource scarcity

The relationship between resource scarcity and vulnerability to human impact needs to be recognized by resource users. If the resource users' belief system does not link human impact (such as overhunting) with resource depletion (for example, as occurs amongst Algonquin Indians in the Boreal forests of North America), then this poses a problem that may even exacerbate overexploitation.

Resource commercialization

Customary controls break down rapidly with the shift from subsistence use to commercial harvest, particularly when commercialization is accompanied by an influx of outsiders.

Multiple-use lands, resources and multiples of users

CBNRM is favoured with fewer, rather than more, users and where resources have fewer rather than multiple uses. The more uses and users there are of a particular landscape or resource, the more complex and potentially conflicting management becomes.

Composition of the User Group(s)

Group size

Smaller numbers of users are better than larger groups, but groups should not be so small that they have no social influence.

Group identity

The more clearly defined the user group, the greater the chance of success (eg local beekeepers, herbalists, midwives, basket makers; see Figures 7.2b and c).

Location of resource users

Ideally, resource users need to live near the resource, or amongst mobile or semi-nomadic communities, and to frequent the resource area regularly. In either case, this simplifies the monitoring of who is using the resource or resource area, and helps restrict access by outsiders.

Community homogeneity

Although no community is completely homogeneous in outlook, many are far more divided in terms of socio-economic status and diverse interests. Social control over resource use is more likely to occur in homogeneous than in heterogeneous communities. Homogeneity breaks down with the influx of outsiders into the area. Religious/ritual belief systems are widely accepted; these systems maintain group pressure for actions that encourage short-term individual sacrifice in favour of longer-term group benefit.

Setting and Maintaining Limits

Users' knowledge

Users' knowledge is best built on existing local knowledge of sustainable yields and resource status.

Rules for resource use

These need to be simple, practical, enforceable and appropriate (see Figure 7.2f).

Maintaining obligations

Mutual agreements reached on resource use need to be kept and there need to be disincentives against individuals exploiting resources at the expense of the group.

Free riders

People who try to abuse the system need to be easy to detect. This largely depends upon having small, clearly defined boundaries around the resource, and a small and identifiable group of resource users who live near the resource.

Punishments against rule breaking

Consensus needs to be reached on punishments for breaking agreed rules. There should be a sliding scale of punishments, but punishments for serious offences require 'bite' in social or material terms.

Conflict Resolution

Well-developed mechanisms for conflict resolution should be established. Mediation may be brokered by outside institutions such as non-governmental organizations (NGOs), or there may be internal mechanisms, such as conflicts which are expressed through witchcraft accusations and resolved by cleansing rituals and therapy.

Resource Management Groups and the State

The state should support and encourage, and be careful not to undermine, decentralized control. Where resource groups are effective in preventing an open-access situation and are managing resource use on a sustainable basis, state control should be minimized. It can play a crucial role, however, when local institutions need support – whether in law enforcement or through technical input.

Source: adapted from Wade, 1987

where there is a greater likelihood of success or failure. Community-based natural resource management is often an experimental process, and it is far better to experiment where success, rather than failure, is most likely. Both broad and fine-scale processes need to be taken into account in this process. It is tempting to focus on local circumstances, but this is rarely sufficient to assess local systems of

Figure 7.2 *(a) Ecological impacts and land-use conflicts increase as savanna and grasslands used by pastoralists are encroached upon by wheat farmers (Rift Valley, Kenya). (b) Stretcher-bearer societies (ekibiina by'engozi) are strong local institutions which form the basis of forest societies (ekibiina kya'beihamba) linked to smaller groups of resource users (herbalists, midwives, beekeepers, basket makers) licensed to harvest specific forest products within multiple-use zones of Bwindi-Impenetrable National Park. (c) Group identity: user groups are first nominated by the community and then each issued with cards for that user group, building on the memorandum of understanding (MOU) between the national park and community, and avoiding conflict with park patrol rangers. (d) Ritual boundaries, tenure and timing: Nuxia congesta fuel wood shifted from virtual 'open access' before harvest in Mount Kilum Forest Reserve, Cameroon, to private rights after harvest through placing charms (ju-jus) on sticks next to logs. (e) Mapping 'invisible' boundaries: John Makombo's work with local elders enabled customary boundaries to be mapped within and around Rwenzori Mountains National Park. (f) Private rights to bee hives are strictly enforced by magic and customary law. (g) Community game guards in northern Namibia are at the forefront of local conservation efforts facilitated by the integrated rural development and nature conservation (IRDNC) programme*

resource use and management. All are obviously influenced by ecological determinants (climate, soils) on land use, and very few (if any) local communities are isolated from wider economic and political systems. These factors strongly influence the potential to develop comanagement systems or community-based management systems. This provides the background for developing site-specific methods and approaches to community-based natural resource management.

Approaches that have been acclaimed in one part of the world, such as CAMPFIRE (Communal Areas Management Programme for Indigenous Resources) in Zimbabwe or Joint Forest Management (JFM) programmes in West Bengal, India, cannot simply be transferred to closed-canopy tropical forest, for example. What can be done is to get insights into what failed or succeeded in other places, since there are often common principles that structure the way that people in different parts of Africa, or different parts of the world, see particular issues, events or places (see Box 7.1). In addition, a legacy of past research and thought by ecologists, economists and social scientists provides important theoretical background for understanding the social processes behind establishing access rights to land or resources. These are summed up in Box 7.2 for those interested in further reading.

In your study area, it is important to identify where consensus and conflicts of interest occur in terms of the following.

Land use

What are the current land-use systems and land-use potential? This is a good measure of habitat change and the lost opportunity costs if land is set aside for conservation purposes (aerial photograph analysis, cost-benefit analysis of land-use options,

overlapping users such as hunter-gatherers, pastoralists, farmers, traders). What are the conflicts (with wildlife, access to water points, grazing versus farming)? What is the direction and rate of change? What is the gap between conservation and other forms of land use, or between exploitation now or sustainable use in the long term? Cost-benefit analysis is a useful tool for assessing who pays the real costs of conservation. Where the 'lost opportunity costs' of communities are low, there is more chance that community-based management will succeed. Where they are large, then local-level management is unlikely to succeed unless 'lost opportunity costs' are met through international and national support.

Institutions and stakeholders

How many institutional 'layers' exist, and where do these conflict? In today's world, resource use and conservation are influenced at multiple levels, from global to local, and it is important to record where these are supportive or in conflict. Is the level international or regional (eg transfrontier parks or land uses such as migratory pastoralists); national (eg national parks and forestry departments); district or subdistrict (eg parishes such as Uganda, or *taluk* such as India); community or group level (eg stretcher-bearer societies – *abataka* – in Uganda, groups of beekeepers, herbalists, midwives); household; or individual? Who has access? Are resource users the local people, 'outsiders' or both? Who authorizes access? Are they women, men or children? Is this changing, and why?

As discussed elsewhere in this chapter, political power is derived or sought through control over key resources. If a comanagement system is desired, then the question of 'who controls what?' needs to be carefully considered. In several cases in

Box 7.2 Access Rights, Environment and Cultural Practice

Although well known by anthropologists and social scientists, few biologists are aware of important studies on tenure and territoriality. These can be broadly divided into three groups.

Group 1

The first group, starting with Julian Steward (1936, 1938), 'the father of human ecology', developed hypotheses on how human territorial behaviour would be influenced under different conditions of resource distribution. Key contributions are the papers developing two important conceptual models. The first model is spatial boundary defence, proposed by Rada Dyson-Hudson and Eric Smith (1978), which makes a cross-cultural comparison of hunter-gatherer territoriality. Dyson-Hudson and Smith termed this the 'economic defensibility model', which was elaborated on in later papers (Dyson-Hudson and Dyson-Hudson, 1980; Smith, 1983). The second model is social boundary defence. This was hypothesized on the basis of optimal foraging theory and field work with foraging societies by Elizabeth Cashdan (1983) from studies with bushmen (San) peoples in Southern Africa, and Nicholas Peterson's (1975) work with Aboriginal communities in Australia. The social boundary defence model suggested that as resources become more sparsely distributed and less predictable, it is not a defence on the basis of territorial space, but on the basis of social groups.

Group 2

The second group includes key studies that contribute to our understanding, and offer a structure for analyses, of how people conceptualize the world, how moral order is maintained and how this is evident in religion, behaviour and natural symbols. This enables, for example, a cross-cultural understanding of land and resource tenure in social terms – how, when and why boundaries are maintained in order to keep outsiders out – and leads to an incentive to manage those resources. Major contributors in this group are Claude Levi-Strauss (1963), Mary Douglas (1973, 1984) and Reichel-Dolmatoff (1996) in Amazonia; Victor Turner (1967, 1969), J M Schoffelleers (1985) and W M J van Binsbergen (1985) in Central Africa; and Monica Wilson (1957), Alex-Ivar Berglund (1976), Robert Thornton (1980) and David Hammond-Tooke (1981) in East and Southern Africa.

Group 3

The third major contribution is made by Anthony Giddens (1984) and Pierre Bourdieu (1973, 1977), who elaborate on how social practices and cultural concepts link to people's use of space – its creation, control and maintenance over time – and who explain the processes through which people in authority exercise power. Two contributions are particularly useful in linking institutional controls to resource management. Firstly, there is the link between social action and spatial arrangements through different forms of control (see 'Boundaries and Tenure, Meaning and Mapping' below). Secondly, there is the recognition that social meaning is produced and maintained through specific activities. The frequency of these practices, such as boundary-marking rituals (whether within or around households, or at larger spatial scales) is one measure of the continued social recognition of these 'invisible' boundaries (see 'Ritual, Religion and Resource Control' below).

Africa, for example, forestry or conservation legislation has been formulated to conserve valuable resources (such as indigenous fruit-bearing trees) that were already conserved under customary law. This overlap between national legislation and customary law, although intended as a conservation mechanism by the state (by forest guards, for example), can be seen by local institutions as a mechanism for undermining local control.

Economic factors

What scale of commerce is associated with local communities? Even the most remote villages are usually linked in some way to national, regional and international trade. One measure is the proportional contribution of income from external sources (through labour migrancy, for example) compared to different local sources (such as agriculture, livestock, gathering, hunting). Based on his work in Lesotho, Steven Lawry (1990) suggests that reliance on external sources of income contributed to local lack of interest in intensifying resource management. Another measure of association with external markets is commercial trade.

Culture

Mutual obligations between people, households and different groups are at the core of cultural logic behind land and resource tenure. This is reflected in, and influenced by, local religions and the way they are changing. This change strongly affects what is locally viewed as ethical. Concepts of tenure and boundary demarcation are strongly linked to belief systems and symbolism. Supernatural power, such as through the use of traditional medicines, is drawn on to enforce socially acceptable behaviour, and social conflicts are played out in the idiom of witchcraft. Again, this occurs at different spatial scales.

Change

No researcher or resource manager, whether local or an outsider, is starting at the 'beginning' of things. Inevitably, there will be a dynamic situation of overlapping interests and forms of control at different spatial scales (global, national, district, ward, household, individual). Some of these situations are 'traditional', others recent, and all will probably change in the future. Whether you are in the field or examining aerial photographs, ask yourself: how have things changed? What factors appear to determine change or resilience in tenure, or social controls over natural resources? Just as formerly isolated villages have been opened to wider economic markets, so they are changing in response to religious and political change. This, in turn, strongly influences inadvertent conservation practices, such as prohibitions on entry to hills that are rainmaking ritual sites, or seasonal restrictions on some medicinal species.

Ecological factors, land use, tenure and territoriality

The factors influencing success or failure of community-based natural resource management programmes have to be seen against the background of climate, land form and land use (see Box 7.1 and Table 7.1).

Climate, soil type and land form can be valuable predictors of:

- the likely level of conflict between conservation and other forms of land

Table 7.1 *Opportunities for community-based wildlife management (CWM) vary with rainfall, soils and land use, socio-economic factors and the composition of local communities*

Band	Ecological characteristics	Distribution of income	Comparative wildlife value	Stakeholder structure	Opportunities for CWM
1	High amounts of well-spread rainfall, year-round supplies of surface water, moderate slopes and fertile soils	Skewed towards the better-off, or outside interests	Low	Diverse interests, differentiated communities	Low
2	High amounts of well-spread rainfall, year-round supplies of surface water, moderate slopes and fertile soils	Skewed towards the better-off, or outside interests	High	Diverse interests, differentiated communities	Possible
3	Uncertain and low levels of rainfall, poor or seasonal supplies of surface water, steep slopes and poor soils	Equitable	High	Strong linkages between and within communities, reciprocal access rights, mobile livelihood strategies	High
4	Uncertain and low levels of rainfall, poor or seasonal supplies of surface water, steep slopes and poor soils	Equitable	Low	Strong linkages between and within communities, reciprocal access rights, mobile livelihood strategies	Possible

Source: IIED, 1994

use (such as agriculture);
- resource predictability; and
- local people's territoriality and tenure systems.

On the basis of work in Tanzania and Malawi, for example, ecologist Richard Bell (1984) points out that in general there is a link between lifestyle and land form (see Chapter 6). In Malawi, subsistence cultivators in areas with poor soils tended to be the heaviest poachers, while fishing communities (with alternative protein sources) and cash-crop farmers were less involved in poaching. Climate, soil type and land form also influence people's territorial behaviour and tenure. All of these are elements in the success or failure of buffer zone establishment or community-based natural resource management (CBNRM).

They also highlight the need for very different approaches in conservation and

resource management work in different habitats such as tropical forest, savanna or semi-desert. Based on their work with hunter-gatherers in Southern Africa and Australia respectively, Elizabeth Cashdan (1983) and Nicholas Peterson (1975) suggest that as resources become more sparsely distributed and less predictable, territories are not maintained on the basis of space ('perimeter defence'), but on the basis of social groups ('social boundary defence') (see Figure 7.3). A similar situation is suggested by Michael Casimir (1992), based on his analysis of factors which determine the rights of 'traditional' pastoralists to grazing areas. Since plant biomass production is closely linked to rainfall (Lieth, 1975), Casimir analysed anthropological studies of pastoralists to determine whether territorial behaviour was related to the amount and predictability of rainfall. He found that few communities grazing their flocks in areas

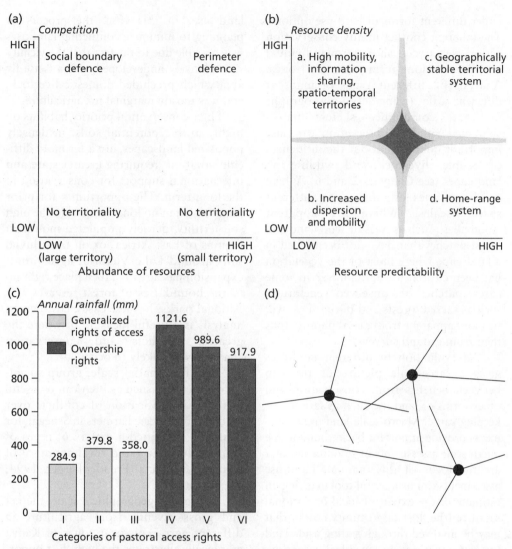

(a)
Competition

HIGH	Social boundary defence	Perimeter defence
	No territoriality	No territoriality
LOW		

LOW (large territory)　　HIGH (small territory)
Abundance of resources

(b)
Resource density

HIGH	a. High mobility, information sharing, spatio-temporal territories	c. Geographically stable territorial system
	b. Increased dispersion and mobility	d. Home-range system
LOW		

LOW　　HIGH
Resource predictability

(c)
Annual rainfall (mm)

Generalized rights of access
Ownership rights

284.9　379.8　358.0　1121.6　989.6　917.9

I　II　III　IV　V　VI
Categories of pastoral access rights

(d)

Sources: (a) Cashdan, 1983; (b) Dyson-Hudson and Smith, 1978; (c) Casimir, 1992; (d) Smith, 1994

Figure 7.3 *Conceptual models and variation in access rights amongst hunter-gatherers and 'traditional' pastoralists. (a) The effects of competition and territory size on territoriality. (b) The conceptual model of economic defensibility linking resource distribution and defensibility. (c) Long-term annual rainfall averages and different levels of access rights to grazing. (d) What boundaries? Beware of imposing Western concepts of tenure: a map of three !noresi (resource areas on which !Kung groups depend, drawn by a !Kung man showing what has been termed 'zero dimensional tenure')*

with rainfall of less than 600mm per year attached fixed ownership rights to their pasture, confirming the hypotheses of Rada Dyson-Hudson and Eric Smith (1978) and Elizabeth Cashdan (1983) with respect to hunter-gatherer territoriality.

Conservation is just one form of land use, and it is important and useful to evaluate and compare benefits that could be expected from the same piece of land

235

under different forms of land-use options. The inherent conflict in any conservation action is between short-term individual benefits and long-term communal ones. Analysis of different types of maps at different scales (using aerial photographs or local community sketch maps), combined with field observation, can raise important questions about the influences of people, livestock and wildlife on landscapes (see Chapters 2 and 6). Where are boundaries established at different spatial scales? Where are apparent 'anomalies', such as trees or woodland and forest patches that have not been felled in a landscape where most of the vegetation has been cleared for agriculture? In some cases, patches of conserved vegetation, such as sacred forests and burial sites, will be more apparent from aerial photographs than from ground surveys.

An evaluation of different land-uses gives a large-scale picture of the gap between benefits from conservation and other forms of land use such as farming or keeping cattle. Macro-scale land-use assessments provide important background to the micro-scale assessments of resource use that are the focus of this manual. Land-use assessments can be a useful tool in giving an estimate of the extent of local or national sacrifice (the 'lost opportunity costs') that may be involved through setting aside land for conservation. In an ideal situation, CBNRM programme planning should be preceded by a regional land-use planning process. In the 40,000km^2 Sebungwe region of Zimbabwe, for example, at an early stage of what was to become the CAMPFIRE programme, ecologists Russell Taylor and Rowan Martin (1983) carried out a land-use planning process prior to recommending buffer zones outside of national parks. These buffer zones were suggested for land of low agricultural potential. Where arable land occurred, it was set aside for dryland cropping, rather than for any other form of land use. In this case, the process of planning to minimize conflicting land uses was possible due to the fact that the vicinity was relatively undeveloped, was a tsetse fly area which precluded domestic livestock, and was mostly marginal for agriculture.

High-conservation priority habitats on highly arable potential soils, in densely populated landscapes, are a far more difficult situation, requiring greater state and international support for conservation in the long term. The opportunity for prior planning often no longer exists. In the high soil fertility, densely populated mountain regions of East Africa, or on the alluvial soils around Lake Victoria, agricultural expansion has already taken place right up to the boundaries of forest reserves and national parks. In these cases, cost-benefit analysis is a useful measure of where the greatest conflicts and conservation challenges are likely to occur.

At a fine spatial scale, group social-survey methods such as PRA can be useful in initial identification of conflicts over land and resources. Farmers in Senegal, for example, identified a matrix of types of conflict during a rapid rural appraisal of resource conflicts (Freudenberger, 1994; see Figure 7.4).

At a broad geographical scale, the net and gross revenue from agriculture in different agro-ecological zones in Kenya graphically illustrates the high 'lost opportunity costs' of land set aside for conservation in higher rainfall sites (Norton-Griffiths and Southey, 1995). Norton-Griffiths and Southey (1995), for example, estimated that the cost of wildlife conservation in Kenya already exceeds the benefits from it, and that by maintaining wildlife conservation areas, instead of using the land in some other way, Kenya may be losing up to US$161 million per year.

Non-monetary cultural values cannot be ignored, however. While cost-benefit exercises are useful, it is important to bear

Nature of Conflict \ Disputants	Between villagers	With neighbouring villages	With strangers	With the State
Trees	1	—	6	—
Land	1	—	4	—
Grass/pastures	6	8	—	—
Water	—	—	—	—
Animals	60	90	75	—

Source: Freudenberger, 1994

Figure 7.4 *A matrix of types of conflict over different natural resources at various institutional levels developed during a rapid rural appraisal of resource conflicts*

in mind that although economic rationalism may be the goal of governments, minimizing risk rather than maximizing profit often characterizes pastoralist (Coughenour et al, 1985) and small-scale farming communities.

Using participatory scoring methods (see Chapter 2) with separate groups of men, women and boys from Jinga village in Zimbabwe, for example, researchers showed that non-monetary benefits, such as water retention and rain-making rituals, were rated far more important than products such as building poles, fruits or fuelwood to which monetary values could be attached (Hot Springs Working Group, 1995; see Figure 7.5). For this reason, modelling based on 'economic rationalism' does not present the full picture.

Diversifying activities in a risk-prone environment is a rational approach. To achieve this, many small-scale farming families and pastoralists prefer to minimize risk through involvement in a range of activities rather than aiming to maximize profits by focusing on a single activity. Access to harvestable resources and religious links to ancestors or ritual control of rainfall are all considered to minimize risk. It is also important to recognize that while the 'lost opportunity costs' of conservation may be low on a national scale, they can be very high locally. A basic principle behind multiple use is to help off-set some of these lost opportunity costs, and to better justify conservation as a form of land use.

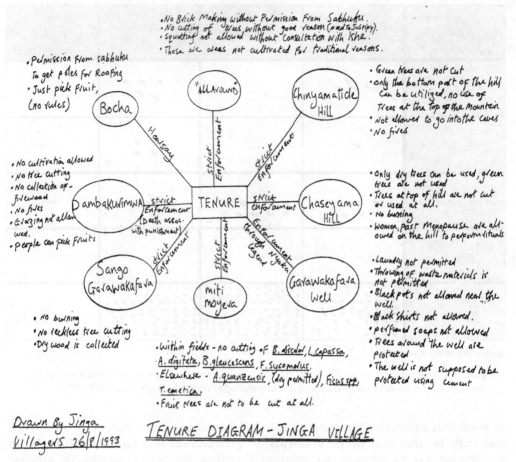

- No Brick Making without Permission From Sabhuku.
- No cutting of trees without good reason (need to Justify).
- squatting not allowed without Consultation with Ishe.
- These are areas not cultivated for traditional reasons.

- Permission from sabhuku to get poles for Roofing
- Just pick Fruit, (no rules)

Bocha

"ALL AROUND"

Chinyamatidie Hill

- Green trees are not Cut
- only the bottom part of the hill can be utilized, no use of trees at the top of the mountain
- Not allowed to go into the caves
- No fires

- No cultivation allowed
- No tree cutting
- No collection of firewood
- No fires
- Grazing not allowed
- people can pick Fruits

Dambakurimwa

strict Enforcement (Death assoc. with punishment)

TENURE

strict enforcement

Chaseyama Hill

- Only dry trees can be used, green trees are not used
- Trees at top of hill are not cut or used at all.
- No burning
- Women, past Menopause are allowed on the hill to perform rituals

- No burning
- No reckless tree cutting
- Dry wood is collected

Sango Garawakafara

strict Enforcement

miti moyera

Enforcement through Nhoka Legend

Garawakafara well

- Laundry not permitted
- Throwing of waste materials is not permitted
- Black pots not allowed near the well
- Black shirts not allowed
- perfumed soaps not allowed
- Trees around the well are protected
- The well is not supposed to be protected using cement

- Within fields - no cutting of *B. discolor*, *L. capassa*, *A. digitata*, *B. glaucescens*, *F. sycomorus*.
- Elsewhere - *A. quanzensis* (dry permitted), *Ficus spp*, *T. emetica*.
- Fruit trees are not to be cut at all.

Drawn By Jinga Villagers 26/8/1993

TENURE DIAGRAM - JINGA VILLAGE

Source: Hot Springs Working Group report, 1995

Figure 7.5 *A diagram drawn by villagers showing the location of sites around Jinga village in Zimbabwe and restrictions on land and resource use in those sites that lead to maintenance of habitat and species in these localities*

Property rights: land and resource tenure

Secure tenure is considered an important ingredient for resource management and conservation. In some cases, the opposite can also be true. Based on years of field work, anthropologist Paul Richards (1996) is convinced that many forests in West Africa survived not because they were under the control of a single, central authority, but because they are old contested domains ('boundary wildernesses') over which undisputed control had not been established (see Box 7.4). Many of these forests are now proclaimed as forest reserves or national parks.

Whether you are working in areas that are privately owned, in a national park belonging to the state, or in a communal area, it is crucial not to fall into the trap of simplistic assumptions or simple classi-fication of different types of tenure. This is particularly important where local people or indigenous communities have established complex rules controlling access to communal land, which in turn has been overlapped by state control (as in the case of many national parks or forest reserves). It is also important to recognize, firstly, that land tenure can take many different forms (anthropologist Paul Bohannan's 1963 paper is still recom-mended reading on this issue), and secondly, that land tenure and resource tenure may differ.

It is equally important to avoid misun-derstandings about the term 'common property'. These have raged on for 30 years in the belief that they inevitably lead to a 'free for all' situation of resource exploitation. A centre of much of the confusion was the famous essay by human ecologist Garrett Hardin (1968), entitled 'The Tragedy of the Commons', which intended to show that freedom to have any number of children would lead to overpopulation. To do this, he used the example of a common grazing area, where:

> *'The rational herdsman concludes that the only sensible course for him to pursue is to add another animal to his herd. And another; and another...but this is the conclusion reached by each and every rational herdsman sharing a commons. Therein lies the tragedy. Each man is locked into a system that compels him to increase his herd without limit – in a world that is limited...Freedom in a commons brings ruin for all.'*

This essay was as controversial as it was influential; but it was unfortunate in that common property resources were confused with open-access resources. To avoid similar misunderstandings, a useful step is to analyse types of tenure. Different ways of doing this are described in the sections that follow.

Basic types of tenure and tenurial niches

In order to clarify the differences between open-access and common property resources, Daniel Bromley and Michael Cernea (1989) distinguished four basic types of property rights (see Box 7.3).

These basic definitions are useful in making this distinction, but it is essential to understand that the situation is far more complex. Tenure and property rights clearly have to be seen in cultural context. It is important to look beyond the politi-cal, economic and legal aspects of tenure and examine the cultural logic and social rules that support local tenure systems.

It is also useful to explore cases of conflict over land or resources and identify the systems of conflict resolution. Records of conflict from district courts, or conflict dealt with by traditional leadership under customary law, can also provide useful insights into rule-breaking and fines. Where the same issues are dealt with through an overlap between customary law and constitutional law, it may also be useful to compare the severity of these different processes. There can be a great variation between the two processes, with customary law being far more severe than state law, or vice-versa, reflecting different perceptions of the interest groups in each case. Who are the different groups involved in the conflict? Is the conflict within families (men/women, immediate or extended family)? Is it between long-estab-lished people and 'newcomers'? What is the severity of punishment for infringe-ments and what form does this take? Who are the beneficiaries of these fines?

BOX 7.3 FOUR TYPES OF PROPERTY RIGHTS

Property rights comprise the following:

1 *Private property resources:* an individual has a right to exclude all others from using that resource. Decisions are made by the single owner.
2 *Common property resources:* this may be thought of as private property for a social unit or community, where outsiders are excluded. This is the main form of property right in sub-Saharan Africa. Decisions require consensus between members of the group before actions such as exclusion are taken; consensus must be established, generally through a community meeting.
3 *State property resources:* in order to prevent overuse and/or to gain revenue, the government restricts the way that people may use a resource.
4 *Open-access resources:* there are no property rights and no rights of exclusion. For this reason, this is sometimes known as a no property regime. Without any rights of exclusion, individual resource users ignore the costs that their resource use will have for future users, often leading to the inevitable resource degradation described by Garrett Hardin (1968).

Source: adapted from Bromley and Cernea, 1989

Specific court cases can provide a very useful illustration of the complexity of tenure. Melissa Leach (1994), for example, describes a local court case where palm wine was stolen from a *Raphia* palm tree being tapped for palm wine in Sierra Leone. Two levels of tenure were involved in this case. Firstly, those held by the palm-wine tapper and secondly, those held by the farmer who granted rights to the palm-wine tapper in exchange for periodic gifts or labour. Somewhat counter to what might have been expected, it was not the palm-wine tapper who took the suspected thief to court, but the farmer who granted the right to tap the trees in the first place.

Two useful approaches have been used to get beyond the simple classification shown in Box 7.3. The first identifies tenurial niches and the second (see the following section) analyses different types of tenure in terms of specific characteristics.

The tenurial niche approach was developed by John Bruce and Louise Fortmann of the University of Wisconsin Land Tenure Centre (Bruce and Fortmann,

1989). It was used to describe different property relationships in terms of categories of land used by different groups of people for a range of purposes. A tenurial niche is defined as 'a space in which access to and use of a resource is governed by a common set of rules' (Bruce et al, 1993). Identifying tenurial niches is a useful way of categorizing different property regimes where systems of state control are superimposed over 'traditional' tenure systems. This is a common situation in Africa, for example, where state control, based on Western notions of tenure, and traditional tenure systems often occur side-by-side. The tenurial niche approach is also useful in defining the different claims to plant resources – such as trees, tree products (fruits, medicines from roots or bark) or thatching grass – by different groups of people on land under different forms of tenure (see Figure 7.7). On the basis of field work in communal areas in Zimbabwe, for example, Calvin Nhira and Louise Fortmann (1996) identified six different

Box 7.4 Eleven Characteristics of Tenure Systems

In order to understand complex forest tenure systems, David Haley and Martin Luckert (1990) chose the following 11 characteristics to describe and compare different forest tenure systems used in Canada because of the link they made between economic behaviour and tenure. Most (94 per cent) forest land in Canada is public land controlled by the state. In many cases, timber-harvesting rights and, in some instances, forest management responsibilities are allocated to the private sector. Just as with other plant resources and tenure systems in communal areas in Africa, the complex tenure systems controlling access to timber in Canada are an important influence on how tenure holders behave.

1 Exclusiveness

To what extent are tenure holders able to control access? Exclusiveness, referring to the right of tenure holders (individuals or a group) to exclude others through controlled access, is a crucial means for tenure holders to derive benefits from a valuable resource. In an open-access situation, there is no exclusivity. Exclusivity is also difficult to maintain with mobile resources such as migratory birds, fish or mammals, and much easier for plants, which generally stay in one place! For this reason, controlled access may apply to traps or trapping sites for birds or fish, rather than to these mobile resources themselves. Amongst many farming communities throughout Southern Africa, private rights are also accorded to wild fruit trees conserved in cleared fields or near to homesteads, whereas anyone can collect fruits in uncleared woodlands. Clear boundaries around the resource or land area and a clearly identified group of users are important factors in controlling access (see Box 7.1).

2 Comprehensiveness

Over what range of resources does the tenure holder have control? In Canada, rights are granted to harvest timber, but not to wildlife resources. Similarly, on the Mozambique coastal plain in Southern Africa, palm-wine tappers have exclusive rights to tap *Hyphaene* palms in a particular area, but this does not apply to grazing rights or rights to fruits from trees in that area.

3 Rights of the Tenure Holder to Benefits

In the Canadian case, the economic benefits flowing to the private companies who had rights to harvest timber were limited by various taxes and fees (such as stumpage fees) levied by the state. In Southern Africa, 50 litres of palm wine had to be provided to the local headman at the start of tapping a newly granted area. In addition, income to men tapping *Hyphaene* palm wine in palm savanna to which they had tapping rights was split in a 2:1 ratio with women who transported the palm wine (see Chapter 3). The flow of benefits to the tenure holder may also be influenced by social rules which affect how the benefits are divided up. In Sierra Leone, for example, anthropologist Melissa Leach describes a common situation where Mende wives have rights to use the fruits and fuel wood from trees their husbands conserve in coffee and cocoa farms (Leach, 1994).

4 Transferability

In addition to the right of the tenure holder to the benefits discussed above is the important issue of allocating use rights to other people. In the Canadian example, monetary benefits dominated the transfer of timber licences, subject to state (minister-ial) approval; but in other circumstances, a much wider range of benefits may be involved, such as political allegiance, barter goods or services. It is important to identify locally or nationally established rules that place limits on how (or to whom) tenure holders are able to pass on rights to resources or land to someone else. This transfer of property or products can take place in various ways, such as through sale, barter or inheritance.

In the Namib desert of Namibia, for example, inherited rights by extended Topnaar (≠Aunin-Nama) family groups (!hao-!nas) are attached to !nara melon patches (*Acanthosicyos horridus*) in the Khuiseb delta (Budack, 1983; Dentlinger, 1977). Topnaar councillors are called 'fathers rich in !naras' (!naraaxa //gun) due to their role in settling boundary disputes about !nara 'fields' (Budack, 1983). Another example of inheritable rights are those applying to fish trapping sites in Kosi lake system and Phongolo flood-plain, South Africa. In both cases, the barriers, which are built to accommodate the fish traps, are erected only after discussion, leading to approval of the prospective trapper with nearby trappers. This agreement is formalized by the headman and thereafter the site is 'owned' by the trapper and is inheritable. Although there are still numerous potential sites available to erect barriers in both wetlands, the trappers limit access, making it difficult for new trappers to enter the fisheries. Both systems have been in operation for centuries and both are believed to be sustainable fisheries. The limited entry into the fishery through site ownership is one of the reasons for this.

Complex social rules that affect who gets which benefits often exist and need to be recorded. When you investigate transferability, it is important to take extended family relationships and gender issues into account, and how these may be changing over time. Inheritance may be passed on to men within a lineage, but not to men outside that lineage, or even women within it. Working in Mhondoro district, a communal area in Zimbabwe, for example, Fortmann and Nabane (1992) investigated how transferabil-ity was affected when women who had planted trees when married were later widowed or divorced. The method they used to investigate transferability was to inter-view widows and divorcees. They found that all 18 divorcees had lost the rights to the trees they planted while they were married, even if they continued to live nearby. They felt unable to do anything about this, and regretted planting the trees in the first place. The only exception applied to trees they had planted when they were part of a women's group, leading the researchers to identify this as a potential opportunity for strengthening women's rights to trees on land controlled by women's groups. Nine of 15 widows interviewed, however, had retained rights to family trees. The main reason for this was that they remained in the family home. Those that left the family home lost all rights to the trees.

5 Use Restrictions and Changes in Tenure Types

Does any form of zoning apply? For example, can garden plots controlled by women be converted to agricultural fields controlled by men? Restrictions may also apply to how or when a resource is used. Closed seasons are a common way in which resource use is limited under customary law. Closing particular sites to any use is also widespread. Both closed seasons and closed areas are often linked to religious belief systems. Bans on setting fires, collection of fuel wood and building poles, and cultivation or entry by menstruating women commonly apply in Southern Africa to sites of religious significance such as burial sites or hills used for rain-making rituals. In South Africa, for example, collection of the medicinal plants *Siphonochilus aethiopicus* (Zingiberaceae), *Alepidea amatymbica* and *Peucedanum thodei* (Apiaceae) only takes place during winter due to fear that collection during the growing season (spring/summer) will attract lightning. Enforcement of post-growing season gathering of *Siphonochilus* and *Alepidea* through the fear of causing storms and lightning is likely to be intentional development of an avoidance practice by specialists (diviners and herbalists) in response to depletion resulting from trade.

6 Duration

How long does right of tenure apply? This is a key issue in resource management and conservation when providing incentives to prevent short-term exploitation by individuals at the expense of maintaining long-term benefits for the wider social group. Tenure over a longer time span is an important incentive for conservation and resource management. Based on his experience in developing joint forest management (JFM) systems in Nepal, Robert Fisher (1995) suggests that the longer the period during which resource users are confident that they have use of a resource, the more likely they are to manage it sustainably. Duration of tenure is closely linked to security of tenure.

7 Security

Both duration and security are key factors affecting resource management behaviour and both depend upon the level of trust and extent of mutual obligations between those granting tenure (whether individuals, a community group or the state) and resource user group(s). Secure tenure is also influenced by perception (how easy is it to detect rule-breaking 'free-riders'), which in itself is influenced by how well the boundaries of the resource and the resource user group are defined (see Box 7.1). A process leading to a written memorandum of understanding (MOU) between the state and resource-user groups within the local community is one way of increasing the level of trust between resource users and the state through a set of mutually agreed rules and obligations. This can be useful where collaborative management or multiple-use arrangements are being developed for protected areas.

8 Operational Stipulations

To what extent can tenure holders make the more detailed rules and develop their own management plans? In the Canadian forestry case, this covered three categories: management, harvesting and processing. Management requirements are there to ensure sustainable use. In this case, reafforestation and protection were required. Harvesting requirements focus on efficient resource use and limits to ensure sustainable yield. In Canada, a common requirement for processing was that tenure holders needed to construct or maintain a particular type of timber-processing plant. Limits based on the need for processing can also apply to tropical non-timber forest products, such as carving timber, rattan and medicinal bark.

9 Operational Control

Although the Canadian forestry example refers specifically to the ways and extent to which the state ensured that the tenure holders followed operational requirements, size specifications and the allotment type agreed on, operational controls may also be devolved to other levels. In protected areas (national parks, forest reserves), this will be between the state and resource users (individuals, groups). Outside protected areas, management responsibilities and operational controls are checked by locally based authorities, with minimal intervention by the state.

10 Size Specifications

How big is the area for which tenure is granted? Size of the area under tenure influences management costs. David Haley and Martin Luckert (1990) point out that in a free-market system, if property rights are transferable and divisible, then the area under tenure tends to change to a point that suits a private economy of scale. This is not possible with public land, such as Crown forest tenure in Canada; but a balance has to be reached between size of the area for which tenure is granted and the creation of monopolies over very large areas.

11 Allotment Type

On what basis are tenure rights granted? This may incorporate one or several of the following limitations on the basis of area, quantity of material harvested, defined user group and defined number of users. In some cases, limitations are granted for a specific area (area-based). Alternatively, the limit is on the quantity of resource extracted (resource quantity-based). It may also be based on user groups and numbers of resource users. Depending upon the context and resource involved, quantities will be measured in different ways: volume (m^3) in the cases of commercial timber, kilograms or tonnes in the case of formal medicinal bark extraction, or in local units such as bundles or handfuls.

Outside protected areas, and particularly within fields or the homestead area, rights to resources are also affected by their location. This is an important factor to bear in mind during field work. In Sierra Leone, for example, Melissa Leach (1994) found that the small gardens behind kitchens were places where women acquired and retained control through individualized tenure. These spaces were intensively cultivated and composted, with medicinal plants and 'wildings' (self-sown seedlings transplanted from natural habitat) of indigenous trees such as *Dialium guineense* and oil palms planted alongside other fruit trees.

Source: adapted from Haley and Luckert, 1990

tenurial niches where savanna woodland management occurred:

- indigenous woodland in communal and resettlement areas;
- trees controlled by district councils on communal land;
- woodland and forest controlled by the state (forest reserves and national parks);
- trees planted by groups and institutions;
- trees planted and protected by individuals on individually controlled land;
- trees on commercial farms.

Characteristics of tenure types

A second method provides a finer classification of different tenure types or niches. This is useful in avoiding simple classification of tenure into just four types (as shown in Box 7.3), and provides a far better basis for comparing and contrasting different types of tenure. This method was used in Canada by David Haley and Martin Luckert (1990) to analyse different forest tenures which were employed as mechanisms to transfer timber-cutting rights from state control to private harvesters (see Box 7.4). Using these characteristics enabled them to distinguish 34 different types of forest tenure in Canada. The method has also been used in Zimbabwe to develop a framework for classifying different types of tenure in communal areas. Each of the characteristics is explained in Box 7.4, with the addition of African examples to emphasize the wider applicability of this approach.

Secure tenure is an important ingredient in natural resource management, but it is not a 'cure all'. Neither weak tenure nor high-value harvest, strong tenure nor low resource values provide much incentive for locally based resource management. In addition, when resource values are very high, so is the temptation for resource 'mining' rather than resource management, even if tenure is strong. Funds from quick, high returns may be invested within other areas, such as education or the cash economy. Nevertheless, sustainable harvesting systems and resource management are both more likely where land and resource tenure is strong and the benefits from sustainable harvest are high.

Recognition of boundaries that demarcate particular resources or parts of the landscape is a key aspect of tenure. Although obvious to local people, many of these boundaries are 'invisible' to the outsiders who are so often involved in land-use planning or conservation. Examples of such boundary markers are stone cairns, paths, river valleys, ridge tops or specific species planted at strategic points across the landscape, all forming boundaries which do not appear on any map. To avoid misunderstanding and land-use conflicts, it is crucial to try to see the world from a local perspective and to understand where such boundaries are and why they are widely recognized and respected. This is covered in the following sections.

Boundaries and tenure, meaning and mapping

Effective establishment and local acceptance and recognition of boundaries around a resource area are an important basis for avoiding an open-access, 'free-for-all' scramble for scarce resources. This applies to private and state rights, as well as to common property resources. When many people think of boundaries, they think of boundary demarcation using fences, walls, lines of planted trees or natural features. There is a second type of 'boundary marking' which it is equally important to recognize. These boundaries are widely known within the local community, yet are often 'invisible' to outsiders, including urban-oriented researchers in rural development or conservation. Physical structures used to demarcate boundaries, as well as trees conserved in fields, are therefore linked to social practice and belief systems that are associated, in turn, with rules of behaviour

Figure 7.6 *(a) Patch-burning of spinifex (*Triodia*) grasslands in Australia reduces the chances of wildfires and creates vegetation varying in age, composition and resource richness. (b) A painting of spinifex landscape, with black patches where the Nyananan men hunted for wallabies at Tjikari, is rich in symbolic meaning and reflects the joy of the artist, Johnny Warangula Tjupurrula, at returning to his country*

at various spatial scales – from the individual through to the district level.

The main reason why this is relevant to resource management is that it involves some of the key requirements for resilient common property resource-management systems shown in Box 7.1: the need for clearly defined boundaries of the resource or resource area, a defined user group, widespread acceptance of the rules governing access to the resource, and effective ways of detecting and punishing rule breakers or of resolving conflicts.

For anyone interested in resource management, it is crucial to develop an understanding of what institutional and religious factors stop people, either individually or in groups, from depleting a resource in the short-term and favour the establishment of managed long-term harvests. To understand people's conservation behaviour, it is important to understand their 'worldview' or cultural perspective. This also is closely linked to the relationship between people and the landscape. The best examples of people's powerful sense of place are those held by nomadic pastoralists and hunter-gatherer societies (see Figure 7.6).

Insight into the social, symbolic and economic significance that land and resources have for people provides a better understanding of what induces people to keep to local rules about harvesting, where they apply, or what happens to rule breakers as a result of unethical behaviour.

'Invisible' boundaries, unwritten rules

Developing an understanding of the social processes that delimit space can be done using a range of social survey methods described in Chapters 2 and 6.

These include field observation of people's everyday activities, participatory mapping and participant observation of special occasions such as boundary-marking rituals. The challenge is to understand what you see or are being told – not an easy task for outsider researchers. Ethnobotanists have many opportunities to observe activities directly linked to cultural control over land, resources and their harvesting, yet often neither 'see' nor analyse those activities. Amos Rapoport (1977) has suggested that any social activity can be analysed into four components:

- the activity itself;
- the specific way of doing it, and where it is done;
- additional, adjacent or associated activities which become part of the activity system;
- the symbolic aspects and meaning of the activity.

These are useful to bear in mind during field work aimed at unravelling the social, economic, ethical, religious and political factors that either encourage resource conservation or lead to resource depletion. Five important tools which can be used in this process include the following:

1 Mapping

Local recognition and acceptance of boundaries is a key determinant of who is allowed to do what, when and where. As Figure 7.7 shows, 'invisible' boundaries are locally recognized at a range of spatial scales. While most anthropological work has recorded how household space is subdivided (such as Adam Kuper's 1980 Southern African work, Pierre Bourdieu's 1977 study of Kabyle houses in North Africa and Henrietta Moore's 1996 anthropological study in Kenya), maps can also be produced at a broader spatial scale. Mapping these boundaries is a useful starting point, which can lead to a better understanding of past land use. Ideally, use recent aerial photographs as a starting point since they give a very useful perspective on patterns of land use and tenure (Figure 7.8).

2 Identifying different social groups and working with key assistants

The complex social groupings involved in establishing boundaries at frontiers need to be recognized. So do the pitfalls of working through a few people (see Box 7.5). However, local leaders and ritual specialists will often have a more detailed knowledge of cultural codes and meanings that delimit space; the fact that someone is unable to explain these does not mean that they are unaware of them. Based on her field work with Marakwet people in Kenya, Henrietta Moore (1996) points out that most people are rarely able to explain cultural codes, but can be very aware of the practical aspects that these codes imply for social behaviour. For this reason, working in western Uganda, John Makombo (1998), a local researcher, mapped the boundaries controlled by ridge-leaders using aerial photographs (see Figure 7.2e). Field work with ridge-leaders (*omuhulha wa balhombo*) was a crucial part of this process. Ridge-leaders also provided information on the frequency with which boundary-marking rituals took place.

3 Recording how and when people use space

Glen Mills (1986), an architect who has studied the social meaning of domestic space, has suggested it is necessary to know: what activities take place; who is involved; where this is done; when; in what order; and for how long. The same approach can be applied to ritual activities which lead to habitat protection, such as sacred forests, or to boundary marking.

Changes in the frequency of boundary-marking rituals is one indicator of how 'clear' and controlled the edges of territories are likely to be. The *masay* rituals described by Robert Thornton (1980) took place annually. By comparison, as a consequence of political and religious change, John Makombo recorded that boundary-marking rituals had not taken place for 10 to 20 years in parts of the Rwenzori Mountains, Uganda. With low and declining frequency of renewal, control can be expected to be weak.

4 Plants and boundaries

Plants are commonly used as boundary markers, either planted at strategic points such as entrances, boundaries of fields, or in fences of cattle pens, or pounded and sprinkled around the homestead. For this reason, planting certain trees is synonymous with claiming land, and the 'simple' process of tree planting can result in bitter disputes (see earlier section on 'Characteristics of Tenure Types').

5 Toponymic surveys

Place names can be easy to record and say a lot about the past history of land and resource use (see the following section on 'Toponymic Surveys: Meanings of Place Names'). Geo-referenced place names can also be a valuable guide in transferring resource-use information from participatory sketch maps or the field observations of local people onto topographic map sheets.

Toponymic surveys: meanings of place names

The study of local place names and their meanings (termed toponymy) as part of the mapping process is a useful way of getting insight into the past history of land and resource use. If this includes geo-refer-

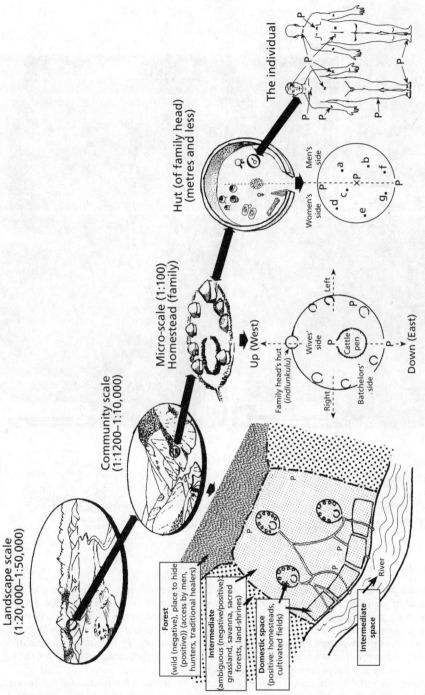

Figure 7.7 *'Ritual topography' at different spatial scales influences tenure and access to different people. The symbolic division of the homestead after Kuper (1980) and of the hut after Davison (1991), where* a = *homestead head;* b = *other men of the homestead (*umzi*);* c = *primary woman of* umzi*;* d = *bride;* e = *other women of* umzi*;* f = *visiting men;* g = *visiting women;* x = *hearth;* P = *strategic points (entrances, boundaries) where protected charms are placed*

Source: (a) and (c)–(e) Mills, 1984, reproduced with permission

Figure 7.8 *Aerial photograph analysis, combined with 'ground-truthing' with local people, is an excellent method of gaining insight into the 'nested layers' of tenure, boundaries and local institutions and how these are changing. (a) A family homestead and farm in the Tsandi area, Namibia, demarcated with brushwood, where private (family) rights are attached to the Hyphaene palms. Space within the family compound (eumbo) is further subdivided. (b) 'Privatization' with scarcity and local political change: former communal grazing on a drainage channel (oshana) fenced off for exclusive use by a local person with economic (and local political) power. (c) Part of a neighbourhood (omikunda) in Ongwediva district showing farms as 'islands' divided by drainage lines, each farm with a distinct boundary. Each family has strict rights to clay from termitaria, water from the hand-dug well and fruit from trees (eg Disopyros mespiliformis) within the farm boundary, whereas fruit from trees within communal grazing areas is available to the wider community. (d) At a broader scale, neighbourhoods within part of a district (oshilonga). (e) Diagrams showing the nested hierarchy of space, each governed by rules of access and rights*

BOX 7.5 MAPPING METHODS: POTENTIAL AND PITFALLS

A recurrent problem facing the development of conservation or resource management programmes is that, while boundaries are widely recognized locally as part of a cultural landscape, they are often not recognized by the state. Participatory mapping with different groups to produce sketch maps (Chapters 2 and 6) is a useful starting point. In Zimbabwe, for example, field workers worked with local villagers who mapped out hills to which access was restricted for ritual purposes such as rainmaking (see Figure 7.5).

Another starting point is to map boundaries by walking with representatives of all local interest groups using aerial photographs and a global positioning system (GPS) to locate and obtain coordinates for points on the landscape (geo-referencing). The use of aerial photographs in developing community forestry-management plans in Nepal (see Box 6.3) is a good example of this. Cheaper, hand-held GPS systems, costing US$300–$400, have a limited accuracy. Differential GPS, which has a greater accuracy (to around 5m) requires a base unit with verified coordinates and a field unit, so is very expensive (around US$10,000). An advantage of GPS is that this technology enables very large areas to be covered. In the Amazon, for example, 470 Mengraknoti Kayapo demarcated their 4.4 million-hectare territory (Poole, 1995). Based on his recent survey of the opportunity for applying this mapping technology to community-based conservation, Peter Poole (1995) concluded that mapping technology (GPS and GIS) enabled local communities to achieve five objectives:

1   Conserve and reinforce local/traditional knowledge.
2   Enhance community capability to manage and protect lands.
3   Raise and mobilize local awareness of environmental issues.
4   Increase local capacities to deal with external agencies.
5   Enable local and global groups to play reciprocal roles in global programmes for biodiversity conservation.

Alternatively, if you do not have access to a GPS, then place-name surveys (see the above section on 'Toponymic Surveys'), combined with topographic maps (which show contour lines), are useful in linking local knowledge to mapping scale. Both are effective methods for mapping parts of the landscape under strong customary controls, working towards resolution of local boundary disputes or for understanding whether locally recognized boundaries can be used to demarcate multiple-use zones or rotational harvest areas.

It is crucial to be aware of three things, however. Firstly, boundary mapping can be a sensitive issue and it is important to avoid becoming a pawn in territorial disputes that worsen the situation. Participatory mapping of the same area by different interest groups can produce very different results. Secondly, some conservation areas are not placed within customary boundaries, but in 'separation zones' between social groups. This is not an uncommon or unfamiliar situation in many parts of the world. The march lands of medieval Europe, such as the disputed borderlands between Wales and England, are one example. African equivalents are the mopane woodlands between different pre-colonial kingdoms in what today is northern Namibia/southern Angola and the 'boundary wildernesses' between pre-colonial African states (Erkkila and Siiskonen, 1992; Richards, 1996). Due to their no-man's land status, these areas are frontiers settled by people from many places and backgrounds. The net result, as anthropologist Paul Richards (1996) points out:

'...is that the margins of most West African forests are extraordinarily complex from a sociological point of view. Typically, they will comprise a complex mix of old refugee populations with new (colonial, post-colonial) migrant popula-tions. Each group in this mix will tend to seek to establish, to legitimize and to maintain its own rights of occupancy and usage of forest resources reflecting the circumstances of arrival of the group founders, and the history of the subse-quent incorporation of their descendants...to my mind, there can be no doubts that if conservationists are to devise effective schemes for the sustainable management of forest reserve margins in West Africa, the careful study and analysis of the cultural processes involved in creating these multi-layered, multi-valent identities is a pre-requisite.'

Probably the single biggest obstacle to understanding these complex cultural processes effectively is a prevailing belief among some conservation agencies that forests and forest margins have a single "true" owner with whom a once-and-for-all resource management deal might be struck, and that all other local groups are in some sense "impostors".'

Under these circumstances, care and a healthy amount of scepticism need to accom-pany the interpretation of participatory maps. The outcome of the mapping process may say more about the history and negotiating skills of the people who drew that map than about the geographic boundaries. Good examples are some of the maps drawn by local Solomon Islanders in the process of trying to resolve boundary disputes. These maps were studied by Peter Larmour (1979), who pointed out how two maps of exactly the same land may be very different.

Thirdly, linked to the above point, boundaries and separation zones change. In 1866 in northern Namibia, for example, missionary Hugo Hahn recorded a 60km wide belt of mopane woodland between the Uukwanyama and Ondonga kingdoms. Fifty years later, this woodland was 40km wide, and in the 1950s 10km wide. Today, this 'boundary woodland' no longer exists (Erkkila and Siiskonen, 1992).

---

encing of place names, then this can provide a network of geographic informa-tion points across the landscape which will enable the transfer of information on resource use from participatory sketch maps, or the transfer of field observations onto topographic map sheets. As part of a survey of potential multiple-use zone boundaries around the northern portion of Rwenzori Mountains National Park, Uganda, for example, John Makombo (1998) conducted a toponymic survey of local place names. With the enormous advantage of being a Mukonjo researcher working in his home area, he worked with four to six people locally known to have the deepest knowledge of place names, sometimes stopping every 200m during

'transect walks' when surveying each mountain ridge. He also held group meetings where he cross-checked place names to confirm their meanings and whether any names had been left out.

In total, 38 focus group interviews were followed later by site walks to places which were identified during the meetings. Not all names had meanings, but 79 of the recorded names did, and their analysis provides interesting results. Thirty-one (39 per cent) of the names described the terrain (steep, rocky, boggy, infertile soils), 28 (35.4 per cent) described places of resource harvest, 14 (17.7 per cent) described cultural/historical sites, and 6 (7.7 per cent) referred to habitat. Examples of place names on the mountain ridge known as

Kakuka, for example, are places referring to resource use, the first outside the national park boundary, the rest inside the park: Malindi ('wild animal traps'), Bihya ('pit-fall traps for wild animals'), Kamusonge ('source of honey'), Masule ('place of the liana *Smilax anceps*' – used for basketry) and Bukungunia ('place for resource harvest' – bamboo). Forty-three (54.4 per cent) of the place names with specific meanings are located inside the national park. In addition, out of the 28 names that describe places of resource harvest, 24 (85.7 per cent) are located inside the park, with harvesting still taking place in most of these today. Of the 43 places located inside the park, 24 (55.8 per cent) describe places whose names refer to resource harvest/utilization; 3 (7.0 per cent) refer to cultural/ historical sites.

Ritual, religion and resource control

If we are to understand people's conservation behaviour, we have to understand the 'worldview' that people have – that is, the way that people conceptualize particular events, such as health or disease, good luck and misfortune, or 'good' or 'bad' behaviour. If harvesting restrictions are going to be employed, it also makes sense to identify which restrictions will 'resonate' with local people in terms of existing cultural controls on resource harvesting.

Just as many societies have ritual rites of transition from one stage of life to another, so there are 'invisible' boundary markers for individuals, men and women within households, extended families, or neighbourhoods. These boundaries are clearest and most strongly enforced at finer spatial scales (the house, the household, a burial site, spring or a hill) and tend to weaken 'outwards' with increase in area from the neighbourhood to the community, to the broader landscape occupied by other communities ' (see Figures 7.8 and 7.9). People's behaviour, sometimes with a conservation outcome, is linked to these boundaries. Some mountains, for example, are land-shrines with a ban on access by menstruating women. Single women are commonly discouraged from entering forests, although access by hunters (men) or divin-

ers gathering medicines is acceptable. At a home level, coding of spatial divisions is strong but still dynamic. The smallest spatial scale is the individual whose skin is a boundary crossed by incisions (symbolic 'doors') where protective medicines (known as *insizi* in Zulu) have been applied at strategic points on the body, at strategic times of his or her life. Rituals for boundary marking and protection are linked by a common worldview at all spatial scales (see Figure 7.7). In many societies, the human body and the land are conceptually linked through ritual practice and metaphor (van Binsbergen, 1988; Tamasari, 1995).

Entrances are the strategic points where protective medicines are placed and replaced in a process of social recognition of boundaries and control over the space inside them. Each of these domains (wild, domesticated) 'pushes' against the boundary, requiring regular reinforcement through ritual process. Similar worldviews are held by other agricultural societies, such as Aouan farmers in the Côte d'Ivoire (van den Beemer, 1994) and amongst Bakiga farmers around Bwindi-Impenetrable National Park who have felled forest to 'domesticate' this wild part of the landscape: it is no coincidence that Bwindi means 'dark'.

Ritual control is strongest and its renewal most frequent at the homestead or individual level. In South Africa, for example, Zulu traditionalists would undertake ritual cleansing (using *Scilla natalensis* bulbs and several other species mentioned below in the section on 'Metaphor and Meaning, Botany and Boundaries') every one to two months (and even more frequently in cities). Ritual cleansing and strengthening of the household would be less frequent (once or twice a year). The lower frequency of renewing boundaries, and weaker control at larger spatial scales, clearly has conservation implications, where large areas are more viable in terms of maintaining ecological and genetic processes than small areas. In Kenya, for example, the average size of sacred kaya forests is about 70ha. In Zambia and Zimbabwe, the area set aside by wild places used as 'land-shrines', such as large trees or spectacular hills, waterfalls or caves, is also small and localized (van Binsbergen, 1985). In Nepal, forests under community management average only 23ha (Wily, 1995). A consequence of this is that while these small sites can be very important for the conservation of plant species, they have limited value in terms of maintaining minimum viable populations of large mammals.

Reaffirmation of boundaries, ritual and control

Many landscapes in which conservation areas have been proclaimed are overlain by a 'ritual topography' dotted by far older ritual features, such as hills and mountains of religious significance, or at a smaller scale, by trees, piles of stones or watering points that demarcate boundaries and tenure (see Figure 7.9). These have direct links to land or resource tenure and customary restrictions motivated by local belief systems.

Establishing boundaries is important, but it is not by itself enough. Just as the paint that marks lines on a tar road has to be repainted, so the boundaries and entrances at all spatial scales, from the individual level to that of the neighbourhood, need to be periodically renewed (see Figure 7.7). Without this, they gradually lose their significance and, if this occurs, weaken one of the mechanisms through which local authorities exercise power (Giddens, 1984; Bourdieu, 1973, 1977). The frequency of these practices, such as boundary-marking rituals, is an important measure of the continued social recognition of these 'invisible' boundaries and culturally significant sites that are markers across a cultural landscape.

Political control, whether through traditional leadership or, in many cases in Africa, through political leadership in government, is linked to symbolic or religious power, where ritual specialists, such as diviners or shamans, mediate with ancestor spirits to maintain social order. Table 7.2 shows a useful framework for thinking about ways in which controls are placed on access to land or resources.

Ritual boundary demarcation not only divides 'wild' from 'domesticated' space, it can also be used to expand and establish control over new territories, in addition to maintaining old ones (see Figure 7.10). A good example of this is anthropologist Robert Thornton's (1980) field work with Iraqw agropastoralists in Tanzania, which illustrates the links between land, religion and tenure:

> 'The ritual condition of the land is influenced most greatly by the acts of men and the events that involve men. These acts and events endanger the condition of the land in all respects, interfering not only with the order imposed on it by the performance of the masay ritual

Source: (c) Y Aumeeruddy

Figure 7.9 *Ritual topography, boundaries and tenure: the frequency of reaffirming key points in the landscape through religious practice is an important 'field measure' of the social significance of boundaries that cross the landscape. (a) A pile of stones in* Colophospermum mopane *woodland says little to an outsider, but speaks volumes to local people. This type of cairn, added to stone-by-stone by passers-by, is found widely in Southern Africa. Like many things of symbolic significance, their local names have multiple meanings. (b) Situated inside a high-diversity tropical forest conservation area, Etinde Mountain ('Small Mount Cameroon') retains strong religious significance to the Bakweri people, with libations to the ancestors made by everyone climbing to the summit. (c) Each of these figures (thorma), made of barley, yak butter and water, represents landscape features of the Gunasa high pasture of Dolpo region, Nepal. These are made during a special ceremony called Yulsa Cholsa, during which lamas propitiate the deities and demons inhabiting the landscape in order to bring peace and prosperity to the local people, agriculture and natural resources*

Table 7.2 *A schematic way in which Nguni people structure the world: a 'traditionalist' view which has resonance in several other agricultural societies, such as Aouan farmers in the Côte d'Ivoire and Bakiga farmers who have felled ('domesticated') much of Bwindi (meaning 'dark') Forest in western Uganda*

	Wild space (wild = bad) negative	Intermediate (ambiguous) negative/positive	Domesticated space (domestic = good) positive
Spatial	forest	savanna/grassland/river (sacred forests, land-shrines and grave sites)	cultivated fields, homestead
Animal	wild animals (carnivores, inedible)	river crocodiles (negative) cattle (positive)	domestic animals (cattle, goats (edible))
Social	individualism	social freedom	community
Ethical	unmerited misfortune	fortuity	merited misfortune
Spirit	witches familiars	river people mythical snakes, spirits	ancestral spirits
Human	witches	diviners/shamans	moral people
Sexual	forbidden, evil sex (witches with familiars)	foreplay between unmarried adults	accepted marital relations

Sources: Hammond-Tooke, 1975; van den Beemer, 1994

itself, but also with fertility, the germination of seeds, predations of birds, and with the rain itself. The object of the ritual is the land itself.

Of course, the land is the primary productive resource of the inhabitants of the aya, and the order and control of the land must therefore be political by its very nature. The masay ritual is therefore political. Ritual is politics and politics is ritual: these two spheres that are distinct in other societies are scarcely separable in Iraqw life. The performance is political in at least two arenas: within the community of the aya itself, and within the larger arena of interaction that includes all other Iraqw and all other ethnic groups in the region.

First of all, since the ritual is conducted by the elders and by the kahamuse ("the speakers of the community"), who are ultimately responsible in disputes over land rights, the ritual legitimates their offices by virtue of the fact that they "create the aya" in the first place. The ritual thus reaffirms the political status quo. But since it also draws up boundaries between the inhabitants of the aya and other groups, thereby laying claim to a portion of land, the ritual also has important bearing on the political ecology of the whole region. Where the Iraqw have expanded onto lands formerly grazed, cultivated or hunted on by other peoples, they have used the masay rituals as the chief political instrument by which they gain control over land, and to legitimate their claim to it. Once the masay ceremony has been performed for a piece of land, "creating" it, as it were, out of the bush, the settlers who inhabit it

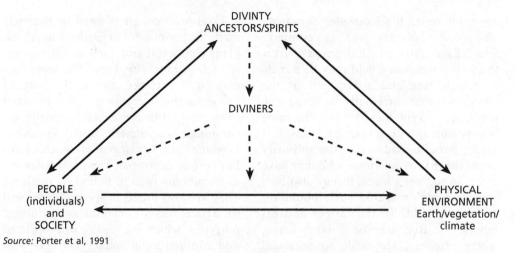

Source: Porter et al, 1991

Figure 7.10 *Diagrammatic representation of the mediating role of an African ritual specialist (diviner). This conceptual model is widely applicable in East and Southern Africa, in this case relating to Giriama diviners whose ritual space, the kaya, has played a crucial role in conserving important small remnants of East African coastal forest*

> *cling to it in the face of repeated raids and adversity. The masay ceremony is in such cases their deed to land.'*

Moral authority relates not only to territories, but also to valued resources or sites within territories. Examples are customary restrictions against the felling of certain tree species; the hunting of totemic animals; seasonal restrictions of hunting, fishing or gathering valuable commodities such as salt; bans on hunting or collection of products such as fuelwood; or even total exclusion from places of ritual significance. People who break these rules are anti-social, and lay themselves open to public sentiment against them, played out in the form of misfortune through witchcraft. Ritual specialists mediate between the two main dangerous realms of wildlands (forest and bush, the source of predatory animals) and heavens (the source of lightning). Fear of lightning and destructive storms, wild predatory animals or the direct accusation of witchcraft by other people in the community all

maintain moral order, including people 'doing the right thing' by conforming to restrictions on resource use. Ritual specialists also play a key role in resolving conflicts that result from anti-social activity. If these cannot be resolved, then exile from that community can follow, either temporarily, with people returning after ritual cleansing, or permanently.

These links may seem strange to conservation biologists or protected area managers who come from a biological sciences background. With our interest in resource management, however, it is crucial that we develop an understanding of what institutional and religious factors constrain people, either individually or in groups, from depleting a resource in favour of managed harvests for long-term gain.

Metaphor and meaning, botany and boundaries

There are many ways of seeing the world, and seeing the world in different ways can avoid misunderstanding and conflict – including conflict over conservation areas.

257

To a botanist, for example, a marula (*Sclerocarya birrea*) tree (a common South-East African indigenous fruit species) in someone's field may be a male or female tree and a remnant of the woodland that originally covered the landscape. To the local farmer, the same tree is not only a source of fruits and shade, but also evidence of the authority he (or she) has to determine who may have access to the tree's fruits. It may also be a 'property peg', marking out a boundary within the field. To the farmer and his family, the tree may be a land-shrine, where offerings are made to ancestral spirits who influence their lives. To the district, this and other trees are a source of *ubuganu* beer, which acts as a 'social glue', linking the community together at the annual first fruits ceremony.

It is important to realize that conservation and resource management are directly linked to social behaviour and, through this, to ritual practice and religion. In many societies around the world, ancestor spirits, through ritual specialists, are a source of moral authority over the living. This creates strong social pressure to conform, and is a powerful motivation behind maintaining control over land and over valued, scarce resources within those boundaries. Following these rules plays a crucial role in maintaining social harmony and community health. Rule breaking then negatively influences the production of crops, cattle, and children, as well as success in hunting and fishing (Berglund, 1976; Knight, 1991; Reichel-Dolmatoff, 1996).

While an understanding of tenure or belief systems is unfamiliar to biologists, they have an advantage: that of recognizing 'invisible' boundaries through botany. In her work in Sumatra, for example, Yildiz Aumeeruddy (1994) records how betel nut palms (*Areca catechu*), whose fruits are used in offerings and chewed as a social practice, are planted to discretely mark the boundaries of gardens. In Africa, plant characteristics such as succulence, spinyness, longevity, vegetative reproduction from cuttings, and leaf colour all influence the selection process. In many cases, several of these characteristics are combined in genera such as *Aloe*, *Commiphora*, *Crassocephalum*, *Dovyalis*, *Euphorbia*, *Erythrina*, *Ficus* and *Solanum*, all commonly used in boundary marking. They are also found in species introduced to Africa for ornamental or economic purposes, which are rapidly appropriated and adopted as boundary markers with symbolic significance (such as *Agave*, *Pereskia* and many Cactaceae). Selection of these same species for demarcating national park boundaries, as is common around forests in western Uganda, has a cultural 'resonance' which results in wide recognition of the boundary-marking process. Boundary-marking species also link symbolism and social practice.

Less obvious, but equally important, is the selection of certain tree species for entrances or as protective charms. This process, the plant medicines and the meanings of the names of the plant ingredients often all have highly significant multiple meanings (polysemy). Sprinkling medicines around the home boundary for protection against lightning or misfortune is termed *ukubethelela* in Zulu, but can also mean to hammer, to put up a fight or to bind the affections of a girl through use of a charm. The term for this type of medicine is *intelezi*, which means 'to smooth over a difference (*theleza*)' or 'to counteract' (other charms). The names of plants commonly used as protective charms also reveal this strong link with boundaries and belief systems: *Drimea elata* (*indongana izibomvana*) means 'red walls', where red is a symbolic colour which consolidates action; *Rapanea melanophloeos* (*umaphipha*) means 'wipe away dirt' and 'help through difficulty' as a result of its ritual cleansing function; *Scilla natalensis* (*inguduza*) means 'make a beaten track or path' or 'grope about in the dark'.

This polysemy is also worth noting by field researchers, for three reasons. Firstly, lack of recognition of polysemy can lead to misinterpreting records from local people. Secondly, the meanings of symbolic objects, such as plants used to demarcate 'invisible' boundaries, say a lot about the belief systems that contribute to social and moral order. Thirdly, just as overdifferentiation in plant names reflects their higher value within that society, so multiple meanings of things reflect symbolic power. The 'memorial heaps' of stone (cairns) found in many parts of Southern Africa

and known in Zulu as *isivivane* are one example (see Figure 7.9). The word *isivivane* not only refers to the cairns that mark points on the landscape (to which passers-by have to add a small stone or suffer the consequences of misfortune); the root word *viva* refers directly to mobilization and to social groups of people (such as a company of soldiers). Survey beacons or pegs marking a boundary are another example. Known in Zulu as an *isikhonkhwane*, this word also refers to the foundation of a house, a wooden stake for tethering livestock, a boundary-marking peg, or a wooden peg (often made of *Ptaeroxylon obliquum* wood) treated with symbolic medicines to ward off lightning.

Who are the stakeholders?

Identifying areas or resources to which different forms of tenure apply is an important step. Equally important, and as complex in terms of resource management, is the process of identifying who the stakeholders are. The view that 'people living adjacent to protected areas have found themselves deprived of resources which for thousands of years they had a right to utilize' (IIED, 1994) has caught the imagination of policy makers and 'biopoliticians'. However, this is more often the exception than the rule. To understand changes in tenure and access rights to land or resources, it is useful to find out what proportion of the local community really fit the image of long-time residents of land within or adjacent to protected areas. This is often fewer than one might expect. Using household survey methods, for example, a 1990 survey around Liwonde National Park, Malawi, showed that only 5 per cent of inhabitants living around the national park were there

in the late 1960s, 13 per cent had moved into the area during the 1970s, and 70 per cent of the 1990 population had moved in the 1980s from other parts of Malawi or had arrived as refugees from Mozambique (Hall-Martin, 1993). The social complexity of West African forest areas is another example (see Box 7.5).

Important questions in this process are: who are the resource users; what local institutions would be most appropriate and representative? The answers to these questions will vary depending upon whether we are dealing with people living within a protected area or adjacent to it, and whether they are sedentary or semi-nomadic. Should the beneficiaries be those people who are the most disadvantaged from proximity to the protected area? Or should they be the 'locals', rather than 'outsider' settlers? Discerning who is 'local' and who is not, in terms of access to land or resources, however, is obscured by the many ways in which people access

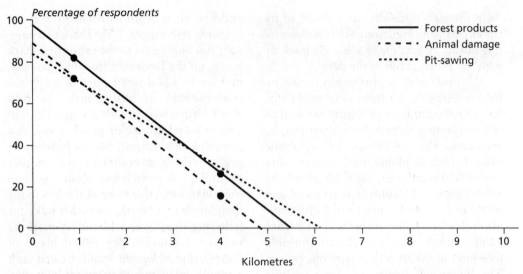

Percentage of respondents

— Forest products
‑ ‑ ‑ ‑ Animal damage
········· Pit-sawing

Kilometres

Source: Wild and Mutebi, 1996

Figure 7.11 *Mean percentage of people from communities adjacent to Bwindi-Impenetrable National Park (n = 978) who were involved in collecting forest products or pit-sawing, or who were affected by crop-raiding animals prior to park closure compared to those further away (n = 1405)*

land: for example, by settlement, birthright, 'creating' extended family links to people already resident there, or by getting land through allocation from local government, traditional authority, loan, rental or direct sale.

In principle, benefits need to be directed to those living closest to the protected area. In most cases, these are the people who are most affected by crop-raiding animals and loss of access to plant resources inside protected areas. This is well illustrated by the household surveys which Rob Wild and his colleagues with CARE-Uganda conducted. Wild and Mutebi (1996) recorded the number of respondents from communities adjacent to Bwindi-Impenetrable National Park who were involved in collecting forest products and pit-sawing, or who were affected by crop-raiding animals prior to park closure, compared to those away from the forest (see Figure 7.11).

In theory, resource-sharing arrangements should take place through local community institutions set up for this purpose, which should be representative of the communities and of resource users. This is often easier said than done. Protected areas are often located in more remote areas, where literacy skills may be limited. In many cases, resource users are from a sector of the local community with the least economic or political power. For these reasons, local resource users are generally not well represented – even at the lowest level of formal local government – although they may be highly influential members of their own communities. In addition, the administrative boundaries that form the basis for local government within the nation state rarely conform to the territorial boundaries of local communities. This may further skew the relationship of who 'represents' communities surrounding protected areas.

Three participatory rural appraisal (PRA) methods which are useful in this process during short-term surveys are the use of household mapping, wealth

Table 7.3 *Criteria for identifying the most significant stakeholders in sustainable forest management: an example from East Kalimantan, Indonesia*

Stakeholders	Proximity	Pre-existing rights	Dependency	Dimensions Indigenous knowledge	Culture/forest integration	Power deficit	Value
Dayak	1	1	1	1	1	1	1.00
Kutai	1	1	1	1	1	1	1.00
Transmigrant	1	variable	1	variable	variable	1	1.00
Forest workers	1	3	1	variable	variable	1	1.50
Small scale entrepreneur	2	variable	2	2	2	2	2.00
Company officials	2	3	1	3	3	3	2.50
Forestry officials	3	3	1	3	3	3	2.67
Environmentalists	3	3	2	3	2	3	2.67
National citizens	3	3	2	3	3	variable	2.80
Consumers	3	3	3	3	3	variable	3.00

Source: Colfer, 1995

ranking and Venn (or 'chapatti') diagrams (see Chapter 2). One example is the result of the Venn diagram exercise facilitated by Moses Saranta at Olorosoito Emurua in Transmara district, Kenya, where local institutions and leaders were identified by the Maasai participants. This example illustrates how close (or far) several local institutions are from the local community.

Carol Pierce Colfer, an anthropologist at the Centre for International Forestry Research (CIFOR), has proposed a method for identifying and defining the most significant stakeholders in sustainable forest management (Colfer, 1995). This has been field-tested in the Côte d'Ivoire, West Africa, in North America and in Kalimantan (Borneo), Indonesia. It is based on a matrix, with different stakeholders on one axis and six factors considered most relevant to the relations between forests and groups of people on the other axis. The factors defining the most significant stakeholders are:

- proximity to the forest;
- pre-existing rights of tenure (recognizing that this varies from place to place);
- dependency on the forest (for products such as food, fibre and medicines);
- level of local/indigenous knowledge about the forest;
- culture/forest integration in terms of symbolic links with the forest; and
- power deficits (people with little power compared to other stakeholders).

Using a rating system on a scale of 1–3 (1 = high, 2 = medium, 3 = low, with an additional category for 'var' = variable), based on field observation and experience, Colfer then calculated mean scores for different stakeholders (see Table 7.3). She found this a quick and easy method, but points out that problems may arise with identifying and defining the six factors that describe stakeholders, the weighting of those dimensions and the level of detail of the scoring method and cut-off point. Although refinements are needed, this is an interesting approach to a truly knotty problem.

Although Rob Wild and Jackson Mutebi (1996) did not use the rating system suggested by Carol Colfer, the characteristics she employed were common to the stakeholders and community groups with whom they worked in Bwindi-Impenetrable National Park, Uganda. It also illustrates the point that local institutions involved in the process can be recent, rather than 'traditional' ones. New organizations should not be discounted: in some cases, religious groups, rural women's savings clubs, even soccer clubs may have a role to play. In the case of Wild and Mutebi's study (1996), three community organizations were identified by the local community as the most appropriate to deal with multiple use, forming a 'forest society' which would coordinate the multiple-use activities. Two of these, the local (formerly resistance) council (LC) and the stretcher-bearer societies (*ebibiina by'engozi*) are recent organizations, while the third, the *abataka*, has a longer history. Due to their different history and social and political links, each is briefly described here.

The LC system is a form of government introduced to Uganda by the current National Resistance Movement (NRM) government of President Yoweri Museveni, which came to power in 1986 after a long period of civil war. The LC system allows significant local self-determination and consists of five levels, from the village (LC1) level to the parliamentary level (LC5). At the LC1 level, every adult member of the community (approximately 150 households) is a member of the LC1 council, which elects a committee of 9 to manage the day-to-day running of the village. The *ebibiina by'engozi* are stretcher-bearer societies which were formed in the 1980s, possibly following the idea of similar groups in Rwanda. The motivation for stretcher societies came when individuals found it increasingly difficult to mobilize their friends and relatives to carry their sick to the clinic. Membership within each community and the attendance at meetings is compulsory, and there is a small monthly fee. To maintain this level of support, discipline is very tough. The penalty for being absent without a good excuse when a patient needs to be carried can be a drum of local banana beer (200 litres), a fine representing the wage-labour equivalent of US$30.

The *abataka* is the traditional community organization amongst the Bakiga people of western Uganda. Loosely translated, *abataka* refers to responsible adults within a geographical area, such as on a ridge or hill, who form citizens' groups. In some cases, therefore, the word *abataka* refers to an extended family group related to one great-grandfather. *Abataka* leadership is drawn from elders in the community, frequently with a hierarchical structure of chairman, secretary and treasurer.

The forest society liaises at the interface between the local community and the national park management and is the 'umbrella' organization under which specialist user groups have formed. Prior to this, most categories of resource user, such as herbalists, midwives, basket makers or beekeepers, worked on an individual basis and did not belong to any formal association.

The signed 'memorandum of understanding' (MOU) reached between the community and the national park authority on multiple use in the national park was an important step once agreement had been reached on rules, rights and responsibilities. The MOU includes the agreement that the community controls activities incompatible with the goals of the conservation area, such as gold mining, commercial logging and illegal hunting. Also important is the request for identification cards by specialist users (beekeeper, herbalist, midwife, etc), which have the mutually agreed rules and responsibilities printed on them. To date, for example, nearly 500 beekeepers in four parish beekeeping societies are registered to keep an estimated 3000 hives within multiple-use zones. In addition, the CARE-Development through Conservation (DTC) project assists beekeepers with processing and marketing surplus honey. Initial ethnobotanical surveys with traditional healers and basket makers have been followed up with PRA surveys in three pilot-study parishes, leading to harvesting of selected species. Each of these activities falls within joint forest management (JFM) agreements developed within the parishes and signed by the forest societies and the Uganda Wildlife Authority, including access to certain footpaths through the forest and to a hot spring site considered to have spiritual healing qualities.

Each of these factors – clear boundaries, group size, group identity, agreed rules, conflict-resolution mechanisms, and so on – relates to the 'ingredients' for community-based conservation given at the start of this chapter (see Box 7.1).

The question is: how successful is this experiment? In answering this, as with any similar project, it is important to resist the temptation to claim early success. I suggest that a ten-year minimum period is needed before this can be done. Too many well-publicized text-book cases fail after a few years. There are positive signs, however. The incidence of fires has been greatly reduced, and so has the problem of beekeepers setting snares (Wild and Mutebi, 1996). The Mpungu Forest Society has also been remarkably tough on rule breakers. In one example in 1994, the forest resource users alerted park staff to illegal hunting in the forest and a ranger patrol apprehended one person while another ran away. The person who was apprehended was fined 4000 Uganda Shillings (about US$4) in the local police court. By contrast, the man who ran away was identified to the community by his own stretcher society, through the medium of the LCs and the local forest society, and was fined 60 litres of beer and a goat (the equivalent of about US$20), a five times larger penalty.

There have also been changes within the Uganda Wildlife Authority. Just as the community has built on its existing system by forming a forest society, the Uganda Wildlife Authority has added to its own network, strengthening its own capacity to interact with the community through a community conservation unit. Patient and participatory conservation work around these parks is bearing fruit. Park staff no longer interact just with law-breakers, but also with responsible members of the community who are constructively involved in multiple-use areas. As a result, instead of a situation where a mere 30 patrol rangers are faced with policing a rugged 330km^2 of forest surrounded by 100,000 people, there are the beginnings of a more promising future emerging out of a complex and conflict-ridden past.

Chapter 8

Striving for Balance: Looking Outward and Inward

Introduction

The beginning of Chapter 7 mentions that conservation behaviour requires three basic conditions before an area or a resource is conserved: appreciation of value, the realization of scarcity, and appropriate social or political institutions to implement conservation or resource management regulations. Recognizing that conservation practice requires an understanding of social and cultural factors, economic driving forces and ecological principles, the preceding chapters have described a variety of tools for identifying, and in some cases for measuring, these three ingredients of conservation behaviour in more detail. The ingredients are: value, monitoring scarcity of the most valued and vulnerable categories of species, and the cultural factors underpinning control of access to land or resources. In particular, this manual has focused on steps used in priority setting when making decisions on conservation and management of wild plant resources. These can be condensed into 15 basic steps, hopefully a mid point between overcomplication (a 'horrendo-gram') and oversimplification (see Figure 8.1).

Two key themes of Chapter 7, tenure and boundaries, have a message for all of us: there are limits to how much demand can be met from sustainably managed harvests. These limits can be extended with more intensive management or cultivation (Tiffen et al, 1994; Netting, 1993; Boserup, 1965), but there are boundaries to this as well. Slow-growing, slowly reproducing, habitat-specific species which are destructively harvested – the very category most vulnerable to overexploitation – are the least likely to be cultivated because of biological attributes: returns per unit time are just too low, unless values are extraordinarily high.

The Brazilian economist Alfredo Homma's (1992) analysis of forest-product harvesting in the Amazon is equally applicable in Africa and to other vegetation types (see Figure 8.2). This shows **four phases** in the harvesting of forest resources: an **expansion phase** at the resource-rich frontier (or when a monopoly is held on the resource in the market); a **stabilization phase** where there is an equilibrium between supply and demand; a **decline phase** brought about by resource depletion; and for some species, a subsequent **domestication** phase.

Prices begin to rise during the stabilization phase when there is no increase in

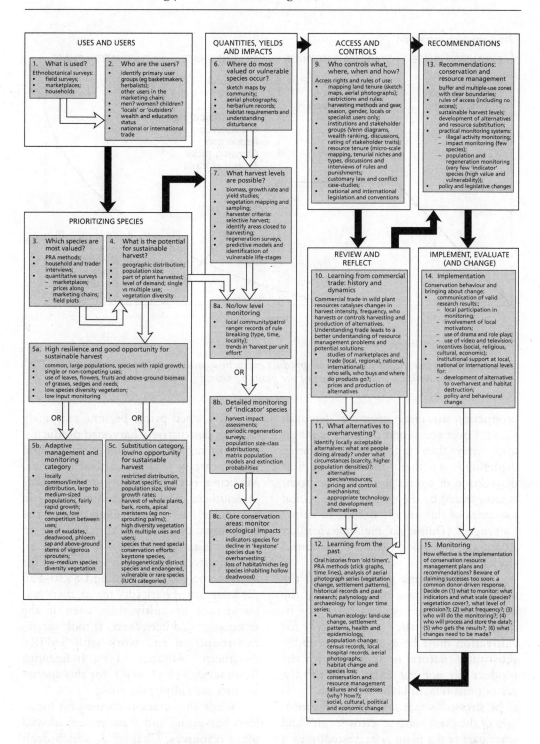

Figure 8.1 *Fifteen basic steps towards resource management. Setting priorities on the basis of ecological principles, social and cultural factors and economic driving forces is essential. So is the recognition and review of past mistakes, successes and political context*

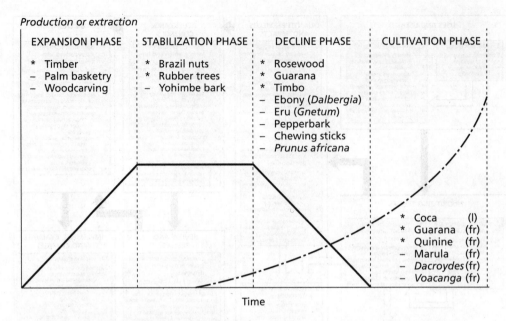

Production or extraction

EXPANSION PHASE	STABILIZATION PHASE	DECLINE PHASE	CULTIVATION PHASE
* Timber	* Brazil nuts	* Rosewood	
– Palm basketry	* Rubber trees	* Guarana	
– Woodcarving	– Yohimbe bark	* Timbo	
		– Ebony (*Dalbergia*)	
		– Eru (*Gnetum*)	
		– Pepperbark	
		– Chewing sticks	
		– *Prunus africana*	

* Coca	(l)
* Guarana	(fr)
* Quinine	(fr)
– Marula	(fr)
– *Dacroydes*	(fr)
– *Voacanga*	(fr)

Time

Source: modified from Homma, 1992

Figure 8.2 *The historical cycle of forest product extraction, with examples from Amazonia (*) and Africa (–) showing part of the plant harvested (l = leaves, fr = fruits)*

production to meet growing demand. Control over access and resource management may then take place. Resource depletion, whether through habitat destruction or overexploitation (or both) is represented by the decline phase. Good examples of this are the decline of ebony ('*mpingo*') (*Dalbergia melanoxylon*) in Africa and rosewood (*Aniba rosaeodora*) stocks in Brazil.

Alfredo Homma points out that the **domestication phase** occurs during the **decline phase** but requires three conditions. Firstly, the technology for cultivation must be available. Secondly, substitutes (natural or synthetic) for the product do not yet exist, and thirdly, prices must remain high. What also needs to be stressed is that the biological attributes of the plant (such as growth rates and what part of the plant is harvested) play a crucial role. These are summarized in Boxes 5.1 and 5.2 (see Chapter 5).

Only when prices become extremely high for destructively harvested products – often in response to high demand and great scarcity – does cultivation start. Medicinal bark from *Warburgia salutaris* in Southern Africa (and Zimbabwe, in particular), is a good example. In the Zimbabwe case, local extinction due to overexploitation resulted in loss of all growing stock. Even with local prices for local medicinal use reaching US$30–$50 per kilogram of bark (dry mass), there was no chance of cultivation, even if the technology had been there. It took species reintroduction and work with SAFIRE (Southern Alliance for Indigenous Resources), a local NGO, for this species to enter the cultivation phase.

While this manual focuses on local-level harvesting and management of wild plant resources, Chapter 3, which dealt with marketplaces and trade, was a reminder that even the remotest areas and plant species can be linked with international trade networks. For this reason, although the methods for analysing macro-economic issues are beyond the scope of this manual, it is important,

briefly, to look outward at the wider context. Unless these wider issues are addressed, conservation programmes end up winning at the local level but losing at a global one.

Looking outward

Harvesting of wild plant resources, often carried out by rural people with little access to political or economic power, is directly linked to the wider issues: macro-economic factors, per capita consumption rates, population growth, technological development and living standards. The recent problems in the Asian economies, where events on New York Stock Exchange computer screens can affect harvesting of forest products in South-East Asia, are a good illustration of one of these global linkages.

The point that wild plant resources are the 'green social security', providing a buffer against drought or economic decline, was made at the start of this manual. One measure of the extent to which these plant resources are under increasing pressure in Africa is the proportion of the total population in formal employment. In Zimbabwe, this has fallen steadily from 15.6 per cent in 1977 to 11.6 per cent in 1993, and the real average, including wages in the farming sector, dropped by 35 per cent between 1985 and 1993 (Bond, 1996). Many other African countries are in a similar situation, as are parts of South-East Asia which were hit by the financial crisis in 1998. This boosts the number of people relying on wild plant resources, including their sale in local, regional and international markets. It can also result in weaker tenure, with the influx of 'outsiders' who arrive to harvest commercially valuable resources or to clear frontier land bordering on conservation areas.

Other measures of environmental impact are human population density, population growth rates and consumption levels. These are emotive, highly politicized issues, but they cannot be ignored (Meffe et al, 1993; Baltz, 1999). Neither can each of these factors be taken in isolation: they have to be considered together as important indicators of loss of habitat or increase in demand for resources. Over 30 years ago, Paul Erlich and others summarized this into the simple equation: $I = PAT$, indicating that environmental impact (I) is a function of population size (P), affluence (A) and technology (T) (Erlich and Holdren, 1971). Energy consumption rates are a good example of environmental impact: a North American family of 4 people has the same environmental impact as 80 Costa Ricans and 280 Bangladeshis (Erlich et al, 1995). In order to present a realistic picture of human consumption on the environment, the *WWF Living Plant Report* (1998) combines population numbers and consumption rates as an index of the pressures people put on the environment (see Figure 8.3).

Projected world-population growth rates under different fertility rates suggest that if global fertility rates stabilize at just over 2 children per woman, the world's population will expand from 5.7 billion people in 1995 to 9.4 billion in 2050, and will reach a maximum of almost 11 billion by about 2200. However, even small differences in fertility rate can make a huge

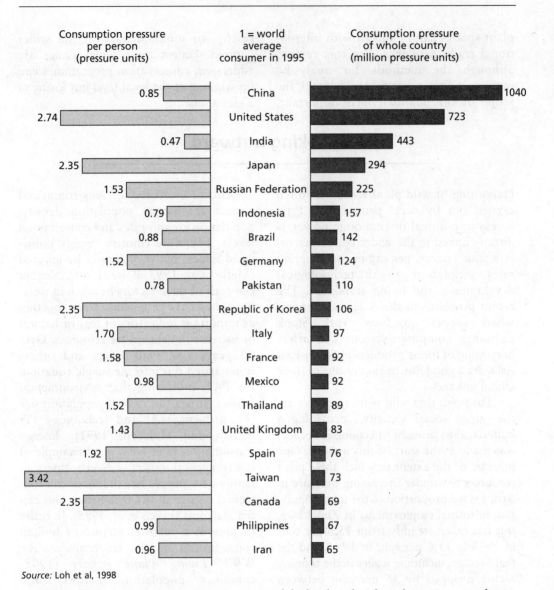

Consumption pressure per person (pressure units)	1 = world average consumer in 1995	Consumption pressure of whole country (million pressure units)
0.85	China	1040
2.74	United States	723
0.47	India	443
2.35	Japan	294
1.53	Russian Federation	225
0.79	Indonesia	157
0.88	Brazil	142
1.52	Germany	124
0.78	Pakistan	110
2.35	Republic of Korea	106
1.70	Italy	97
1.58	France	92
0.98	Mexico	92
1.52	Thailand	89
1.43	United Kingdom	83
1.92	Spain	76
3.42	Taiwan	73
2.35	Canada	69
0.99	Philippines	67
0.96	Iran	65

Source: Loh et al, 1998

Figure 8.3 *Consumption pressure: a measure of the burden placed on the environment by people, 1995*

difference to these projections (see Figure 8.4a). In Africa, for example, the population would treble over the next 50 years under the 'medium fertility scenario'. In 1995, 700 million people lived in Africa; by 2050 there will be just over 2 billion (see Figure 8.4b).

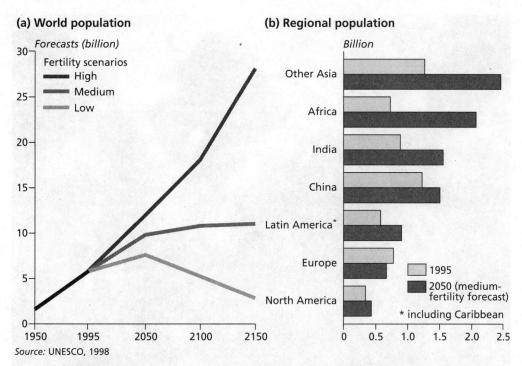

Figure 8.4 *(a) World population, projected to 2150. (b) Population by region, 1995 and projection for 2050 under a medium-fertility scenario*

Looking inward; examining innovative local approaches

Ethics are at the core of conservation behaviour, and ethical change, in this case ethics that constrain individual action for long-term benefits to a wider group, often arises through crisis. One of the requirements, however, is that claims about crisis are validated and popularized. In societies with high literacy levels, this can be done through posters or books, such as Aldo Leopold's classic, *A Sand County Almanac* (1949). In other cases, verbal and visual communication, through the use of songs, theatre, drama, film or video, is a far more powerful tool for communicating research results.

Religious practice can play a powerful role in instilling (or re-instilling) a land ethic. In Zimbabwe, for example, projects through ZIRRCON (Zimbabwean

Institute of Religious Research and Ecological Conservation), which was initiated by anthropologist Enus Daneel, and AZTREC (Association of Zimbabwean Traditional Ecologists) – both working with the African Independent Churches and traditional healers – have developed a theology of the environment with links to tree planting. Using practices which have links to traditional practices of blessing seeds and the ecological religion of territorial cults studied by Schoffeleers (1978) and van Binsbergen (1985) (see Chapter 7), congregations are held where people contribute tree seeds, not money, into a collection. These are then blessed and planted. Ceremonies conducted by traditionalists, separately from the Independent Church members, also offer sorghum beer

Figure 8.5 *Encouraging conservation through drama, rather than through the barrel of a gun: woodcarvers and their relatives from Wamunyu, Kenya, toured carving centres in Kenya, acting out a drama which communicated research results about the depletion of favoured wild species and the cultivation of viable alternatives*

to their ancestors, sprinkling snuff and mixing beer into the water for the seeds (Holt-Biddle, 1994).

Drama has also been used very successfully in Kenya. Actors from woodcarving families (or the woodcarvers themselves) tour woodcarving centres, acting out a drama in Kikamba written by local Kamba playrights Fidelma Kyalo and Vinette Mbaluto (see Figure 8.5). The use of low-cost, but high-quality, video footage – taken by programme staff but professionally edited to scripts they have written – has also been a successful method used by the People and Plants Initiative to transfer knowledge of resource management methods, problems and solutions.

In the South Pacific, the Wan Smolbag Theatre (translated as 'one small bag'), based in Vanuatu, has produced plays, videos and songs related to marine conservation issues. In Southern Africa, Nicholas Ellenbogen's 'Theatre for Africa' has sent an equally powerful message about local communities and conservation issues, including a play on the controversial issue of the Southern African position on elephant culling and the ivory trade, acted at the recent CITES (Convention on International Trade in Endangered Species of Wild Fauna and Flora) congress in

Harare, Zimbabwe.

Creative projects give signs of hope, even under the bleakest of circumstances (see Figure 8.5). One of the strongest tests of conservation strategies is how resilient they are in the face of civil conflicts. Recent tests of this stem from conservation areas in Rwanda and Zaire (now the Democratic Republic of Congo), engulfed by conflict (Hart and Hart, 1997; Fimbel and Fimbel, 1997). These Central African examples highlight the crucial need for appropriately training hand-picked local people at various levels (rangers, technical staff, research professionals and managers) to take responsibility for conservation programmes. International non-governmental organizations have a key role in this process, and one of these is to support this training process. In both cases, international funding was disrupted and expatriate staff left or were evacuated due to conflicts in or around the Nyungwe Forest Conservation Project in Rwanda and four World Heritage Sites in the Democratic Republic of Congo. What preserved these conservation areas during the conflicts were local people connected to the projects.

Innovative, decentralized approaches to buffer zones and landscapes outside protected areas also have a way of catching on and spreading. Two examples are CAMPFIRE (Communal Areas Management Programme for Indigenous Resources) in Zimbabwe (Child, 1996) and Joint Forest Management programme projects spread across India and Nepal (Poffenberger et al, 1992a, b; Fischer, 1995). In both cases, however, the context is crucial.

CAMPFIRE has succeeded mainly in areas such as the Zambezi Valley, where there are big populations of large mammals (from which revenue is derived through trophy hunting), low arable potential and low densities of people. In India, Joint Forest Management has worked best in 'tribal' areas such as West Bengal, which also have poor lateritic soils and where the dominant tree species, *Shorea robusta* (*sal*), has vigorous resprouting ability.

The multiple effect of innovative approaches also applies to the marine environment. In Vanuatu (Johannes, 1998) and in Fiji (Biodiversity Support Programme, 1998), experiments in village-based marine conservation, including monitoring of key resources (such as trochus shells and edible mussels), in collaboration with local government and NGOs, have led to the development of controlled harvests of other valued species and the closure of some areas to harvesting. Although small, and begun in isolation, these programmes have built up experience and common ground that have been more widely applied.

The practical methods covered in this manual can similarly be used by trained local people. What is essential is to review and reflect on these successes and failures and to work out what made them succeed or fail – whether social (see Chapter 7), ecological (see Chapters 4 to 6) or economic factors (see Chapter 3).

The final important ingredient for successful projects is the one mentioned in the preface to this manual: long-term institutional support, independent of political constraints. Applied ethnobotanical studies can be a catalyst in this process – it is clear that useful plants are a key to opening people's minds to seeing the world in different ways so that a land ethic may grow.

Acronyms and Abbreviations

AI	artificial intelligence
ANPWS	Australian National Parks and Wildlife Service
AVHRR	Advanced Very High Resolution Radiometer
AZTREC	Association of Zimbabwean Traditional Ecologists
ba	basal area
bd	basal diameter
BP	before present
BSP	Biodiversity Support Programme
CAMP	Conservation Assessment and Management Plan
CAMPFIRE	Communal Areas Management Programme for Indigenous Resources
CBNRM	community-based natural resource management
CFA	Communauté Financière Africaine
CIFOR	Centre for International Forestry Research
CITES	Convention on International Trade in Endangered Species of Wild Fauna and Flora
CLC	Community Land Companies, India
cm	centimetre
CNES	Centre National d'Études Spatiales, France
dbh	diameter at breast height
DFID	Department for International Development, UK
DTC	Development through Conservation project
FAA	formalin-acetic acid alcohol
FAO	Food and Agriculture Organization
gbh	girth at breast height
GIS	geographic information system
GPS	global positioning system
ha	hectare
IAWA	International Association of Wood Anatomists
ICDP	Integrated Conservation and Development Project
ICS	index of cultural significance
IGBP	International Geosphere-Biosphere Programme
IIED	International Institute for Environment and Development, UK
ILDIS	International Legume Database and Information Service
IRDNC	integrated rural development and nature conservation
ISD	initial size-class distribution
IUCN	The World Conservation Union
JCM	Joint Forest Management programme
kg	kilogram

km	kilometre
LC	local council
LEAP	*List of East African Plants*
MAB	Man and the Biosphere programme
MVP	minimum viable population
MOU	memorandum of understanding
NASA	National Aeronautics and Space Administration, US
NGO	non-governmental organization
NLCB	National Lottery Charities Board, UK
NRM	National Resistance Movement, Uganda
ODI	Overseas Development Institute
PAME	participatory assessment, monitoring and evaluation
PAR	participatory action research
PC	personal computer
PCQ	point-centred quarter method
PRA	participatory rural appraisal
PSP	permanent sample plot
RBG	Royal Botanic Gardens, Kew
RRA	rapid rural appraisal
SAFIRE	Southern Alliance for Indigenous Resources
SARARES	Southern African RARES database
SE	standard error
SLA	specific leaf area
SPOT	Système pour l'Observation de la Terre
SSD	stable-stage distribution
UNEP	United Nations Environment Programme
UNESCO	United Nations Educational, Scientific and Cultural Organization
WCMC	World Conservation Monitoring Centre, Cambridge
WCU	World Conservation Union
WRI	World Resources Institute
WWF	formerly the World Wide Fund For Nature
ZIRRCON	Zimbabwean Institute of Religious Research and Ecological Conservation

Further Reading

The following key references are recommended for pursuing the subjects covered in Chapters 2–8.

Chapter 2 Local inventories, values and quantities of harvested resources

Baker and Mutitjulu Community (1992) 'Comparing two views of the landscape: aboriginal ecological knowledge and modern scientific knowledge', *Rangeland Journal* 14(2): 174–189

Bernhard, H R, P Killworth, D Kronenfeld and L Sailer (1984) 'The problem of informant accuracy: the validity of retrospective data', *Annual Review of Anthropology* 13: 495–517

Carlquist, S (1991) 'Anatomy of vine and liana stems: a review and synthesis' in F E Putz and H A Mooney (eds) *The Biology of Vines*. Cambridge University Press, Cambridge, pp53–71

Chambers, R (1992) *Rural appraisal: rapid, relaxed and participatory*. Discussion Paper 311, Institute of Development Studies, University of Sussex

Dufour, D L and N I Teufel (1995) 'Minimum data sets for the description of diet and measurement of food intake and nutritional status' in E F Moran (ed) *The Comparative Analysis of Human Societies*. Lynne Reiner Publishers, London, pp98–128

Hoskins, M (1990) 'The Community Toolbox: the idea, methods and tools for participatory assessment, monitoring and evaluation in Community Forestry', *FAO Community Forestry Field Manual 2*. FAO, Rome

IAWA (1957) 'International glossary of terms used in wood anatomy', *Tropical Woods* 107: 1–36

IAWA (1981) 'Standard list of characters suitable for computerized hardwood identification', *International Association of Wood Anatomists (IAWA) Bulletin* 2(2–3): 99–110

IAWA (1989) 'IAWA list of microscopic features for hardwood identification', *International Association of Wood Anatomists Bulletin* 10: 219–332

Junikka, L (1994) 'Survey of English macroscopic bark terminology', *International Association of Wood Anatomists (IAWA) Bulletin* 15(1):1–45

Miller, R B (1981) 'Explanation of coding procedure', *International Association of Wood Anatomists (IAWA) Bulletin* 2(2–3):111–145

Mori, S A and G T Prance (1990) 'Taxonomy, ecology and economic botany of the Brazil nut (*Bertholletia excelsa* Humb & Bompl: Lecythidaceae)', *Advances in Economic Botany* 8: 130–150

Nichols, P (1991) *Social Survey Methods: a Field-Guide for Development Workers*. Development Guidelines No 6, Oxfam, Oxford

Phillips, O L (1996) 'Some quantitative methods for analysing ethnobotanical knowledge' in M N Alexiades (ed) *Selected Guidelines for Ethnobotanical Research: a field manual*. New York Botanical Garden, New York, pp171–197

Phillips, O and A H Gentry (1993a) 'The useful plants of Tambopata, Peru: I. Statistical hypotheses tests with a new quantitative technique', *Economic Botany* 47: 15–32

Phillips, O and A H Gentry (1993b) 'The useful plants of Tambopata, Peru: II. Additional hypothesis testing in quantitative ethnobotany', *Economic Botany* 47: 33–43

Pratt, B and P Loizo. (1992) *Choosing Research Methods: Data Collection for Development Workers*. Development Guidelines No 7, Oxfam, Oxford

Pretty, J N, I Guijt, I Scoones and J Thompson (1995) *Participatory Learning and Action: a trainer's guide*. IIED Participatory Methodology Series, International Institute for Environment and Development, London

Toledo, V M, A I Batis, R Bacerra, E Martinez and C H Ramos (1992) 'Products from the tropical rain forests of Mexico: an ethnoecological approach' in M Plotkin and L Famolare (eds) *Non-Wood Products from Tropical Rainforests*. Conservation International, Washington, DC

Turner, N J (1988) 'The importance of a rose: evaluating the cultural significance of plants in Thompson and Lilooet Interior Salish', *American Anthropologist* 90: 272–290

Weller, S C and A K Romney (1988) *Systematic Data Collection*. Qualitative Research Methods, vol 10. Sage Publications, Newbury Park, California

Chapter 3 Settlement, commercialization and change

Bye, R A and E Linares (1985) 'The role of plants found in Mexican markets and their importance in ethnobotanical studies', *Journal of Ethnobiology* 3: 1–13

Smith, C A (1985) 'How to count onions: methods for a regional analysis of marketing' in S Plattner (ed) *Markets and Marketing*. Society for Economic Anthropology, University Press of America, Lanham, MD, pp49–77

Trager, L (1995) 'Minimum data sets in the study of exchange and distribution' in E F Moran (ed) *The Comparative Analysis of Human Societies*. Lynne Reinner Publishers, London, pp75–96

Chapter 4 Measuring individual plants and assessing harvesting impacts

Enright, N J and A D Watson (1992) 'Population dynamics of the nikau palm, *Rhopalostylis sapida* (Wendl et Drude), in a temperate forest remnant near Auckland, New Zealand', *New Zealand Journal of Botany* 30: 29–43

Green, D F and E A Johnson (1994) 'Estimating the mean annual seed production of trees', *Ecology* 75: 642–647

Lamont, B B, D C le Maitre, R M Cowling and N J Enright (1991) 'Canopy seed storage in woody plants', *The Botanical Review* 57: 277–317

Peters, C M (1996) 'Beyond nomenclature and use: a review of ecological methods for ethnobotanists' in M N Alexiades (ed) *Selected Guidelines for Ethnobotanical Research: a field manual*. New York Botanical Garden, New York, pp 241–276

Ruiters, C, B McKenzie and L M Raitt (1993) 'Life-history studies of the perennial geophyte *Haemanthus pubescens* (Amaryllidaceae) in lowland coastal fynbos, South Africa', *International Journal of Plant Science* 154: 441–449

Rutherford, M C (1979) 'Plant-based techniques for determining available browse and browse utilisation: a review', *The Botanical Review* 45: 203–228

Chapter 5 Opportunities and constraints on sustainable harvest: plant populations

Alder, D and T J Synnott (1992) *Permanent Sample Plot Techniques for Mixed Tropical Forest*. Oxford Forestry Institute, University of Oxford, Oxford

Alvarez-Buylla, E R (1994) 'Density dependence and patch dynamics in tropical rain forests: matrix models and applications to a tree species', *The American Naturalist* 143(1):155–191

Bell, A D (1998) *Plant Form: an illustrated guide to flowering plant morphology*. Oxford University Press, Oxford

Bernal, R (1998) 'Demography of the vegetable ivory palm *Phytelephus seemannii* in Colombia, and the impact of seed harvesting', *Journal of Applied Ecology* 35: 64–74

Caswell, H (1989) *Matrix Population Models*. Sinauer Associates, Sunderland, Massachusetts

Desmet, P G, C M Shackleton and E R Robinson (1996) 'The population dynamics and life-history attributes of a *Pterocarpus angolensis* DC. Population in the northern province, South Africa', *South African Journal of Botany* 62(3): 160–166

Enright, N J and Watson, A D (1992) 'Population dynamics of the nikau palm, *Rhopalostylis sapida* (Wendl et Drude) in a temperate forest remnant near Auckland, New Zealand', *New Zealand Journal of Botany* 30: 29–43

Midgley, J J, M C Cameron and W J Bond (1995) 'Gap characteristics and replacement patterns in the Knysna forest, South Africa', *Journal of Vegetation Science* 6: 29–35

Nantel, P, D Gagnon and A Nault (1996) 'Population viability analysis of American ginseng and wild leek harvested in stochastic environments', *Conservation Biology* 10(2): 608–621

Peters, C M (1994) *Sustainable Harvest of Non-Timber Forest Plant Resources in Tropical Moist Forest: an ecological primer*. Biodiversity Support Program, Washington, DC. Available from Biodiversity Support Program, 1250 24th Street, NW, Washington, DC, 20037, US

Peters, C M (1996a) 'Beyond nomenclature and use: a review of ecological methods for ethnobotanists' in M N Alexiades (ed) *Selected Guidelines for Ethnobotanical Research: a field manual*. New York Botanical Garden, New York, pp241–276

Sheil, D (1995) 'A critique of permanent plot methods and analysis with examples from Budongo forest, Uganda', *Forest Ecology and Management* 77: 11–34

Chapter 6 Landscapes and ecosystems: patterns, processes and plant use

Bond, W J and B W van Wilgen (1996) *Fire and Plants*. Chapman & Hall, London

Clark, D B (1996) 'Abolishing virginity', *Journal of Tropical Ecology* 12: 735–739

Fairhead, J and M Leach (1996) *Misreading the African Landscape: society and ecology in a forest-savanna mosaic*. Cambridge University Press, Cambridge

Hubbell, S P and R B Foster (1986) 'Commonness and rarity in a neotropical forest: implications for tropical tree conservation' in M E Soulé (ed) *Conservation biology: the science of scarcity and diversity*. Sinauer Associates, Sunderland, Massachusetts, pp205–231

IUCN (1994) *IUCN Red List Categories*. IUCN Species Survival Commission, Gland, Switzerland

Lewis, H T (1989) 'Ecological and technological knowledge of fire: Aborigines versus park rangers in Northern Australia', *American Anthropologist* 91: 940–961

Mather, R, M de Boer, M Gurung and N Roche (1998) *Aerial Photographs and 'Photo-Maps' for Community Forestry*. Overseas Development Institute (ODI), London. Rural Development Forestry Network 2e: 13–22

Miller, K R (1996) *Balancing the Scales: guidelines for increasing biodiversity's chances through bioregional management*. World Resources Institute, Washington, DC

Noss, R F (1990) 'Indicators for monitoring biodiversity: a hierarchical approach', *Conservation Biology* 4: 355–364

Pickett, S T A and P S White (1985) *The Ecology of Natural Disturbance and Patch Dynamics*. Academic Press, New York

Poole, P (1995) *Indigenous Peoples, Mapping and Biodiversity Conservation: an analysis of current activities and opportunities for applying geomatics technologies*. Biodiversity Support Program (BSP), Peoples and Forest Program Discussion Paper series. BSP/WWF/The Nature Conservancy, Washington, DC

Rabinowitz, D, S Cairns and T Dillon (1986) 'Seven forms of rarity and their frequency in the flora of the British Isles' in M E Soulé (ed) *Conservation Biology: the science of scarcity and diversity*. Sinauer Associates, Sunderland, Massachusetts, pp182–204

Rundstrom, R A (1990) 'A cultural interpretation of Inuit map accuracy', *The Geographical Review* 80: 155–168

Sharpe, B (1998) 'Forest people and conservation initiatives: the cultural context of rainforest conservation in West Africa' in B Goldsmith (ed) *Tropical rain forest: a wider perspective*. Chapman & Hall, London

Wagener, W W (1961) 'Past fire incidence in Sierra Nevada forests', *Journal of Forestry* 59: 739–748

Whitmore, T C (1988) 'The influence of tree population dynamics on forest species composition' in A J Davy, M J Hutchings and A R Watkinson (eds) *Plant Population Biology*. Blackwell, Oxford, pp271–291

Chapter 7 Conservation Behaviour, Boundaries and Beliefs

Bohannan, P (1963) '"Land", "tenure" and land-tenure' in D Biebuyck (ed) *African Agrarian Systems*. Oxford University Press, Oxford, pp101–111

Bromley, DW and M M Cernea (1989) *The Management of Common Property Natural Resources: some conceptual and operational fallacies*. World Bank Discussion Paper 57. World Bank, Washington, DC

Bruce, J and L Fortmann (1989) *Agroforestry: tenure and incentives*. Land Tenure Centre Report 135, Land Tenure Centre, Madison, Wisconsin

Casimir, M J (1992) 'The determinants of rights to pasture: territorial organisation and ecological constraints' in M J Casimir and A Rai (eds) *Mobility and Territoriality: social and spatial boundaries among foragers, fishers, pastoralists and peripatetics*. Berg, New York, pp153–203

Colfer, C J Pierce (1995) *Who Counts Most in Sustainable Forest Mmanagement?* Working Paper No 7, Centre for International Forestry Research (CIFOR), Bogor, Indonesia

Fischer, R (1995) *Collaborative Management of Forests for Conservation and Development*. Issues in Forest Conservation. IUCN, Gland, Switzerland

Ostrom, E (1990) *Governing the Commons: the evolution of institutions for collective action*. Cambridge University Press, Cambridge

Poole, P (1995) *Indigenous Peoples, Mapping and Biodiversity Conservation: an analysis of current activities and opportunities for applying geomatics technologies*. Biodiversity Support Program, Washington, DC

Richards, P (1996) 'Forest indigenous peoples: concept, critique and cases', *Proceedings of the Royal Society of Edinburgh* 104B: 349–365

Shipton, P (1994) 'Land and culture in tropical Africa: soils, symbols and the metaphysics of the mundane', *Annual Review of Anthropology* 23: 347–377

Wade, R (1987) 'The management of common property resources: collective action as an alternative to privatisation or state regulation', *Cambridge Journal of Economics* 11: 95–106

Chapter 8 Striving for balance: looking outward and inward

Baltz, M E (1999) 'Overconsumption of resources in industrial countries: the other missing agenda', *Conservation Biology* 13: 213–215

Homma, A K G (1992) 'The dynamics of extraction in Amazonia: a historical perspective', *Advances in Economic Botany* 9: 23–31

Meffe, G K, A H Erlich and D Ehrenfeld (1993) 'Human population control: the missing agenda', *Conservation Biology* 7:1–3

References

Acevedo-Rodriguez, P (1990) 'The occurrence of piscicides and stupefactants in the plant kingdom', *Advances in Economic Botany* 8: 1–23

Adu-Tutu, M, Y Afful, K Asante-Appiah, D Liebermann, J B Hall and M Elvin-Lewis (1979) 'Chewing stick usage in Ghana', *Economic Botany* 33(3): 320–328

Agnew, A D Q (1985) 'Cyclic sequences of vegetation in the plant communities of the Aberdare mountains, Kenya', *Journal of the East Africa Natural History Society and National Museum* 75: 1–12

Ake-Assi, L (1988) 'Plantes medicinales: quelques Legumineuses utilisées dans la medecine de tradition Africaine en Côte d'Ivoire', *Monogr. Syst. Bot Gard.* 25: 309–313

Alder, D and T J Synnott (1992) *Permanent Sample Plot Techniques for Mixed Tropical Forest.* Tropical Forestry Papers No 25. Oxford Forestry Institute, University of Oxford, Oxford

Alvarez-Buylla, E R (1994) 'Density dependence and patch dynamics in tropical rain forests: matrix models and applications to a tree species', *The American Naturalist* 143(1): 155–191

Anderson, J C (1984) 'The Political and Economic Basis of Kuku-Yalanji Social History'. Unpublished PhD thesis, Department of Archaeology and Sociology. University of Queensland, Queensland

Anderson, A B and D A Posey (1989) 'Management of a tropical shrub savanna by the Gorotire Kayapo of Brazil', *Advances in Economic Botany* 7: 159–173

Ankei, Y (1985) 'A comparative study of the barter markets of the upper Zaire river', *Africa Study Monographs Supplementary Issue* 4: 89–101

Ankei, Y (1981) 'Agricultural livelihood and economic activities of the Songola–slash and burn agriculturalists in the tropical rainforest, central Africa', *Kikan Jinruigku* 12: 96–178

Antos, J A and G A Allen (1988) 'Relative reproductive effort in males and females of the dioecious shrub *Oemleria cerasiformis* (Rosaceae)', *Oecologia* 76: 111–118

Arnold, J E M and W C Stewart (1991) *Common property resource management in India.* Tropical Forestry Papers No 24. Oxford Forestry Institute, University of Oxford, Oxford

Ash, J (1986) 'Demography and production of *Leptopteris wilkesiana* (Osmundaceae), a tropical tree-fern from Fiji', *Australian Journal of Botany* 34: 207–215

Ash, J (1987) 'Demography of *Cyathea hornei* (Cyatheaceae), a tropical tree-fern in Fiji', *Australian Journal of Botany* 35: 331–342

Austin, D D and P J Urness (1980) 'Response of Curlleaf Mountain Mahogany to pruning treatments in northern Utah', *Journal of Range Management* 33: 275–277

Baker and Mutitjulu Community (1992) 'Comparing two views of the landscape: aboriginal ecological knowledge and modern scientific knowledge', *Rangeland Journal* 14 (2): 174–189

Balee, W and D C Daly (1990) 'Resin classification by the Ka'apor Indians', *New Directions in the Study of Plants and People. Advances in Economic Botany* 8: 24–34 (New York Botanical Garden)

Balee, W (1989) 'The culture of Amazonian forests', *Advances in Economic Botany* 7: 1–21

Baltz, M E (1999) 'Overconsumption of resources in industrial countries: the other missing agenda', *Conservation Biology* 13: 213–215

Barnes, R F W (1990). 'Deforestation trends in tropical Africa', *African Journal of Ecology* 28: 161–173

Beentje, H (1994) *Kenya Shrubs, Trees and Lianas.* National Museum of Kenya, Nairobi

Bell, A D (1998) *Plant Form: an illustrated guide to flowering plant morphology.* Oxford University Press, Oxford

Bell, R H V and T O McShane (1984) 'Landscape classification' in R H V Bell, T O McShane and E Caluzi (eds) *Conservation and Wildlife Management in Africa*, US Peace Corps, Washington, DC, pp95–106

Bennett, B C (1992) 'Plants and people of the Amazonian rainforests', *BioScience* 42: 599–607

Berglund, A-I (1976) *Zulu Thought Patterns and Symbolism*. David Phillip, Cape Town

Berlin, B (1992) *Ethnobiological Classification: principles of categorization of plants and animals in traditional societies*. Princeton University Press, Princeton, New Jersey

Bernal, R (1998) 'Demography of the vegetable ivory palm *Phytelephas seemannii* in Colombia, and the impact of seed harvesting', *Journal of Applied Ecology* 35: 64–74

Bernhard, H R, P Killworth, D Kronenfeld and L Sailer (1984) 'The problem of informant accuracy: the validity of retrospective data', *Annual Review of Anthropology* 13: 495–517

Berry, M I (1996) 'The use of chewing sticks, khat and Indha kuul amongst the Somali population of Liverpool', poster abstract. Society for Economic Botany Meeting, London, 2–3 July

Biodiversity Support Program (1998) 'Fiji Case Story: accounting for success in community-based monitoring', *Lessons from the Field* 1: 6–7

Bird, N M and G Shepherd (1989) *Charcoal in Somalia: a woodfuel inventory in the bay region of Somalia*. Somali Forestry Series No 2. NRA/ODA, Somalia

Bohannan, P (1963) '"Land", "tenure" and land-tenure', in D Biebuyck (ed) *African Agrarian Systems*. Oxford University Press, Oxford, pp101–111

Bond, I (1996) 'Employment, population growth and the demand for land in communal areas' in B M Campbell (ed) *The Miombo in Transition: woodlands and welfare in Africa*. Centre for International Forestry Research (CIFOR), Bogor, p88

Bond, W J and B W van Wilgen (1996) *Fire and Plants*. Chapman & Hall, London

Boom, B M (1989) 'Use of plant resources by the Chacabo', *Advances in Economic Botany* 7: 78–96

Boom, B M (1990) 'Giving native people a share of the profits', *Garden* 14: 28–31

Borrini-Fyerabend, G (1996) *Collaborative Management of Protected Areas: Tailoring the Approach to the Context*. Issues in Social Policy. IUCN, Gland, Switzerland

Bourdieu, P (1973) 'The Berber house' in M Douglas (ed) *Rules and Meanings*. Penguin, Harmondsworth, pp98–110

Bourdieu, P (1977) *Outline of a Theory of Practice*. Cambridge University Press, Cambridge

Bridson, D and L Forman (1992) *The Herbarium Handbook*. Royal Botanic Gardens, Kew

Bromley, D W and Cernea, M M (1989) *The Management of Common Property Natural Resources: some conceptual and operational fallacies*. World Bank Discussion Paper 57. World Bank, Washington, DC

Bromley, R J (1971) 'Markets in the developing countries: a review', *Geography* 56: 124–132

Bromley, R J (1974) 'The organization of Quito's urban markets: towards a reinterpretation of periodic central places', *Institute of British Geographers Transactions* 62: 45–70

Bruce, J and L Fortmann (1989) *Agroforestry: tenure and incentives*. Land Tenure Centre Report 135. Land Tenure Centre, Madison, Wisconsin

Bruce, J, L Fortmann and C Nhira (1993) 'Tenures in transition, tenures in conflict: examples from the Zimbabwe social forest', *Rural Sociology* 8:626–642

Budack, K F R (1983) 'A harvesting people along the south Atlantic coast', *South African Journal of Ethnology* 6: 1–7

Bulatao, R A, E Bos, P W Stephens, and M T Vu (1990) *World Population Projections 1989–1990 edition; short- and long-term estimates*. Johns Hopkins University Press, London

Buwai, M and M J Trlica (1977) 'Multiple defoliation effects on herbage yield, vigour and total non-structural carbohydrates of five range species', *Journal of Range Management* 30: 164–171

Bye, R A and E Linares (1985) 'The role of plants found in Mexican markets and their importance in ethnobotanical studies', *Journal of Ethnobiology* 3: 1–13

Campbell, D G (1989) 'Quantitative inventory of tropical forests' in D G Campbell and H D Hammond (eds) *Floristic Inventory of Tropical Countries*. New York Botanical Garden, New York, pp524–533

Carlquist, S (1991) 'Anatomy of vine and liana stems: a review and synthesis' in F E Putz and H A Mooney (eds) *The Biology of Vines*. Cambridge University Press, Cambridge, pp53–71

Carpenter, S G and G Cottam (1982) 'Growth and reproduction of American ginseng (*Panax quinquefolius*) in Wisconsin, USA', *Canadian Journal of Botany* 60: 2692–2696

Casas, A and J Caballero (1996) 'Traditional management and morphological variation in *Leucaena esculenta* (Fabaceae: Mimosoideae) in the Mixtec region of Guerrero, Mexico', *Economic Botany* 50: 167–181

Cashdan, E (1983) 'Territoriality among human foragers: ecological models and an application to four Bushman groups', *Current Anthropology* 24: 47–66

Casimir, M J (1992) 'The determinants of rights to pasture: territorial organisation and ecological constraints' in M J Casimir and A Rai (eds) *Mobility and Territoriality: social and spatial boundaries among foragers, fishers, pastoralists and peripatetics*. Berg, New York

Caswell, H (1989) *Matrix Population Models*. Sinauer Associates, Sunderland, Massachusetts

Chambers, R (1992) *Rural Appraisal: rapid, relaxed and participatory*. Discussion Paper 311. Institute of Development Studies, University of Sussex, Sussex

Chapman, M (1987) 'Traditional political structure and conservation in Oceania', *Ambio* 16: 201–205

Chazdon, R L (1992) 'Patterns of growth and reproduction of *Geonoma congesta*, a clustered understorey palm', *Biotropica* 24: 43–51

Child, B (1996) 'The practice and principles of community-based wildlife management in Zimbabwe: the CAMPFIRE programme', *Biodiversity and Conservation* 5: 369–398

Christaller, W (1966) *Central Places in Southern Germany*. Prentice-Hall, Englewood Cliffs

Clark, D B (1996) 'Abolishing virginity', *Journal of Tropical Ecology* 12: 735–739

Clark, R L (1990) 'Ecological history for environmental management', *Proceedings of the Ecological Society of Australia* 16:1–21

Cole, M M and R C Brown (1976) 'The vegetation of the Ghanzi area of western Botswana', *Journal of Biogeography* 3: 169–196

Coley, P D, J P Bryant, and F S Chapin III (1985) 'Resource availability and anti-herbivore defence', *Science* 230: 859–899

Colfer, C J Pierce (1995) *Who Counts Most in Sustainable Forest Management?* Working Paper No 7. Centre for International Forestry Research (CIFOR), Bogor, Indonesia

Conelly, W T (1985) 'Copal and rattan collecting in the Philippines', *Economic Botany* 39: 39–46

Connah, G and A Jones (1983) 'Photographing Australian prehistoric sites from the air' in G Connah (ed) *Australian Field Archaeology: a guide to techniques*. Australian Institute of Aboriginal Studies, Canberra, pp73–81

Cooke, H B S (1964) 'The Pleistocene environment in southern Africa' in D H S Davis, B de Meillon and J S Harington (eds) *Ecological Studies in Southern Africa*. Junk, The Hague, pp1–23

Coppen, J J W (1995) *Flavours and Fragrances of Plant Origin. Non-Wood Forest Products 1*. Food and Agriculture Organization (FAO), Rome

Coughenour, M B, J E Ellis, D M Swift, D L Coppock, K Galvin, J T McCabe and T C Hart (1985) 'Energy extraction and use in a nomadic pastoral ecosystem', *Science* 230: 619–625

Crouse, D T, L B Crowder and H Caswell (1987) 'A stage-based population model for loggerhead sea turtles and implications for conservation', *Ecology* 68: 1412–1423

Crumley, C L and W H Marquardt (eds) (1987) *Regional Dynamics: Burgundian landscapes in historical perspective*. Academic Press, San Diego

Cunningham, A B (1985) 'The Resource Value of Indigenous Plants to Rural People in a low Agricultural Potential Area'. Unpublished PhD thesis. University of Cape Town, Cape Town

Cunningham, A B (1988a) 'Collection of wild foods in Tembe-Thonga society: a guide to Iron Age gathering activities?' *Annals of the Natal Museum* 29: 433–466

Cunningham, A B (1988b) *Botswana Basketry Resources: research and management of plant resources supporting the Ngamiland basketry trade, 1982–1988*. Botswanacraft Marketing Company (Pty) Ltd, Gaborone

Cunningham A B (1988c) 'Leaf production and utilization in *Hyphaene coriacea*: management guidelines for commercial harvesting', *South African Journal of Botany* 54: 189–195

Cunningham, A B (1988d) *An Investigation of the Herbal Medicine Trade in Natal/KwaZulu*. Investigational Report No 29. Institute of Natural Resources, University of Natal, Pietermaritzburg, South Africa

Cunningham, A B (1989) 'Indigenous plant use: balancing human needs and resources' in B J Huntley (ed) *Biotic Diversity in Southern Africa: concepts and conservation*. Oxford University Press, Cape Town, pp93–106

Cunningham, A B (1990a) 'Income, sap yield and the effects of tapping on palms in south-eastern Africa', *South African Journal of Botany* 56: 137–144

Cunningham, A B (1990b) 'The regional distribution, marketing and economic value of the palm wine trade in the Ingwavuma district, Natal, South Africa', *South African Journal of Botany* 56: 191–198

Cunningham, A B (1991) 'Development of a conservation policy on commercially exploited medicinal plants: a case study from southern Africa' in O Akerele, V Heywood, H Synge (eds) *Conservation of Medicinal Plants.* Cambridge University Press, Cambridge, pp337–358

Cunningham, A B (1993) *Ethics, Ethnobiological Research and Biodiversity.* WWF-International, Gland, Switzerland

Cunningham, A B (1996a) 'Professional ethics and ethnobotanical research' in M N Alexiades and J W Sheldon (eds) *Selected Guidelines for Ethnobotanical Research: a field manual.* Advances in Economic Botany, New York Botanical Garden, New York, pp19–51

Cunningham, A B (1996b) *People, Park and Plant Use: recommendations for multiple-use zones and development alternatives around Bwindi-Impenetrable National Park, Uganda.* People and Plants Working Paper 4. UNESCO, Paris

Cunningham, A B, E Ayuk, S Franzel, B Duguma and C Asanga (in press) *An economic valuation of medicinal tree cultivation: Prunus africana in Cameroon.* Working Paper, WWF/UNESCO/Kew People and Plants Initiative. UNESCO, Paris

Cunningham, A B and B R Gwala (1986) 'Plant species and building methods used in Tembe-Thonga hut construction', *Annals of the Natal Museum* 27: 491–511

Cunningham, A B and Milton, S J (1987) 'Effects of the basket weaving industry on the mokola palm (*Hyphaene petersiana*) and on dye plants in NW Botswana', *Economic Botany* 42: 386–402

Dallmeier, F (1992) *Long-Term Monitoring of Biological Diversity in Tropical Forest Areas: methods for establishment and inventory of permanent plots.* MAB Digest 11. UNESCO, Paris

Davis, S D, S J M Droop, P Gregerson, L Henson, C J Leon, J L Villa-Lobos, H Synge and J Zantovska (1986) *Plants in Danger: what do we know?* IUCN, Gland, Switzerland

Davison, P (1991) 'Material, Context and Meaning: a critical investigation of museum practice, with particular reference to the South African Museum'. Unpublished PhD thesis, University of Cape Town, Cape Town

Dawkins, H C (1958) *The Management of Natural Tropical High Forest with Special Reference to Uganda.* Institute Paper, Imperial Forestry Institute, University of Oxford, No 34. University of Oxford, Oxford

Dentlinger, U (1977) *The !Nara plant in the Topnaar Hottentot culture of Namibia.* Munger Africana Library Notes, No 38. California Institute of Technology, Pasadena

Desmet, P G, C M Shackleton and E R Robinson (1996) 'The population dynamics and life-history attributes of a *Pterocarpus angolensis* DC population in the northern province, South Africa', *South African Journal of Botany* 62(3): 160–166

Digernes, T H (1979) 'Fuelwood crisis causing unfortunate land-use – and the other way around', *Norsk. geogr. Tidsskft* 33: 23–32

Dinerstein, E, D M Olson, J Graham, A L Webster, S A Primm, M P Bookbinder and G Ledec (1995) *A Conservation Assessment of the Terrestrial Ecoregions of Latin America and the Caribbean.* The World Bank, Washington, DC

Donaldson, J (in press) *Changes in Abundance of South African Cycads during the 20th Century: preliminary data from the study of matched photographs.* Proceedings of the 4th International Conference on Cycad Biology, Panzihua, People's Republic of China

Douglas, M (1966) *Purity and Danger: an analysis of concepts of pollution and taboo.* Routledge and Kegan Paul, London

Douglas, M (1970) *Natural Symbols.* Pantheon Books, New York

Douglass, A E (1914) 'A method of estimating rainfall by the growth of trees' in E Huntington (ed) *The Climatic Factor as Illustrated in Arid America.* Carnegie Institute of Washington, Publ, 192, Washington, DC, pp100–122

Douglass, A E (1936) *Climatic Cycles and Tree Growth.* Carnegie Institute of Washington, Vol III, Washington, DC

Dransfield, J (1981) 'The biology of Asiatic rattans in relation to the rattan trade and conservation' in H Synge (ed) *The Biological Aspects of Rare Plant Conservation*. John Wiley & Sons, Chichester, pp 179–186

Dufour, D L and N I Teufel (1995) 'Minimum data sets for the description of diet and measurement of food intake and nutritional status' in E F Moran (ed) *The Comparative Analysis of Human Societies*. Lynne Reiner Publishers, London, pp98–128

Durr, P C, L Richmond and C Eagar (1988) *Site Classification and Field Measurements: Methods Manual*. Science Division, Great Smoky Mountains National Park, Gatlinburg, Tennessee

Dyson-Hudson, R and Dyson-Hudson, N (1980) 'Nomadic pastoralism', *Annual Review of Anthropology* 9: 15–61

Dyson-Hudson, R and E A Smith (1978) 'Human territoriality: an ecological assessment', *American Anthropologist* 80: 21–41

Enright, N J and Watson, A D (1992) 'Population dynamics of the nikau palm, *Rhopalostylis sapida* (Wendl et Drude) in a temperate forest remnant near Auckland, New Zealand', *New Zealand Journal of Botany* 30: 29–43

Erkkila, A and H Siiskonen (1992) *Forestry in Namibia 1850–1990. Silva Carelica 20*. Faculty of Forestry, University of Joensuu

Erlich, P R and P Holdren (1971) 'Impact of population growth', *Science* 171: 1212–1217

Erlich, P R, A H Erlich and G C Daily (1995) *The Stork and the Plow: the equity answer to the human dilemma*. G P Putnam and Sons, New York

Everard, D A (1992) 'On the feasibility of developing a functional classification as a decision support system for the management of indigenous forests in Natal'. Unpublished report. FOR-DEA 458, CSIR, Pretoria

Fairhead, J and M Leach (1996) *Misreading the African Landscape: society and ecology in a forest-savanna mosaic*. Cambridge University Press, Cambridge

Fimbel, C and R Fimbel (1997) 'Conservation and civil strife. Rwanda: the role of local participation', *Conservation Biology* 11: 309–310

Fischer, J B (1981) 'Wound healing by exposed secondary xylem in *Adansonia* (Bombacaceae)', *International Association of Wood Anatomists Bulletin* 2(4): 193–199

Fischer, R J (1995) *Collaborative Management of Forests for Conservation and Development*. Issues in Forest Conservation. IUCN, Gland, Switzerland

Fjeldså, J, D Erlich, E Lambin and E Prins (1997) 'Are biodiversity "hot-spots" correlated with current ecocolimatic stability? A pilot study using the NOAA-AVHRR remote sensing data', *Biodiversity and Conservation* 6: 401–422

Flannery, T F (1994) *The Future Eaters: an ecological history of Australasian lands and people*. Reed Books, Chatswood

Fleuret, A (1980) 'Non-food uses of plants in Usambara', *Economic Botany* 34: 320–333

Fortmann, L and J Bruce (1988) *Whose Trees? Proprietary dimensions of Forestry*. Westview Press, Boulder, Colorado

Fortmann, L and N Nabane (1992) *The fruits of their labour: gender, property and trees in Mhondoro District*. CASS Occasional Paper Series 6/1992. Centre for Applied Social Sciences, University of Zimbabwe, Harare

Fuegelsang, A (1982) *About Understanding – ideas and observations on cross-cultural communication*. Media Books, Inc, New York

Freudenberger, K S (1994) *Tree and Land Tenure: Rapid Appraisal Tools*. Community Forestry Field Manual 4. Food and Agriculture Organization (FAO), Rome

Geldenhuys, C J (1992) *The use of diameter distributions in sustained use management of forests: examples from southern Africa*. Paper presented at the SAREC/Zimbabwe Forestry Commission Symposium: Ecology and Management of Indigenous Forests in Southern Africa, Victoria Falls, July 1992

Geldenhuys, C J (1994) 'Bergwind fires and the location of forest patches in the southern Cape landscape, South Africa', *Journal of Biogeography* 21: 49–62

Gentry, A H (1993) *A Field Guide to the Families and Genera of Woody Plants of Northwest South America (Colombia, Ecuador, Peru) with Supplementary Notes on Herbaceous Taxa*. Conservation International, Washington, DC

Gerstner, J (1938) 'A preliminary checklist of Zulu names of plants', *Bantu Studies* 13: 49–64; 131–149; 307–326

Ghimire, K B and M P Pimbert (eds) (1997) *Social Change and Conservation: environmental politics and impacts of national parks and protected areas.* Earthscan Ltd, London

Giddens, A (1984) *The Constitution of Society: outline of a theory of structuration.* Polity Press, Cambridge

Glowka, L, F Burhenne-Guilmin and H Synge (1994) *A Guide to the Convention on Biological Diversity.* Environmental Policy Paper 30. World Conservation Union, Cambridge

Gluckman, M (1965) *The Ideas in Barotse Jurisprudence.* Yale University Press, New Haven

Godoy, R and K S Bawa (1993) 'The economic value and sustainable harvest of plants and animals from the tropical forest: assumptions, hypotheses and methods', *Economic Botany* 47(3): 215–219

Gomez-Pompa, A and S del Amo (eds) (1985) *Investigaciones sobre la Regeneracion de Selvas Atlas en Veracruz. Mexico. II.* Editorial Alhambra Mexicana, SA de CV, Mexico

Good, C M (1975) 'Periodic markets and travelling traders in Uganda', *Geographical Review* 65: 49–72

Gourlay, I D (1995) 'Growth ring characteristics of some African *Acacia* species', *Journal of Tropical Ecology* 11: 121–140

Gourlay, I D and R D Barnes (1994) 'Seasonal growth zones in the wood of *Acacia karroo* Hayne: their definition and implications', *Commonwealth Forestry Review* 73: 121–127

Green, D F and E A Johnson (1994) 'Estimating the mean annual seed production of trees', *Ecology* 75: 642–647

Gregory, M (1980) 'Wood identification: an annotated bibliography', *International Association of Wood Anatomists Bulletin* 1(1–2): 3–41

Grosenbaugh, L R (1991) 'Tilted tree hypsometry', *Forest Science* 37(6): 1581–1590

Grossman, D, A A Ferrar and P C du Plessis (1992) 'Socio-economic factors influencing conservation in southern Africa', *TRAFFIC Bulletin* 13: 29–31

Grundy, I M (1995) 'Regeneration and Management of *Brachystegia spiciformis* Benth and *Julbernardia globiflora* (Benth) Troupin in Miombo Woodland, Zimbabwe'. Unpublished PhD thesis. University of Oxford, Oxford

Haley, D and M K Luckert (1990) *Forest Tenures in Canada: a framework for policy analysis.* Information Report E-X-43. Forestry Canada, Ottawa

Hall, M (1987). *The Changing Past: farmers, kings and traders in southern Africa 200–1860.* David Philip, Cape Town

Hall, J B (1983) 'Positive management for strict nature reserves: reviewing effectiveness', *Forest Ecology and Management* 7: 57–66

Hall, R C (1944). 'A vernier tree-growth band', *Journal of Forestry* 42: 742–743

Hallé, F, R A A Oldeman and P B Tomlinson (1978) *Tropical Trees and Forests: an architectural analysis.* Springer Verlag, Berlin

Hallé, F (1985) 'Modular growth in seed plants', *Phil. Trans. R. Soc. London* B(313): 77–87

Hall-Martin, A (1993) 'Liwonde: Malawi's National Park of the future', *Africa Environment and Wildlife* 1: 71–79

Hames, R (1987) 'Game conservation or efficient hunting?' in B McCay and J M Acheson (eds) *The question of the commons: the culture and ecology of communal resources.* The University of Arizona Press, Tucson, Arizona

Hamilton, A C and R Bensted-Smith (1989) *Forest Conservation in the East Usambara Mountains, Tanzania.* IUCN Tropical Forest Programme, Gland, Switzerland

Hamilton, A C (1981) 'The quaternary history of African forests: its relevance to conservation', *African Journal of Ecology* 19: 1–6

Hammond, J E (1933) *Winjan's People.* Imperial Printing, Perth

Hammond-Tooke, W D (1975) 'The symbolic structure of Cape Nguni cosmology' in M G Whisson and M West (eds) *Religion and Social Change in southern Africa.* David Philip, Cape Town

Hammond-Tooke, W D (1981) *Boundaries and Belief: the structure of a Sotho worldview.* Witwatersrand University Press, Johannesburg

Hansen, A, J S Pate and A P Hansen (1991) 'Growth and reproductive performance of a seeder and resprouter species of *Bossiaea* as a function of plant age after fire', *Annals of Botany* 67: 497–509

Hardin, G (1968) 'The tragedy of the commons', *Science* 162: 1244

Harper, J L (1977) *Population Biology of Plants*. Academic Press, New York

Harris, D R (1989) 'An evolutionary continuum of people-plant interaction' in D R Harris and G C Hillman (eds) *Foraging and farming: the evolution of plant exploitation*. One World Archaeology Series. Unwin Hyman, London, pp11–26

Hart, T and J Hart (1997) 'Conservation and civil strife. Zaire: new models for an emerging state', *Conservation Biology* 11: 308–309

Hart, T B, J A Hart, R Dechamps, M Fournier and M Ataholo (1994) 'Changes in forest composition over the last 4000 years in the Ituri basin, Zaire' in L J G van der Maesen, X M van der Burgt and J M van Medenbach de Rooy (eds) *The Biodiversity of African Plants*. Kluwer Academic Publishers, Dordrecht, pp545–559

Hartshorn, G S (1989) 'Application of gap theory to tropical forest management: natural regeneration on strip clear-cuts in the Peruvian Amazon', *Ecology* 70: 567–569

Hecht, S B and D A Posey (1989) 'Preliminary results in soil management techniques of the Kayapo Indians', *Advances in Economic Botany* 7: 174–188

Hersh-Martinez, P (1995) 'Commercialisation of wild medicinal plants from south-west Puebla, Mexico', *Economic Botany* 49: 197–206

Hill, P and R H T Smith (1972) 'The spatial and temporal synchronisation of periodic markets: evidence from four emirates in northern Nigeria', *Economic Geography* 47: 345–355

Hilton-Taylor, C (1996) *Red Data List of Southern African Plants*. Strelitzia 4, National Botanical Institute, Pretoria

Hitchcock, R K (1978) *Kalahari Cattle Posts: a regional study of hunter-gatherers, pastoralists and agriculturalists in the western sandveld region, Central District, Botswana*. Ministry of Local Government and Lands, Gaborone

Hobbs, R J and H A Mooney (1991) 'Effects of rainfall variability and gopher disturbance on grassland dynamics in northern California', *Ecology* 72: 59–68

Hodder, B W and R Lee (1974) *Economic Geography*. Methuen and Co Ltd, London

Holmgren, P K et al (1990) *Index Herbariorum: Part 1. The Herbaria of the World*. 8th edition. Regnum Vegetabile vol 120. New York Botanical Garden, New York

Holt-Biddle, D (1994) 'Hondo yemiti: Zimbabwe's "war of the trees"', *Africa Environment and Wildlife* 2: 59–63

Homma, A K G (1992) 'The dynamics of extraction in Amazonia: a historical perspective', *Advances in Economic Botany* 9: 23–31

Hoskins, M (1990) *The Community Toolbox: the idea, methods and tools for participatory assessment, monitoring and evaluation in Community Forestry*. FAO Community Forestry Field Manual 2, Food and Agriculture Organization (FAO), Rome

Hot Springs Working Group (1995) *Local-level economic valuation of savanna woodland resources; village cases from Zimbabwe*. IIED Research Series 3(2). Sustainable Agriculture Programme, International Institute for Environment and Development, London

Howard, P C (1991) *Nature Conservation in Uganda's Tropical Forest Reserves*. IUCN, Gland, Switzerland

Hubbell, S P and R B Foster (1986) 'Commonness and rarity in a neotropical forest: implications for tropical tree conservation' in M E Soulé (ed) *Conservation Biology: the science of scarcity and diversity*. Sinauer Associates, Sunderland, Massachusetts

Huntley, B J (1977). *Savanna Ecosystem Project – progress report 1975/76*. South African National Scientific Programme Report 12, CSIR, Pretoria

IAWA (1957) 'International glossary of terms used in wood anatomy', *Tropical Woods* 107: 1–36

IAWA (1981) 'Standard list of characters suitable for computerized hardwood identification', *International Association of Wood Anatomists (IAWA) Bulletin* 2(2–3): 99–110

IAWA (1989) 'IAWA list of microscopic features for hardwood identification', *International Association of Wood Anatomists Journal* 10: 219–332

IIED (1994) *Whose Eden? An overview of community approaches to wildlife management*. International Institute for Environment and Development, London

IUCN (1980) *World Conservation Strategy: living resource conservation for sustainable development*. IUCN/UNEP/WWF, Gland, Switzerland

IUCN (1994) *IUCN Red List Categories*. IUCN Species Survival Commission, Gland, Switzerland

Jacoby, G C (1989) 'Overview of tree-ring analysis in tropical regions', *International Association of Wood Anatomists Bulletin* 13(4): 359–379

James, S (1984) 'Ligno-tubers and burls – their structure, function and ecological significance in Mediterranean ecosystems', *The Botanical Review* 50: 225–266

Jenkins, M and S Oldfield (1992) *Wild plants in trade*. TRAFFIC International, Cambridge

Johannes, R E (1981) *Words of the Lagoon: fishing and marine lore in the Palau district of Micronesia*. University of California Press, Berkeley

Johannes, R E (1998) 'The case for data-less marine resource management: examples from tropical nearshore fisheries', *TREE* 13: 243–246

Johns, T, J O Kokwaro and E K Kimanani (1990) 'Herbal remedies of the Luo of Siaya district, Kenya: establishing quantitative criteria for consensus', *Economic Botany* 44: 369–381

Johnson, D (1996) *Palms: their conservation and sustained utilisation*. Status Survey and Conservation Action Plan. IUCN, Gland and Cambridge

Joyal, E (1996) 'The palm has its time: an ethnoecology of *Sabal uresana* in Sonora, Mexico', *Economic Botany* 50: 446–462

Junikka, L (1994) 'Survey of English macroscopic bark terminology', *International Association of Wood Anatomists (IAWA) Journal* 15(1): 1–45

Kamatenesi, M (1997) 'Utilization of the medicinal plant "nyakibazi" (*Rytigynia* spp) in the multiple-use zones of Bwindi-Impenetrable National Park, Uganda'. Unpublished MSc thesis. Makerere University, Kampala

Kawano, S, A Hiratsuka and K Hayashi (1982) 'The productive and reproductive biology of flowering plants. V. The life characteristics and survivorship of *Erythronium japonicum*', *Oikos* 38: 129–149

Kingdon, J (1990) *Island Africa: the evolution of Africa's rare animals and plants*. Collins, London

Kingston, B (1967) *Working plan for Mgahinga Central Forest Reserve, Kigezi District, Uganda (1967–1977)*. Uganda Forest Department, Kampala

Klee, G A (1980) *World systems of traditional resource management*. V H Winston & Sons with Edward Arnold

Kloos, H (1976/1977) 'Preliminary study of medicinal plants and plant products in markets of Central Ethiopia', *Ethnomedizin* IV(1/2): 63–102

Knight, C (1991) *Blood Relations: menstruation and the origins of culture*. Yale University Press, New Haven

Kremen, C, A M Merenlender and D D Murphy (1994) 'Ecological monitoring: a vital need for integrated conservation and development programs in the tropics', *Conservation Biology* 8: 388–397

Kruger, L M, J J Midgley and R M Cowling (1997) 'Resprouters vs reseeders in South African forest trees; a model based on forest canopy height', *Functional Ecology* 11: 101–105

Kuper, A (1980) 'Symbolic dimensions of the southern Bantu homestead', *Africa* 50: 8–23

Kurita, K (1982) 'A market on boundary: the economic activities of the Pokot and the Marakwet in Kenya', *Africa Study Monographs, Supplementary Issue* 1: 71–103

Lamont, B B and S Downes (1979) 'The longevity, flowering and fire history of the grasstrees *Xanthorrhoea preissii* and *Kingia australis*', *Journal of Applied Ecology* 16: 893–899

Lamont, B B, D C le Maitre, R M Cowling and N J Enright (1991) 'Canopy seed storage in woody plants', *The Botanical Review* 57: 277–317

Lange, D (1997) 'Trade in plant material for medicinal and other purposes: a German case study', *TRAFFIC Bulletin* 17(1): 21–32

Lange, D and U Schippmann (1997) *Trade survey of medicinal plants in Germany: a contribution to international species conservation*. Bundesamt für Naturschütz. LV Druck, Münster

Langholz, G (1996) 'Economics, objectives and success of private nature reserves in sub-Saharan Africa and Latin America', *Conservation Biology* 10: 271–280

Larmour, P (1979) 'Customary maps' in Institute of South Pacific Studies *Land in Solomon Islands*. Fiji Times and Herald, Suva, pp28–40

Latz, P (1995) *Bush Fires and Bushtucker: Aboriginal plant use in Central Australia*. IAD Press, Alice Springs

Lawry, S (1990) 'Tenure policy toward common property natural resources in sub-Saharan Africa', *Natural Resources Journal* 30: 403–422

Lay, D W (1965) 'Effects of periodic clipping on yield of some common browse species', *Journal of Range Management* 18: 181–184

Leach, M (1994) *Rainforest Relations: gender and resource use among the Mende of Gola, Sierra Leone*. Edinburgh University Press, Edinburgh

Leakey, R and D O Ladipo (1996) 'Trading on genetic variation – fruits of *Dacroydes edulis*', *Agroforestry Today*. April–June: 16–17

Lefkovitch, L P (1965) 'The study of population growth in organisms grouped in stages', *Biometrics* 21: 1–18

Leloup, S (1984) *The grapple plant project: an ecophysiological approach of the influence of harvest on the population dynamics of the Grapple plant* Harpagophytum procumbens DC. National Institute for Development Research and Documentation, Gaborone, Botswana

Leopold, A (1949) *A Sand County Almanac and Sketches of Here and There*. Oxford University Press, New York

Leslie, P H (1945) 'On the use of matrices in certain population dynamics', *Biometrika* 33: 183–212

Levin, D A and H W Kerster (1978) 'Rings and age in *Liatris*', *American Naturalist* 112: 1121–1122

Levi-Strauss, C (1963) *Structural Anthropology*. Basic Books, New York

Lewis, H T (1989) 'Ecological and technological knowledge of fire: Aborigines versus park rangers in Northern Australia', *American Anthropologist* 91: 940–961

Liebenberg, L and L Steveton (1989) *Cybertracker Software: Field computer system for trackers*. Noordhoek, Cape Town (http://www.icon.co.za/~ctracker)

Lieth, H (1975) 'Primary production of the major vegetation units of the world' in H Lieth and H Whittaker (eds) *Primary Productivity of the Biosphere*. Springer Verlag, Berlin, pp203–215

Liming, F G (1957) 'Homemade dendrometers', *Journal of Forestry* 55: 575–577

Lock, J M (1989) *Legumes of Africa: a check-list*. Royal Botanic Gardens, Kew

Loh, J, J Randers, A Macgillivray, V Kapos, M Jenkins, B Groombridge and N Cox (1998) *Overconsumption is Driving the Rapid Decline of the World's Natural Environments*. WWF-International/New Economics Foundation/WCMC

Lösch, A (1954) *The Economics of Location*. Yale University, New Haven

Makombo, J (1998) 'Mapping traditional resource use zones around Rwenzori Mountains National Park, Uganda'. Unpublished MSc thesis. Makerere University, Kampala

McConnell, B R and J G Smith (1977) 'Influence of grazing on age-yield interactions in bitterbush', *Journal of Range Management* 30: 91–93

McKim, W (1972) 'The periodic market system in north-eastern Ghana', *Economic Geography* 48: 333–344

MacNally, R and G P Quinn (1998) 'Symposium introduction: the importance of scale in ecology', *Australian Journal of Ecology* 23: 1–7

McNeely, J A, J Harrison and P Dingwall (eds) (1994) *Protecting Nature: regional reviews of protected areas*. IUCN, Morges

McPherson, K and K Williams (1996) 'Establishment growth of cabbage palm, *Sabal palmetto* (Areaceae)', *American Journal of Botany* 83: 1566–1570

Mace, G, N Collar, J Cooke, K Gaston, J Ginsberg, N Leader-Williams, M Maunder and E J Milner-Gulland (1993) 'The development of new criteria for listing species on the IUCN Red List', *Species* 19: 16–22

Mann, C C and M L Plumme (1993) 'The high cost of biodiversity', *Science* 260: 1868–1871

Marsh, A C and M K Seely (eds) (1992) *Oshanas: sustaining people, environment and development in Central Owambo, Namibia*. Typoprint, Windhoek, Namibia

Marshall, L (1976) *The !Kung of Nyae-nyae*. Harvard University Press, Cambridge, Massachusetts

Martin, G J (1995) *Ethnobotany: a methods manual*. Chapman and Hall, London

Martin, R B (1994) *Alternative Approaches to Sustainable Use; what does and doesn't work*. Paper presented at the conference on Conservation through Sustainable Use of Wildlife. University of Queensland, Brisbane

Martinez-Ramos, M (1985) 'Claros, ciclos vitales de los arboles tropicales y regeneracion natural de las selvas atlas perennifolias' in A Gomez-Pompa and S del Amo (eds) *Investigaciones sobre la Regeneracion de Selvas Atlas en Veracruz, Mexico. II.* Editorial Alhambra Mexicana, S A de CV, Mexico, pp191–239

Martinez-Ramos, M, J Sarukhan, and D Pinero (1988) 'Treefall age determination and gap dynamics: the case of *Astrocaryum mexicanum* at Los Tuxlas tropical rain forest' in A J Davy, M J Hutchings and A R Watkinson (eds) *Plant population Ecology*. Blackwell Scientific Publications, Oxford, pp293–313

Mason, L R and G S Hutchings (1967) 'Estimating foliage yields on Utah juniper from measurements of crown diameter', *Journal of Range Management* 20: 161–166

Mason, P M (1995) 'Wildlife conservation in the long term – Uganda as a case-study'. Unpublished MSc thesis in environmental economics. University of Oxford, Oxford

Mather, R, M de Boer, M Gurung and N Roche (1998) 'Aerial photographs and "photo-maps" for community forestry', *Rural Development Forestry Network* 2e: 13–22. Overseas Development Institute (ODI), London

Mattos, M, D C Nepstad and I C M Vieira (1992) *Cartilha sobre mapeamento de area, cubagem de maderia e inventario florestal*. Woods Hole Research Centre, Belem, Brazil

Maxwell, S E and H D Delaney (1989) *Designing Experiments and Analysing Data: a model comparison perspective*. Wadsworth Publishing Company, Belmont, California

Meffe, G K, A H Erlich and D Ehrenfeld (1993) 'Human population control: the missing agenda', *Conservation Biology* 7: 1–3

Menke, J W and M J Trilica (1981) 'Carbohydrate reserves, phenology and growth cycles of nine Colorado range species', *Journal of Range Management* 34: 269–277

Mentis, M T (1980) 'Towards a scientific management of terrestrial ecosystems', *South African Journal of Science* 76: 536–540

Mialoundama, F (1993) 'Nutritional and socio-economic value of *Gnetum* leaves in Central African Forest' in C M Hladik, A Hladik, O F Linares, H Pagezy, A Semple and M Hadley (eds) *Tropical Forests, People and Food: biocultural interactions and applications to development*. Man and the Biosphere Series, vol 13, UNESCO, Paris, pp177–182

Midgley, J J, M C Cameron and W J Bond (1995) 'Gap characteristics and replacement patterns in the Knysna forest, South Africa', *Journal of Vegetation Science* 6: 29–35

Midgley, J J (1996) 'Why is the world's vegetation not totally dominated by resprouters: an architectural hypothesis', *Ecography* 19: 92–95

Midgley, J J and R M Cowling (1993) 'Regeneration patterns in a subtropical transition thicket: where are all the seedlings?' *South African Journal of Botany* 59: 496–499

Midgley, J J, A Seydack, D C Reynell and D McKelly (1990) 'Fine grain patterns in southern Cape plateau forests', *Journal of Vegetation Science* 1: 29–35

Miller, K R (1996) *Balancing the Scales: guidelines for increasing biodiversity's chances through bioregional management*. World Resources Institute, Washington, DC

Miller, R B (1981) 'Explanation of coding procedure', *International Association of Wood Anatomists (IAWA) Bulletin* 2(2–3): 111–145

Mills, G T (1984) 'An inquiry into the structure and function of space in indigenous settlement in Ovamboland'. Unpublished MArch thesis. University of Cape Town, Cape Town

Milton, S J (1987) 'Effects of harvesting on four species of forest ferns in South Africa', *Biological Conservation* 41: 133–146

Milton, S J (1991) 'Slow recovery of defoliated seven-weeks fern *Rumohra adiantiformis* in Harkerville forest', *South African Journal of Forestry* 158: 23–27

Mkanda, F X and S M Munthali (1994) 'Public attitudes and needs around Kasungu National Park, Malawi', *Biodiversity and Conservation* 3: 29–43

Moll, E J (1981) *Trees of Natal*. Eco-Lab Trust Fund, University of Cape Town, South Africa

Molur, S and S Walker (1996) *Conservation Assessment and Management Plan (CAMP II) for Selected Species of Medicinal Plants of Southern India*. 12–14 February 1996. Zoo outreach organization/CBSG, India, Coimbatore

Moore, H L (1996) *Space, Text and Gender: an anthropological study of the Marakwet of Kenya*. The Guildford Press, New York

Mori, S A and G T Prance (1990) 'Taxonomy, ecology and economic botany of the Brazil nut (*Bertholletia excelsa* Humb. & Bompl: Lecythidaceae)', *Advances in Economic Botany* 8: 130–150

Muir, D P (1990) 'Indigenous forest utilization in KwaZulu: a case study of the Hlatikulu forest, Maputaland'. Unpublished MSc thesis. University of Natal, Pietermaritzburg

Murphree, M (1995) *Optimal principles and pragmatic strategies: creating an enabling politico-legal environment for community-based natural resource management – CBNRM*. Keynote Address, Conference of the National Resources Management Programme, SADCC Technical Coordination Unit, USAID-NRMP. Chobe, Botswana

Mustart, P J and R M Cowling (1992) 'Impact of flower and cone harvesting on seed banks and seed set of serotinous Agulhas Proteaceae', *South African Journal of Botany* 58: 337–342

Nantel, P, D Gagnon and A Nault (1996) 'Population viability analysis of American ginseng and wild leek harvested in stochastic environments', *Conservation Biology* 10(2): 608–621

Nhira, C and L Fortmann (1993) 'Local woodland management: realities at the grass roots' in P N Bradley and K McNamara (eds) *Living with Trees: policies for forestry management in Zimbabwe*. World Bank Technical Paper 210, World Bank, Washington, DC, pp139–156

Nichols, P (1991) *Social Survey Methods: a Field-Guide for Development Workers*. Development Guidelines No 6. Oxfam, Oxford

Norton-Griffiths, M and C Southey (1995) 'The opportunity costs of biodiversity in Kenya', *Ecological Economics* 12: 125–139

Noss, R F (1990) 'Indicators for monitoring biodiversity: a hierarchical approach', *Conservation Biology* 4: 355–364

Obermeyer, A A (1978) '*Ornithogalum*: a revision of the southern African species', *Bothalia* 12: 323–376

Obeso, J R (1997) 'Costs of reproduction in *Ilex aquifolium*: effects at tree, branch and leaf levels', *Journal of Ecology* 85: 159–166

Ogle, B M and L E Grivetti (1985) 'Legacy of the chameleon: edible wild plants in the kingdom of Swaziland, southern Africa. A cultural, ecological, nutritional study. Part II – demographics, species availability and dietary use, analysis by ecological zone', *Ecology of Food and Nutrition* 17: 1–30

Oldfield, S (1997) *Cactus and Succulent Plants: status survey and Conservation Action Plan*. IUCN, Gland and Cambridge

Olmsted, I and E R Alvarez-Buylla (1995) 'Sustainable harvesting of tropical trees: demography and matrix models of two palm species in Mexico', *Ecological Applications* 5(2): 484–500

Olson, D M and E Dinerstein (1998) 'The Global 200: a representation approach to conserving the earth's most biologically valuable ecoregions', *Conservation Biology* 12: 502–515

O'Neill, A L, L M Head and J K Marthick (1993) 'Integrating remote sensing and spatial analysis techniques to compare Aboriginal and pastoral fire patterns in the East Kimberly, Australia', *Applied Geography* 13: 67–85

Osborne, R, A Grove, P Oh, T Mabry, J Ng and A Seawright (1994) 'The magical and medicinal usage of *Stangeria eriopus* in South Africa', *Ethnopharmacology* 43: 67–72

Ostrom, E (1990) *Governing the Commons: the evolution of institutions for collective action*. Cambridge University Press, Cambridge

Oyama, K (1993) 'Are age and height correlated in *Chamaedorea tepejilote* (Palmae)?' *Journal of Tropical Ecology* 9: 381–385

Padoch, C (1988) 'Aguaje (*Mauritia flexuosa*), L.f., in the economy of Iquitos, Peru', *Advances in Economic Botany* 6: 214–224

Park, S (1981) 'Rural development in Korea', *Economic Geography* 57: 113–126

Parker, E, D Posey, J Frechione and L F Da Silva (1983) 'Resource exploitation in Amazonia: ethnoecological examples from four populations', *Annals of Carnegie Museum* 52: 163–203

Pate, J and K Dixon (1982) *Tuberous, Cormous and Bulbous Plants: biology of an adaptive strategy in western Australia*. University of Western Australia Press, Nedlands

Pate, J S, R H Froend, B J Bowen, A Hansen, and J Kuo (1990) 'Seedling growth and storage and characteristics of seeder and resprouter species of Mediterranean-type ecosystems of south-western Australia', *Annals of Botany* 65: 585–601

Pate, J S, K A Meney, and K W Dixon (1991) 'Contrasting growth and morphological characteristics of fire-sensitive (obligate seeder) and fire-resistant (resprouter) species of Restionaceae (S. Hemisphere Restiads) from south-western Australia', *Australian Journal of Botany* 39: 505–525

Pellew, R A (1980) 'The production and consumption of Acacia browse and its potential for animal protein production' in H N le Houerou (ed) *Browse in Africa*. International Livestock Centre for Africa, Addis Ababa, Ethiopia, pp223–231

Peterken, G F (1993) *Woodland Conservation and Management*. Chapman & Hall, London

Peters, C M (1994) *Sustainable Harvest of Non-Timber Forest Plant Resources in Tropical Moist Forest: an ecological primer*. Biodiversity Support Program, Washington, DC

Peters, C M (1996a) 'Beyond nomenclature and use: a review of ecological methods for ethnobotanists' in M N Alexiades (ed) *Selected Guidelines for Ethnobotanical Research: a field manual*. New York Botanical Garden, New York, pp241–276

Peters, C M (1996b) *Pedoman inventarisasi dan Penghasilan Sumber Daya Alam Non-Kayu [Inventory and yield manual for non-wood forest products]*. Social Forestry Development project, GTZ and departemen Kehutanan, Sanggau, West Kalimantan, Indonesia

Peters, C M and E Hammond (1990) 'Fruits from the flooded forests of Peruvian Amazonia: yield estimates for natural populations of three promising species', *Advances in Economic Botany* 8: 159–176

Philip, M S (1994) *Measuring Trees and Forests*. Second edition. CAB International, Wallingford

Phillips, O (1993) 'The potential for harvesting fruits in tropical rainforests: new data from the Peruvian Amazon', *Biodiversity and Conservation* 2: 18–38

Phillips, O L (1996) 'Some quantitative methods for analysing ethnobotanical knowledge' in M N Alexiades (ed) *Selected Guidelines for Ethnobotanical Research: a field manual*. New York Botanical Garden, New York, pp171–197

Phillips, O and A H Gentry (1993a) 'The useful plants of Tambopata, Peru: I. Statistical hypotheses tests with a new quantitative technique', *Economic Botany* 47: 15–32

Phillips, O and A H Gentry (1993b) 'The useful plants of Tambopata, Peru: II. Additional hypothesis testing in quantitative ethnobotany', *Economic Botany* 47: 33–43

Pickett, S T A and P S White (1985) *The Ecology of Natural Disturbance and Patch Dynamics*. Academic Press, New York

Picton, J and J Mack (1989) *African Textiles*. British Museum Publications, London

Pinard, M (1993) 'Impacts of stem harvesting on populations of *Iriartea deltoidea* (Palmae) in an Extractive Reserve in Acre, Brazil', *Biotropica* 25(1): 2–14

Pinard, M A and F E Putz (1992) 'Population matrix models and palm resource management', *Bull. Inst. Fr. Études Andines* 21(2): 637–649

Pitman, N C A, J Terborgh, M R Silman and P Nuñez (1999) 'Tree species distributions in an upper Amazonian forest', *Ecology* 80(8): 2651–2661

Poffenberger, M, B McGean, A Khare and J Campbell (1992) *Field Methods Manual, volume 2: community forest economy and use patterns*. Joint Forest Management Support Programme, Society for Promotion of Wastelands Development, New Delhi, India

Poffenberger, M, B McGean, N H Ravindranath and M Gadgil (1992) *Field Methods Manual, volume 1: diagnostic tools for supporting joint forest management systems*. Joint Forest Management Support Programme, Society for Promotion of Wastelands Development, New Delhi, India

Polak, A M (1992) *Major Timber Trees of Guyana: a field guide*. Tropenbos Series 2. Tropenbos Foundation, Wageningen

Poole, P (1995) *Indigenous Peoples, Mapping and Biodiversity Conservation: an analysis of current activities and opportunities for applying geomatics technologies*. Biodiversity Support Program (BSP), Peoples and Forest Programme Discussion Paper Series. BSP/WWF/The Nature Conservancy, Washington, DC

Porter, D, B Allen and G Thompson (1991) *Development in Practice: paved with good intentions*. Routledge, London

Posey, D A (1984) 'A preliminary report on diversified management of tropical forest by the Kayapo Indians of the Brazilian Amazon', *Advances in Economic Botany* 1: 112–126

Prance, G T, W Balee, B M Boom and R L Carneiro (1987) 'Quantitative ethnobotany and the case for conservation in Amazonia', *Conservation Biology* 1(4): 296–310

Pratt, B and P Loizos (1992) *Choosing Research Methods: Data Collection for Development Workers*. Development Guidelines No 7. Oxfam, Oxford

Pretty, J N, I Guijt, I Scoones and J Thompson (1995) *Participatory Learning and Action: a trainer's guide*. IIED Participatory Methodology Series. International Institute for Environment and Development, London

Prinsloo, J (1982) 'Construction of a questionnaire on poverty; lessons from an urban survey' in SALDRU (ed) *Questionnaires Are No Short Cut*. SALDRU Working Paper 43. South African Labour and Development Research Unit, University of Cape Town, Cape Town, pp29–41

Prior, J A B and P E Gasson (1990) 'Comparative wood anatomy of Afromontane and bushveld species from Swaziland', *IAWA Bulletin* 11: 319–336

Rabinowitz, D, S Cairns and T Dillon (1986) 'Seven forms of rarity and their frequency in the flora of the British Isles' in M E Soulé (ed) *Conservation Biology: the science of scarcity and diversity*. Sinauer Associates, Sunderland, Massachusetts, pp182–204

Rapoport, A (1977) *Human Aspects of Urban Form: towards a man-environment approach to the urban form and design*. Pergamon, New York

Raunkiaer, C (1934) *Life Forms of Plants and Statistical Plant Geography*. Clarendon Press, Oxford

Rebelo, T (1995) *Proteas: a field guide to the Proteas of southern Africa*. Fernwood Press, Vlaeberg

Rebelo, A G and P M Holmes (1988) 'Commercial exploitation of *Brunia albiflora* (Bruniaceae) in South Africa', *Biological Conservation* 45: 195–207

Reichel-Dolmatoff, G (1996) *The Forest Within: the world-view of the Tukano Amazonian Indians*. Themis Books, Dartington

Reynolds, N (1981) *The design of rural development: proposals for the evolution of a social contract suited to conditions in southern Africa. Parts 1 and 2*. SALDRU Papers Nos 41 and 42. University of Cape Town, South Africa

Richards, P (1996) 'Forest indigenous peoples: concept, critique and cases', *Proceedings of the Royal Society of Edinburgh* 104B: 349–365

Ruiters, C, B McKenzie and L M Raitt (1993) 'Life-history studies of the perennial geophyte *Haemanthus pubescens* (Amaryllidaceae) in lowland coastal fynbos, South Africa', *International Journal of Plant Science* 154: 441–449

Rundstrom, R A (1990) 'A cultural interpretation of Inuit map accuracy', *The Geographical Review* 80: 155–168

Rutherford, M C (1979) 'Plant-based techniques for determining available browse and browse utilisation: a review', *The Botanical Review* 45: 203–228

Rutherford, M C (1982) 'Woody plant biomass distribution in *Burkea africana* savannas' in B J Huntley and B H Walker (eds) *Ecology of Tropical Savannas*. Ecological Studies 42. Springer Verlag, Berlin, pp121–141

Rykiel, E J, R N Coulson, P J H Sharpe, T F H Allen and R O Flamm (1988) 'Disturbance propagation by bark beetles as an episodic landscape phenomenon', *Landscape Ecology* 1: 129–139

Sada, P O, M L McNulty and I A Adelemo (1978) 'Periodic markets in a metropolitan environment: an example of Lagos, Nigeria' in R H T Smith (ed) *Marketplace Trade*. University of British Columbia Centre for Transportation Studies, Vancouver

Sakai, A, S Sakai and F Akiyama (1997) 'Do sprouting tree species on erosion-prone sites carry large reserves of resources?' *Annals of Botany* 79: 625–630

Salick, J (1992) 'Amuesha forest use and management: an integration of indigenous forest use and natural forest management' in K Redford and C Padoch (eds) *Conservation of Neotropical Forests: working from traditional resource use*. Columbia University Press, New York, pp305–332

Salick, J, A Meija and T Anderson (1995) 'Non-timber forest products integrated with natural forest management, Rio San Juan, Nicaragua', *Ecological Applications* 5: 878–895

Scharfetter, H (1987) 'Timber resources and needs in southern Africa', *South African Journal of Science* 83: 256–259

Schoffeleers, J M (1978) *Guardians of the Land*. Mambo Press, Gwelo

Schupp, J R (1992) 'Effect of root pruning and summer pruning on growth, yield, quality, and fruit maturity of McIntosh apple trees', *Acta Hort.* 322: 173–183

Schuster, J L and J George (1976) 'Redberry juniper response to top removal', *Journal of Range Management* 29: 258–259

Schutte, A L, J H J Vlok and B-E van Wyk (1995) 'Fire-survival strategy –a character of taxonomic, ecological and evolutionary importance in fynbos legumes', *Plant Systematics and Evolution* 195: 243–259

Schweingruber, F H (1992) 'Annual growth rings and growth zones in woody plants in southern Australia', *International Association of Wood Anatomists Bulletin* 13(4): 359–379

Scifres, C J, Kothmann, M M and Mathis, C W (1974) 'Range site and grazing system influence on regrowth after spraying honey mesquite', *Journal of Range Management* 27: 97–100

Scott, P J (1993) 'Fringe benefits: national park boundaries as areas for local community utilization: the case of the Impenetrable (Bwindi) forest'. Unpublished MSc thesis. Agricultural University of Norway, Bergen

Scott, P J (1995) 'Progress report on multiple-use management to Uganda National Parks'. Unpublished report. WWF Rwenzori Mountains Conservation and Development Project, Fort Portal, Uganda

Scudder, T and T Conelly (1985) *Management Systems for Riverine Fisheries*. International Development Association Report. International Development Association, Washington, DC

Seydack, A H W (1995) 'An unconventional approach to timber yield regulation for multi-aged, multi-species forests. I. Fundamental considerations', *Forest Ecology and Management* 77: 139–153

Seydack, A H W, W J Vermeulen, H E Heyns, G P Durrheim, C Vermeulen, D Willems, M A Ferguson, J Huisamen and J Roth (1995) 'An unconventional approach to timber yield regulation for multi-aged, multi-species forests. II. Application to a South African forest', *Forest Ecology and Management* 77: 155–168

Shackleton, C M (1993) 'Demography and dynamics of the dominant woody species in a communal and protected area of the eastern transvaal lowveld', *South African Journal of Botany* 59: 569–574

Shackleton, C M (1993) 'Fuelwood harvesting and sustainable utilization in a communal grazing land and protected area of the eastern Transvaal lowveld', *Biological Conservation* 63: 247–254

Shackleton, C (1998) 'Annual production of harvestable deadwood in semi-arid savannas, South Africa', *Forest Ecology and Management* 112: 139–144

Shackleton, S (1990) 'Socio-economic importance of *Cymbopogon validus* in Mkambati Game Reserve, Transkei', *South African Journal of Botany* 56: 675–682

Shafer, C L (1990) *Nature Reserves – island theory and conservation practice*. Smithsonian Institution Press, Washington, DC

Shankar, U, K S Murali, R U Shaanker, K N Ganeshaiah and K S Bawa (1996) 'Extraction of non-timber forest products in the forests of Biligiri Rangan hills, India. 3. Productivity, extraction and prospects of sustainable harvest of Amla (*Phyllanthus emblica*), Euphorbiaceae', *Economic Botany* 50: 270–279

Shanley, P and L Luz (in press) 'Eastern Amazonian medicinals: marketing, utilisation and implications for conservation', *BioScience*

Shanley, P, J Galvao and L Luz (1997) 'Limits and strengths of local participation: a case-study in Eastern Amazonia', *PLA Notes (IIED, London)* 14: 64–67

Shanley, P, M Cymerys and J Galvao (1998) *Fruitiferas da mata na Vida Amazonica*. Editora Supercores, Chaco, Belem-Para

Sharpe, B (1998) 'Forest people and conservation initiatives: the cultural context of rainforest conservation in West Africa' in B Goldsmith (ed) *Tropical Rain forest: a wider perspective*. Chapman & Hall, London, pp75–97

Sheil, D (1995) 'A critique of permanent plot methods and analysis with examples from Budongo forest, Uganda', *Forest Ecology and Management* 77: 11–34

Shiokura, T (1989) 'A method to measure radial increment in tropical trees', *IAWA Bulletin* 10: 147–154

Shipton, P (1994) 'Land and culture in tropical Africa: soils, symbols and the metaphysics of the mundane', *Annual Review of Anthropology* 23: 347–377

Schonau, A P G (1982) 'Models for Stand Development in a Short Rotation crop'. Paper delivered at the Symposium on Growth Modelling, University of Stellenbosch, South Africa

Siegfried, W R, G A Benn and C M Gelderblom (1998) 'Regional assessment and conservation implications of landscape characteristics of African national parks', *Biological Conservation* 84: 131–140

Singh, L and J S Singh (1991) 'Species structure, dry matter dynamics and carbon flux of a dry tropical forest in India', *Annals of Botany* 68: 263–273

Skinner, G W (1964) 'Marketing and social structure in rural China. Part 1', *Journal of Asian Studies* 24: 3–43

Skinner, G W (1965) 'Marketing and social structure in rural China. Part 2', *Journal of Asian Studies* 24: 195–228

Smith, A B (1994) 'Metaphors of space: rock art and territoriality in southern Africa' in T A Dowson and D Lewis-Williams (eds) *Contested Images: diversity in southern African rock art research*. Witwatersrand University Press, Johannesburg, pp373–384

Smith, C A (1985) 'How to count onions: methods for a regional analysis of marketing' in S Plattner (ed) *Markets and Marketing*. Society for Economic Anthropology, University Press of America, pp 49–77

Smith, R L (1980) *Ecology and Field Biology*. Harper and Row, New York

Soetprayitno, T, T L Tobing and E A Widjaja (1988) 'Why the Sundanese of West Java prefer slope inhabiting *Gigantochloa pseudoarundinacea* to those growing in the valley', *BAMBOOS Current research*. Proceedings of the International Workshop, 14–18 November 1988, pp215–217

Sokal, R R and F J Rohlf (1987) *Introduction to Biostatistics*. Freeman, New York

Southwood, T R E, U K Brown and P M Reader (1986) 'Leaf palatability, life expectancy and herbivore damage', *Oecologia* 70: 544–548

Steiner, K E (1993) 'Has *Ixianthes* (Scrophulariaceae) lost its special bee?' *Plant Systematics and Evolution* 185: 7–16

Stern, W L (1978) 'Index Xylariorum. Institutional wood collections of the world. 2', *Taxon* 27 (2/3): 233–269

Stockdale, M C and J D Power (1994) *Forest Ecology and Management* 64: 47–57

Sussman, R W, G M Green and L K Sussman (1994) 'Satellite imagery, human ecology, anthropology and deforestation in Madagascar', *Human Ecology* 22: 333–354

Swart, J P J (1980) 'Non-destructive wood sampling methods from living trees: a literature survey', *International Association of Wood Anatomists Bulletin* 1(1–2): 42

Tailfer, Y (1989) *La forêt dense d'Afrique tropicale. Identification practique des principaux arbres*. Tome 1, ACCT, Paris

Tait, N G and A B Cunningham (1988) 'An identification guide to commonly sold medicinal plants'. Unpublished report. Institute of Natural Resources, University of Natal, Pietermaritzburg, South Africa

Tamasari, F (1995) *Body, names and movement: images of identity among the Yolngu of north-east Arnhem Land*. Unpublished PhD thesis. London School of Economics, University College, London

Taylor, D M (1990) 'Late quaternary pollen records from two Ugandan mires: evidence for environmental change in the Rukiga highlands of south-west Uganda', *Paleogeography, Paleoclimatology, Paleoecology* 80: 283–300

Thorsen W, W R J Dean and S J Milton (1997) 'Simulated plant population responses to small-scale disturbances in semi-arid shrublands', *Journal of Vegetation Science* 8: 163–176

Tietema, T (1993) 'Biomass determination of fuelwood trees and bushes of Botswana, Southern Africa', *Forest Ecology and Management* 60: 257–269

Tinley, K L (1987) 'Achieving a balance between long and short term research' in D A Saunders, G W Arnold, A A Burbidge and A J M Hopkins (eds) *Nature Conservation: the role of remnants of native vegetation*. Surrey Beatty and Sons Pty Ltd, Chipping-Norton, NSW, Australia, pp347–350

Toledo, V M, A Batis, R Bacerra, E Martinez and C H Ramos (1992) 'Products from the tropical rain forests of Mexico: an ethnoecological approach' in M Plotkin and L Famolare (eds) *Non-Wood Products from Tropical Rainforests*. Conservation International, Washington, DC, pp99–109

Trager, L (1995) 'Minimum data sets in the study of exchange and distribution' in E F Moran (ed) *The Comparative Analysis of Human Societies*. Lynne Reiner Publishers, London, pp75–96

Trapnell, C G (1953) *The Soils, Vegetation and Agricultural Systems of North-Eastern Rhodesia*. Government Printer, Lusaka, Zambia

Trlica, M J, M Buwai, and J W Menke (1977) 'Effects of rest following defoliations on the recovery of several range species', *Journal of Range Management* 30: 21–27

Trollip, A-M (1995) 'Meaning of blankets, towels and T-shirts in the context of acculturation', *South African Journal of Ethnology* 18: 150–154

Turner, M G (1989) 'Landscape ecology: the effect of pattern on process', *Ann. Rev. Ecol. Sys.* 20: 171–197

Turner, N J (1988) 'The importance of a rose: evaluating the cultural significance of plants', *American Anthropologist* 90: 272–290

Turner, R M 1990 'Long-term vegetation change at a fully protected Sonoran desert site', *Ecology* 71: 464–477

Turner, V (1967) *The Forest of Symbols*. Cornell University Press, Ithaca, New York

Turner, V (1969) *The Ritual Process*. Aldine, Chicago

Ukwu, U I (1969) 'Markets in Iboland' in B W Hodder and U I Ukwu (eds) *Markets in West Africa*. Ibadan University Press, Ibadan

UNESCO (1998) *The Economist*, 14 March

van Binsbergen, W J (1985) *Theoretical Explorations in African Religion*. Kegan Paul International, London

van Binsbergen, W J (1988) 'The land as body: an essay on the interpretation of ritual among the Manjaks of Guinea-Bissau', *Medical Anthropological Quarterly* 2: 386–401

van den Beemer, J P M (1992) 'Ideas and usage. Environment in Aouan society, Ivory Coast' in E Croll and D Parkin (eds) *Bush Base: Forest Farm. Culture, Environment and Development*. Routledge, London, pp97–109

van Laar, A and C J Geldenhuys (1975) 'Tariff tables for indigenous tree species in the southern Cape Province', *Forestry in South Africa* 17: 29–36

van Wyk, G F, D A Everard, J J Midgley and I G Gordon (1996) 'Classification and dynamics of a southern African subtropical coastal lowland forest', *South African Journal of Botany* 62(3): 133–142

Vance, J E (1970) *The Merchant's World: the geography of wholesaling*. Foundations of Economic Geography Series. Prentice-Hall, Englewood Cliffs, New Jersey

Vasquez, R and A H Gentry (1989) 'Use and misuse of forested harvested fruits in the Iquitos area', *Conservation Biology* 3: 350–361

Viljoen, A J (1988) 'Long-term changes in the tree component of the vegetation in the Kruger National Park' in I A MacDonald and R J M Crawford (eds) *Long-term data series relating to southern Africa's renewable natural resources*. South African National Scientific Programmes Report 157. CSIR, Pretoria, pp310–315

Wade, R (1987) 'The management of common property resources: collective action as an alternative to privatisation or state regulation', *Cambridge Journal of Economics* 11: 95–106

Waddy, J A (1982) 'Biological classification from a Groote eylandt Aborigine's point of view', *Journal of Ethnobiology* 2: 63–77

Wagener, W W (1961) 'Past fire incidence in Sierra Nevada forests', *Journal of Forestry* 59: 739–748

Walsh, F J (1990) 'An ecological study of traditional use of "country": Martu in the Great and Little Sandy deserts, Western Australia', *Proceedings of the Ecological Society of Australia* 16: 23–37

Walsh, F J (1993) 'The relevance of some aspects of Aboriginal subsistence to the management of national parks; with reference to Martu people of the Western Desert', in J Birkhead, T de Lacy and L Smith (eds) *Aboriginal involvement in parks and protected areas*. Australian Institute of Aboriginal and Torres Strait Islander Studies, Canberra, pp75–97

Walter, S and J-C R Rakotonirina (1995) *L'exploitation de Prunus africana à Madagascar*. PCDI Zahamena et la Direction des Eaux et Forêts. Antananarivo, Madagascar

Watkinson, A R and J White (1985) 'Some life-history consequences of modular construction in plants', *Phil. Trans. Roy. Soc. Lond.* B313: 31–51

Weller, S C and A K Romney (1988) *Systematic Data Collection*. Qualitative Research Methods, vol 10. Sage Publications, Newbury Park, California

Werner, P A (1978) 'On the determination of age in *Liatris aspera* using cross-sections of corms: implications for past demographic studies', *American Naturalist* 112: 1113–1144

White, F (1976) 'The underground forests of Africa: a preliminary review', *Gardens Bull. (Singapore)* 29: 55–71

Whitmore, T C (1988) 'The influence of tree population dynamics on forest species composition' in A J Davy, M J Hutchings and A R Watkinson (eds) *Plant Population Biology*. Blackwell, Oxford, pp271–291

Wild, R G, A B Cunningham and J Mutebi (1995) 'People, parks and plant use: networks to enhance the conservation of montane forests in Uganda, East Africa' in D A Saunders, J L Craig and E M Mattiske (eds) *Nature Conservation 4: the role of networks*. Surrey Beatty & Sons, Sydney, pp112–121

Wild, R G and J Mutebi (1996) *Conservation through Community Use of Plant Resources*. People and Plants Working Paper 5. UNESCO, Paris

Williams, V L (1996) 'The Witwatersrand muti trade', *Veld & Flora* 82(1): 12–14

Wilmsen, E N (1978) 'Seasonal effects of dietary intake on Kalahari San', *Federation Proceedings* 37: 65–72

Wilson, M (1957) *Rituals of Kinship Among the Nyakusa*. Oxford University Press, London

Wily, E (1995) 'What future for community forestry in Nepal?' *Social Development Newsletter* 3, Overseas Development Administration, London

Witkowski, E T F, B B Lamont and F J Obbens (1994) 'Commercial picking of *Banksia hookeriana* in the wild reduces subsequent shoot, flower and seed production', *Journal of Applied Ecology* 31: 508–520

Witkowski, E T F and B B Lamont (1996) 'Nutrient losses from commercial picking and cockatoo removal of *Banksia hookeriana* blooms at the organ, plant and site levels', *Journal of Applied Ecology* 33: 131–140

World Conservation Union, United Nations Environment Programme, World Wide Fund For Nature (1991) *Caring for the Earth: a strategy for sustainable living*. WCU, UNEP, WWF, Gland, Switzerland

World Resources Institute (1992) *Global Biodiversity Strategy: guidelines for action to save, study and use Earth's biotic wealth sustainably and equitably*. WRI/IUCN/UNEP, Washington, DC

Wyatt-Smith, J and A J Vincent (1962) 'The swing from qualitative to quantitative assessment of individual tree crown parameters in the Malayan Forest Service', *Malayan Forester* 25: 276–291

Yeaton, R I (1988) 'Porcupines, fire and the dynamics of the tree layer of the *Burkea africana* savanna', *Journal of Ecology* 76: 1017–1029

Zar, J H (1998) *Biostatistical Analysis*. Fourth edition. Prentice-Hall Biological Sciences, Englewood Cliffs, New Jersey

Index

Page numbers in *italics* refer to figures and tables